The Media
and the
Persian Gulf War

**Recent Titles in the Praeger Series
in Political Communication**
Robert E. Denton, Jr., General Editor

Political Empiricism: Communication Strategies in State and Regional
Elections
Rita Kirk Whillock

Contemporary Apocalyptic Rhetoric
Barry Brummett

Televised Presidential Debates: Advocacy in Contemporary America
Susan Hellweg, Michael Pfau, and Steven Brydon

Vietnam-on-the-Potomac
Moya Ann Ball

The Political Pundits
Dan Nimmo and James E. Combs

Visions of Empire: Hollywood Films on the Political Landscape of the
1980s
Stephen Prince

Postmodern Political Communication: The Fringe Challenges the
Center
Edited by Andrew King

Broadcasting Propaganda: International Radio Broadcasting and the
Construction of Political Reality
Philo C. Wasburn

Enacting the Presidency: Political Argument, Presidential Debates,
and Presidential Character
Edward A. Hinck

Citizens, Political Communication and Interest Groups: Environmental
Organizations in Canada and the United States
John C. Pierce, Mary Ann E. Steger, Brent S. Steel, and Nicholas P. Lovrich

Media and Public Policy
Edited by Robert J. Spitzer

American Rhetoric and the Vietnam War
J. Justin Gustainis

THE MEDIA
AND THE
PERSIAN GULF WAR

Edited by
Robert E. Denton, Jr.

Praeger Series in Political Communication

Westport, Connecticut
London

Library of Congress Cataloging-in-Publication Data

The Media and the Persian Gulf War / edited by Robert E. Denton, Jr.
    p.   cm.—(Praeger series in political communication, ISSN
1062–5623)
    Includes bibliographical references and index.
    ISBN 0–275–94232–5 (alk. paper)
    1. Persian Gulf War, 1991—Journalists.   2. Persian Gulf War,
1991, in mass media.   I. Denton, Robert E., Jr.   II. Series.
DS79.739.M44   1993
303.6'6—dc20   92–36554

British Library Cataloguing in Publication Data is available.

Library of Congress Catalog Card Number: 92–36554
ISBN: 0–275–94232–5
ISSN: 1062–5623

First published in 1993

Praeger Publishers, 88 Post Road West, Westport, CT 06881
An imprint of Greenwood Publishing Group, Inc.

Printed in the United States of America

The paper used in this book complies with the
Permanent Paper Standard issued by the National
Information Standards Organization (Z39.48–1984).

10 9 8 7 6 5 4 3 2 1

The editor and publisher gratefully acknowledge Brian P. Lamb, Chairman and
Chief Executive Officer, and Susan Swain, Senior Vice President, of C-SPAN,
for permission to reprint interview material in chapter 7.

This book is dedicated to my aunt and uncle,
Nellie and Dudley Stallings,
who always took time to share and care.
With my love, appreciation, and admiration.

Contents

Illustrations   ix

Series Foreword
    Robert E. Denton, Jr.   xi

Preface
    Robert E. Denton, Jr.   xv

Acknowledgments   xix

1. The Rules of the Game: The Military and the Press in
    the Persian Gulf War
    Gary C. Woodward   1

2. Television as an Instrument of War
    Robert E. Denton, Jr.   27

3. The Natural, and Inevitable, Phases of War Reporting:
    Historical Shadows, New Communication in the
    Persian Gulf
    Donald L. Shaw and Shannon E. Martin   43

4. Media Perspectives on World Opinion During the
    Kuwaiti Crisis
    Frank Louis Rusciano   71

5. Vox Populi: Talk Radio and TV Cover the Gulf War
    Dan Nimmo and Mark Hovind   89

6. Constructing News Narratives: ABC and CNN Cover
    the Gulf War
    Bethami A. Dobkin   107

7. C-SPAN's Coverage of the Gulf War: Television as
    Town Square
    Janette Kenner Muir   123

8. News Viewing, Authoritarianism, and Attitudes
    Toward the Gulf War
    *Mary Beth Oliver, Marie-Louise Mares, and
    Joanne Cantor*   145

9. War in the Global Village: A Seven-Country
    Comparison of Television News Coverage of the
    Beginning of the Gulf War
    David L. Swanson and Larry David Smith   165

10. Media Coverage of Women in the Gulf War
    Anne Johnston   197

11. "What Did You Advertise with the War, Daddy?":
    Using the Persian Gulf War as a Referent System in
    Advertising
    Matthew P. McAllister   213

12. Celluloid Heroes and Smart Bombs: Hollywood at War
    in the Middle East
    Stephen Prince   235

13. From the Great War to the Gulf War: Popular
    Entertainment and the Legitimation of Warfare
    James Combs   257

Selected Bibliography   285

Index   295

About the Editor and Contributors   299

Illustrations

Figures

3.1. The Key Relationships in Public Support for the War   46

3.2. A Balanced Situation   55

3.3. An Unbalanced Situation   55

3.4. Phase I of War Reporting   56

3.5. Phase II of War Reporting   57

3.6. Phase III of War Reporting   57

4.1. Percentage of Total References to World Opinion on Kuwaiti Crisis, by Date   75

4.2. Percentage of Total References to Isolation on Kuwaiti Crisis, by Date   82

8.1. News Stories Used in the Experimental Portion of the Second Study   157

8.2. Separate Regression Slopes of War Attitudes on Story Perceptions as a Function of Story Version   160

Tables

3.1.   Number of Stories Citing Bush and Congress in the
       Washington Post During Specific Time Periods
       Surrounding the Persian Gulf War   51

3.2.   Number of Stories Citing Pentagon Sources in the
       Washington Post During Specific Time Periods
       Surrounding the Persian Gulf War   52

3.3.   Number of Stories Citing Saddam Hussein and Adolf
       Hitler, and the New World Order, in the *Washington
       Post* During Specific Time Periods Surrounding the
       Persian Gulf War   53

3.4.   Number of Stories Citing the Kurds and Oil and the
       Gulf in the *Washington Post* During Specific Time
       Periods Surrounding the Persian Gulf War   54

8.1.   Regression Analysis of Perceptions of the News Story
       as a Function of War Attitudes and Story Version   159

Series Foreword

Those of us in the field of communication studies have long believed that communication comes before all other fields of inquiry. In several other forums I have argued that the essence of politics is "talk" or human interaction.[1] Such interaction may be formal or informal, verbal or nonverbal, public or private, but it is always persuasive, forcing us consciously or subconsciously to interpret, to evaluate, and to act. Communication is the vehicle for human action.

From this perspective, it is not surprising that Aristotle recognized the natural kinship of politics and communication in his writings *Politics* and *Rhetoric*. In the former, he establishes that humans are "political beings [who] alone of the animals [are] furnished with the faculty of language."[2] In the latter, he begins his systematic analysis of discourse by proclaiming that "rhetorical study, in its strict sense, is concerned with the modes of persuasion."[3] Thus, it was recognized over 2,300 years ago that politics and communication go hand in hand because they are essential parts of human nature.

In 1981, Dan Nimmo and Keith Sanders proclaimed that political communication was an emerging field.[4] Although its origin, as noted, dates back centuries, a "self-consciously cross-disciplinary" focus began in the late 1950s. Thousands of books and articles later, colleges and universities offer a variety of graduate and undergraduate coursework in the area in such diverse departments as communication, mass communication, journalism, political science, and sociology.[5] In Nimmo and Sanders' early assessment, the "key areas of inquiry" included rhetorical analysis, propaganda analysis, attitude change studies, voting studies, government and the news media, functional and systems analyses, technological changes, media technologies, campaign techniques, and research techniques.[6] In a survey of the state of field in 1983, the same authors plus Lynda Kaid found additional, more specific areas of concerns such as the presidency, political polls, public opinion, debates, and advertising, to name a few.[7] They also noted a shift away from the rather strict behavioral approach they had seen at the time of the first study.

In the early 1990s, Dan Nimmo and David Swanson assert that "political communication has developed some identity as a more or less distinct domain of scholarly work."[8] The scope and concerns of the area have further expanded to include critical theories and cultural studies. While there is no precise definition, method, or disciplinary home of the area of inquiry, its primary domain is the role, processes, and effects of communication within the context of politics broadly defined.

In 1985, the editors of *Political Communication Yearbook: 1984* noted that "more things are happening in the study, teaching, and practice of political communication than can be captured within the space limitations of the relatively few publications available."[9] In addition, they argued that the backgrounds of "those involved in the field [are] so varied and pluralist in outlook and approach, . . . it [is] a mistake to adhere slavishly to any set format in shaping the content."[10] And more recently, Swanson and Nimmo called for "ways of overcoming the unhappy consequences of fragmentation within a framework that respects, encourages, and benefits from diverse scholarly commitments, agendas, and approaches."[11]

In agreement with these assessments of the area and with gentle encouragement, in 1988 Praeger Publishers established the series entitled "Praeger Studies in Political Communication." The series is open to all qualitative and quantitative methodologies as well as contemporary and historical studies. The key to characterizing the studies in the series is the focus on communication variables or activities within a political context or dimension. Scholars from the disciplines of communication, history, political science, and sociology have participated in the series.

I am, without shame or modesty, a fan of the series. The joy of serving as its editor is in participating in the dialogue of the field of political communication and in reading the contributors' works. I invite you to join me.

Robert E. Denton, Jr.

NOTES

1. See Robert E. Denton, Jr., *The Symbolic Dimensions of the American Presidency* (Prospect Heights, Ill.: Waveland Press, 1982); Robert E. Denton, Jr., and Gary

Woodward, *Political Communication in America* (New York: Praeger, 1985, 2nd ed., 1990); Robert E. Denton, Jr., and Dan Hahn, *Presidential Communication* (New York: Praeger, 1986); and Robert E. Denton, Jr., *The Primetime Presidency of Ronald Reagan* (New York: Praeger, 1988).

2. Aristotle, *The Politics of Aristotle*, trans. Ernest Barker (New York: Oxford University Press, 1970), 5.

3. Aristotle, *Rhetoric*, trans. Rhys Roberts (New York: The Modern Library, 1954), 22.

4. Dan Nimmo and Keith Sanders, "Introduction: The Emergence of Political Communication as a Field," in *Handbook of Political Communication*, Dan Nimmo and Keith Sanders, eds. (Beverly Hills, Calif.: Sage, 1981), 11–36.

5. Ibid., 15.

6. Ibid., 17–27.

7. Keith Sanders, Lynda Kaid, and Dan Nimmo, eds. *Political Communication Yearbook: 1984* (Carbondale, Ill.: Southern Illinois University, 1985), 283–308.

8. Dan Nimmo and David Swanson, "The Field of Political Communication: Beyond the Voter Persuasion Paradigm" in *New Directions in Political Communication*, David Swanson and Dan Nimmo, eds. (Beverly Hills, Calif.: Sage, 1990), 8.

9. Sanders, Kaid, and Nimmo, xiv.

10. Ibid., xiv.

11. Nimmo and Swanson, 11.

Preface

On June 8, 1991, the United States held a victory day parade in Washington, D.C. The troops were officially welcomed home, praised for their bravery and sacrifice. America, after the embarrassment of the Korean and Vietnam conflicts, had at last "won" another "war." We felt good.

In actuality, however, the war was really not much of a war. If was too quick, too easy, and too successful. The conflict lasted only weeks instead of months or years. American casualties were incredibly low, less than 300 rather than hundreds of thousands or even millions. This acknowledgment is not meant to diminish the efforts of the Allied forces but is an expression of relief and historical fact.

Now, two years later, to the general public the war is mostly forgotten and seldom mentioned. For future generations, the conflict will probably be only a footnote in American history. President George Bush, who received national and international acclaim and who enjoyed a 90 percent approval rating, lost his reelection bid. While the war did not play a role in the 1992 presidential campaign, we still remember the evening of January 16, 1991. At home, in our dens and living rooms, we witnessed the beginnings of the "mother of all battles."

At first, the nation was mesmerized by the immediacy. Half a world away, we saw the bombs drop, heard the sirens blare, and shared the fear as reporters prepared for possible gas attacks. Throughout the ordeal there was no escape or comfort. For many, it was rather awkward, even surreal, to be sitting in our homes witnessing live the initial phases of the conflict. This was not a movie but a real life drama.

The Gulf War has been widely characterized as "the global village's"

first "prime-time war." It was, according to the editors of *U.S. News &
World Report* (1992),

a see-it-now, hear-it-now electronic spectacular that filled the world's television
screens with images of battle in the age of the microprocessor and the memory
chip. . . . And yet for all of the air time and newsprint and magazine coverage
devoted to the war, only an extremely incomplete and limited picture of the
war was conveyed to the people on whose support the effort relied. (vii, 414)

Thus, although the conflict was quickly resolved, there still remain many
questions and concerns about the role of the press and of the military,
social, and political use of modern communication technologies in times
of war.

This book is an attempt to aid understanding of the role and impact
of the media during the Persian Gulf War. The chapters benefit from
the passage of time and initial reflection. Broad in scope and varied in
methodologies, this collection spans across the media of television, radio, print, and film.

Gary Woodward surveys the historical relationship between the press
and the military in times of war. He provides a comprehensive review
of the Pentagon's guidelines that were enforced during the Persian Gulf
War and concludes by examining several important organizational and
political factors that shaped the broadcast and print coverage of the
conflict.

In my chapter, I explore the notion of television as an instrument of
war by examining some unique characteristics of the medium and associated issues of national military engagement. In the Gulf War, I argue
that television became a strategic tool and an essential weapon in the
military's arsenal. I conclude by addressing the dilemma of how to preserve freedom of the press as well as national security in times of war.

Donald Shaw and Shannon Martin investigate the relationships
among the military, White House, reporters, editors, and the public
during the conflict. By reviewing models and phases of war reporting,
they provide a rationale for why the military and the White House were
so successful in controlling the "pictures" of the war, and they speculate
on the challenges of covering modern warfare with modern communication technologies.

Frank Rusciano presents a content analysis of the manner in which
the *New York Times* and the *Times of India* referenced world opinion during
the pre-war Kuwaiti crisis. Topics of discussion include the comparative
agendas for world opinion in the papers, the timing of references to
world opinion, the importance attached to the moral component of world
opinion in the crisis, the importance attached to the pragmatic component of the world opinion, and the role of isolation as viewed as pun-

ishment for violating the wishes of world opinion. Interestingly, while the perspectives on world opinion were similar between the two newspapers for the first eight weeks, variations existed relevant to the positions of the United States and India in the world community.

Dan Nimmo and Mark Hovind explore the role of television and radio call-in talk shows during the gulf crisis. They discovered three general formats of coverage of agreement, confrontation, and instruction. They argue that regardless of format, the talk shows constructed an overall favorable consensus in support of American involvement and for the war. Key in the process of consensus building was the role of the talk show host who either bonded with or disputed views expressed by guest experts and callers.

Bethami Dobkin compares and contrasts the ways in which ABC and CNN covered the Gulf War. Similarities between the two include the structural narrative framework of romantic quest and reliance upon speculation, experts, and hypothetical scenarios to tell the story. CNN relied less on character development, however, and more on military and strategic information. The ultimate challenge is for television journalism to use structural frames that provide thematic continuity and aid audience understanding without bias.

Janette Muir discusses C-SPAN's unique role in covering the war. With over 500 calls coded, three major areas of public attitudes emerged regarding: attitudes about the war, the president's performance, and the anti-war protesters. In addition, Professor Muir analyzes the styles of discourse and the way callers presented their arguments. Argument by example, analogy, and storytelling were the dominant approaches. The study concludes that the C-SPAN network served a vital role in providing unique coverage of the war in the Gulf and a forum for the public to express their viewpoints.

Mary Beth Oliver, Marie-Louise Mares, and Joanne Cantor provide an empirical study that explores the variables that predicted supported for the war and how support for the war affected interpretations of media coverage of the conflict. They found a positive link between authoritarianism and support for the war as well as news viewing and supportive attitudes.

David Swanson and Larry David Smith compare television coverage during the first week of the war offered by services in Chile, Germany, India, Jordan, Malaysia, the United Kingdom, and the United States. The comparisons show that all the services followed similar journalistic conventions and drew upon similar information and pictures to create seven different stories of the war, each reflecting national sentiment and involvement in the war.

Anne Johnston explores media coverage of women in the gulf conflict by discussing how various issues were framed by the print media. Although women have always played a role in war, Desert Storm renewed public discussion about the role of women in combat. The chapter concludes by identifying what Americans learned by the experience and discussing future implications.

Matthew McAllister analyzes the themes common in advertising, which used the war as a referent system, discussing how the war was presented, how it compared to advertising during previous wars, and what are the implications for the consumer's view of the war and the role of advertising in society. Hundreds of ads attempted to associate companies and products with the popular war effort at both the national and local levels for products ranging from cars to pizza. The author concludes that the pervasiveness of Persian Gulf War advertising expands the purview of what advertisers may legitimately link with their products and presents an image of war that is pure and apolitical.

Stephen Prince looks at the impact of Hollywood upon American views of Arabs and the Middle East region. He argues that by the time of the Gulf War, Arabic cinematic representation was well established in American culture. These representations shared a number of similarities with the terms and images used in political discourse to explain, justify, and interpret the war itself. In effect, Hollywood's historical representations inhibited American understanding and sympathy for peoples of the Middle East.

Finally, James Combs explores how popular entertainment legitimizes warfare. Historically, there has been a great deal of cooperation between Washington and Hollywood during times of war with generally favorable and noble presentations of warfare. In other periods, however, movies and television tend to present more critical perspectives of our nation's activities. The danger, of course, is that gripping war stories that invite vicarious audience interest and that solicit popular support offer a new opportunity for national security elites to conduct warfare in a media age without undue criticism or restraint stemming from negative or critical ideas and images generated independent of war communications control.

War and international conflict seem inevitable. The challenge is how to continue to cultivate an active, democratic citizenry in light of our heavy dependence upon the media. We need greater public understanding of the role, function, and power of the media in our society. Thus, we offer these studies in the hope that they may inform our future, especially in times of war.

                                                                Robert E. Denton, Jr.

BIBLIOGRAPHY

U.S. News & World Report. 1992. *Triumph Without Victory*. New York: Times Books.

Acknowledgments

The joy of editing a book is working with outstanding colleagues across the nation. In the past, I have been informed by their analyses, discussions, and, in some cases, personal friendships. It has been a genuine pleasure working with each author, and I appreciate their participation in this volume and their insightful contributions.

Serving as department head can be a difficult and very time-consuming task. I am most fortunate, however, to have wonderful and supportive colleagues in the Department of Communication Studies at Virginia Polytechnic Institute and State University. I want to thank them for their encouragement to pursue projects of interest and in many ways for protecting me from the bureaucratic abyss and administrative nightmares of academic life.

I also appreciate the folks at Praeger who, after nearly a decade, continue to be interested, helpful, and most supportive in so many ways. A special thanks goes to Anne Davidson Kiefer, an outstanding editor and friend.

Finally, I want to thank Paula, Bobby, and Chris for their love, encouragement, and support. They understand that such projects are essential to my very being. They provide, as always, the basis of my hope for the future, my joy of the present, and the purpose of all my endeavors.

The Media
and the
Persian Gulf War

Chapter One

The Rules of the Game: The Military and the Press in the Persian Gulf War

Gary C. Woodward

It was a war that came—as perhaps most do—with a number of disquieting contradictions.✦Live television coverage would be extensive, but so would on-screen disclaimers and newspaper sidebars reminding Americans that the reporting had been "cleared by military censors." A sea of facts would be available in press handouts—we learned that 800 chaplains served the 532,000 troops of Operation Desert Storm and that the total cost of the 45-day air war was $13.3 billion—but few reporters actually witnessed any combat. The objective of the U.S.-led military coalition was to free a sliver of country with an embarrassing wealth of oil, a state known more for its feudal monarchy and exclusionary immigration policies than any lasting contributions to the region's stability and culture. There was also irony in the fact that George Bush had decided to punish a former recipient of American aid and a sometime ally. Just months earlier Saddam Hussein had been reassured by the American ambassador and visiting senators that the hostility of the "conceited" American press toward Iraq did not reflect their views (Mathews 1991, 56). In the end, an uneasy peace would be achieved after the destruction of over half of the Iraqi army. Perhaps 100,000 or more people died,[1] most of them Iraqis, many as unwilling conscripts to a huge military that consumed most of the nation's wealth and distorted much of its rich history. And Saddam would survive to destroy many of Iraq's internal enemies in the northern part of the country, at the same time tormenting leaders of the military coalition who had set out to defeat and discredit his regime.

✦ Wars come with built-in contradictions. The press seeks rapid and complete disclosure of all but the most sensitive of information; yet military leaders generally want to control the flow of news. It is also the business of journalism to offer quick-but-tentative versions of the truth. Pentagon planners, in contrast, believe they must try to manipulate public opinion for their own ends, and they know that the mortal business of conflict gives them a considerable rhetorical advantage against the press. War involves the highest of stakes, including the lives of the young men and women who fight, the treasure of the nation that sponsors it, and the fantasies of national honor that are put at risk. We want to hear about war heroes and courageous fighters, but not about soldiers who dislike their commanders or the casualties of friendly fire. Wars must always seem to enact the best instincts that we have defined as part of our national character.

And so the contradictions surfaced again in the Persian Gulf as they had in the past decades that defined the eras of Vietnam, Korea, and the two world wars. Technology has made it increasingly possible for journalists to notify the rest of the world instantaneously of what they know. Still, they often know very little. Many ended up covering the desert war from places like the plush-red hotel ballroom or the roof terrace of the Dhahran International Hotel, relaying pieces of second-hand information given to them by cautious briefers and "pool" reporters authorized to be with combat units. In this six-week conflict in the first two months of 1991, the single-most-common image was not of troops slogging through the desert, or of bombs falling silently on the distant grids of an Iraqi city. It was perhaps of a reporter—Charles Jaco of CNN or his counterparts at the other television networks—reporting from their designated spaces on the terrace of the Dhahran International. Against the background of the blue canopies over the lower-level swimming pool they did their best to sketch in the details of briefings and to grope for partial answers. Guidelines laid down by the Department of Defense greatly limited the access that the roughly 1,000 journalists gathered in Saudi Arabia would actually have to combat areas and military units. These rules required that visits to military sites would be limited to small press pools who would be accompanied at all times by escorts. Many reports from these journalists would be reviewed by military censors in advance of their release.

These restrictions eventually opened a second and unlikely front during the war, pitting many—but certainly not all—in the national news media against the Pentagon. A number of reporters and magazines filed suit against the Department of Defense, arguing that First Amendment guarantees for freedom of the press had been violated by these rules. Pulitzer Prize–winning foreign correspondants such as Sidney Schanberg and David Halberstam wrote cautionary jeremiads about the dangers of using "national security" as a cover for managing war news. And sympathetic senators held hearings to query Pentagon officials about the restrictions (U.S. Senate, 1991). For his part, the assistant secretary for Defense for Public Affairs, the affable Pete Williams, concluded that "the press gave the American people the best war coverage they ever had" (*New York Times* 1991: A16). News executives around the country, however, asserted that they had been hindered by "real censorship" that tended to confirm "the worst fears of reporters in a democracy" (DeParle 1991b: A4). They shared concerns that had begun to crystallize after the 1983 American invasion of Grenada, where press access had been denied for over two days. As NBC's John Chancellor noted at the time:

✝ It is not only the privilege of the American press to be present at moments of historic importance, it is the responsibility of the press to be there. The men who died . . . were representing values in American life; one of those values is the right of the citizenry to know what their government is doing. (Braestrup 1985: 118)

✝ By May of 1991 the representatives of fifteen news organizations ranging from the *Wall Street Journal* to The Associated Press complained in an angry letter to Secretary of Defense Dick Cheney that the Pentagon had exercised "total control" over what they broadcast and wrote.

✝ Virtually all major news organizations agree that the flow of information to the public was blocked, impeded or diminished by the policies and practices of the Department of Defense. These conditions meant we could not tell the public the full story of those who fought the nation's battle. . . .
Pools did not work. Stories and pictures were late or lost. Access to the men and women in the field was interfered with by a needless system of military escorts and copy review. The pool system was used in the Persian Gulf war not to facilitate news coverage but to control it. (*New York Times* 1991: A16)

If this conflict was not inevitable, it was at least predictable; it had many Americans again pondering the well-known observation attributed to California's Senator Hiram Johnson that "the first casualty when war comes is truth."

This chapter explores the uneasy relationship that exists between the press and the military in a time of war. Many members of news organizations believed that their work had never been so severely restricted by the actions of the commanders overseeing a military action. As the first section suggests, however, there is a long tradition of governmental news management in times of military conflict. The second section reviews the Pentagon's guidelines that were enforced in the Persian Gulf, with particular attention to how members of the press adapted or adhered to them. The concluding section examines several organizational and political factors that were important as shapers of broadcast and print coverage of the war, if generally beyond the control of the American military.

MILITARY NEWS MANAGEMENT: A SHORT SUMMARY OF A LONG HISTORY

Military journalism takes several distinct forms, each coming with various freedoms and constraints in times of war. The most graphic reporting has always come from the relatively few reporters who have been willing to accept the risk of joining frontline troops or combat pilots. In his landmark study of war reporting from the Civil War to Vietnam, Phillip Knightley provides a vivid picture of journalists who sought to bring the terror of battle to readers and viewers. Every age has identified with some of these colorful figures: photographer Mathew Brady with the Union armies at Bull Run and Gettysburg; Ernest Hemingway seeking out stories from the battle lines in the Spanish Civil War; Ernie Pyle with infantry units in World War II; and CBS's Jack Laurence covering an ambush and firefight in Vietnam (Knightley 1975). Such frontline correspondents have always provided the most vivid images of war. In unexpected ways they humanize war by showing its ugly and often senseless consequences. The more accurate the reporting from the field, the more likely it is to serve as a valuable check on the lofty political rhetoric that initially justifies the decision to commit forces to combat.

A second kind of coverage is provided by writers who specialize in the strategies and technologies available to military commanders. For these journalists, war is a chessboard full of dangerous or decisive options. Covering the military through the prolonged Cold War has created a small core of specialists who have been able to describe complicated weapons systems, intramilitary frictions, the views of Pentagon dissidents, the politics of the North Atlantic Treaty Organization (NATO), and the biases of particular commanders or congressional power brokers. In recent years the emphasis of journalists such as Drew Middleton of the *New York Times* and Charles Corddry of the *Baltimore Sun* has been less on eyewitness reporting from military hotspots than on explaining the behavior of those who made key military decisions.

A third and largely neglected form of reporting on defense affairs involves the cultural forces that have shaped the conflict. Arguably no information is more important than the political, bureaucratic, and social contexts that can provide vital frames of reference. These will usually continue to exert their influence long after the fighting ceases. For example, at least one comprehensive analysis of the Korean and Vietnam wars was done far from Southeast Asia, in the New York City office of the independent-minded I. F. Stone. By engaging in very close reading of government documents, transcripts of congressional hearings, and official reports, Stone was often able to provide a better picture of the evolution of these wars than those who were on the scene (Knightley 1975: 422). Even an aggressive combat journalist like David Halberstam came to believe that war reporting in the absence of a strong historical context was not very useful. As a frontline reporter, he noted,

The problem was trying to cover something every day as news when in fact the real key was that it was all derivative of the French Indo-China War, which is history. So you really should have had a third paragraph in each story which would have said, "All of this is shit and none of this means anything because we are in the same footsteps as the French and we are prisoners of their experience." But given the rules of newspaper reporting you can't really do that. Events have to be judged by themselves, as if the past did not really exist. (Knightley 1975: 423)

In actual fact, few national reporters who operate under daily deadlines have the luxury of focusing on only one style of reporting. But these different approaches to the reporting of military actions are useful in understanding how news has been managed in wartime. The third kind of reporting, emphasizing background information and analysis, offers journalists the greatest freedom. Often, individual facts matter less than broad historical patterns that are not easily concealed. Those attempting to function in the first two modes—actually covering the planning and execution of wartime actions—have always been subject to various degrees of censorship and misinformation. The reason is obvious but important. They usually have little choice but to seek the active cooperation of the military in pursuit of their objectives, a fact that produces an uncomfortable combination of realism and rebellion within many members of the press corps.

Since World War I, few journalists have bothered to argue with what has become a standard list of restrictions regarding military actions. These prohibitions have included detailed information on the location of troops or weapons; discussions of planned tactics; the location of missing troops, planes, or ships still subject to possible rescue; and news about operational weaknesses that could be used by the enemy. With the partial exception of the Vietnam War, however, there has been little agreement between commanders and reporters on less strategic types of information.

Edward R. Murrow's experiences with Britain's Ministry of Information in 1940 is illustrative. He sought permission to do several live broadcasts to his huge CBS audiences in the United States during the massive German air attacks on London. Permission was initially denied. It is difficult to figure out what kind of news might have been broadcast that would have compromised British secrecy; the devastation of the night-time raids on central London's docks and homes would have been obvious to the German air crews. More likely, the ministry was bothered by the prospect of the world witnessing the nightly pounding that the capital city was taking from the Luftwaffe's five hundred-pound incendiary bombs. Murrow kept asking and agreed to record his reports in a number of practice runs, attempting to prove to the ministry that he would not expose vital military secrets (Sperber 1986: 161–74). In the end the ministry finally relented, slow to realize that Murrow's accounts of the stoic resolve of the city's residents would help achieve Winston Churchill's objective of motivating Americans to come to Britain's aid.

Murrow and other reporters were often less successful in getting stories cleared through American military censors. Drew Middleton recalls that "total censorship prevailed. Everything written, photographed, or broadcast was scrutinized by censors. Anything that did not meet the high command's considerations of security was deleted" (Middleton 1984: 37). In the Pacific Theater, for example, Americans were not told initially of the heavy damage to the U.S. Navy inflicted by the Japanese at Pearl Harbor. Even at the end of the war information about the desperate kamikaze attacks of the Japanese Air Force against U.S. ships was largely kept out of the American press by military censors (Knightley 1975: 273–74, 297).

In spite of strict censorship rules in World War II, the press generally gave the military and its planners high marks. Several factors explain why. One reason is that the skeptical adversary model that is so common today was less clearly a part of the journalistic *ethos*. Members of the press suffered less from the antipolitical bias that is now a fixture in contemporary American life. In addition, most reporters were personally committed to the broad political objectives of the Allies, and they were routinely allowed to join particular units, talk to their members, and fly on bombing and supply missions. Key commanders from Dwight D. Eisenhower to George C. Marshall were willing to provide thorough briefings "off the record" on the effects of particular campaigns. Control over what was reported usually came *after* reporters had been given extensive information. Then, censors restricted what they allowed journalists to reveal in news reports and newsreels. As in World War I, correspondents soon learned to engage in their own form of self-censorship to avoid the delays that rewriting stories sometimes entailed (Steele 1985: 707–12).

The stalemated and deadly "police action" in Korea signaled a gradual shift away from this pattern of broad access but strong official censorship, a pattern that would be complete by the time the Vietnam War had escalated into a major conflict. Partly because Vietnam was an undeclared war, journalists had a freer rein in determining for themselves what they would file to their editors and producers.

Vietnam has been called the "uncensored war," a label that is technically accurate but also misleading. In the second half of the 1960s correspondents in Vietnam found that they had wide access to individual units in the field. Many became effective chroniclers of the peculiar hell that results when the "enemy" becomes indistinguishable from the inhabitants of jungle villages. UPI's Neil Sheehan, the AP's John Wheeler, NBC's Greg Harris, and many others captured in words and images much of the incredible horror of the Vietnam conflict, usually shipping their reports back to their offices without prior military screening. A Harris television story in 1967 about the destruction of Cong Phu, a village that was thought to harbor the Viet Cong, was not unusual in its vividness and raw accuracy:

The Army calls this an "insertion" [troops are being dropped by helicopter at a landing zone in "the bush"]. As gunships saturate the landing zone with rockets and machine-gun fire, scout helicopters seek out the VC or sport suspects. Then a squad of the assault, or "blue," platoon is lifted into the location to either engage the enemy or surprise and capture a suspect. . . .

We then see the unit move into and search a village. Ammunition is found, and that was enough proof of its being used by the Vietcong. Cong Phu was burned and blasted to death. We see American medics treating sick and injured civilians, then Harris speaks with the platoon commander. The Vietcong, the lieutenant says, had been moving in and the only way to stop it is to eliminate the area. . . . "[We are] razing these houses so we'll avoid Charlie coming in and spending his nights."

Harris begins his summation over film first of a body being pulled out of a hole by the hair, then of burning huts. (Hallin 1986: 138)

The increasing intensity of this kind of reporting left Americans with few illusions about the high costs and muddled objectives of the war. But the absence of military censorship of outgoing dispatches and film stories conceals what Drew Middleton describes as the common practice of "censorship at the source" (Middleton 1984: 61). Especially in the case of Vietnam, an enormous credibility gap developed that increasingly pitted journalists—and soon, a sizeable minority of the American public—against the president and military commanders in Saigon. The gap was created by the enormous discrepancies between what reporters were seeing and relaying to Americans from the villages in the countryside and what briefers were more optimistically describing in Saigon and Washington. The daily afternoon sessions between journalists and representatives of the Joint U.S. Public Affairs Office became for many Americans a notorious symbol of purposeful equivocation. What was dubbed "the five-o'clock follies" provided abundant evidence to journalists that the bureaucracy was intentionally attempting to manage news about the overall scope of the conflict, often by claiming that

information was not available or by inflating estimates such as the number of enemy soldiers killed in combat. After 1968 it was obvious that
optimistic military estimates about South Vietnamese control over its
own regions did not square with what frontline journalists were seeing
and reporting.

The later years of the Vietnam conflict saw an unprecedented degree
of stunningly vivid combat reporting. If the graphic imagery was not
matched by a clarity about the United States's objectives and policy, it
was perhaps the first and last time Americans would confront the gritty
realities of combat as they unfolded (Braestrup 1977: 156–60; Arlen 1969).
One reason was that many officers in the field welcomed reporters as
potential allies. Many of those engaged in fighting in Vietnam wanted
the American public to see the difficulties and daily frustrations of combat against an enemy of uncertain origins in obscure locations. The press
was also able to develop its coverage because of the extended period of
time it had to organize its own infrastructure. In organizing its resources
for long-term coverage, journalism organizations were able to overcome
one of their major liabilities: the fact that the press is naturally a *reactive*
institution. As the Nieman Foundation's Bill Kovach has observed, the
press typically responds only after other organizations have already put
their plains in motion (Kovach 1991). At least in the short term, the press
is easily led. It has a strong tendency to cover an event initially from
the perspective of those who have orchestrated it. Only because the
Vietnam conflict grew incrementally and over nearly a decade, the press
had the luxury of time to be able to establish a stronger independent
presence than would be possible in more rapidly moving events.

Ironically, it was a small operation on the island of Grenada in 1983
that would signal the weakness of the media to cover short-term military
actions, a weakness that could be exploited by defense planners. The
Grenada invasion was a quick military strike—White House Chief of
Staff James Baker accurately described it as a commando raid—centered
on the airport of that small Caribbean island. Its primary objective was
the rescue of American students thought to be held by a government
friendly to Cuba. The invasion occurred without the press, and was
virtually over before any were able to fly to the island. Although there
were strong objections from the press about Defense Secretary Caspar
Weinberger's decision to exclude journalists in the initial landing, most
had no choice but to grudgingly provide after-the-fact accounts of the
invasion provided by the Pentagon and the White House (Hertsgaard
1989: 205–37). Even Pete Williams later conceded that it was a "journalistic disaster" (Williams 1991: 2).

The political consequences of the Grenada invasion may have been
as important as its strategic value. It pushed the military into meetings
with news executives and reporters about how to arrange coverage of

the smaller combat operations that were now predicted in a world no longer dominated by East–West tensions. The primary result of these meetings was the so-called Sidle Commission Report, named after retired army general Winant Sidle who oversaw the deliberations. At the request of the chairman of the Joint Chiefs of Staff, General John W. Vessy, Jr., Sidle worked with retired military officers and journalists to establish a set of recommendations governing press–military planning in future operations. The most basic included the following:

- That public affairs planning for military operations be conducted concurrently with operational planning.

- When it becomes apparent during military operational planning that news media pooling provides the only feasible means of furnishing the media with early access to an operation, planning should provide for the largest possible press pool . . . and minimize the length of time the pool will be necessary.

- That a basic tenet governing media access to military operations should be voluntary compliance by the media with security guidelines or groundrules established and issued by the military. These rules should be as few as possible.

- Public affairs planning for military operations should include sufficient equipment and qualified military personnel whose function is to assist correspondents in covering the operation adequately. (Sidle 1984: 166–67)

On this last point members of the panel were less clear on whether staff support should include "escorts" who would have the power to censor reports under the direction of the commander in charge of the operation. Sidle noted that "all of the media were against escorts if their goal was to try to direct, censor, or slant coverage" (Sidle 1984: 175). He also observed that there was no consensus on whether commanders had the right to "embargo" stories or delay their release to the public (Sidle 1984: 172).

The first combat test of the guidelines proposed by the panel was in 1987, after the United States agreed to escort merchant ships through the Persian Gulf. Iran—then nearly at the end of its long and deadly war with Iraq—had threatened to attack any commercial vessels in the region that it deemed to be a threat. Several pools were placed on navy destroyers that would escort Kuwaiti tankers that had recently been re-registered under the American flag. For example, joining the escort on the USS *Fox* were several print reporters, a radio journalist, and a *Time* photographer. Most of their reports made during their time aboard the *Fox* were approved for release. But according to Knight Ridder's Mark Thompson, several were held up for nearly two days, and at least one was changed by the *Fox*'s commander before he would allow it to be published. Near the end of the operation the pool witnessed what the navy had sought to avoid when the supertanker *Bridgeton* hit a mine near Iran's Farsi Island. The journalists' reports of the accident were immediately released to the press, but *Time*'s photographer was denied permission to photograph the *Bridgeton* scene from an available helicopter, a shot that would have revealed that the navy ships were behind the wounded tanker they were supposedly escorting (Thompson 1987: 40–45).

This first test of the pool system was not a resounding success for the Sidle Commission rules, even though Thompson conceded that "our audiences were better served for our having been there, rather than at our Washington desks" (Thompson 1987: 45). Even so, the same general guidelines remained in effect for the American invasion of Panama in December 1990. Few journalists who covered that operation felt that the new rules granted them adequate access to the military planners and units during the operation.

As the invasion to capture and disarm General Manuel Noriega and his soldiers began, the military agreed to fly a pool of sixteen reporters to the scene. Members of the pool reported, however, that they were consistently delayed from covering the fighting. Incongruously, during the early hours of what was officially dubbed "Operation Just Cause," the pool was escorted first to a room to watch CNN's television coverage of the war and then on to a lecture by the U.S. chargé d'affairs on the history of Panama. Over the next four days, the group was generally kept at some distance from the fighting in Panama City, and only escorted into an area after combat had mostly ceased. The AP's Steven Komarow noted that it was "frustratingly apparent the invasion we were sent to witness was blazing forth without us" (Komarow 1990: 45), and the Pentagon's Pete Williams again conceded that "it took too long to get reporters to the scene of the action" (Williams 1991: 2). One disgruntled member of a pool under military escort came up with his own motto: "Semper Tardis." Always late.

We missed what could have been some great stories, including stuff which, ironically, Southern Command brass should have been scrambling to let us see. A case in point was the U.S. Military's entrance into Colon, the port city at the Atlantic end of the canal, in response to uncontrolled looting. This was on Friday, more than two full days after the initial invasion. We were only a short helicopter ride away, but they kept us away from the operation until evening, when it was nearly over. (Cranberg 1990: 49)

For their part, the few journalists who were already in Panama before the invasion began found it difficult to do much more than provide phone reports from a Marriott hotel that was periodically raided by Noriega loyalists. Several were taken from the hotel as hostages. Photographers Patrick Chauvel and Juan Rodriquez fared even worse when they were shot after venturing out to cover the fighting around Noriega's headquarters. Rodriquez later died from his wounds (Vasquez 1990: 44, 46). Reflecting a pattern that would be soon repeated by CNN's crew at Baghdad's Al-Rashid Hotel in the opening hours of war in Iraq, CBS and NBC news crews attempted to provide coverage to American audiences from the upper floors of the Marriott. In the days that followed, reporters such as CBS's Juan Vasquez also had the added advantage of using their local contacts and limited mobility to provide the semblance of a frontline perspective. In contrast to official reports from the Southern Command announcing the end of the fighting, they continued to send a less-simplified picture that included evidence of continued resistance from Noriega's troops and massive civilian looting of businesses in Panama City (Vasquez 1990: 46).

Throughout the Persian Gulf escort mission and the Panama invasion, news organizations tended to go along with the Sidle Commission Rules, perhaps underestimating the damage that one of its most troubling aspects would later cause. Few would dispute the need to travel with military escorts in the early hours or days of invasion. There were practical reasons to limit the size of the pool that should accompany the first wave of troops into a hostile area. But conceding the right to final review of stories to the military now seems like an inordinately high quid-pro-quo. Gilbert Cranberg, who was a member of a pool in Panama, noted that "military review of pool stories went smoothly, with no censorship problems" (Cranberg 1990: 52). Indeed, at that point he had no choice but to work through the military clearance machinery or not file his stories. But as the Persian Gulf War loomed, members of the press would have good reason to rethink the wisdom of ceding the editorial prerogative of prior restraint to Pentagon planners. A general silence on this key point throughout the tanker escort operation in 1987 and the later Panama invasion meant that coveted slots in press pools would come at a very high price.

MILITARY GROUNDRULES IN THE GULF

"With an arrogance foreign to the democratic system," CBS's venerable Walter Cronkite told readers of *Time* magazine, "the U.S. military in Saudi Arabia is trampling on the American people's right to know" (Cronkite 1991: 43). What he and other journalists objected to was a series of specific guidelines laid down to the approximately 1,000 accredited reporters and technicians who covered the war from Saudi Arabia. Of this number, no more than 126 were ever assigned to pools for coverage of the half-million Americans in the area during the five-week air war. During the three days of ground combat that began on

February 24, 1991, approximately 250 journalists were allowed to join combat pools (Lamb 1991: 33).

Many Americans were angered, but not particularly surprised, when CNN's Peter Arnett and other reporters working in the region were heavily restricted in what they could write or show. Arnett was not allowed to show or discuss any military damage in and around Baghdad, nor was he permitted to talk freely to ordinary citizens without a government escort. His on-the-air copy was also approved by Iraqi censors prior to broadcast (Goodman 1991: 30–31). Even the relatively open government of Israel imposed strict limits on reports. In the first ten days of the air war the cities of Haifa, Tel Aviv, and Ramallah came under attack from Iraqi Scud missiles. Television viewers were regularly treated to live broadcasts from network correspondents who clearly knew more about the effects of the damage caused by these Soviet-made missiles— their location, payloads, and civilian casualties—than they were permitted to report. Americans were more surprised, if not especially bothered, by complaints from the press that their reporting was heavily restricted by the Department of Defense.

Built on the Sidle Commission model, the military's rules in the Middle East put heavy and burdensome restrictions on members of the press. Even before the massive air offensive began on January 16, Pentagon rules issued to the Washington bureaus of news organizations required that all reports not disclose sensitive military information, that access to combat units would be limited to preselected pools of reporters, and that reports from members within a pool would have to be submitted to "security review." Pete Williams wrote to the press corps on January 14, reminding them that tight rules "intended to meet the specific operational environment of the Persian gulf" would be enforced by public affairs officers working in Riyadh and Dhahran.[2] The small number of reporters who ignored them in the weeks that followed, such as the *New York Times*'s Chris Hedges, discovered that they sometimes gained protection from commanders who were sympathetic to their desire to break free of Pentagon restrictions. At other times, however, these so-called unilaterals were rounded up by military M.P.s, shipped back to rear-staging areas, and detained for short periods of time (Hedges 1991: 27–29). The most unlucky of the unilaterals was CBS's Bob Simon, who was captured along with his crew by Iraqi troops and held until the end of the war.

The two-page list of restrictions that would be placed on the press included the obvious and traditional limits on coverage. Reporters were reminded to restrict the use of lights at night. They were told that they would have to carry their own gear, such as batteries and cameras, and were cautioned against giving out information regarding the names of casualties, the movements of troops, and specific information on individuals or aircraft down behind enemy lines. They were generally cautioned about reporting anything that "could jeopardize operations and endanger lives"; for example:

- Any information that reveals details of future plans, operations, strikes, including postponed or cancelled operations.
- Information, photography, and imagery that would reveal the specific location of military forces or show the level of security at military encampments.
- Information on operational or support vulnerabilities that could be used against U.S. forces, such as details of major battle damage or major personnel losses of specific U.S. or coalition units.

Some journalists were bothered by the stipulation that "at U.S. tactical or field locations and encampments, a public affairs escort may be required because of security, safety, and mission requirements, as determined by the host commander."[3] Reporters do not want to be told where they can go and to whom they may talk. But the decision to rely on censored pool reports as a primary conduit of battle and combat information was even more controversial.

The idea of using a representative group of journalists in a specific setting is not new. In some cases the sheer number of accredited reporters in a given location makes it impossible for press offices to arrange access for all who wish it. The White House, presidential campaigns, the National Aeronautics and Space Administration (NASA), and other agencies have often put limits on coverage by selecting a limited number of reporters to cover a story. Those who are selected relinquish the right to claim an "exclusive" on the events they witness. Much like wire-service reporters, their job is to provide a factual running narrative of what took place and to make it available to all other members of the press. A pool report—in pictorial or written form—may be used by various media as is or incorporated into a rewritten story.

In Dhahran, several days before the first Tomahawk Missile was launched toward Baghdad, combat pools were set up by the Central Command—in Pentagon jargon, CENTCOM—and administered with the help of the Joint Information Bureau (JIB). Williams's January 14 memo laid out the basic structure of the pools:

To the extent that individuals in the news media seek access to the U. S. area of operation, the following rule applies: Prior to or upon commencement of hostilities, media pools will be established to provide initial combat coverage of U.S. forces. U. S. news media personnel present in Saudi Arabia will be given the opportunity to join CENTCOM media pools, providing they agree to pool their products. News media personnel who are not members of the official CENTCOM media pools will not be permitted into forward areas. Reporters are strongly discouraged from attempting to link up on their own with combat units.[4]

Faithful to the Sidle Commission rules, Williams went on to clarify how pool reports would be cleared for general release:

In the event of hostilities, pool products will be subject to review before release to determine if they contain sensitive information about military plans, capabilities, operations, or vulnerabilities. . . . Material will be examined solely for its conformance to the attached ground rules, not for its potential to express criticism or cause embarrassment. The public affairs escort officer on scene will review pool reports, discuss ground rule problems with the reporter, and in the limited circumstances when no agreement can be reached with a reporter about disputed materials, immediately send the disputed materials to JIB Dhahran for review.[5]

In this period less than ten groups were initially established, with sizes ranging from seven to eighteen members. The largest pools were assigned to the army and marines. Smaller groups were established to cover the air force, navy, military hospitals, and any unexpected events. Approximately 71 individual slots were available, growing to about 126 reporters (including support technicians in video-news crews) when the air war was well under way (Lamb 1991: 33–34). Even so, large gaps remained. Many army units had no journalists with them. According to the *New York Times*'s R. W. Apple, out of a total of eight army or marine divisions numbering over 100,000 men and women on the ground near Kuwait, only thirty spots existed for the press just days before the ground war (Apple 1991: A14). Most of the approximately 1,000 journalists who wanted to cover the war in the Persian Gulf were left at the Dhahran International Hotel or the Riyadh Hyatt, able to receive only pool reports and the daily military briefings issued by representatives of the Joint Command (Lamb 1991: 34). Many key commanders apparently did not share Dwight Eisenhower's belief that the media could be an asset to the military. "I'm not a great fan of the press," began one operational commander in a Dhahran pool briefing, "and I want you to know where we stand with each other. I suppose the press has its purpose. But one thing is certain; you can't do me any good, and you sure as hell can do me harm" (Browne 1991: 30).

The problem of limited access to specific units in the field was compounded by the fact that journalists largely set up their own mechanism for selecting pool reporters, with preferences going to major newspapers and broadcast outlets. This process quickly created tensions within a news community that has always thrived on large egos and intense competition. Small publications claimed that major news outlets took too many of the coveted pool slots. The *Times*'s Apple argued the reverse, noting that no reporter from his paper had been selected for a pool assignment with American ground forces during the first five weeks of Operation Desert Storm.[6] He noted ruefully that among those selected over the *New York Times* were reporters for *Mirabella*, a women's magazine, and the military's own semi-official *Stars and Stripes* (Apple 1991: A14).

In practice, the pool/escort system did sometimes work. No reporter could easily defend the premise that in a military campaign all members of the press should be accommodated in specific locations. Some escorts were helpful in getting reporters to key locations and helping them see particular aspects of a military operation, especially in its early phases. But more aggressive members of the press frequently viewed the system as an efficient filter that worked against the press and in favor of the ostensible news management objectives of the military. A few reporters described helpful escorts and sympathetic field commanders (Lamb 1991: 33; Massing 1991: 23). Many more, however, sensed that their reporting was often unlikely to survive the intrusive presence of the military. They saw several levels of filters. First, reporters needed to obtain accreditation from the Pentagon. Second, they had to get into a pool—at best, a considerable long shot. Finally, if they managed that hurdle they were then dependent—as in Panama—on their escort's choice of a location for a story.

The apparent intention to keep pilots and members of the press apart is a case in point. Members of a pool hoping to interview or fly with the crews of the massive B–52 bombers and other crews that flew in some of the estimated 72,000 air sorties during the war were instead given ground interviews with air force commanders or a single preselected pilot. At one point they ended up interviewing drivers in a motor pool, where the commander suggested stories about the "unsung" role of military truck drivers in combat. Apparently only one reporter during the Persian Gulf conflict actually flew on an actual bombing mission, even though many types of aircraft—including B–52 bombers—had ample space. ABC's Forrest Sawyer, who abandoned pool arrangements in frustration, was able to find a Saudi pilot who was willing 'to go beyond the limits set by the American military (DeParle 1991a: A9). Even considering the fact that many fighters could not carry an additional passenger, this was in stark contrast to World War II, when reporters like Edward R. Murrow repeatedly flew on bombing runs over Germany.

Another pool was escorted to the outskirts of the Saudi border town of Khafji, which had been the scene of heavy fighting some eighteen hours earlier. They were told—and they reported—that the battle had been between Saudis and Iraqis. It was only because of several unauthorized reporters who went out on their own, in violation of Pentagon rules, that Americans learned of the involvement of U. S. troops in the bloody street fighting (DeParle 1991b: A4).

To National Public Radio's Deborah Amos, the power of military public information officers to select individuals and sites to be covered almost made them the equivalent of assignment editors who could dictate particular story lines (DeParle 1991a: A9). An escort could either pave the way to broad access for the band of journalists he accompanied—and many did—or he could impose further obstacles. Some escorts read or listened to pool reports without making changes. Others demanded alterations of wording or the deletion of material. In one instance a reporter who described returning fighter pilots as "giddy" was asked to note instead that they were "proud." In other instances harmless but revealing details were excised by military censors: that navy pilots relaxed by watching sex films, that church services were held in Saudi Arabia for groups of marines, that army chaplains found conditions difficult (Levinson 1991: 28).

One of the most troubling problems was that stories sent through military channels were often delayed or lost. Few news outlets could find or afford the direct-to-satellite phones that were leased at great expense by a few major news organizations such as the *New York Times*.[7] Most news organizations relied on the military to deliver stories that—under pool rules—had to be made available to all members of the press. No doubt many stories were lost in the confusion and understandable difficulties of combat. Others may have been delayed on purpose. A Seattle reporter described a rebuke by an escort on February 22 for talking to members of an army ranger unit without permission. The piece he then filed was later lost in transit back to Dhahran (Boot 1991: 25). Others similarly found that their reports disappeared for one or two days, thus increasing the likelihood that they would be discarded altogether in favor of more current reporting (Browne 1991: 45).

In late February Pete Williams conceded there had been problems, among them the delay of a reporter's story about the performance of the Stealth bombers, which was effectively killed when it was sent to a Stealth base in Nevada for clearance (Williams 1991: 6). "But," he went on, "I believe the system we have now is fair, that it gets a reasonable number of journalists out to see the action, and that the American people will get the accounting they deserve" (Williams 1991: 8). In testimony before the Senate's Committee on Governmental Affairs he defended the press rules as necessary for the safety of the troops and the security of military operations. "The rules are not intended to prevent journalists from reporting on incidents that might embarrass the military or to make military operations look sanitized," he noted.

The main concern of the military is that information not be published which would jeopardize a military operation or endanger the lives of the troops who must carry it out. The preamble to the rules for reporters covering World War II summarized the issue by saying that editors, in wondering what can be published, should ask themselves, "Is this information I would like to have if I were the enemy?" (Williams 1991: 4)

Williams even found at least lukewarm support among some journalists. Writing in the *Columbia Journalism Review* at the end of the conflict, one of its contributing editors complained that too many members of the press "seemed to be fighting the last war." According to Michael Massing, the Persian Gulf was not Vietnam, but rather a "fully conventional conflict, and it required something other than traditional on-the-ground reporting." While the press rules and restrictions may have been "burdensome," they hardly amounted to the denial of access: "A sanitized adjective, an altered airplane description, a story delayed for a day. Not exactly the Pentagon Papers" (Massing 1991: 23) Most of the American public apparently agreed, indicating in several polls acceptance of restrictions on the press as the legitimate price for conducting a major military campaign (Zoglin 1991: 52–53).

Even so, these elaborate guidelines for war coverage might have looked less threatening if they didn't so easily mesh with a larger picture of intensive news management. Most obviously, many soldiers who had entered the services during the Vietnam War, and now occupied senior military positions in the Persian Gulf, viewed Vietnam as a struggle with the media as well as the North Vietnamese. The message of television after the Tet Offensive of 1968 was often that the war was a logistical and political disaster, and some military leaders privately blamed the messenger (Turner 1985: 232–33). With some justification they concluded that the conflict became tougher to wage as the reporting and analysis of journalists like Walter Cronkite, Morley Safer, and Charles Mohr soured American public opinion. In General William Westmoreland's words, "the war that Americans saw was almost exclusively violent, miserable or controversial" (Braestrup 1985: 68).

Then, too, the Pentagon seemed to take a page from the Reagan stylebook in using news management as a tool for effecting public opinion. The television-oriented public relations techniques developed during the Reagan presidency by Michael Deaver, David Gergen, Roger Ailes, and others became a model for many federal agencies. Their interest in controlled press arrangements completed a shift in emphasis toward the needs of television news that had begun in the late 1960s under Richard Nixon. Americans had also acquired a thirst for interesting "visuals," a fascination that was captured in the grainy videos of "smart bombs" zooming in to their targets. This fact was not lost on the military's public relations directors. It probably figured in their decision to declare Delaware's receiving center for soldiers killed in combat off limits to the press. Pictures of coffins laid out in even rows within Dover Airforce Base's white hanger had always dramatized the human costs of military operations undertaken in Southeast Asia, Lebanon, and else-where. No issue of military security could be easily invoked to defend this decision. Only a desire to numb the American public over the actual costs of war could justify denying them the experience of witnessing the return of those lost to combat. Finally, there was the early decision of Secretary of Defense Dick Cheney to impose a news blackout on the first two days of the massive air attacks against Iraq. Echoing the logic that excluded the press from the Grenada invasion, Cheney apparently concluded that the press should see only the effects rather than the process of a massive military strike. Even General Norman H. Schwarz-kopf was unhappy with this rule, and the embargo ended after less than a day (DeParle 1991a: A9).

SPECIAL PROBLEMS IN THE GULF

Even without tight Defense Department restrictions, covering events in the Middle East has never been especially easy. Part of the difficulty originates in the United States, where news organizations have re-sponded to leaner times by cutting budgets for foreign reporters and bureaus. And part of the problem lies in the nature of the Middle East itself. While many states like Jordan have been hospitable to Western observers, others have been controlled by governments that are deeply suspicious of the motives of foreign journalists. These and other factors can be briefly catalogued.

1. Before the Gulf War, the American media had a very limited pres-ence in Saudi Arabia, Kuwait, and Iraq; nearly all were then forced to shift staffers to the region on relatively short notice. A number of news organizations—especially the three traditional network powerhouses—had cut back on their foreign reporting staffs in the last half of the 1980s. CBS, for example, had always been regarded by broadcasters as a net-work that fostered excellence in foreign reporting, but after its takeover by the Loews Corporation's Laurence Tisch, the division that Edward R. Murrow built was radically downsized. After 1985, reporters were fired and bureaus were closed in several devastating rounds of reduc-tions. One of those let go in a recent $33 million budget cut was their permanent Middle East correspondent (Boyer 1988: 326).[8]

As new arrivals in an unfamiliar setting, many reporters lacked the local contacts that would have helped them function outside of the umbrella of the Pentagon's Joint Information Bureau. In the best of conditions, the press is usually dependent on the military for basic sup-port. In the Persian Gulf, however, circumstances combined to intensify this unequal relationship. Few journalists spoke Arabic. Many had never been in a war, let alone a war zone; and few had connections to local residents or institutions who could provide opportunities to travel or present alternate perspectives. The press had to depend on the goodwill of the military for many basic privileges and services, including the necessary accreditation that gave them the modest right to attend briefings. With some exceptions, the military also retained control over most of the essential services journalists would need in order to function, including transportation, housing, essential field equipment such as gas masks, and access to fax equipment and satellite up-links.

In a relatively short war in a remote location, the relationship of the press to the military is fundamentally hierarchical, with the press functioning as a client of the larger bureaucracy it is attempting to cover. *Harper's* Lewis Lapham captured this dilemma when he compared reporters on the scene to the network's television announcers who must cover football games according to the rules laid down by the National Football League. "Like the sportscasters in the glass booth on the fifty-yard line," he noted, "the newscasters standing in front of the palm tree or the minaret understood themselves to be guests of the management" (Lapham 1991: 11).

2. Working in Saudi Arabia and most other states in the region is not easy for the press, even in times of relative peace. The *World Press Encyclopedia* notes that Riyadh has a reputation among journalists as "among the top discomfort stations" in the world (Kurian 1982: 783). Western reporters have always had difficulties obtaining permission to report from within Saudi Arabia, Syria, Iran, and Iraq. Saudi customs and laws, for example, remain largely antithetical to the idea of a free press (Theroux 1990). Even during the early weeks of the American military buildup that was ostensibly for the defense of the Saudis, the Saudi government was extremely reluctant to issue visas to members of the foreign press. Saudi journalists remain under severe restrictions for their reporting, with the threat of jail terms or death for libelous or defamatory comments about their government or its restrictive interpretations of Islamic law.

To some extent the American military was also caught in the middle of an enormous cultural chasm. It did not wish to offend the Saudis on their own soil, but thousands of troops reflecting the diversity and pluralism of the United States could not easily blend in to Saudi Arabia's very different cultural landscape. Visitors carried the burden of adapting to different customs that have the force of law, especially in fundamentalist enclaves such as Riyadh.

The problem was especially accute for women, who were a significant part of the American military presence. Saudi custom prohibits any woman from driving an automobile or moving around with male escorts who are not relatives. Thus, reporters such as National Public Radio's

Deborah Amos were often at the mercy of male journalists who risked censure for simply giving a woman a ride to the scene of a story. Her "crimes" for leaving a press center were potentially twofold: for violating American military "guidelines" that prohibited venturing out beyond preselected areas without military authorization, and for violating Saudi religious laws that forbade her to be with a man who was not her husband (Amos 1991). Even Bob Hope had to skip his traditional USO-sponsored shows to the troops. Saudi officials apparently made it clear to American commanders that his jokes and company of beautiful women would have caused offense.

A Department of Defense pamphlet distributed to troops in the country went to great lengths to placate the Saudi monarchy, citing a host of topics and activities that would have to be curtailed during the joint military operation. Among the taboos:

- material deemed immoral or critical of state policies or action, such as pictures of men and women embracing, dancing, kissing, in sexual encounters, or nude;
- sensual advertisements for perfume, blue jeans, women's lingerie, gambling, alcohol, and so forth;
- discussing U.S. involvement in supporting Israel and Israel's current presence in Lebanon;
- discussing the host country's reservations about the peaceful intentions of other Arab states;
- proselytizing for non-Islamic religions;
- implying that any Arab country is totally dependent on foreign manpower for its economic and military structure;
- criticizing Islamic religious customs, women's rights, enforced dress and moral standards, and media coverage and censorship;
- photographing women, religious sites, or anything that would cast a negative light on the host country. (Fund For Free Expression 1991: 37–38)

3. With notable exceptions, American reporting from the Middle East has often focused on immediate events rather than the deeper ideological or social contexts. War reporting offers a few opportunities to construct a background for understanding the cultural origins of Middle Eastern problems. By its very nature news focuses on crises rather than the contexts that could put them in perspective. Unlike most of his colleagues, for example, the *New York Times*'s Chris Hedges could speak Arabic and thus was able to more easily shun Pentagon restrictions on pool reporting and blend into the local landscape. Over the course of the war Hedges reported the reactions of Saudi shopkeepers, Kuwaitis who survived the occupation, and fleeing Iraqi soldiers (Hedges 1991: 28).

The problem of thin and uninformed reporting from the Middle East has a considerable history and many causes. An emphasis on spot news, the enormous cultural differences between Western and Islamic states, press dependence on frames of reference defined by the American government, and a long history of insularity have all contributed to ignorance about the region (Altheide 1981: 128–57). Iran is an obvious example. After the overthrow of the shah in 1979, and during the prolonged hostage crisis that consumed the final years of the Carter administration, many members of the press conceded that little ground work existed for giving these events a needed perspective. In 1973 the television networks had devoted an average of only four-and-a-half minutes *over the entire year* to news about Iran, but their coverage jumped to over 700 minutes after Americans were taken hostage in Teheran (Barrett 1982: 20). As Bill Moyers observed at the time, we had become used to "taking one-dimensional snapshots of a complex culture." Thus, "we were surprised that politics and religion were so tightly meshed in Persian life. We were surprised when one of the best-equipped armies in the world could not keep the Shah in power. . . . We were surprised they hated us so" (Barrett 1982: 25). In the same period the networks similarly gave virtually no attention to the cultural and military activities of Syria and Iraq. Between 1972 and 1979, for example, mentions of Iraq in ABC's nightly newscasts were almost nonexistent. James Larson's content analysis of broadcasts from that period found that Iraq represented a tiny seven-tenths of one percent of ABC's on-air references to all foreign states (Larson 1982: 30).

4. Working in a largely treeless desert environment with few villages beyond the major cities, the press was left with a scarcity of safe outposts near forward military units. This problem was heightened by the fact that most journalists were officially unwelcome in units unless they were a part of a formally designated press pool. In other war zones ranging from Europe to Asia, reporters have often been able to retain some freedom of movement by using the protective cover of local villages and hamlets near the fighting. For example, Sydney Schanberg's insightful reporting on the fall of Cambodia in 1976—dramatized in the film "The Killing Fields"—would have probably been impossible without the protection of the forested terrain and his ability to gain the confidence and quiet access of many villagers. As one reporter noted in contemplating striking out on his own in the desert, "the Saudi hinterlands, unlike those of Vietnam, India or Central America, do not favor news coverage by stealth. Only a handful of roads cross the naked desert—mostly six lane highways on which traffic is sparse and a press vehicle is conspicuous" (Browne 1991: 45).

5. Although it is difficult to quantify the effect, there can be little doubt that editors and reporters were overwhelmed and perhaps intimidated by the rapid accumulation of public support for the military solution of extension bombing over Iraq. The arrogance of Saddam Hussein's invasion of Kuwait—along with the certain knowledge that the thirty-eight nations allied against his military would prevail—contributed to the general feeling that this was a just war. The possibility that there might be significant American casualties created strong initial doubts, but those also eased as rumors of defections from the Iraqi army began to circulate and as it became apparent in the second week of the war that Saddam could not mount a massive counter offensive. (Less than 200 U.S. troops died in the air and ground campaigns.)

Against this backdrop of rising euphoria over the course of the war, members of the press faced the dilemma of expressing their displeasure with Pentagon restrictions. For much of the public the criticisms seemed ungrateful: the equivalent of threatening to bring a malpractice suit against a doctor who had just saved someone's life. Editors around the nation quickly sensed that the press was in danger of appearing to be in the unsavory company of Saddam Hussein as an adversary to the American military. To the apparent delight of the White House, for example, NBC's "Saturday Night Live" opened its February 9 program with a lampoon of the Riyadh military briefings. Yet the object of the jokes was not the briefer, but a press that was portrayed as complaining and inept (DeParle 1991a: A9). Polls in late January and early February confirmed the worse. In a Times Mirror survey, over three quarters of the respondents felt that the military was not hiding information, and nearly 60 percent thought the Pentagon should exert even tighter controls over the press (Boot 1991: 24). CNN's Atlanta headquarters was flooded with thousands of letters critical of their coverage. Well over half the 55,000 pieces of mail they received were negative (Zoglan 1991: 53). As David Gergen wrote after the cease fire, "No public forum about the war seems to end without a denunciation of whining reporters badgering the military with goofy questions" (Gergen 1991: 57).

Many forces shaped coverage of the Persian Gulf War in the early months of 1991: the organizational realities of newsgathering, the legacy of Vietnam, the remarkable popularity of the war, the desire by the military to protect lives and sometimes mistakes, and the long but checkered tradition of American press independence. In the next conflict these and additional events will produce a different mix of pressures on military planners and the news media. Yet the stakes will remain the same, including the public's right to know and the nation's judgment about the political and military wisdom of the decision.

The prospect for the future is by no means certain, but several patterns found here will no doubt carry over in the years to come. For many reasons, military planners have committed themselves to imposing strict groundrules on press activities.╪Short wars depend on a certain degree of surprise: a tactical advantage commanders are unlikely to risk to even a select group of pool reporters. Therefore the press will continue to learn of military initiatives after they have actually begun. They can only submit to military guidelines for most subsequent reporting—at least for the short term. Panama, Grenada, and the initial days of the air assaults on Iraq are all consistent with this pattern.

The advantage that military planners hold over the mass media at the beginning of a conflict, however, begins to recede as time passes. The reasons are partly technological, but also rooted in the anarachic nature of the news business. Distance is increasingly irrelevant to newsgatherers, who will find it even easier in the future to establish phone, fax, and video links—even when they are reporting from remote areas. Like the government of East Germany, whose propaganda increasingly fell victim to Western television and print media, defense officials will probably be unable to enforce a single "cleared" perspective on journalists over an extended period of time. To do so would eventually mean placing military censors at the side of journalists in the field and next to editors in the nation's newsrooms. The internationalization of the news business—typified in television by CNN's acceptance in foreign capitals, and its use of reports by foreign journalists—represents the progressive irrelevance of national boundaries in the flow of information.

In addition, there is a considerable psychological distance that separates foreign correspondents from the officials and bureaucracies that they cover. There is both romance and truth to the image of journalism as a profession that naturally leans toward anarchy, but the fact that the pool system put in place in the Persian Gulf was within days of complete collapse was evidence of their resistance to control. After only three days of the ground campaign many journalists abandoned the safety of the Pentagon's restrictions and joined Allied units approaching Kuwait. The apparent collapse of the Iraqi army obviously contributed to the breakdown of the pool system. But it was also evident that a vital core of independent journalists were no longer willing to function as conduits for official conclusions that they could not confirm for themselves.

NOTES

The author would like to thank Nancy Dimeo for editorial suggestions and Howell Raines of the *New York Times* and Nelson Evans and the Roscoe West Library for their assistance in locating certain materials.
  1. Estimates have ranged from less than 65,000 to nearly 200,000.

2. Memorandum for Washington Bureau Chiefs, from Assistant Secretary of Defense for Public Affairs Pete Williams, Washington, January 15, 1991.

3. Department of Defense, Operation Desert Shield Ground Rules and Guidelines for News Media, photocopy, 2 pages, January 14, 1991.

4. Ibid.

5. Ibid.

6. Apple overlooked the fact that *Times* correspondent Malcom Browne did participate with a rapid reaction pool on January 17.

7. In future operations this will probably change. Small and lightweight telephone and television systems that will be able to function as direct uplinks to communications satellites will soon mean that many reporters will be able to transmit their stories from any location directly to their broadcast and editorial offices. Ministries of telecommunications in most countries still regulate the use of their own uplinks, but in most cases cost rather than censorship is what concerns most news executives who arrange for satellite services for their own outlets. See "News Drives Global Uniformity," *Broadcasting*, July 29, 1991, 49–51.

8. At a time of increased Middle Eastern tension in 1987, for example, CBS maintained foreign bureaus in China, Egypt, England, France, West Germany, Hong Kong, Israel, Italy, Japan, Lebanon, South Africa, and the USSR. Interestingly, with the exception of non-Arab Egypt, none of the bureaus was based in one of the large and predominantly Moslem countries in the Middle East. Source: *TV and Cable Factbook No. 55, Part II, 1987 Edition* (Washington: Television Digest, 1987), 88–89.

BIBLIOGRAPHY

Altheide, David. "Iran vs. TV News: The Hostage Story Out of Context." In William C. Adams, ed. *Television Coverage of the Middle East*. Norwood, N.J.: Ablex, 1981, 128–57.

Amos, Deborah. Interview on "Fresh Air." National Public Radio. July 9, 1991.

Apple, R. W. "Correspondents Protest Pool System." *New York Times*, February 12, 1991, A14.

Arlen, Michael. *Living Room War*. New York: Viking, 1969.

Barrett, Marvin. ed. *Broadcast Journalism: 1979–1981*. New York: Everest House, 1982.

Boot, William. "The Pool." *Columbia Journalism Review* (May/June 1991): 24–27.

Boyer, Peter J. *Who Killed CBS?* New York: Random House, 1988.

Braestrup, Peter. *Battle Lines: Report of the Twentieth Century Fund Task Force on the Military and the Media*. New York: Priority Press, 1985.

Braestrup, Peter. *Big Story*. Vol. 1. Boulder, Colo.: Westview Press, 1977.

Browne, Malcolm W. "The Military vs. The Press." *New York Times Magazine*, March 3, 1991, 27–30, 44–45.

Cranberg, Gilbert. "A Flimsy Story and a Compliant Press." *Washington Journalism Review* (March 1990): 48–49, 52–53.

Cronkite, Walter, "What Is There to Hide?" *Newsweek* (February 25, 1991): 43.

DeParle, Jason. "Keeping the News in Step: Are the Pentagon's Gulf War Rules Here to Stay?" *New York Times*, May 6, 1991(a), A9.

DeParle, Jason. "17 News Executives Criticize U.S. for 'Censorship' of Gulf Coverage." *New York Times*, July 3, 1991(b), A4.

Fund for Free Expression. "Freedom to Do as They're Told." *Index on Censorship* 4 and 5 (1991): 36–38.

Gergen, David. "Why America Hates the Press." *U.S. News and World Report*, March 11, 1991, 57.

Goodman, Walter. "Arnett." *Columbia Journalism Review* (May/June 1991): 29–31.

Hallin, Daniel C. *The "Uncensored War:" The Media and Vietnam*. New York: Oxford, 1986.

Hedges, Chris. "The Unilaterals." *Columbia Journalism Review* (May/June 1991): 27–29.

Hertsgaard, Mark. *On Bended Knee: The Press and the Reagan Presidency*. New York: Schocken, 1989.

Knightley, Phillip. *The First Casualty*. New York: Harcourt, Brace Jovanovich, 1975.

Komarow, Steven. "Pooling Around in Panama." *Washington Journalism Review* (March 1990): 45, 49.

Kovach, Bill. Speech to the Cambridge Forum. National Public Radio. July 26, 1991.

Kurian, George Thomas. ed. *World Press Encyclopedia Vol. 2, 1982*. New York: Facts on File, 1982.

Lamb, David. "Pentagon Hardball." *Washington Journalism Review* (April 1991): 33–36.

Lapham, Lewis H. "Notebook: Trained Seals and Sitting Ducks." *Harpers Magazine* (May 1991): 10–14.

Larson, James F. "International Affairs Coverage on US Evening Network News." In William C. Adams, ed. *Television Coverage of International Affairs*. Norwood, N.J.: Ablex, 1982, 15–41.

Levinson, Nan. "Snazzy Visual, Hard Facts, and Obscured Issues." *Index on Censorship*, 4 and 5 (1991): 27–29.

Massing, Michael, "Another Front." *Columbia Journalism Review* (June 1991): 23–24.

Mathews, Tom. "The Road to War." *Newsweek* (January 28, 1991): 54–65.

Middleton, Drew. "Barring Reporters From the Battlefield." *New York Times Magazine*, February 5, 1984, 37, 61, 69, 92.

New York Times. "15 Top Journalists See Cheney and Object to Gulf War Curbs." May 2, 1991, A16.

Sidle, Winant. Report by CJCS Media-Military Relations Panel, appendix. In Peter Braestrup, ed. *Battle Lines: Report of the Twentieth Century Fund Task Force on the Military and the Media*. New York: Priority Press, 1985, 161–78.

Sperber, A. M. *Murrow: His Life and Times*. New York: Freundlich, 1986.

Steele, Richard W. "News of the 'Good War': World War II News Management." *Journalism Quarterly* (Winter 1985): 707–83.

Theroux, Peter. *Sandstorms: Days and Nights in Arabia*. New York: Norton, 1990.

Thompson, Mark. "With the Press in the Persian Gulf." *Columbia Journalism Review* (November/December 1991): 40–45.

Turner, Kathleen J. *Lyndon Johnson's Dual War: Vietnam and the Press*. Chicago: University of Chicago, 1985.

United States Senate. Hearing Before the Committee on Governmental Affairs, February 20, 1991. Washington: U.S. Government Printing Office, 1991.

Vasquez, Juan. "Panama: Live From the Marriott!" *Washington Journalism Review* (March 1990): 44–47.

Williams, Pete. Statement before the Committee on Governmental Affairs. United States Senate, Washington, Photocopy. February 20, 1991.

Zoglin, Richard. "Just Whose Side Are They On?" *Time* (February 25, 1991): 53.

Chapter Two

Television as an Instrument of War

Robert E. Denton, Jr.

Vietnam was the first television war. With the Persian Gulf conflict, television became an instrument of war—an instrument of war as powerful and targeted as any cruise missile. Television is an effective weapon not simply because of any specific rules of journalism or agreements between networks and government, but because of the unique characteristics and requirements of the medium and contemporary technologies.

The dilemma becomes how to preserve national security and the freedom of the press in times of war. The press is caught in a balancing act between providing adequate information for informed citizen action (i.e., approval or disapproval) and the security and integrity of national interests. As with any democracy, there will be a natural tension between the two objectives.

As the Persian Gulf conflict progressed, I, like most Americans, was on an emotional roller coaster. I agreed that Saddam Hussein should be stopped, but at what price? When I saw the "video postcards"—mothers saying goodbye to young children, interviews with members of grieving families, then later charred bodies of innocent people—my will to fight and to support military action was automatically questioned. Saddam noted American sensitivity to human life and openly asserted that the public would not tolerate a protracted military conflict. According to conventional wisdom and myth, television coverage of the Vietnam War contributed to the erosion of public support for the conflict. Thus, a pragmatic question arises: Can a nation, with today's technologies, fight a war, much less win one, by showing the instantaneous battles or the bodies—the horrors of killing and destroying people? In this age of satellite and instant communication, can a nation engaged in combat risk openness and access of media to any military operations?

This chapter explores the notion of television as an instrument of war by examining some unique characteristics of the medium and associated issues of national military engagement. Television is an instrument of power and control. To control content is to control public perceptions and attitudes. Today, television is the primary instrument of political campaigning and governing (Denton 1988). In the Gulf War, television became a strategic tool and an essential weapon in the military's arsenal.

My approach is intuitive, qualitative, and conceptual. I offer no empirical evidence. While perhaps less satisfying to my social science colleagues, I think the influence of the media is so subtle and complex that mere quantitative data alone cannot reveal all aspects of their nature or function in society. From my perspective, I am equally concerned about political and public policy issues related to media and society.

TELEVISION AND POLITICS: IS THE MEDIUM THE MESSAGE?

Marshall McLuhan (1967) was one of the first theorists to recognize fully the impact of communication media upon society. He argued that "societies have always been shaped more by the nature of the media by which men communicate than by the content of the communication" (8). At the heart of McLuhan's argument is the now-famous notion that "the medium is the message." In a simplistic way, what this means is that what we think of as the "message" is transmitted by some medium that, because of its mechanical nature, also sends a simultaneous "message." This implies that perception and interpretation of a message will be affected by the simultaneous message that is inherent in the mechanical nature of the medium. This perspective does not deny the importance of content; rather, it emphasizes the importance of the sensory ratios present in any given medium. As McLuhan (1967) explains, "the extension of any one sense alters the way we think and act—the way we perceive the world . . . when ratios change, men change" (41, 47).

The rather obvious point is that we "interact" with the media. Media becomes a pervasive environment that provides both action and reaction in a continuous fashion. This new environment encourages unification and involvement. For McLuhan, we move from being separate individuals with unique points of view to one of many, returning us as members of the "global village," losing identity and separate action.

What many scholars are attempting to understand is the relationship between message content and media. Of course any message should be designed to best use the uniqueness of the medium. Thus, the interaction of the message and the media impacts our message reception and consequent behavior. According to Tony Schwartz (1973), constant exposure to television results in the sharing of common "TV stimuli" by everyone in society. This process creates a reservoir of common media experiences that are stored in our brains. Mediated communication evokes meaning and each medium conditions the brain to receive and to process information in specified ways.

Schwartz further argues that "experience with TV and radio stimuli are often more real than first-hand, face-to-face experiences" (44). He even asserts that the "captured reality" of media is preferred to personal experience. Like McLuhan, Schwartz also argues that the role of audiences is altered. Audiences become participants rather than serving as targets of mediated communication.

From this perspective, there are several implications of the televised coverage of the Persian Gulf War.

Instant History

Vietnam may well have been America's first television war, but the Persian Gulf was America's first "real time" television war (Pavlik and Thalhimer 1991: 34–38). With the latest computer and satellite technologies, we were able to see events as they happened, not as recorded for some later presentation. Perspective and analyses were left to newspapers and news weeklies. Immediacy as measured by minutes became the standard for the war coverage and the major criterion for media quality (Dennis 1991: 4).

Instant history, according to George Gerbner (1991),

[i]s made when access to video-satellite-computer technologies blanket the world in real time with selected images that provoke immediate reactions, influence the outcome, and then quick-freeze it into the official text of received history. Instant history is simultaneous, global, mass, living, telling, and making history in brief and intensive bursts. (3)

Images of Vietnam were prepackaged, days old. Images of the Persian Gulf were instantaneous.

Gerbner (1991) explains that there is a danger to "instant history." It forces the pace of events. "The crisis unfolds before our eyes, too fast for thoughtful consideration of antecedents, alternatives, or long-range consequences, but just in time for conditioned reflex. . . . Images reveal what presumably happens; they do not need logic to build the case" (3). Instant history making is potentially dangerous. The stakes are high.

Political Information and Television News

Television news is the prime source of political information for the majority of Americans (Kaid and Davidson 1986: 185). This fact was also true for news about the Gulf War. According to a Gallup poll in January 1991, television was the main source of information about the war for 89 percent of all Americans (Fitzsimon 1991: 89).

News on television is more believable, exciting, and dramatic than in other media. The nightly news is the single most important element in impacting political cognitions in America. As a result, according to Dan Nimmo and James Combs (1983), few people learn about politics from direct experience. They argue that political realities are mediated through mass and group communication. The result is the "creation, transmission, and adoption of political fantasies as realistic views of what takes place" (xv). They define fantasy as

a credible picture of the world that is created when one interprets mediated experiences as the way things are and takes for granted the authenticity of the mediated reality without checking against alternative, perhaps contradictory, realities so long as the fantasy offers dramatic proof for one's expectations. (8)

Murray Edelman (1988) concurs. He argues that

the spectacle constituted by news reporting continuously constructs and reconstructs social problems, crises, enemies, and leaders and so creates a succession of threats and reassurances. These constructed problems and personalities furnish the content of political journalism and the data for historical and analytic political studies. They also play a central role in winning support and opposition for political causes and policies. (1)

Thus, the press does more than inform; it literally creates the reality toward which we act. Television evening news, for most people, is their window to the world. The presentations and visuals of the thirty-minute broadcasts are critical in the formation of American attitudes and subsequent political actions.

From Nimmo and Combs' perspective, television news is storytelling and employs the elements of dramatic narrative. Largely because of the demands of the medium, television journalism must be entertaining and highly visual. News crews often trim stories to support film and visual elements. Peter Jennings, anchor for ABC's World News Tonight, states that "television is afraid of being dull. . . . In television, you're obligated to write to the pictures" (Schram 1987: 58). Thus, film footage is seldom used to illustrate stories but is used to tell the story (Altheide and Snow 1979: 109–10).

Eric Vollmer (1991) argues that "television structured this historical event around its own fascination with images instead of older social forms of reasoned discourse" (14). The industry looks for and shares "news that wiggles." Unfortunately, the more in-depth the coverage, the less "wiggle." Elements of action and movement are stressed over more cognitive elements. According to Edelman (1988), "accounts of political issues, problems, crises, threats, and leaders now become devices for creating disparate assumptions and beliefs about the social and political world rather than factual statements" (10).

The public's thoughts on issues are influenced by "sound bites and rapid-fire visuals rather than through extended dialogue and exchange of views" (Vollmer 1991: 14). Emotional responses are the ones the public remembers and help define future reactions to people and events. With little perspective or analysis, pictures tell the story contributing to more simplistic, stimulus-response audience reactions.

Public viewing and entertainment values were clearly in the minds of network executives during the Gulf War. The entire coverage of the war was more of a race for ratings, personalities, and scoops than for citizen information, context, and understanding. In the early days of the conflict, it was a media spectacle on the scale of a miniseries or the Olympics. The nation was treated to play-by-play analyses, human interest features, special music, graphics, and animation. The emphasis of the networks, according to Everette Dennis (1991), was on "quality of coverage and on editing otherwise disparate coverage into coherent, well-produced reports" while CNN, for example, served as a continual feed of information and footage for both networks and independent stations (4).

For media scholar Dan Hallin, television coverage was very sensitive to public opinion. In the beginning, reporters generally approached the conflict from an antiwar perspective. The tone and nature of the questioning were hostile, reflecting governmental distrust and predictions of great casualties. When it became clear that the public supported the war effort, the coverage shifted "from treating the war as a political policy and toward treating it as a kind of national celebration—like a moon shot or something" (Dennis et al. 1991: 66). Indeed, of the 2,855 minutes of network coverage of the Gulf from August 8, 1990, when troops were committed to the region, until January 3, 1991, only 29 minutes dealt with public opposition to the military build up (Lee and Devitt 1991: 20).

Hallin also thought the coverage was similar to an election campaign with the quantity of strategic analysis equivalent to the "horse race" coverage of most political elections (Dennis et al. 1991: 72). *Newsweek* media critic Jonathan Alter agrees and observed that "the entertainment values that are so much a part of the medium created really unseemly cheer leading such as the video postcards and the willingness to congratulate commanders on screen" (Dennis et al. 1991: 67). The networks approached the war, according to Robert Rhodes, a journalism professor at the University of Alaska, as a "military super bowl" sending 1,600 reporters—one for every 325 soldiers (Atwood Lecture 1991: 2). CBS, in an effort to increase advertising sales, reassured sponsors that war specials would be tailored to provide good lead-ins to commercials with "upbeat images" prior to station breaks.

TELEVISION AND THE GULF WAR: IS THE MESSAGE THE MEDIUM?

What exactly was conveyed through the televised coverage of the Gulf War? There was certainly no shortage of visuals and information. Never before had the networks and news organizations assembled such a cadre of experts of retired generals, diplomats, politicians, and academics all quite willing to define terms, explain military concepts and strategies, as well as to offer opinions and guesses of future actions. As a critical viewer, I often wondered if any experts were left to conduct the field operation itself.

Was the coverage really informative? There were hours of live coverage, expert speculations of often dubious accuracy, and constant repetition. Recall Dan Rather's "tears and fears" as I call it—"real bombs, real fighting, real death." The nation also discovered new heroes, Bernard Shaw and John Holliman of CNN. But did we understand more, have a better perspective with Shaw risking his life describing the first night of the bombing of Baghdad? His hiding and crawling on the floor were certainly exciting, high drama. Was his description of the bombing that "looks like the Fourth of July" a visual photograph we really needed? If he had been killed, would it have been worth the risk? Is seeing or hearing *something* better than *nothing*? Is restricted reporting better than no reporting?

Was the war really televised? Did we really witness the war? No. There was lots of live coverage—not of the war but of talking heads, briefings, and human interest stories. Reports from correspondents on rooftops soon became dull and redundant. At best, the war was something akin to "televised radio reports." We heard more about the war than we saw. There was much speculation but little information. All the satellite technology did very little to speed the flow of real information.

For months, the Persian Gulf War naturally dominated news stories at the expense of major domestic issues. For example, for the three month period of December 1990 through February 1991, Desert Storm generated 2658 minutes of coverage, 47 times more than the next ranking story of Soviet foreign minister Edward Shevardnadze's resignation with only 56 minutes of total coverage. A national energy strategy unveiled by the White House ranked twenty-first in coverage with only 12 minutes (LaMay 1991: 48).

With all the hours of coverage, what did we learn? Researchers from the University of Massachusetts discovered that heavy viewers of television were more likely to support the war and less likely to be well informed of its history, causes, or consequences (Silver 1991: 2). According to William Fore (1991), we saw "a great deal of interpretation as opposed to documentation. . . . Never was so much stock footage used to convey so little" (3). Thus, the more people watched television, the less they knew.

What media did do was to influence how the public viewed issues of war and peace. Rosalind Silver (1991), editor of *Media & Values*, faults the news coverage of the conflict for favoring the "flashy technology while ignoring its impact on humankind," for "stifling of alternative views resulting from limited or unbalanced coverage by critics of the war," and for the "dehumanization and demonization of a stereotyped enemy" (2). For Silver, the "Gulf War TV coverage provided one of the best examples yet of the misleading selectivity of instant satellite feeds and the ability of authorities (in this case the military) to command a platform "(2).

What we saw from the coverage was images of technology; powerful futuristic planes, smart bombs, and fast, highly equipped tanks. We saw images of our soldiers, dedicated, cheerful, and confident. We saw the hardships of those loved ones at home waiting for their spouses and family members to return as heroes. We did not see Iraqi victims. We were not told that "smart bombs" constituted only 10 percent of the total bombs dropped in Iraq (Fore 1991: 4) or that 70 percent of our bombs missed their targets (Vollmer 1991: 15).

What we learned from the coverage was the power of technology and the conduct of a humane war. We learned, according to William Fore (1991), that "war can be relatively safe, sanitary (surgical), and not terribly costly either in personnel or material" (4). Phillip Knightley (1991) argues that the successful news management by the government resulted in the view of "a war almost without death, a sanitized version of what has gone before. . . . the idea was to suggest that hardly any people were involved in modern warfare, only machines" (5). The coverage met some of our most deep-rooted psychological needs:

to feel powerful and in control, to experience extreme emotions in a guilt-free, non-threatening environment, to share emotionally charged experiences with others, to gain a sense of identity, to gain information, to satisfy a belief in justice, to see others make mistakes, to participate in the drama of history (vicariously and without risk) and to affirm moral values. (Fore 1991: 4)

Television is a medium of impact.┼In agreement with the agenda-setting function of media, television tells us not only *what* to think about but also *how* to think, about the subject of presentation. To ignore the power of television to influence the beliefs, attitudes, and values of the public is simply naive. Pictures do make a difference. The small sliver of reality is not the larger landscape, however. Academics continue to debate the extent that media shapes public opinion or merely reflects it. The fact that it does both argues for the perspective of television as an active instrument of impact rather than simply a passive conduit of information.

TELEVISION AS AN INSTRUMENT OF WAR

George Gerbner (1991) identifies five essential elements in today's age of instant history: control, orchestration, witness, feedback, and quick-freeze (3). It is important to quickly gain access and control of the "real-time" imagery portrayed on television. The goal is to mobilize before opposition voices can be heard or network counter-perspectives are generated. Orchestration requires coordination of efforts and actions designed to bolster public support. Single events do not motivate or saturate the public environment. A campaign consists of multiple, coordinated events with a single focus. Vicarious audience participation is enhanced with carefully planned events as press conferences, panel discussions, and briefings that appear spontaneous. Once the "outcome" is achieved, it is to be celebrated, communicated, even ritualized.

These elements were very much a part of the Gulf War media campaign waged by the government. Television became the medium for disinformation and propaganda for both sides of the conflict. President Bush and American leaders acknowledged their reliance on the media for early developments in the conflict. Both Secretary of Defense Dick Cheney and Joint Chiefs of Staff Chairman Colin Powell dubbed CNN the best source for discovering the extent of the Baghdad bombing. Air Force Lt. General Charles Horner, the architect of the air war, confessed that because of the detail of CNN reports, he installed a television at his command post. Peter Tarnoff, president of the Council on Foreign Relations, was quoted as saying that CNN was "the most efficient way for one government to speak to another during the crisis" (Cooper 1991: 44).

Saddam Hussein even watched the war on CNN in his headquarters (Dennis 1991: 1). Iraqi officials often delayed press conferences until CNN reporters arrived. The network enjoyed special treatment and access to Iraqi officials, events, and city locations. CNN reporters were the only ones allowed to stay in their hotel rooms early in the conflict. Peter Arnett became the world's window on Iraq. Saddam had hoped that CNN's controlled coverage would result in world sympathy and Arab support. In one report, an Iraqi woman, wailing in perfect English about civilian casualties, turned out, as even reported by CNN, to be an Iraqi official. She also showed up on French television wailing in French (Alter et al. 1991: 38). Iraqi officials knew the power of televised reports on American and world opinion.

For centuries wartime propaganda took months of preparation and execution. Today, thanks to modern technology and CNN, it takes mere minutes. Television provides instant access to the enemy's camp and into the public's psyche, ranging from troop maneuvers to world opinion. Governments must be concerned about military information as well as public perceptions. There is a real danger of "telediplomacy" that may encourage leaders to become overemotional or may cause overreaction to foreign statements or actions.

In theory, of course, journalists are supposed to work independently of propaganda. In the Gulf War, however, the form and content of the medium dominated and became a player in the conflict. Television became a *strategic* tool of diplomacy, of troop and resource allocation, and of national and international public motivation. Thus, television became an essential weapon in the military's arsenal (O'Heffernan 1991: 6).

A report of the Gannett Foundation (Dennis et al. 1991) acknowledges that the military was most successful in managing the media and information.

The military supplied much of the news that came out of the gulf through briefings and videotapes, therefore what Americans saw on their screens (and television was the main source of gulf news for the vast majority of Americans) reflected the government's viewpoint. . . . It is evident, not the least by its own admission, that the military used the press to promulgate its own policies as well as to spread disinformation to the Iraqis. (xi–xii)

Journalists did not find the daily briefings very helpful or informative (Pavlik and Rachlin 1991: 38). More importantly, the briefings determined the priority and focus of stories. For example, the dramatic video of targeted bombing became the lead story on the evening news rather than any informed battlefield information or action. In some cases, the Pentagon released so much trivial information that the press could not keep up or digest the information in any useful way. Such a tactic diverted attention away from more sensitive or media-initiated issues or stories.

The American public was misled about the strength and ability of Iraqi forces, about Iraq's nuclear and chemical capabilities, about possible military assault locations, and about the accuracy and superiority of American bombing efforts. While there was little direct censorship, there was a great deal of information that was never shared with the public. Even today, there are no "official" counts of Iraqi casualties although most estimates are well over 100,000. Essentially, according to Gerbner (1991), "the deception, suppression, misinformation, and disinformation that characterized the buildup overwhelmed and disoriented the public and defused the opposition" (5).

The military was ready for this "televised war." Since Vietnam, war colleges have trained officers to become more media-savvy. Even young officers receive training in media and community and public relations. At the Pentagon, detailed plans for handling the media were developed and awaiting implementation. The military needed television to build and sustain public support for the war. They realized pictures were powerful weapons and could easily help the enemy and lower morale of the troops as well as the general public.

Members of the press were less prepared to cover the conflict. In general, the military press people actually came across better than the journalists. Many reporters seemed rude, uninformed, and, in some cases, rather stupid. Newspaperman Robert Rhodes (1991) characterized the coverage as

amateur night. Times Square on New Year's Eve. How many of those reporters would you guess knew even the first thing about weaponry, about military strategy, about war? And how many were on assignment there only because they were their organization's star, and this was their reward, their chance to add a line to their resume that said, "War Correspondent".... Some of the questioning during those military briefings came in on the low side of sophomoric. ... Some of the personal interviews done by TV personalities were embarrassing in their ineptitude. (3)

Pentagon officials referred to the journalists as "tourists." The sign on the Pentagon press room read "Welcome temporary war experts." According to Stephen Hess of the Brookings Institute, the American public saw trained briefers who knew something and were experts in their areas, in contrast to "reporters who often don't know anything, who are tongue-tied and often inarticulate. The setting doesn't leave you with a sense that the journalists are terribly in command of their profession" (Rosenstiel 1991: 5). One of the principal recommendations of the Gannett Foundation Report (Dennis et al. 1991) is that "media organizations that covered the war must carefully assess their performance and the performance of their correspondents with an eye toward improvement" (xii).

Ted Koppel (1991) of ABC's "Nightline" provides a different perspective, however:

One of the problems is that the American public was treated to the journalistic equivalent of watching sausage being made. And just as you probably don't want to eat a sausage once you've seen how it's made, you're going to have kind of queasy feelings about journalism once you've seen how it's made. . . . It always amazes me that the American public does not realize an underlying reality of American journalism. Anyone in the country can become a journalist. There is no exam. If you want to be a journalist, you're a journalist. For some reporters in the Gulf, this may have been the first time in their lives they had the opportunity to ask a three-star general a question on live television. And they were just intoxicated by the experience. But that's the price of a free press. Anyone can ask any dumb question. (3)

The general public fully supported the military's actions and handling of the press. Although the public generally approved of the media's coverage of the war, a Roper opinion poll found that a majority of the people favored even more military control of information (FitzSimon 1991: 91). In a Times Mirror survey in late February 1991, 79 percent of the public approved of the Pentagon's restrictions (Levinson 1991: 29). Furthermore, in a *Newsweek* poll in late January 1991, 64 percent of Americans thought that media coverage of the war "makes it harder for U.S. officials to conduct war" and 55 percent thought that "live coverage leads to impatience for a quick ending" (Alter and Manegold 1991: 61).

The point is rather obvious. Television is more than a channel of information. Television, as a communication medium, is immediate, of limited perspective, and, as a personalizing medium, prefers people over things. The picture is stronger than the abstract idea. It best demonstrates rather than argues in the classical sense. Drama and emotion are favored over reason. Its portrayal of the world has consequences.

Thus, the issues of what we see, when we see it, and how we see it have direct implications in terms of national interests that demand consideration of perspective, long-term goals, and the notion of general welfare rather than personal convenience. Television is a powerful weapon of war. And if the nation is committed to war, it should be used as strategically, as efficiently, and as effectively as any other weapon. But as any weapon, television can harm both friend and foe. It does not discriminate between "good" and "bad." As a weapon, television is only as "good" or "bad" as the people who use it.

The dangers are obvious. For Gerbner (1991)

bombarding viewers by violent images of a mean and dangerous world without illuminating the real costs of violence and war, is, in the last analysis, an instrument of intimidation and terror. It was indispensable to the triumph of instant history in the Persian Gulf. . . . An overkill of violent imagery helps to mobilize support for taking charge of the unruly at home and abroad. (8)

CONCLUDING OBSERVATIONS

I realize that my argument is somewhat bothersome. On the surface, it implies that by showing the "realities" of war (or instant history) will, by the nature of the medium and our cultural norms, jeopardize the likelihood of "winning" a war. In addition, today's instant global communication encourages the use of television as a tool of propaganda.

I confess to being more interested in domestic politics and policy than media studies. Thus, for me the larger issue is how much constraint to place upon media in times of crises or issues of national security.

In my opinion, the purpose and intent of the First Amendment is to enhance and to secure the practice of democracy. The First Amendment was originally designed for the benefit of the general public. The First Amendment provides the essence and philosophical basis for democracy because in reality, human communication is the way we participate in the political decision making of self-government. Freedoms of speech and of the press are means of attaining truth, exercising our democratic prerogative of self-government and satisfying our yearnings for self-expression.

Unfortunately, rather than a principle of democratic government, the concept of freedom of speech today has become a legal principle to protect extremist speech. As citizens we have failed in our responsibility to not only engage in social interaction but also to sustain the quality of that interaction. Instead of serving as a stimulus for public discussion of vital issues, free speech has become, for most Americans, merely one of our foremost cultural symbols. It was Mark Twain who observed that "it is by the goodness of God that in our country we have those three unspeakably precious things: freedom of speech, freedom of conscience, and the prudence never to practice either of them."

Three important characteristics of a democratic form of government are accountability, information, and the "marketplace of ideas." Information is critical for citizens to make informed judgments and evaluations of issues and elected officials. Democracy is a process of collective deliberation. It is the national and public debate that should determine the collective wisdom and will of the people. In the classic sense, a true democracy is founded on an informed and active citizenry. A democratic society assumes that all citizens vote, speak, and participate politically as equals. Civic culture, responsibility, and initiative should once again become a keystone of social life.

From this idealistic perspective, the role of the press is obvious. Media, broadly defined, provides forums through which individuals and groups may express opinions. As governmental "watchdogs," the press keep citizens informed of governmental actions and of events. In addition, not only may people learn about government actions in order to control them, but by monitoring the contents of the media, government officials are able to gauge public sentiment.

I do not think free speech and free press are the same thing, however. As Michael Parenti (1986) notes, freedom of the press is for those who own the presses (27). The press is a structured institution that enjoys special access, resources, and power not granted or available to individuals. Broadcast companies are not in the business to serve First Amendment principles. They are profit-making businesses that exhibit many of the same characteristics as any other enterprise whose goal is to maximize profits. Thus, the need for checks and balances are just as great for the media as for the government.

Of course, freedom of expression is not absolutely unlimited. The majority of legal officials and officers, as well as most Americans for that matter, support limited abridgment of the First Amendment in times of war and issues of public security and safety. But somehow we have lost sight of the fundamental goal and purpose of the First Amendment: the enhancement and fulfillment of democracy. The primary justifications for protecting free speech and the press tend to divide into two main groups: those that stress the values to the individual and those that stress the values to the society. We have focused so much on the former that we have largely ignored the latter. Few politicians and certainly younger generations of Americans have no concept of "the common good."

At the heart of my disappointment is the failure of the citizenry to simply engage one another in public debate and issue discussion—not just media celebrities and politicians on Sunday morning talk shows. Instead of viewing politics as *talk*, maybe we should view politics as *people engaged in talk*. It must be person to person. We need more of a communitarian conception of democracy that would reverse the current trend toward centralization of politics and of political communication (Abramson et al. 1988: 24–26). We need community participation in debate at the local level. Thus, the key is to insure that national interests are clearly defined, articulated, and formulated as a result of national debate and discussion. Quite simply, before we go to war, we need full and open debate. Prior to the Gulf War, there simply was not enough public knowledge or debate.

On issues of national security, I tend to favor a more "conservative" view than a more "liberal" free speech orientation. Once war is declared, I, like most Americans, am inclined to defer to governmental needs and desires for news control and management. In the early stages of an operation, for example, a "news blackout" seems reasonable and appropriate. Likewise, it's too late to begin a national debate about the wisdom of initial military action once the first shot has been fired. The stakes are simply too high. There is also a difference between a genuine national policy debate and a mediated theatrical coverage of an event. My confidence, therefore, in broadcast journalism to act as arbitrators of a national debate is rather low, especially in times of national crises.

Cleve Mathews (1991), a print journalism professor at Syracuse University, strongly disagrees. For him, the essential question is "whose war is it—the military's, the government's, the people's? . . . The government and its military arm act in behalf of the people and serve at their consent. Wars belong to the people, who pay for them in lives and money" (4). The press serves to inform the people of how their agents are doing their job. The "pool reporting" system, according to Mathews, was designed by the military only to support the mission of "an efficient victory rather than as an agreed, temporary expedient for informing the people how that mission was being achieved" (4).

The difficulty becomes in determining when news management is censorship, when briefings are propaganda events, or when official information is simply lies and misinformation. Can there really be a "democratic war," or are we doomed to being pawns of ill-advised or despot leaders?

There is, of course, a real danger of "throwing out the baby with the bath water." We need to have greater public understanding of the role, function, and power of the media in our society. Media literacy should become a goal of public education. Len Masterman asserts that "without media education a society cannot have the critically informed citizenry necessary for a functioning democracy" (Thoman 1991: 24). As satellite and communications technologies develop and increase in sophistication, we must carefully plan for their usage within the context of democratic values. Walter Cronkite (1989) suggests that

we could benefit by a journalism course for consumers. If we could teach people how to read a newspaper, how to listen to radio and watch television . . . we could create an understanding of media, of the individual strengths and weaknesses of each medium. We could lead them away from a dependence on television, back to good newspapers, magazines, and books. (7)

Finally, television has been blamed for far too many social ills. It simply cannot take a largely uneducated, uninformed electorate and transform them into model democratic citizens. Such a responsibility belongs to the citizens, not to a primarily entertainment medium. The challenge is how to continue to cultivate an active, democratic citizenry in light of the heavy dependence upon television, an undemocratic medium (Denton 1991: 91–114). Terry Sanford (1981) warns of the "danger of democracy" where "we will use its name in vain, and in its name so unstructure our political institutions that nothing can be decided, or decided wisely"

(100). Television, at best, is an *individual* medium that produces *mass* responses. It serves many masters. It can also be a powerful and effective instrument of war.

BIBLIOGRAPHY

Abramson, Jeffrey, et al. *The Electronic Commonwealth*. New York: Basic Books, 1988.

Alter, Jonathan, and C. S. Manegold. "Showdown at 'Fact Gap.' " *Newsweek*, February 4, 1991, 61–62.

Alter, Jonathan, et al. "The Propaganda War." *Newsweek*, February 25, 1991, 38, 39.

Altheide, David, and Robert Snow. *Media Logic*. Beverly Hills, Calif.: Sage, 1979.

Cooper, Matthew. "The Very Nervy Win of CNN." *U.S. News & World Report*, January 28, 1991, 44.

Cronkite, Walter. Acceptance Speech for the Allen H. Neuharth Award for Excellence in Journalism. University of South Dakota, 1989. Pamphlet.

Dennis, Everette. "Introduction." In *The Media at War: The Press and the Persian Gulf Conflict*, Everette Dennis et al., eds. 1–4. New York: Gannett Foundation Media Center, 1991.

Dennis, Everette, et al., eds. *The Media at War: The Press and the Persian Gulf Conflict*. New York: Gannett Foundation Media Center, 1991.

Denton, Jr., Robert E. "Primetime Politics: The Ethics of Teledemocracy." In *Ethical Dimensions of Political Communication*, Robert E. Denton, Jr., ed., 91–114. New York: Praeger, 1991.

Denton, Jr., Robert E. *The Primetime Presidency of Ronald Reagan*. New York: Praeger, 1988.

Edelman, Murray. *Constructing the Political Spectacle*. Chicago: University of Chicago Press, 1988.

FitzSimon, Martha. "Public Perception of War Coverage." In *The Media at War: The Press and the Persian Gulf War*, Everette Dennis, ed., 86–95. New York: Gannett Foundation Media Center, 1991.

Fore, William. "The Military-News Complex." *Media & Values* 56 (Fall 1991): 3–5.

Gerbner, George. Acceptance Address of the Wayne Danielson Award for Outstanding Contributions to Communication Scholarship. The University of Texas at Austin, 1991. Pamphlet.

Kaid, Lynda, and Dorthy Davidson. "Elements of Videostyle." In *New Perspectives on Political Advertising*, Lynda Kaid et al., eds., 184–209. Carbondale, Ill.: Southern Illinois University Press, 1986.

Koppel, Ted. "Koppel Shares Insights on War in Persian Gulf." *Newhouse Network* 6 (Spring 1991): 1, 3.

Knightley, Phillip. "Here is the Patriotically Censored News." *Index on Censorship* 20 (April/May 1991): 4–5.

LaMay, Craig. "By the Numbers: Measuring the Coverage." In *The Media at War: The Press and the Persian Gulf Conflict*, Everette Dennis et al., eds., 45–50. New York: Gannett Foundation Media Center, 1991.

Lee, Martin, and Tiffany Devitt. "Gulf War Coverage: Censorship Begins at Home." *Newspaper Research Journal* 12 (Winter 1991): 14–22.

Levinson, Nan. "Snazzy Visuals, Hard Facts and Obscured Issues." *Index on Censorship* 20 (April/May 1991): 27–29.

Mathews, Cleve. "Wartime Censorship." *Newhouse Network* 6 (Spring 1991): 4.

McLuhan, Marshall. *The Medium Is the Message*. New York: Bantam Books, 1967.

Nimmo, Dan, and James Combs. *Mediated Political Realities*. New York: Longman, 1983.

O'Heffernan, Patrick. "Television and the Security of Nations: Learning from the Gulf War." *Television Quarterly* 25 (1991): 5–10.

Parenti, Michael. *Inventing Reality: The Politics of the Mass Media*. New York: St. Martins Press, 1986.

Pavlik, John, and Seth Rachlin. "On Assignment: A Survey of Journalists Who Covered the War." In *The Media at War: The Press and the Persian Gulf War*, Everette Dennis et al., eds., 26–33. New York: Gannett Foundation Media Center, 1991.

Pavlik, John, and Mark Thalhimer. "The Charge of the E-Mail Brigade: News Technology Comes of Age." In *The Media at War: The Press and the Persian Gulf Conflict*, Everette Dennis et al., eds., 34–38. New York: Gannett Foundation Media Center, 1991.

Rhodes, Robert. 1991 Atwood Lecture. University of Alaska at Anchorage, 1991. Pamphlet.

Rosenstiel, Thomas. "Reporters Viewed as Bumbling Villains of War." *Roanoke Times & World-News*, February 24, 1991, Section D, 5.

Sanford, Terry. *A Danger of Democracy*. Boulder, Colo.: Westview Press, 1981.

Schram, Martin. *The Great American Video Game*. New York: William Morrow, 1987.

Schwartz, Tony. *The Responsive Chord*. New York: Anchor Books, 1973.

Silver, Rosalind. "The More We Watched the Less We Knew." *Media & Values* 56 (Fall 1991): 2.

Thoman, Elizabeth. "Media Literacy: Strengthening Democracy." *Media & Values* 56 (Fall 1991): 24.

Vollmer, Eric. "Untying the Yellow Ribbon." *Media & Values* 56 (Fall 1991): 14–15.

Chapter Three

The Natural, and Inevitable, Phases of War Reporting: Historical Shadows, New Communication in the Persian Gulf

Donald L. Shaw and Shannon E. Martin

NEW SOCIETY, OLD WARS

Each of us lives in at least two worlds—the "real" one around us and the historical one that represents our past and is always whispering to us about how things were done in the past, and perhaps should be done the same way again. These two forces clash with each other in the larger society, as they do within us as individuals. In the Persian Gulf War, key players from President George Bush to congressional leaders, reporters and editors, and members of the public followed their own expectations of what should be expected of each other. Obviously there were clashes.

For President Bush, as for President Franklin Roosevelt in World War II, the expectation was for support from the Congress, press, and public. That was a model from World War II. For members of Congress, the expectation was that members would play a consultative role, as required, in congressional views, by the 1973 War Powers Act. That was a model influenced by the Vietnam War.

For reporters and editors, the expectation was that they could have reasonable freedom to roam the battlefield, develop their own sources, and provide a wide set of perspectives. That model was based on World War II and Korea, with some influence from Vietnam.

For the military, the expectation was that reporters would need to be contained and the news channeled to prevent helping the enemy or hurting American or coalition forces. That model was based on Vietnam, where many junior—now senior—officers developed a suspicion of the press, and from the more recent forays into Grenada in 1983 and Panama in 1989.

In the Persian Gulf, therefore, historical models clashed. When it was over, the president and military—supported by strong initial public opinion—claimed victory. But the press grumbled and Congress remained cowed for a little while (Browne 1991: 27; Harwood 1991). This study concentrates on the relationships among the military, White House, reporters, editors, and public and suggests why the military/White House was, indeed, so successful in controlling the initial picture of the war and why, as coverage continues of that volatile region, the victory is now being seen from many other perspectives.

Cleaning the Window: War Reporting

War reporting continues after a war ends, as a car windshield wiper wipes a few times more before coming to rest. Like the windshield wiper, press coverage of events slightly lags the rain of events. Press coverage, like the windshield wiper, can be manipulated to some extent in terms of the speed with which it moves, or the blades can be improved in some way. But the essential function and characteristics remain the same. Like the windshield wiper, the press helps to improve our view and it responds as we may direct it to changing conditions. We suggest that press coverage of war has three natural and inevitable phases. Those phases, for the press, follow the traditional democracy model from an initial monistic or unified, single point of view, to a final pluralistic or multi-perspective view. The basic characteristics of U.S. press coverage of war remain the same—only the timing and the quality may be changed, as we illustrate with the recent war in the Persian Gulf.

Historical Shadows in the Persian Gulf

When we confront new challenges we use past experience as an initial guide, learning as we go along. In the Persian Gulf, World War II images surfaced because we confronted in Saddam Hussein an opposing leader as we had, for example, in Hitler. Although the analogy somewhat sanitized Hitler—who after all systematically killed his own people, Jews and gentiles alike—it was a convenient model that President Bush borrowed ("Bush Asks"; "President Warns"; "Gulf Crisis"). Historical analogies are convenient, although always wrong to some extent, because they fit political rhetoric. If a leader uses analogies, the press is usually happy with the quotes. In Vietnam, the 1968 Tet Offensive was called a "Battle of the Bulge" by some military leaders, in reference to the 1944 last-ditch counteroffensive by the Germans. Where the Germans failed, the North Vietnamese ultimately succeeded. But the analogy was convenient.

In World War II and the Korean War, reporters moved with troops, and had reasonable access to both soldiers at the bottom and top military leaders. Correspondents wore plain uniforms without rank designations. As did soldiers, reporters often grumbled about conditions. But, like soldiers, they also supported the war effort. In World War II, Eric Sevareid, Walter Cronkite, and many others became famous names back home for skillful writing about war events, issues, and personalities. Ernie Pyle was beloved, and many of his columns were collected into books (1945; 1947). The relationships between the military and press were watchful but supportive; they were not adversarial. And there was some censorship (Mott 1966: 761). These relationships were repeated with little change in the Korean War that broke out five years later. But the model was one of a loosely organized, supportive press that could often be trusted with knowledge of military details.

In Vietnam, these historical models seemed to be changed. When that war began for the United States in the early 1960s, the initial force commitments were small numbers of military advisers to the South Vietnamese Army. There were few journalists, and even those, for a while, knew little of the local political and military situation (Oberdorfer 1984). Most early reporting was supportive. Because the war was mostly a guerrilla conflict, the battlefield was everywhere, potentially, and so reporters arriving in Saigon were automatically in the middle of battle. Reporters did need to catch rides outside battle sites, and the military provided a daily briefing on the war. At first the World War II/Korean model worked well. A society in conflict expects support, even if it initiated that conflict.

In time, however, as casualties rose and the war lingered, public resistance increased, along with official reservations raised in the U.S. Senate and elsewhere (Hammond 1988: 263f). Reporting became more balanced, as reporters found the politics in South Vietnam to be corrupted and began to question the strategic basis for the American commitment. Some questioned the Cold War themes—we were there to stop communism—raised by presidents Johnson and Nixon. By the time of the 1968 Tet Offensive, the political system confronted a divided public opinion, a condition that would remain until the end of the war (Hammond 1988: 366). Lincoln would have understood; modern political leaders did not, nor did military force members who resented fighting a war lacking broad public consensus. There was no censorship. Reporters were free to report events as they saw them, whether or not this news fit well with military strategy or not. In Vietnam, the tactical coverage, in time, helped erode the public support back home for the strategic goals. Or journalists, perhaps, only reflected the shrinking support. But journalists did not lose the war (Summers 1982).

Tactics and strategy are vitally related on the battlefield, but also two broad ways of seeing war are related to public opinion. We can visualize a model that highlights some of the key relationships.

Figure 3.1
The Key Relationships in Public Support for the War

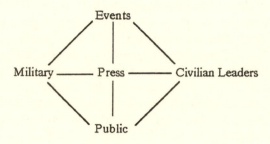

Public Support

Figure 3.1 suggests that reporters can see events for themselves, or they can learn of events and other details from military and civilian leaders. Journalists select constantly among competing perspectives. That is one of the most important aspects of journalism. But Figure 3.1 shows that the public also has separate ties with the military because citizens have fathers, mothers, daughters, and/or sons, or friends in the military—especially in eras in which the draft is used—and they learn of events this way. Also friends and family members get injured or killed. Nevertheless, government and military views necessarily come mostly through newspapers, magazines, radio, television, and/or films. Photographs are potent—millions remember the picture of the five-year-old naked girl, a napalm victim, running down the dusty Vietnam road (Ut 1972), or the picture of the suspected member of the Viet Cong being summarily executed by a pistol-weilding South Vietnamese officer (Adams 1968). Millions remember the AP picture of the flag raising over Iwo Jima in World War II (Rosenthal 1945). Such pictures burn themselves into memory, and—in time—may become the most remembered aspect of that war. Many remember coverage of Vietnam as negative when, in fact, studies show coverage was generally fair and balanced (Johnson 1969; Moody 1970; Wyatt 1986). Journalism, in fact, was much more successful than was civilian leadership, which never sufficiently clarified goals or provided the level of support that the military felt essential to conduct the war (Summers 1982).

By the time of recent conflicts in Grenada, Panama, and the Persian Gulf, Vietnam experiences had influenced military–press relations. In these conflicts the press was organized into press pools of about twenty people. There was an attempt to balance the newspaper, magazine, wire, radio, and television types of coverage. In exchange for obtaining early warning of upcoming conflicts, press pool members agreed to keep details secret. The military also promised to provide early access to events and imposed a mild censorship of news.

A suspicion of the press lingered over this arrangement, as the shadow of one war fell over three smaller wars. Junior military officers in Vietnam, such as Commanding General Norman Schwarzkopf, were now senior and ultimately in charge of press arrangements. Some tests of the press pool had shown journalists could hardly keep a secret ("How Reporters": 61). In Grenada, the press was kept out for the first two days of the battle. In Panama, the delay was for a crucial four to eight hours. In both wars, the press never really caught up. We still do not know how many civilians were killed inadvertently in Panama while trying to capture leader Manuel Noriega, who earlier in his career apparently had worked with the U.S. Central Intelligence Agency.

In the Persian Gulf the press was anxious to gain access to what, in the fall of 1990, was probably a forthcoming battle. The press pool arrangement, by now the model for small wars, was employed, this time challenged by the huge numbers of reporters that wanted to cover activities of local U.S. Army Reserve and National Guard troops activated for the duration of the war. The military said the pool arrangement would control the numbers of reporters, protect them from a fast-moving lethal environment, and still ensure in-depth coverage back home. There was mild censorship, and reporters could not roam freely because accompanying press officers were required to be present at all times. If they struck out on their own, they might be captured, as was Bob Simon and his CBS crew ("CBS News Crew"). Or they might have a foot blown off by a mine. Indeed, the environment was dangerous, and a desert war makes it easy to control reporters. If an enemy tank or soldier can be easily spotted in a desert, so can a reporter.

President Bush pointed out that he, unlike Lyndon Johnson in Vietnam, was not going to micro-manage the war ("Bush Keeps Eye"). He left execution of battle details to General Norman Schwarzkopf and General Colin Powell, chairman of the Joint Chiefs of Staff. Both soon became heroes. Unlike President Johnson, Bush called for the reserves, and he deployed them in great strength, unlike the inch-at-a-time build up that proved ineffective in Vietnam. Like Franklin Roosevelt in World War II and Harry Truman in Korea, Bush worked rapidly, and with skill, to build a coalition, and obtain the United Nations' sanction. He blocked Israel participation and neutralized Syria. The forces employed came overwhelmingly from the United States, yet the presence of sizable forces from England, France, and elsewhere ensured that it was not a go-it-alone battle against Iraq. Bush obtained commitments from Japan and elsewhere to pay for the war. He suggested that—despite early editorial and cartoon criticism ("Yeah, Man")—this was not a war solely to protect the vast oil stores of Saudi Arabia. Instead, it would be a new world order in which unwarranted, unlawful invasions would be collectively and summarily dealt with ("Mitterrand Proposes"). In the Persian Gulf, there were political shadows of World War II and Korea and, especially, Vietnam. The coverage of this war, nevertheless, fit a predictable pattern of singular to multiple views.

WAR AND THE PERSIAN GULF

It always is a challenge to know when a war starts. Some argue that World War II began when both Germany and the Soviet Union sent volunteers to participate in the Spanish Civil War in the mid–1930s. In Vietnam, one could argue that we became engaged in a civil war that stretched back to at least the early 1950s and the failure of the French to maintain their colonial empire after World War II (Fitzgerald 1972).

In the Persian Gulf, one can argue that the war began with the invasion of Kuwait by Iraqi forces on August 2, 1990. There had been posturing before that, with threats and counterthreats. The U.S. ambassador to Iraq, April Glaspie, perhaps signaled that the United States did not care if Iraq invaded Kuwait, a territory that once was part of Iraq ("The Road to August 2"). Whatever the reasons for the invasion, President Bush acted quickly to alert U.S. military forces, call up reserves, and make clear to Iraq authorities that the United States expected the Iraqi military to withdraw immediately ("Bush Wins Support").

The initial Bush goal—Iraqi withdrawal—was clear and unambiguous. Carl Von Clausewitz (1976) had argued that goals need to be clearly laid out; otherwise how do you know if you have or have not achieved your goals? (Howard 1991). In Vietnam, goals had not always been clear and, because Congress never declared war, in a sense that war could not end because it never officially began. In the Persian Gulf Bush insisted that Congress pass a measure of support, although he argued that a declaration of war was not needed because he was acting within his authority ("Special Report" 1991).

Saddam Hussein ignored all threats and hints, and his armed forces, assisted by some members of the Palestine Liberation Forces, engaged in brutal operations within Kuwait. On January 16, as promised, the president initiated an air war, and on February 23, he initiated a ground war that mopped up the pulverized ground forces within about 100 hours. Then, there emerged a period of uncertain peace. The Kurds, with apparent administration approval ("A Moral Failure" 1991), engaged in a short, unsuccessful revolt within Iraq. The war had killed an estimated 10,000 to 100,000 of the Iraqi armed forces (the figure is not yet clear); decimated the Iraqi air force, except for planes that left for Iran; used up the majority of the ineffective—with some tragic exceptions—Scud missile supply; undermined the infrastructure (bridges, roads, schools, hospitals) of Iraq; and allegedly destroyed the nuclear warhead capability of Iraq ("Iraq May Still" 1991). Militarily it was an impressive performance, even if the opposing military surrendered or fought anemically after the ground war opened. Militarily this was no Vietnam.

The Coverage

Back home, audiences peeped into our first real time war. Audiences saw precision guided bombs dropping down elevator shafts (*U.S. News* 60). Pentagon briefings described the performance of weapons systems of unbelievable technical sophistication. There were video and print graphics of all kinds. Many stories illustrated the technological battle field ("Pilots Rely"; "Patriot Missile's Success"; "Oil Spill"; "Six Main Kinds"; "Smart Bombs"; "The Ugly Land War").

The print and television reporters in the field numbered nearly a thousand and local television stations presented downhome views of the local troops. In fact, local television showed how easy it was to displace network television. CNN did as well, as both Secretary Dick Cheney and Bush were at times reported to be tuned into CNN to learn of events ("Frustration Widespread"), and CNN's Peter Arnett was allowed to remain in Baghdad in the early days of the war ("Iraq Will Allow"). We learned of the opening of the war from broadcasters who, as surprised as anyone else, reported an early popping—it turned out to be bombs. From his command bunker, General Schwarzkopf also watched CNN, relieved that the reports he saw were not especially accurate and realizing that the Iraqi high command was watching as well (Pyle 1991). Television did more than cover the war; in a sense it was a full participant.

Although most stories were about actual conflict or preparations for conflict, there were stories about activities in Egypt, Jordan, Syria, and Israel, especially after Scud missiles were used against that nation by Iraq ("Allies Reach Consensus").

Before the war, as one might expect, there were stories that speculated about goals and possible military activities. There was a diversity of opinion. Before the shooting started, for example, some editorials and cartoons questioned the purposes of the war. Was it a war only to preserve oil for the market economies? ("Yeah, Man"). Were coalition troops a mercenary force, paid for by Japan and Germany among others ("World's Poorest"; "Congress Approves"). Did the United States indirectly encourage Iraq by supporting that nation against Iran during a long eight-year war? ("Saudis Press"). Was President Bush merely proving that he was not a "wimp," a charge made by some during his 1988 presidential campaign? (Schanberg). But the fact remains that most coverage during the conflict was oriented on the battle and quite supportive of the U.S. and coalition forces. After the war, as before, the edges of dissent began to appear, as the inevitable phases of war reporting would predict.

Key Actors in the News

One can test the diversity of coverage by looking at how President Bush dominated all phases of the war and Congress "disappeared"—relatively speaking—during the period of actual conflict, to be replaced by General Schwarzkopf and other military leaders. A search of the *Washington Post* with the NEXIS system shows this exchange of civilian for military leadership. See Tables 3.1 through 3.4.

Stories that mention oil, especially the most negative, dropped out as the actual fighting started, as did references to Congress. Stories involving Kurds appeared at the end of the battle, as they began their revolt and created a new challenge for peace in the region.

The tables graphically map the rise and fall of particular leaders and subjects associated with the Persian Gulf crisis beginning during a pre-war period of July 1990, to a post-war period of March 1991. The use of an average number of stories per day is used here to smooth out the varying number of days in discreet periods of the conflict. For example, the pre-war and post-war periods as we have defined them each have thirty-two and thirty-one days respectively, while the threats, air war, and ground war periods each have 167 days, 38 days, and 5 days respectively. The average number of stories per day allows a comparative base across such a wide variance of time. One must be careful to note that the vertical scales in the tables differ quite a bit, so that the results are only suggestive.

In Table 3.1, stories mentioning both President Bush and the Persian Gulf appear slightly more often than does Congress and the Persian Gulf, but as the governments in the Persian Gulf region and the United States begin to spar verbally with one another, Bush takes a significant lead over Congress as a source of information about the conflict. During the air war Bush stories rise to an average number ten times that of Congress stories, and during the ground war thirteen times as many stories. In war, the commander-in-chief is the dominating news source.

In Table 3.2 the comparative dominance of military sources is evident by the peaking of Defense Secretary Cheney at the height of conflict. He was subsequently and slowly overshadowed by stories citing General Schwarzkopf. Schwarzkopf continued as a dominant story source even into the immediate postwar period.

Tables 3.3 and 3.4 demonstrate the rise and fall of news themes that could be somewhat controlled by U.S. government administration sources and those subjects that were more independent news events. There was a dramatic fall of references to oil as a news subject during

Table 3.1
Number of Stories Citing Bush and Congress in the *Washington Post* During Specific Time Periods Surrounding the Persian Gulf War

	Prewar		Threats		Air		Ground		Postwar	
	6/30/90 8/1/90	Average No. of Stories	8/2/90 1/15/91	Average No. of Stories	1/16/91 2/22/91	Average No. of Stories	2/23/91 2/27/91	Average No. of Stories	2/28/91 3/30/91	Average No. of Stories
No. Days	32	Per Day	167	Per Day	38	Per Day	5	Per Day	31	Per Day
Bush	4	0.13	979	5.86	358	9.42	69	13.80	209	6.74
Congress	1	0.03	148	0.89	35	0.92	5	1.00	38	1.23

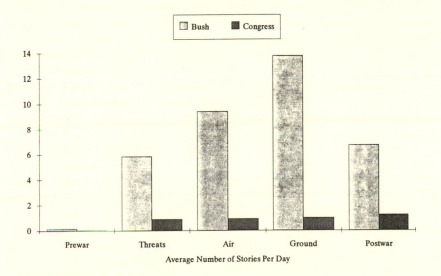

Average Number of Stories Per Day

the height of the Gulf War, and an increase of the administration's emphasis on the Saddam/Hitler image.

"After Action" Reports on Press Performance

The military routinely evaluates major actions when they are over in order to see what might be done better the next time. Pete Williams, spokesman for the Pentagon, concluded that the public was well served by the reporting (Williams 1991). But many journalists concluded differently. Some complained about constraints during that war (Copeland; Schanberg, "Press Lets"). Malcolm Browne lambasted the pool system in an early major article in the *New York Times Magazine*. There were panel sessions, reports, speeches to discuss coverage ("War Over"; "TV and the Gulf War"). Among the conclusions: the pool system was too

Table 3.2
Number of Stories Citing Pentagon Sources in the *Washington Post* During Specific Time Periods Surrounding the Persian Gulf War

	Prewar		Threats		Air		Ground		Postwar	
No. Days	6/30/90 8/1/90 32	Average No. of Stories Per Day	8/2/90 1/15/91 167	Average No. of Stories Per Day	1/16/91 2/22/91 38	Average No. of Stories Per Day	2/23/91 2/27/91 5	Average No. of Stories Per Day	2/28/91 3/30/91 31	Average No. of Stories Per Day
Powell	4	0.13	44	0.26	49	1.29	4	0.80	24	0.77
Schwarzkopf	0	0.00	64	0.38	100	2.63	14	2.80	114	3.68
Cheney	38	1.19	307	1.84	137	3.61	29	5.80	51	1.65

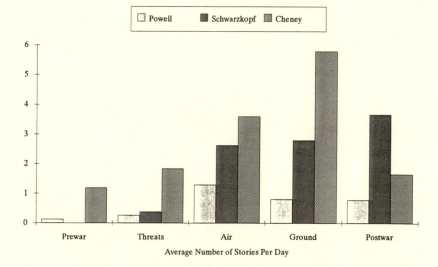

Average Number of Stories Per Day

confining. Some reports had been delayed—excessively in the view of some—while possible security leaks were considered by the military.

The system was not supposed to be adversarial, yet many concluded that the system did in fact become so, and that the military had "won." By controlling what reporters saw, the military controlled what the public saw of the action. By controlling what the public saw, the military ensured that public opinion would not turn against the effort, as had occurred in Vietnam. After the Persian Gulf, troops came home to welcoming crowds who had faithfully worn yellow ribbons. Congressmen who dared to vote for economic sanctions rather than to support the direct action of war were threatened for re-election ("Sanford Facing Backlash"). General Schwarzkopf retired from the army and reportedly could command $50,000 per speech, and when he came home he said, at last, Vietnam veterans could come home. In General Schwarzkopf's mind, apparently, the Vietnam War was finally over through this suc-

Table 3.3
Number of Stories Citing Saddam Hussein and Adolf Hitler, and the New World Order, in the *Washington Post* During Specific Time Periods Surrounding the Persian Gulf War

	Prewar		Threats		Air		Ground		Postwar	
	6/30/90 8/1/90	Average No. of Stories	8/2/90 1/15/91	Average No. of Stories	1/16/91 2/22/91	Average No. of Stories	2/23/91 2/27/91	Average No. of Stories	2/28/91 3/30/91	Average No. of Stories
No. Days	32	Per Day	167	Per Day	38	Per Day	5	Per Day	31	Per Day
Hussein & Hitler	2	0.06	118	0.71	39	1.03	7	1.40	7	0.23
New World Order	0	0.00	50	0.30	45	1.18	5	1.00	21	0.68

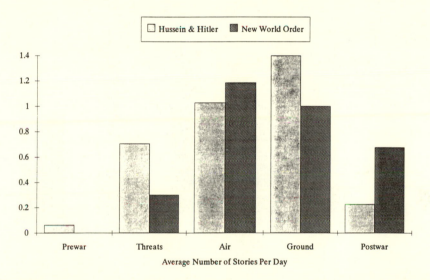

Average Number of Stories Per Day

cessful modern effort in the Persian Gulf. All it had taken was a supportive president, public, and press, all pulling together. The war was over but the reporting, like the windshield wiper, was not.

MODELS: BALANCING OLD WARS AND NEW COMMUNICATION

"Balance" in War News

Why does the press, like the windshield wiper, not stop immediately in war coverage? Reporting requires a balancing of views from a diversity of sources, exemplifying our pluralistic society. War reporting in the Persian Gulf followed the same pattern as in the first period of the Vietnam War and other wars as well. The only major difference was the

Table 3.4

Number of Stories Citing the Kurds and Oil and the Gulf in the *Washington Post* During Specific Time Periods Surrounding the Persian Gulf War

	Prewar		Threats		Air		Ground		Postwar	
	6/30/90 8/1/90	Average No. of Stories	8/2/90 1/15/91	Average No. of Stories	1/16/91 2/22/91	Average No. of Stories	2/23/91 2/27/91	Average No. of Stories	2/28/91 3/30/91	Average No. of Stories
No. Days	32	Per Day	167	Per Day	38	Per Day	5	Per Day	31	Per Day
Kurds	2	0.06	34	0.20	27	0.71	2	0.40	51	1.65
Oil & Gulf	12	0.38	266	1.59	87	2.29	3	0.60	25	0.81

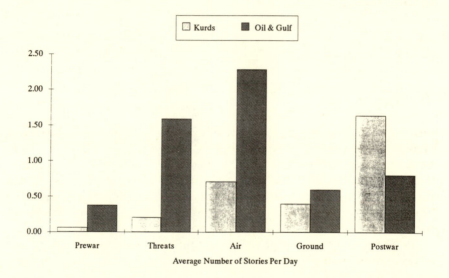

Average Number of Stories Per Day

duration of the initial phase and the successful control of initial coverage. One can argue that if the Vietnam War had been relatively short, coverage would have been neutral or favorable, too. The same model fits both wars, as this chapter briefly sketches for a comparison, and in fact all our wars. The success or failure of the military and/or press was really a success or failure of the larger social system. And as the military has twelve principles of war, such as simplicity, unity, surprise, and so on, a thirteenth principle has become evident—managing the media.

A social system, like a healthy human body, strives to maintain a balance of opinions, just as the body attempts to maintain a moderate and steady temperature. If the body temperature rises, the body reacts to cool itself, and if it is too cool, to heat itself up. This is homeostasis.

Something analogous operates in society. Borrowing from Fritz Heider (1988), Theodore Newcomb argues that we attempt to maintain a balance

Figure 3.2
A Balanced Situation

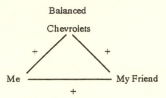

Balanced

Chevrolets

Me ——————— My Friend

Figure 3.3
An Unbalanced Situation

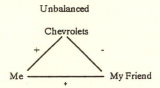

Unbalanced

Chevrolets

Me ——————— My Friend

between our own view of different things or concepts and those of our friends (Newcomb 1965). For example, if we really like Chevrolets, then we want our best friend to like them as well. If the friend does so, then all is balanced. If the friend does not, then we may decide we do not like Chevrolets so much . . . or our friend so much. But at any rate, the situation is unbalanced and we feel pressure to either change our views or our friend. Figure 3.2 and 3.3 illustrate these two conditions.

The point is that our individual perceptions cause us to change our views to remain in balance. We suggest now that this model, by analogy, can explain much of war news coverage in the Persian Gulf or Vietnam, although we need to draw the model with a little more complexity to represent the relevant parties involved. Figure 3.4 sketches the relevant players. We also suggest that war news evolves through three definite phases, exemplified in Vietnam coverage, but perhaps not complete yet in Persian Gulf coverage.

The events of war involve battles, planning for battles, strategy, supply and transport, tactical weapons—the subject list is very long. Reporters who cannot always see the events of war, much less have the military background to understand them, have to rely upon military sources as experts to explain them, until the reporters have more knowledge and contacts in the region. The military briefs reporters on the scene and also officials back in Washington—such as the president and members of the joints chiefs of staff. Reporters meanwhile send stories to editors, who also have ongoing contacts with officials in the White House and Pentagon. Editors ultimately control the amount and direc-

Figure 3.4
Phase I of War Reporting

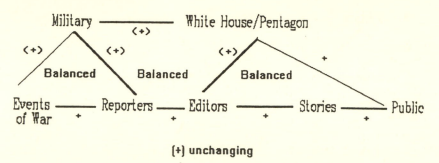

(+) unchanging

tion of coverage because they have veto power. If all perspectives were positive on the war, then the model would be in balance and look like Figure 3.4. Such is Phase I of war reporting.

But that condition is not likely to occur naturally in a pluralistic press system where reporters are free to roam around, dig up news, follow hunches, plum dissent, and in general do what reporters are supposed to do: provide reportorial diversity. Of course, that requires time. The more likely condition is that the system will be in balance at first simply because reporters do not know how to assess war events and simply borrow the perspectives provided by military briefers.

One could argue that Phase I, in fact, did represent most coverage of the Vietnam War in the 1960–1964 periods, despite some probing of other perspectives by David Halberstam, Peter Arnett, and others (Hammond 1988). As U.S. troop commitments grew, so did reportorial sophistication, and so the 1964–1968 years were ones in which reporters began to write both neutral, positive, and negative reports of events (Karnow 1984). Editors, however, found this confusing because their own sources in Washington, the White House and the Pentagon, still held to a positive assessment. This model, Phase II, is portrayed in Figure 3.5.

Within months of the Tet Offensive, U.S. public support for the war began to decline, and in the last years of the war, therefore, editors began to listen to their own reporters more than they did to the things-are-going-great messages they heard from the White House and Pentagon. Editors, finally, resolved the imbalance in views by supporting their reporters, thereby bringing the system at least partially into balance, as represented by Phase III illustrated by Figure 3.6. Phase III provides diversity of perspectives and the public is then aware of difference.

We suggest this view fits the 1968–1972 period in Vietnam and provided more perspectives to the public, but it meant that reporters fol-

Figure 3.5
Phase II of War Reporting

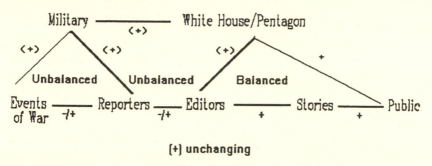

[+] unchanging

Figure 3.6
Phase III of War Reporting

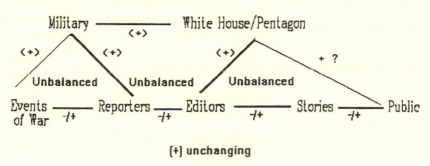

[+] unchanging

lowed their own sources rather than merely those of briefing officers. Those most likely to be getting a distorted view were officials in the White House and Pentagon where their own staff brought favorable views, while the press presented more pluralistic views. In Vietnam the news media did not "fail"; official reporting channels did ("Pentagon Seems Vague"). This led some high-ranking military officers in Vietnam, such as General William Westmoreland, to condemn the press for lack of support of the troops. Many other officers came to the same conclusion, as a sort of American version of the stab in the back that the German military—incorrectly—used to blame civilian leadership for the collapse of the war effort in 1918. Some military officers still cling to this view, despite the efforts of leading military historians and theorists who place the blame on political indirection, lack of public support, or on many other causes. In fact, we argue, what was involved was a communication system attempting to come into some kind of balance, a social attempt at homeostasis. The model suggests that the press-government-public relations move from being unnaturally monistic in Phase I to being

naturally pluralistic in Phase III—unbalanced because the official channels always emphasized publicly "good" news, while the press is obligated in a free system to use diverse sources and present balanced
perspectives.

If war coverage remained fixed in Phase I, it would suggest enormous
consensus—not even World War II met that test—or a totally controlled
press. Phase III represents the final evolutionary stage of an active, free
press. The only way Phase III could, and should, be balanced would be
for official sources to present an open, balanced view to the press and
public. That seldom happens, so Phase III always reflects tension between press and government. In the case of the Vietnam War, that was
enough for some to blame the press for all the political and military
problems of that conflict.

Phase I in the Persian Gulf: Precision Guided Information Bombs

What is the relevance of coverage in Vietnam to coverage in the Persian
Gulf War? We suggest now that early Phase I war coverage in the Persian
Gulf was similar to that of the 1960–1964 years in Vietnam. Reporters,
in a strange land and culture, did not have much knowledge of military
plans; indeed, most young reporters have not served in the military.
Reporters, therefore, as in Vietnam, relied upon military briefings and
access through press pools. It is little wonder that reports were filled
with technological handouts, expert opinions (especially on the networks), and informed guesses about supposed or actual military operations. As President Bush changed war goals, reporters could only hustle
to see if the goals could be met. Over the course of time, for example,
President Bush called for

- withdrawal of Iraqi forces from Kuwait; (then added)
- the destruction of the war-making capability of Iraq; (then added)
- the destruction of the nuclear-capability of Iraq; (then encouraged)
- the removal of Saddam Hussein; (then, apparently, encouraged)
- the revolt of the Iraqi Kurds; (then added, we need)
- a new world order.

As if following Carl Von Clausewitz, President Bush initially announced
clear war goals—Saddam, get out of Kuwait! Unlike Clausewitz's recommendations, he changed goals from time to time. If reporters wanted
to check on these goals, they needed help from the White House and
from the military. Reporters did not have any independent way to de-

termine if the nuclear capability was smashed. Schwarzkopf said it was, for example, when it perhaps was not.

Reporters could ask the president about the New World Order; and they did, drawing some negative views and cartoons as journalists questioned the need for a new world order abroad when the U.S. economic infrastructure is so imperiled (Powell; Smith). During the war itself, public opinion fell so solidly behind the war effort that dissent all but disappeared and so reporters concentrated upon the battlefield rather than on long-range White House strategy.

Most war coverage was factual, supportive of military efforts, and not provocative. Figure 3.4 (Phase I) suggests the positive nature of coverage. Without dissenting views, audience members presumably become even more supportive of the war effort. One communication theorist, a German, Elisabeth Noelle-Neumann (1984) argues that when you read only one point of view in the press, you assume that represents the majority opinion, although it might not. But in order to fit in, you might be silent if you disagree, thereby making that point of view appear to be even more in the ascendancy. We argue that happened in the Persian Gulf War, briefly, in the combat period.

Phase II in the Persian Gulf

There was a subsequent Phase II in the Persian Gulf. When the majority of the troops came home—though many remained a year later—to celebrations, so did sober second assessments. When the war was over the coverage was not. We learned about many war events as reporters added the diversity of perspectives that they could not develop during the short conflict itself.

For example, after the war some reported that:

- about (a record) one-third of American troop deaths resulted from "friendly" fire ("U.S. Works to Cut");
- only about one weapon of ten was a precision-guided weapon; the rest were regular mass destruction weapons ("Pentagon Acknowledges");
- there were many missed targets, including the well-known hit on an elevator shaft, which was part of a telephone exchange ("Nightline");
- collateral damage was very great and the Iraqi infrastructure—roads, schools, hospitals—were destroyed ("Allies Aimed to Kill");
- several thousand civilians died ("Bombing Puts U.S.");
- we, through the White House, may have encouraged the Kurd revolt, implicitly promising aid that we did not deliver ("Saudis Press U.S.");
- the Iraqi capability for nuclear production was not destroyed during the war ("How Iraq Plays");

- the United States tried to destroy Iraq's computer database system by introducing a virus ("U.S. Said to Put");
- the much vaunted equipment, such as the very expensive invisible B2 bomber is, in fact, visible and a poor performer; U.S. tanks, distracted by sand and moving fast, had trouble distinguishing friend from enemy; some technical systems did not perform to par ("Army's Top War Machines");
- our forces buried enemy troops alive ("Nightly News");
- an estimated 80,000 children in Iraq may eventually die as a result of war-related causes, including the lack of medicines resulting from the continuing blockade ("Back from the Living Dead");
- an estimate of Iraqi soldier deaths range from 10,000 to 115,000 with no sure number known ("The Ones That Got Away");
- Egyptian participation and Israeli nonparticipation ended up mostly being expensive buyoffs ("Allies Played Politics");
- the British and the French were not happy with their designated participation among the allies, and asked for a greater share of the fighting ("Coalition Coped with Infighting");
- Japan had been willing and able to pay more for oil, even if the Iraqi takeover of Kuwait did drive up prices ("Developments in Gulf Crisis");
- Kuwait leaders were autocratic and little interested in democratic rights ("Saddam's Staying Power");
- The Kuwaiti government hired an international public relations firm to ensure U.S. participation in the war effort, and the U.S. Congress knew nothing about it ("20/20");
- The story of Kuwaiti babies yanked from incubators and left by Iraqi soldiers to die was not corroborated by the Kuwaiti doctors who remained in the hospital, and this story may have been promulgated by a public relations firm ("Unmasking Kuwait's");
- many Saudi leaders and citizens were more than anxious for U.S. and coalition troops to depart ("Legacy of War");
- the decision-making process in the White House was often slow and uncertain ("The Day We Stopped");
- President Bush said he was not targeting Saddam during the conflict, but U.S. military leaders under his command made repeated efforts to find and destroy him ("The Last-Gasp Effort");
- Saddam Hussein was not personally imperiled during the war; indeed he could not be found and remained perhaps even more firmly than ever entrenched in power ("The Desert a Year Later");
- An American company may have actually supplied the Iraqis with Scud launchers during the Iraq/Iran conflict that were later used against the allied forces of Desert Storm ("U.S. Linked to Iraqi Scud Launchers").

These stories came from diverse sources, not just from the White House or the Pentagon. Of course, much discussion of the technical details of the war discussed in public would have been very helpful to the enemy. But other news seemed to go to the political basis of the war, a legitimate part of the political process, even if such news was, for the moment, bypassed during Phase I.

Even during the war, some of these points were raised here and there in foreign or alternative presses, and there was some coverage of early short-lived main line mass protests against war. But the general press concentrated on the technical aspects of the war ("Some Say U.S."; "Allies Smash"; "The Mother of All"). If these missed points are important, the delay of their publication meant that the public could not evaluate support in terms of the total war but only in terms of its apparent technological success. Apparently, that is what the public did. From the point of view of the White House and Pentagon, Phase I reporting worked well, although not Phase II.

Phase III in the Persian Gulf?

At any rate, the reporting continued after the ground war ended in February—indeed, it still does—and so we have learned about many events and perspectives we did not know during the actual period of conflict. Belatedly, there has been a Phase II and perhaps even a Phase III, as reporters and editors continue to do their job of providing a pluralistic view. At least one presidential candidate in early 1992 openly called the war a mistake (instead of only employing economic sanctions from the start). In reflection, not all was yellow ribbons. Dissent—belatedly—surfaced in Phase II and III of the Persian Gulf reporting.

NEW WARS, NEW COMMUNICATION

Challenges of Covering Modern War

War is one of the most complex activities in which modern societies, unfortunately, engage. For reporters today, as in earlier wars, there are challenges about what to write. You cannot write about everything, even if you had access to every military and political leader and to every battlefield on land, sea, and air. If reporters concentrate on obtaining news from those at the top of political and military leadership, the stories are very strategic—that is, the big picture—in orientation. Such views concentrate on broad goals, not exciting combat details, where men and women live and die. The top view is invaluable, but lacks the drama of confronting war at the tactical level of individual soldiers, sailors, and air combatants. Stories about broad goals provide a view of the mountain, but stories and pictures of fighting individuals give a close view of the mountain's trees. One cannot look at both at the same time, but over time one should have the chance to see both (and other) perspectives of the mountain. In war, the challenge has always been how to present balanced coverage of events and perspectives. Those who remember coverage of War II are likely to remember the sonorous voice of Edward R. Morrow, braving London air raids, to bring a voice picture of Luffwaffe bombers and the terror and destruction they brought, or the word pictures of individual soldiers portrayed by Scipps-Howard reporter Ernie Pyle, or the cartoons of small soldiers drawn by Bill Mauldin (Norton et al. 1986). We remember coverage of tactics because we can relate to them. Tactical stories can displace strategic views.

Modern communication has narrowed the distance between the top and bottom of communication structures and has brought them much closer together. Today people at the top and bottom of military forces can easily talk to each other—and to the press as well—if they choose. This capability, called a feedback revolution by one scholar (Beniger 1986), was used by leaders, such as President Johnson to keep his finger on the military action in the Vietnam War and, more recently, President Bush to keep his finger on the political pulse—if not so clearly on the military trigger—in the Persian Gulf War ("Bush Sees Iraq"; "Conservative Group"; "Emerging Black"; "Clouds Form"; "U.S. War Toll"; "Concerns about Quayle").

A leader at the top can do much in war. President Johnson personally selected key targets during the air war against North Vietnam (Gelb 1991). His orders could be related much more quickly and directly than those of any previous president. Since Vietnam, the president can be commander-in-chief in fact as well as law, should the president choose, as Johnson in frustration did toward the end of the war.

If one could direct bombers to specific targets then, perhaps, one could also limit the collateral damage to public opinion back home. It was precision-guided information. This view is old fashioned because it assumes that audiences do not have access, like the president, to many conflicting sources of information. One could win on the battlefield but lose the public opinion war at home. The three phases of war reporting are likely to happen much more quickly than in past wars. And the wide spread of technology means that no leader can stop reporting at Phase I. Phase II and III will come in a free system.

The Thirteenth Principle of War—Press Management

The Persian Gulf demonstrated the importance that military commanders put on information. General Schwarzkopf himself watched CNN, if only to see what the other side was watching (Pyle 1991). Control of information has become the thirteenth principle of war. The day of the senior commander, such as Admiral David Farragut in another context, saying damn the press, full speed ahead, is over. For all the storming that Norman Schwarzkopf did, he earned much praise for his press briefings, one of which—the overall explanation of the ground war—is considered a kind of masterpiece (Keegan 1991). Even Pentagon briefer Lieutenant General Thomas Kelly was able to retire from the military to earn high fees for his speeches, based on fame earned far from the field of battle ("General Praises Media").

As press organizations assembled teams to cover the war, the military assembled units to fight the war. U.S. and coalition forces assembled to carry out the battle plans of the central command, which actually is a small number of officers. The Persian Gulf was a "modular" war, fought with troops assembled to fit the conflict. It is likely to be the future model. Most major commands are skeletons awaiting flesh. News organizations would be well advised to learn how to fit news teams to different types of conflicts in different parts of the world, perhaps with news teams who work with different U.S. commands around the world. That way reporters at least would not be ignorant of the region in which they could suddenly find themselves, and they would be ready to provide a diversity of perspectives. The press needs to fit better, flexibly, into conflict.

A New Concern: The President's Army

The military force is now a voluntary one. Because the draft ended in 1973, everyone joining the armed forces since then is there by choice. This force is well trained and educated. The force owes first allegiance to the president, as commander-in-chief. The Congress is sometimes viewed as an obstacle to obtaining equipment, supplies, pay raises. We no longer have draftees faithfully keeping one foot in the civilian community and one in the military for a limited tour of duty.

Military members are loyal Americans but they also have both feet planted in their units, with a face turned upward to their commanders, especially the commander-in-chief. The routes of senior commanders to communicate with military members have never been greater. Never before has the American military belonged so much to the president; our army is in a sense the president's army more than it is our army. The Congress did not, for a variety of reasons, resist the president in Panama, Grenada, or the Persian Gulf. And there were no draftees writing home.

The roots of the military, once so deeply a part of the civilian community because of draftees, are different than in World War II, Korea, and Vietnam. President Bush and his subordinate commanders used the military with sensitivity and skill in the Persian Gulf, but one can never be certain that power will be used responsibly, even in a democracy. One brake on the possible abuse of power is provided by a free press that provides reasonable diversity. The press must watch how the president uses his military, for which after all he is not paying.

Old Leaders, New Wars

Balancing strong emotions generated by war challenges leaders, press, and citizens alike. In such times, democracy is most tested. Sometimes democracy fails, as when repressive laws were passed in World War I and socialists and anarchists were crammed into prisons (Stevens 1984), or as in World War II when approximately 120,000 Americans of Japanese background were put into concentration camps although there was not a single piece of solid evidence that these citizens posed any danger of "defecting" to Japan.

In the Revolutionary War era, Isaac Sears and the rough riders did not tolerate the attempt of New York *Gazetteer* editor James Rivington to present both patriot and loyalist points of view (Teeter 1964). A mob ran Boston editor John Mein out of town for trying to present different points of view (Mott 1966: 79). From our earliest days as a nation, we know the public can act to crush dissent—directly, as with Sears in the Revolution or indirectly as the incarceration of the Japanese in World War II. In war (as in other times of crisis), romantic notions of a supportive and tolerant public opinion are inappropriate, even in liberal democracies. On occasion, public reactions may be far more dangerous than actions of the military or government (Lofton 1980). The public is as likely as any king to kill the messenger, and often has, or threatened to do so, in our history.

Historian Fred Siebert (1972), in his important study of 300 years of press freedom in England (1476–1776) concluded that the press confronts the most trouble when there is pressure on the society and government. His thesis argues: "When pressure on the government increases, then pressure on the press increases" (10).

Leaders arise because of ability, drive, opportunity, and luck. Some presidents, like Washington, assumed power reluctantly and humbly. Some, like Truman, assumed power by accident. Some, like Jimmy Carter and Richard Nixon, assumed power after long and ambitious efforts to gain high office. Whatever the route to the top, leaders have to balance support at home with support of troops in the field. This involves listening to concerns at the bottom, adjusting to them, and sending messages back down. Top military leaders are at the center of a complex communication web. In our society, the president is the top commander.

The opportunities for leaders to listen have never been greater. Political leaders routinely use polls, experts, and media to keep up. The ability to send messages back down is also great, although audiences today turn to a variety of media, not just a few major mass media (Shaw, "The Rise and Fall" 1991).

In the eighteenth century leaders could rule by decree, with small professional armies. By the nineteenth century, decrees required the backing of larger armies. By the early twentieth century, leaders could use mass media. By the end of the twentieth century, millions potentially could use some kind of media. In modern war, leaders have to keep in mind the power of opposing opinion to use interconnecting media to collect other views and slow the passing wheels of the national war machine. In 1991, we saw this power demonstrated vividly in the Soviet Union, tragically in Yugoslavia, and politically in the former Soviet Bloc (Shaw & Martin, "David's Slingshot" 1991). Even without Phases II and III reporting, diversity will, eventually, surface. Modern communication gives termites the power to gnaw the strong timbers of leadership, often in unseen corners. Without vigilance and responsiveness, timbers can fall.

In the closing scene of *Patton*, the 1970 movie by 20th Century Fox, George C. Scott plays a thoughtful General Patton walking his dog Willie, as he says:

For over a thousand years, Roman conquerors returning from the wars enjoyed the honor of a triumph, a tumultuous parade. In the procession came trumpeters and musicians and strange animals from the conquered territories, together with carts laden with treasure and captured armaments.

The conqueror rode in a triumphal chariot, the dazed prisoners walking in chains before him. Sometimes his children, robed in white, stood with him in the chariot or rode the trace horses.

A slave stood behind the conqueror holding a golden crown and whispering in his ear a warning . . . that all glory is fleeting.

Indeed, for President Bush, for all of us, modern communication ensures that. Glory cannot just be the talk of high-minded leaders; instead, glory must come from the collective action of all of us, in communication with our leaders and with each other. That way, perhaps, we would not need any bombs, precision-guided or not. But can we listen?

BIBLIOGRAPHY

"20/20." ABC. January 17, 1992.

"A Moral Failure." *Washington Post*. April 5, 1991, A19.

Adams, Eddie. "Vietcong Executed." Associated Press. 1968.

"Allies Aimed to Kill Saddam." *News and Observer*. Raleigh, N.C. January 12, 1992, A1.

"Allies Played Politics as They Fought a War." *News and Observer*. Raleigh, N.C. January 15, 1992, A1.

66   THE MEDIA AND THE PERSIAN GULF WAR

"Allies Reach Consensus on Chemical Weapon Response." *News and Observer*. Raleigh, N.C. February 7, 1991, A1.

"Allies' Scud Hunt Came at a Cost." *News and Observer*. Raleigh, N.C. January 14, 1992, A1.

"Allies Smash Missile Sites." Associated Press. *The Chapel Hill Newspaper*. January 18, 1991, 1A.

"Army's Top War Machines Inconsistent in Iraq, Investigators Find." Associated Press. January 9, 1992.

Arnett, Peter. "Arnett Reflects on Reporting from Iraq." In *News and Observer*. Raleigh, N.C. March 17, 1991, A2.

"Back from the Living Dead." *Newsweek* (January 20, 1992): 28.

Beniger, James R. *The Control Revolution*. Cambridge: Harvard University Press, 1986.

"Bombing Puts U.S. on Defensive." *News and Observer*. Raleigh, N.C. February 14, 1991, A1.

Browne, Malcolm W. "The Military vs. the Press." *New York Times Magazine*. March 3, 1991, 27.

"Bush Asks Nation to Back 'Defensive' Mission." *Washington Post*. August 9, 1990, A1.

"Bush Keeps Eye on Intelligence But Hands off War Plans." [Maureen Dowd], *News and Observer*. Raleigh, N.C. January 24, 1991, 5A.

"Bush Sees Iraq as Nuclear Threat." *Washington Post*. November 23, 1990, A1.

"Bush Wins Support on Hill." *Washington Post*. August 29, 1990, A1.

"CBS News Crew Held in Baghdad." *Washington Post*. February 16, 1991, C1.

Clausewitz, Carl Von. *On War*. Princeton, N.J.: Princeton University Press, 1976.

"Clouds Form over GOP Senate Hopes." *Washington Post*, March 10, 1991, A18.

"Coalition Coped with Infighting." *News and Observer*. Raleigh, N.C. January 15, 1992, A1.

"Concerns about Quayle Appear to Rise." *Washington Post*. May 7, 1991, A17.

"Congress Approves $42.6 Billion to Finance Persian Gulf War." *News and Observer*. Raleigh, N.C. March 23, 1991, A3.

"Conservative Group Lobbies for Gulf Policy." *Washington Post*. November 30, 1990, A18.

Copeland, Larry. "Military Control over Media in Gulf is Unprecedented," Knight-Ridder News Service. *News and Observer*. Raleigh, N.C. January 27, 1991, 9A.

"The Day We Stopped the War." *Newsweek* (January 20, 1992): 16.

"The Desert a Year Later: Still Stormy." *Herald Sun*. Durham, N.C. January 12, 1992, A8.

"Developments in Gulf Crisis." *Washington Post*. January 15, 1991, A1.

"Does Bush Lack Strength to Be Patient?" *News and Observer*. Raleigh, N.C. February 6, 1991, A15.

Dowd, Maureen. "Bush Keeps Eye on Intelligence But Hands off War Plans." *News and Observer*. Raleigh, N.C. January 24, 1991, A5.

"Emerging Black Anti-War Movement." *Washington Post*. February 8, 1991, A27.

Fitzgerald, Frances. *Fire in the Lake*. New York: Vintage, 1972.

Friedman, Thomas L. "Some Say U.S. Should Rethink Ground Plans." New

York Times News Service. *News and Observer*. Raleigh, N.C. January 25, 1991, 3A.

"Frustration Widespread over Lack of Details." *News and Observer*. Raleigh, N.C. January 23, 1991, A5.

Gelb, Leslie H. "Bush Should Be Asking His Generals More Questions." *News and Observer*. Raleigh, N.C. February 7, 1991, A13.

"General Praises Media as He Departs." *News and Observer*. Raleigh, N.C. March 5, 1991, A3.

"Gulf Crisis Tests Baker as Diplomat." *Washington Post*. November 2, 1990, A1.

Hammond, William M. *The Military and the Media 1962–1968*. Washington, D.C.: Center for Military History, 1988.

Harwood, Richard. "In Battle for News, Eyes on Bottom Line." *News and Observer*. Raleigh, N.C. February 13, 1991, 13A.

Heider, Fritz. *Balance Theory*. New York: Springer-Verlay, 1988.

"Hollow Victory." *U.S. News and World Report*. January 20, 1992, 40.

"How Iraq Plays Nuclear Chicken." *U.S. News and World Report*. January 20, 1992, 45.

"How Reporters Missed the War." *Time* (January 8, 1990): 61.

Howard, Michael. "Clausewitz, Man of the Year?" *New York Times*. January 28, 1991, A23.

"Iraq May Still Have Nuclear Capability." *Washington Post*. January 22, 1991, A18.

"Iraq Uses Prisoners as Shields." *News and Observer*. Raleigh, N.C. January 22, 1991, A5.

"Iraq Will Allow CNN Satellite." *News and Observer*. Raleigh, N.C. January 27, 1991, A9.

Jeffres, Leo W. *Mass Media Process and Effects*. Prospect Heights, Ill.: Waveland Press, 1986.

Johnson, DeWayne B. "Vietnam: Report Card on the Press Corps at War." *Journalism Quarterly* 46 (Spring 1969): 9.

Karnow, Stanley. *Vietnam: A History*. New York: Penguin, 1984.

Keegan, John. "How the War Was Won." *Washington Post*. March 3, 1991, C7.

"The Last-Gasp Effort to Get Saddam." *U.S. News and World Report*. January 20, 1992, 42.

"Legacy of War Is Varied." *Herald-Sun*. Durham, N.C. January 12, 1992, A8.

Lofton, John. *The Press as Guardian of the First Amendment*. Columbia, S.C.: University of South Carolina Press, 1980.

Moody, Randall J. "The Armed Forces Broadcast News System: Vietnam Version." *Journalism Quarterly* 47 (Spring 1970): 27.

"Military Control over the Media Is Unprecedented." *News and Observer*. Raleigh, N.C. January 27, 1991, A3.

Military Strategy: Theory and Application. Carlisle Barracks, Pa.: U.S. Army War College, 1983.

"Mitterrand Proposes Peace Plan." *Washington Post*. September 24, 1990, A1.

"The Mother of All Battles." *News and Observer*. Raleigh, N.C. February 10, 1991, 1J.

Mott, Frank Luther. *American Journalism*. New York: Macmillian, 1966.

Newcomb, Theodore. *Social Psychology: The Study of Human Interaction*. New York: Holt, Rinehart & Winston, 1965.

"Nightline." *ABC News*. January 10, 1992.

"Nightly News." ABC. January 16, 1992.

Noelle-Neumann, Elisabeth. *Spiral of Silence*. Chicago: University of Chicago Press, 1984.

Norton, Mary Beth, David M. Katzman, Paul D. Escott, Howard Chudacoff, Thomas G. Patterson, and William M. Tuttle, Jr., eds. *A People and A Nation*, Vol. 2, 2d ed. Boston: Houghton Mifflin, Co. 1986. 791, 800.

Oberdorfer, Don. *Tet!* New York: DaCapo Press, 1984.

"Oil Spill into Gulf Cut to a Trickle." *News and Observer*. Raleigh, N.C. January 30, 1991, A1.

"The Ones That Got Away." *Newsweek* (January 20, 1992): 18.

"Patriot Missile's Success a Boost for Star Wars." *News and Observer*. Raleigh, N.C. January 30, 1991, A1.

"Pentagon Acknowledges Some of Its Bombs Killing Civilians." *Herald-Sun*. Durham, N.C. February 13, 1991, A7.

"Pentagon Seems Vague on the Iraqis' Death Toll." *New York Times*, February 3, 1991, A10.

"Pilots Rely on Flying Traffic Cop." *News and Observer*. Raleigh, N.C. January 30, 1991, A1.

Powell, Dwane. "The New World 'Order.' " *News and Observer*. Raleigh, N.C. March 12, 1991, 8A.

"President Warns Iraq of War Crimes Trials." *Washington Post*. October 16, 1990, A19.

"Press Lets Bush Keep It Caged." *News and Observer*. Raleigh, N.C. February 13, 1991, A13.

Pyle, Ernie. *Here Is Your War*. Cleveland: World Publishing Co., 1945.

———. *Home Country*. New York: William Sloan Associates, 1947.

Pyle, Richard. *Schwarzkopf: In His Own Words*. New York: Signet Books, 1991.

"Rethinking the Lessons of Desert Storm." *Newsweek* (January 20, 1992): 20.

"The Road to August 2." *Washington Post*. January 20, 1991, B7.

Rosenthal, A. M. "What Happened to George Bush? Nothing Much." *Chapel Hill Newspaper*. January 12, 1992, A5.

Rosenthal, Joe. "Old Glory Goes Up On Mt. Suribachi, Iwo Jima." Associated Press. 1945.

"Saddam's Staying Power." *Time* (August 5, 1991): 26–28.

Safire, William. "Unfinished Business with Saddam." *News and Observer*. Raleigh, N.C. January 15, 1992, A9.

"Sanford Facing Backlash over Vote on War Authorization." *News and Observer*. Raleigh, N.C. February 13, 1991, B3.

"Saudis Press U.S. for Help in Ouster of Iraq's Leader." *New York Times*. January 19, 1992, A1.

Schanberg, Sydney H. "Does Bush Lack Strength to be Patient." *News and Observer*. Raleigh, N.C. February 6, 1991, 15A.

Shaw, Donald L. "The Rise and Fall of American Mass Media: Roles of Technology and Leadership." Roy W. Howard Public Lecture, School of Journalism, Indiana University. April 4, 1991.

Shaw, Donald, and Shannon Martin. "David's Slingshot, Goliath's Peril: How Communication is Empowering Audiences and Downsizing Leaders." Paper presented at American Journalism Historians Association Meeting. October 3, 1991.

Siebert, Fred S. *Freedom of the Press in England 1476–1776.* Urbana: University of Illinois Press, 1972.

"Six Main Kinds of Missions Carried Out." *News and Observer.* Raleigh, N.C. January 17, 1991, A1.

"Skirmishes Fill Time Waiting for Ground War." *News and Observer.* Raleigh, N.C. February 7, 1991, A1.

"Smart Bombs Used to Stop Oil Spill in Gulf." *News and Observer.* Raleigh, N.C. January 28, 1991, A1.

Smith, Mike. "The New World Order/McWeapons." *The Chapel Hill Newspaper.* March 21, 1991, A4.

"Special Report." *Congressional Quarterly* (January 5, 1991): 42.

Stevens, John D. *Mass Media Between the Wars: Perception of Cultural Tension.* Syracuse, N.Y.: Syracuse University Press, 1984.

Summers, Harry. *On Strategy: A Critical Analysis of the Vietnam War.* Navato, Calif.: Presidio Press, 1982.

Teeter, Dwight. "King Sears, the Mob and Freedom of the Press in New York, 1765–76." *Journalism Quarterly* 41 (1964): 539–44.

"TV and the Gulf War." *The Quill* (March 1991): 17.

"The Ugly Land War: Iraqi Defenses Built to Drive Up Casualties." *News and Observer.* Raleigh, N.C. January 27, 1991, A1.

"U.S. Armor Did Well in Gulf, but War Ended Just in Time." *News and Observer.* Raleigh, N.C. January 9, 1992, A4.

"U.S. Considers Ways to Target Iraq's Saddam." *News and Observer.* Raleigh, N.C. November 25, 1991, A3.

"U.S. Linked to Iraqi Scud Launchers." *New York Times.* January 26, 1992, A4.

U.S. News and World Report, Special Issue, March 11, 1991, No. 16, 60.

"U.S. Said to Put Bug in Iraqi Computers." *News and Observer.* Raleigh, N.C. January 11, 1992, A8.

"U.S. Says It Will Hold Saddam Accountable." *News and Observer.* Raleigh, N.C. January 22, 1991, A1.

"U.S. War Toll Defines Racial Predictions." *Washington Post.* March 21, 1991, A28.

"U.S. Works to Cut 'Friendly Fire' Deaths." *News and Observer.* Raleigh, N.C. December 9, 1991, A3.

"Unmasking Kuwait's Deception." *News and Observer.* Raleigh, N.C. January 8, 1992, A9.

Ut, Huynh Cong "Nick." "Terror of War." Associated Press. 1972.

"War Over, the Press Looks Back." *Presstime* (April 1991): 40.

Williams, Pete. "This Was the Best War Coverage Ever." *News and Observer.* Raleigh, N.C. March 18, 1991, A2.

Wilson, Stan Le Roy. *Mass Media/Mass Culture.* New York: Random House, 1989.

"World's Poorest Nations Hit Hard by Gulf Crisis, U.N. Says." *Washington Post.* March 21, 1991, A23.

Wyatt, Clarence R. " 'At the Cannon's Mouth': The American Press and the Vietnam War." *Journalism History* 13 (Autumn-Winter 1986): 104.
"Yeah, Man, the Profit Be Praised." *Herald-Sun*. Durham, N.C. February 17, 1991, F4.

Chapter Four

Media Perspectives on World Opinion During the Kuwaiti Crisis

Frank Louis Rusciano

Since the fall of the Berlin Wall and the official acknowledgment of the end of the Cold War, not a week has passed without some reference in the media to the "New World Order" heralded by these events (see Unger 1991: 20); and Ullman 1991: 21 for examples). While the definition of this new order remains vague, it is clearly characterized by two critical features: a *consensus*, real or perceived, about acceptable forms of behavior in international relations, and the tendency of leaders to invoke the sanction of international *isolation* toward nations that violate this consensus. Both features focus our attention upon the concept of "world opinion." Consensus implies that nations generally share an opinion regarding proper behavior in the international sphere, while the threat of isolation implies that nations are willing to act upon this consensus to punish errant nations or leaders.

The concept of "world opinion," however, has remained an elusive and often ill-defined term. As Davidson noted in 1973, "World opinion not only lacks an agreed definition; even its existence is frequently questioned" (Davidson 1973: 871). Indeed, while Davidson defends the usefulness of the idea, such writers as Morgenthau (1962) and Bogart (1966) have argued that the diversity of cultures and ideologies existing among nations renders the concept invalid.

It now seems reasonable to argue, however, that many of the criticisms levelled at the concept were time bound. When the world was still divided into two major, and several minor, competing ideologies, it was doubtful that any form of international consensus on issues was possible. When one nation's "freedom fighters" becomes another nation's "terrorists," general international support for freedom or against terrorism becomes unlikely. With the collapse of the Eastern bloc and the refutation of Marxist interpretations within what is now the former Soviet Union, though, the possibility for a shared language and shared opinions among nations about topics of international concern became more likely.

The Iraqi invasion of Kuwait provides us with a unique opportunity to study the concept of "world opinion" in the new international order. This chapter concerns the concept's relevance to the study of political communication. For while analysts may dispute whether "world opinion" actually exists, it is undeniable that the term enjoys common usage among journalists. In another article, I noted how the *International Herald Tribune* and the *Frankfurter Allgemeine Zeitung*, representing an American newspaper published in Europe and a West German newspaper respectively, tended to use the concept of "world opinion" in a similar manner in news stories and editorials between February and April of 1986 (Rusciano and Fiske-Rusciano 1990: 305–22). The present analysis extends this study to two newspapers during the period of the Kuwaiti crisis, from August 1, 1990 (one day before the Iraqi invasion) to January 16, 1991 (one day after the Persian Gulf War began). The purpose here is to study whether the perspective on "world opinion," and the usage of the term, differed in an American newspaper, the *New York Times*, and a Third World newspaper, the *Times of India*. This chapter will illustrate that while the newspapers shared many perspectives on the content and timing of "world opinion" during this crisis, there were critical differences that point to the position accorded the United States and India in world opinion and the emerging international order.

THE STUDY DESIGN AND QUESTIONS FOR RESEARCH

This chapter analyzes the common usage of the concept of world opinion in the *New York Times* and the *Times of India* by studying its appearance in stories and editorials in the two newspapers. A content analysis of all pieces referencing world opinion during the pre-war Kuwaiti crisis discovered that the concept was commonly used in both papers. World opinion was referenced in some form sixty-seven times in the American daily and sixty-five times in the Indian daily. References occurred in stories 54 percent of the time and editorials 46 percent of the time in the *New York Times*, and in stories 68 percent of the time and editorials 32 percent of the time in the *Times of India*; these differences were not statistically significant.[1]

References to world opinion included explicit and implicit citations. Explicit citations included some direct reference to the phrase or its equivalent; examples include "world opinion," "international opinion," or "world public opinion." Far more common, comprising 93 percent of the references in both newspapers, were implicit citations. These citations did not use synonyms for world opinion, but rather included attitudes, preferences, opinions, or reactions attributed to the world or to all nations considered together. The following serve as examples of such references. (In these excerpts, as with all similar excerpts throughout the chapter, emphasis has been added.)

The *will of the nations around the world* will be to enforce these sanctions. (*New York Times*, August 7, 1990)

There would probably have been little *world reaction* had it not been for the oil and wealth at stake. (*New York Times*, August 11, 1990)

The fighting was reported by Gulf-based diplomats as *world reaction* toughened against Iraq. (*Times of India*, August 4, 1990)

Bowing to *international . . . pressure and condemnation* and threat of punitive economic sanctions, Iraq today started withdrawing its troops from Kuwait, three days after it invaded the country. (*Times of India*, August 6, 1990)

Implicit references were also likely to be active constructions, as if "the world" were stating a preference or judging an action or event: "condemning," "applauding," or "expecting" a result. Such citations include the following (emphasis has been added):

The world is watching what we do and will not be satisfied with vacillation and procrastination. (*New York Times*, August 3, 1990)

All nations have reason to be outraged by a violation of frontiers tantamount to armed robbery . . . *The only rational response is to isolate Iraq* and compel its unconditional pullout. (*New York Times*, August 5, 1990)

What these various pressures add up to is a *refusal by the international community . . . to endorse* the fait accompli that Iraq presented it with by forcibly taking over Kuwait. (*Times of India*, August 11, 1990)

Most of the world still considers the Al-Sabah family, under Emir Jaber Al-Ahmed Al-Sabah, the legitimate rulers of Kuwait, which was invaded by Iraq on August 2 and annexed a week later. (*Times of India*, August 23, 1990)

These references, and others like them, formed the basis for a comparative analysis of the manner in which the two newspapers used the concept of "world opinion" during the pre-war Kuwaiti crisis. This analysis is guided by five major questions. First, to what extent does the Kuwaiti crisis dominate the agenda for world opinion during this period? Are other issues or events also likely to be referenced as subjects for world opinion? Second, how do the timing of references between the two newspapers compare? Do the newspapers tend to reference world opinion in relation to the Kuwaiti crisis at similar times during the six-month period? Third, do the newspapers differ in the emphasis they place on the moral component of world opinion (referring to *values* shared by nations) and the pragmatic component of world opinion (referring to *interests* shared by nations)? Fourth, do the two newspapers tend to evaluate the crisis in different ways, providing different interpretations of world reactions to leaders and events? Finally, how do both newspapers view the role of *isolation* in punishing Iraq for the Kuwaiti invasion? Specifically, do both newspapers tend to agree that the invasion of Kuwait left Iraq effectively isolated in world opinion prior to the Persian Gulf War? The general conclusion reached in this chapter is that while the two dailies tended to be remarkably similar in their perspectives on world opinion in this crisis, there were critical differences that underscore the relative positions of the United States and India in the international community. A few notes will then be added about the possible import of these differences for the status of Third World nations like India in the emerging international order.

EXPLORING THE AGENDA FOR WORLD OPINION

The Kuwaiti crisis unquestionably dominated the agenda for world opinion, as it was perceived by the two newspapers, during the six-month period studied. All sixty-seven references in the *New York Times* dealt with the crisis, as did forty-five (or 69.2%) of the references in the *Times of India*. Despite the Kuwaiti crisis's dominant position in both newspapers' citations, this difference is statistically significant.[2]

Because the Indian newspaper displays a more pluralistic interpretation of the agenda for world opinion, it is useful to study the other subjects it includes. The Palestinian problem was cited in six, or 9.2 percent, of all stories referencing world opinion. Eduard Shevardnadze's predictions about the Soviet Union's future, India's appointment to a seat on the United Nations' Security Council in January, India's status and image as a democracy in light of recent political violence, and discussions of the nuclear capacity of Third World nations were cited in two stories each, representing 3.1 percent of the total. Finally, the awarding of the Nobel Peace Prize to Mikhail Gorbachev, a scientific space shuttle mission, the reunification of Germany, apartheid in South Africa, and civil strife in Cambodia and Sri Lanka were cited in one story each, representing 1.5 percent of the total. Generally speaking, the *New York Times* and the *Times of India* viewed the agenda for world opinion in a similar manner. Specifically, though, the Indian daily described a more diverse agenda—and, in the case of the Palestinian problem, an agenda that included topics at least partially supportive of the Iraqi position.

This pattern of general similarity with specific, yet important, variance, also applies to the dates upon which world opinion was referenced

Figure 4.1
Percentage of Total References to World Opinion on Kuwaiti Crisis, by Date

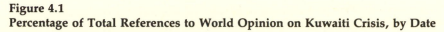

regarding the Iraqi invasion. Figure 4.1 shows the distribution of all citations on the Kuwaiti crisis for the two newspapers, by date; here, the dates are divided into two-week periods.[3] As the graph indicates, the general pattern of references tends to be the same over the period of the crisis; the chi-square value indicates no significant differences between the two newspapers regarding date of reference.[4] However, the correspondence between the dates of reference increases after the fourth two-week period. The similarity exists primarily beyond this period. The symmetric lambda value for the first period is .196, indicating a significant relationship between the newspaper and the date of reference; the symmetric lambda for the second period is .000, indicating no relationship between the two variables.

The significant difference that exists between dates of citations for the two newspapers in the first eight weeks is not a function of the difference in their agendas for world opinion. All of the references in both newspapers during the first eight weeks dealt with the Kuwaiti crisis. The similarity after the first eight-week period is also not a function of similar sources for the news stories and editorials that cite world opinion in the two newspapers. The *New York Times* relied upon its own reporters or wire services for citations to world opinion in 89 percent of the cases; the *Times of India* relied upon its own reporters or wire services for citations in 85 percent of the cases. The two papers only shared sources for stories in 9 percent of cases; hence, the similarities are not due to the newspapers' use of the same stories off the international wire services. These findings apply for the early and later periods in the crisis.

However, other differences in the two newspapers' interpretations of world opinion do offer clues to the early variance in the dates of reference. First, there were significant differences in the *measures* of world opinion used by the two newspapers. The *Times of India* cited leaders' reactions as the primary source of information on world opinion in 64.4 percent of cases; the *New York Times*, by contrast, mentioned leaders' reactions as a measure in only 12 percent of cases. Most frequently, the American newspaper described no measure for world opinion (58.2 percent of cases); by contrast, the Indian newspaper gave no measure in only 9 percent of the cases.[5] These findings apply before and after the first eight weeks of the crisis. But the signals given by other world leaders shifted dramatically between these periods, altering the perception of world opinion described in the Indian newspaper.

In the first eight weeks of the crisis, the *Times of India* was more open to the Iraqi perspective on the invasion. While its stories and editorials condemned the takeover of Kuwait as morally wrong, this paper was more likely to refer to Iraqi public opinion than was the *New York Times* in this early period. The Indian newspaper referenced Iraqi opinion in 50 percent of cases in the first eight weeks; the American newspaper referenced Iraqi opinion in only 4.5 percent of cases.[6] The former also noted how Iraqi public opinion disagreed with commonly perceived notions of world opinion in nine out of ten cases cited. After the first eight weeks, the *Times of India* cited Iraqi public opinion in only 4 percent of cases, while the *New York Times* cited it in 8.9 percent of cases.[7]

Other evidence suggests that the Indian newspaper was more likely to dispute the American interpretation of world opinion regarding the Kuwaiti crisis in the first eight weeks than afterward. The United States was often accused in this first period of attempting to rally international opinion against Iraq. As one story noted:

Iraq's main enemy now, the United States, also has indirect motivations. From the way in which *the U.S. is trying to turn the whole world against Iraq*, it is clear that it is . . . trying to humiliate and overthrow Mr. Hussein because he is an uppity insubordinate Arab . . . *To increase the world's ill will towards Iraq*, the U.S. is propagating that Saudi Arabia is Iraq's next target and much is being made of the fact that Iraqi troops in Kuwait are near the Saudi border . . . but it can at least be said that an invasion of Saudi Arabia is, as of now, improbable. (*Times of India*, August 5, 1990)

The Indian newspaper also described a struggle for world opinion taking place among nations—a struggle one reporter felt was exacerbated by American and British troops in Saudi Arabia:

the effect [of the troops] can only be to raise tensions unduly and to rally Arab states, despite themselves, to Baghdad's side. President Hussein, isolated though he is, would like nothing more than *Arab and world hostility* to his gobbling up of Kuwait dissipated by Western military action *that would make him an underdog and a hero*. (*Times of India*, August 11, 1990)

The evidence suggests that early differences in timing and tone of references to the Kuwaiti crisis relate to the relative positions of India and the United States, the actions taken by Iraq during the early period, and the resulting formation of world opinion. The *New York Times* repeatedly stated that world opinion favored the American position on the invasion, and the resulting demonization of Saddam Hussein, with little reference to specific nations' reactions. The Indian newspaper, representing a Third World nation, cited a greater variety of voices regarding the crisis. The *Times of India* mentioned other world leaders and Iraqi public opinion in its attempts to define world opinion on the crisis. Its reactions were therefore more ambivalent regarding the degree of consensus among nations.

This ambivalence changed after the first eight weeks of the crisis for several reasons. Certainly, Saddam Hussein's appearance on television with two British children being held in Baghdad on August 23 affected this shift. Originally intended to illustrate the humane treatment of the Westerners barred from leaving Iraq, Saddam's appearance with the frightened children only served to present a cruel and tyrannical image to the international media.

A second factor was the agreement of the Soviet Union to support the United States's actions against Iraq when Bush and Gorbachev met in Helsinki on September 9. The agreement of these two former antagonists underscored the unity of world leaders against the Iraqi invasion. This agreement had special significance in India, which has traditionally enjoyed a friendly relationship with the Soviet Union.

Finally, nine United Nations resolutions were passed condemning the Iraqi invasion, and defining the diplomatic and economic isolation of that nation, during the first eight weeks of the crisis. These resolutions underscored the increasing isolation of Iraq and Saddam Hussein from other nations on the U.N. Security Council, and left no doubt regarding these nations' reactions to the Iraqi invasion.

All of these factors point to an apparent crystallization of world opinion, as the concept is measured by leaders' reactions, after the first eight weeks of the crisis. The American newspaper reported and critiqued its nation's assumption of the role of apparent world opinion leader. The Indian newspaper carefully monitored other nations' leaders for its perception of world opinion. It is therefore not surprising that their citations regarding world opinion began to converge as an international consensus appeared to form.

The ramifications of accepting this apparent consensus were different for the United States and India, though. The two nations had different positions and interests during the crisis. These differences are illustrated in the manner in which the two newspapers described the moral and pragmatic components of world opinion, and the role of isolation, in their stories and editorials.

THE MORAL AND PRAGMATIC COMPONENTS OF WORLD OPINION DURING THE KUWAITI CRISIS

A previous analysis of the use of world opinion in major newspapers noted two critical components in the concept. The *moral component* refers to "value judgments shared by nations in their expression of world opinion" (Rusciano and Fiske-Rusciano 1990: 321). Typically, this component is defined as some explicit or implicit reference to right or wrong behavior, in such phrases as "our shared outrage" or "our consciences are bothered" by particular events or actions (ibid.). The *pragmatic component* refers to "interests shared by nations in their expression of world opinion" (ibid.). Typically, this component is defined as some explicit or implicit reference to behavior useful to all nations, in such phrases as "all nations would benefit" or "the world situation would be more stable" due to certain events or actions (ibid.). The use of these two components serves to highlight the patterns of general convergence and specific variance described in the previous section.

There were no differences in the manner in which the *New York Times* and the *Times of India* discussed the moral component of world opinion during the crisis. Both newspapers condemned the Iraqi invasion as morally wrong. Even when the Indian newspaper cited mitigating factors in Iraq's actions, such as the Kuwaiti refusal to adhere to OPEC limitations of oil production, it still condemned the invasion as an affront to all nations' moral sensibilities. The moral component is ubiquitous in references to world opinion in both newspapers, appearing in 95.5 percent of articles on Kuwait in the *New York Times* and in 93.2 percent of articles on Kuwait in the *Times of India*. Also, there were no significant differences between the first eight weeks of the crisis and afterwards in terms of references; the moral component was equally likely to be mentioned in both periods.

Previous research has shown that the moral component tends to be related to the power of world opinion in persuading other nations to accept its judgments. The pragmatic component, though highly correlated with references to the moral component, was less important in building international consensus (see Rusciano and Rusciano-Fiske 1990). World opinion is primarily about moral suasion, and in the case of the Iraqi invasion the moral issues were clear from the beginning.

The pragmatic issues were less clear in the two newspapers studied. While the American newspaper tended to present action against Saddam as in the interests of all nations, the Indian newspaper was more ambivalent about the interests of India and other Third World nations in the crisis. Regarding the move toward war in the Persian Gulf, for instance, one story in the *Times of India* quoted an Indian leader who called for a peaceful solution, expressing "deep consciousness of the many historic, cultural, linguistic and other ties that bind India with the nations and peoples of the Gulf region and the long and friendly relations with them" (*Times of India*, January 12, 1990). In an editorial in the Indian newspaper, the conflict between the moral and pragmatic components of world opinion for India is evident:

India fully endorses the U.N. Security Council's resolutions calling upon Iraq to vacate its occupation of Kuwait . . . India has refrained from any criticism, even indirectly, of the very large forces deployed against Iraq around its borders . . . it recognizes that each state has an *inherent right of self-defense and to take measures it considers necessary towards this end* . . . India is urging Iraq, a friend of long standing to pull back its troops to clear the way for the redress of its grievances against Kuwait. . . . If Iraq refuses to accept the peaceful alternative, the onus will be on it *for the consequences that may follow will be disastrous not only for Iraq but for countries like India.* (*Times of India*, January 7, 1991)

Here one sees clearly illustrated the conundrum in which the Indian newspaper found itself regarding world opinion. On the one hand, it defends the moral principle of the right to self-defense for all nations. On the other hand, however, it notes how this principle, while morally justified, would probably have results in this case that were not in the interests of India and "countries like it"—that is, other Third World nations. Finally, the editorial notes that because of the moral principle involved, India's leaders have refrained from stating that their interests do not coincide with other nations' interests regarding war.[8]

Clearly, the newspaper indicates that the moral issues tended to silence the pragmatic component of world opinion as it was discussed in the Indian newspaper. A comparative analysis of the two newspapers' references to world opinion underscores this observation. The *New York*

Times referenced the pragmatic component of world opinion just about as frequently as the moral component, in 91 percent of cases. The *Times of India* referenced the pragmatic component much less than the moral component, referring to the former in only 61.4 percent of cases. The result shows a significant difference between the two newspapers ($r = .358$, significance $= .000$).

This difference varies by date of reference, however. In the first eight weeks of the crisis, the two newspapers were about equally likely to reference the pragmatic component of world opinion; citations appeared in 72.7 percent of cases in the *New York Times*, and in 60 percent of cases in the *Times of India*. The difference between the newspapers is not statistically significant.[9] After the initial eight-week period, though, the *New York Times* cited the pragmatic component of world opinion in all cases, while the *Times of India* cited the pragmatic component in only 62.5 percent of cases. This difference is statistically significant,[10] and indicates that the American newspaper was more likely to describe interests shared by all nations in the crisis than the Indian newspaper. As the American newspaper increased its tendency to define the pragmatic component of world opinion, the Indian newspaper did not respond in kind after the first eight weeks of the crisis. The relative silencing of the Indian perspective regarding "common interests" shared by all nations probably contributed to the convergence of references to world opinion past the early stages of the crisis.

Why should the moral component of world opinion have this much power, though? Why would the Indian newspaper yield the perspective on the pragmatic issues due to the apparently overwhelming moral issues involved? One answer lies in the power of world opinion to enforce its judgments through the threat of international isolation.

THE THREAT OF ISOLATION AND THE KUWAITI CRISIS

The notion of "isolation" in world opinion refers to "implicit or explicit moves by nations to distance themselves from those who violated the dictates of world opinion" (Rusciano and Fiske-Rusciano 1990: 321). The isolation of Iraq after the Kuwaiti invasion was referenced in 79.1 percent of articles in the *New York Times*, and in 72.7 percent of articles in the *Times of India*. As with the concept "world opinion," "isolation" was referenced in explicit terms (34.7% of cases) as well as implicit terms (65.3% of cases). Explicit references from both papers use the word or its equivalent: "Mr. Saddam Hussein is almost completely isolated," "Hussein . . . struggles to break his international isolation," and "there will be no separate . . . paths for isolated nationalistic efforts" serve as examples of this usage. The more common implicit references convey a sense that a nation or leader is separated from, or shunned by, other countries in the world. References to "embargoes" and "boycotts" of Iraqi goods after the U.N. resolutions barred trade with that nation serve as examples of this usage. So, too, does this statement of the predicted results of the Bush-Gorbachev summit in Helsinki, from the *New York Times* of September 11, 1990:

Conveying to Saddam Hussein the message that Moscow was *standing with Washington and the rest of the world* was meaningful in itself, of course; the chances of persuading him to pull out of Kuwait depend to a considerable degree on penetrating the Iraqi dictator's tough psychological carapace and *making him feel increasingly shunned, cornered, and friendless.*

These examples also serve to illustrate two meanings of isolation. First, isolation may refer to the breaking of tangible relationships of trade, diplomacy, or business. Other nations may close embassies, recall diplomatic personnel, or deny trade with the isolated nation. However, isolation may have a vaguer, more general meaning as well—for example, the sense that a country's citizens and leaders have become pariahs to other nations, unwelcome as visitors or illegitimate as heads of state. The above quotation from the *New York Times* illustrates this notion of isolation—a feeling of being "shunned" and "friendless" in the world, regardless of any specific actions other nations may take against the target of isolation.

Isolation appeared to play a key role in world opinion, helping to explain the power of the moral component in the process. In stories regarding the Kuwaiti crisis, the moral component and the notion of isolation were mentioned together in 74.6 percent of stories in the *New York Times*, and in 68.2 percent of stories in the *Times of India*. Similarly, the moral component of world opinion and the power of world opinion were mentioned together in 67.1 percent of stories in the American newspaper, and in 72.1 percent of stories in the Indian newspaper. Finally, the power of world opinion and the threat of isolation were mentioned together in 58.2 percent of the stories in the *New York Times*, and in 53.3 percent of the stories in the *Times of India*. These common references suggest that the moral component is related to the power of world opinion, and to the threat of isolation by which that power is expressed.

As with the references to world opinion, the pattern of references to the isolation of Iraq tended to be generally similar between the two newspapers. Figure 4.2 shows the pattern of citations for two-week periods during the crisis. Despite some deviations on specific dates, the two newspapers appear to agree generally upon the times when Iraq's actions deserved reference to the threat of international isolation; the chi-square value confirms this correspondence.[11]

Figure 4.2
Percentage of Total References to Isolation on Kuwaiti Crisis, by Date

The references to the isolation of Iraq, however, also follow the specific pattern of variation found in the references to world opinion: Citations in the first eight weeks of the crisis were significantly different between the two newspapers, while citations after the first eight weeks were not. The symmetric lambda for the early period equalled .268, indicating a significant difference between dates of reference; the symmetric lambda for the later period equalled .019, indicating no significant difference between the dates of reference.

It is not surprising that the pattern of references to isolation should display the same characteristics as the pattern of references to world opinion. Directing the threat of isolation toward a nation requires a great degree of international consensus. Indeed, the newspapers' articles were often very specific about the entity from which Iraq had become isolated. Saddam's actions had alienated him from the "international community," the "community of nations," and the "world community." These and other examples present an image of the world as a unit with which Iraq was denied contact.

This pattern does allow for speculation regarding the importance of moral considerations in the threat of isolation. It was only after an international consensus had formed, and the moral issues were seen to dominate the pragmatic concerns of nations like India, that a general correspondence regarding threats of isolation emerged in the news articles of the two papers. The apparent crystallization of world opinion regarding the isolation of Iraq must be evaluated in terms of its effects. Despite Iraq's control of about 20 percent of the world's known oil reserves, the embargo against their goods was deemed 100 percent effective, costing them 48 percent of their GNP in lost trade.[12] Given the traditional barriers to the success of embargoes, this result shows the power of the international consensus against Iraq, reflected in newspaper references during the last sixteen weeks of the crisis.

CONCLUSIONS: MEDIA PERSPECTIVES ON WORLD OPINION IN THE EMERGING INTERNATIONAL ORDER

The preceding analysis presented a portrait of the world opinion process as it was depicted in the *New York Times* and the *Times of India* during the Kuwaiti crisis. Certain key findings stand out from this analysis. First, the *Times of India* appeared to draw its cues from world leaders in evaluating the content of world opinion; the *New York Times* gave little evidence of doing so. Second, the timing of references to world opinion during the Kuwaiti crisis tended to converge after the first eight weeks of the crisis. Third, both papers were likely to emphasize the moral component of world opinion, and they were in agreement regarding the universal condemnation of Iraq's actions. Fourth, however, both papers were not equally likely to reference the pragmatic component of world opinion, nor were they likely to agree on its content. The Indian daily was more likely to raise questions regarding the fate of Third World nations should war break out in the Persian Gulf, even as they accepted the general moral consensus regarding the war. The Indian daily was also less likely than the American newspaper to raise pragmatic issues regarding world opinion on the crisis after the first eight weeks. Finally, references to the isolation of Iraq also tended to follow the same general pattern between newspapers after the first eight weeks of the crisis.

A general definition of world opinion, derived from a previous work, allows for organization of these findings. World opinion was defined as "the moral judgments of observers which actors must heed in the international arena, or risk isolation as a nation" (Rusciano and Fiske-Rusciano 1990: 320). The moral component of world opinion was seen to link with the power of world opinion and the threat of isolation through which that power might be expressed. The success of the embargo against Iraq showed how serious a threat isolation can become when it is expressed in tangible relationships. But tangible expressions of isolation such as boycotts or embassy closings are often accompanied (and preceded) by intangible expressions of isolation.

Consider that the *New York Times* referenced Iraq's image in the world in 99 percent of the cases in which it discussed world opinion. The message was evident: Saddam's actions had lowered Iraq's standing among nations. The *Times of India*, in contrast, mentioned Iraq's negative image in only 21 percent of cases.

The Indian newspaper was generally concerned with the image of India in the world, however, particularly regarding its stance on the Kuwaiti crisis. Stories and editorials in the Indian newspaper discussed how India would appear to the world as it took its seat on the U.N. Security Council, and as a democracy beset by political violence. The *Times of India* was likely to reflect a self-consciousness regarding its nation's image in the world. The *New York Times* was much less likely to reflect a similar self-consciousness regarding the image of the United States during the crisis.[13]

When a nation's image is at risk, however, the power of world opinion—and in particular, its moral component—becomes more manifest. Articles in the *Times of India* were less likely to challenge the emerging consensus regarding Iraq's actions and sanctions against Saddam Hussein after the first eight weeks of the crisis. This relative silence is notable, given the misgivings regarding American and allied intentions, and their effects on Third World nations, reflected in the Indian newspaper's earlier stories. As one group of Indian peace activists stated just before the war began:

We will be representing those *silent countries* whose economy will be most affected by the war. If there is a war, the poor countries of Asia and Africa will suffer the most. . . . However, surprisingly, *these nations have no say in the Gulf controversy*. (*Times of India*, January 12, 1991)

The dissenting opinions and reactions perceived by the Indian newspaper were silenced in the face of an overwhelming moral imperative to condemn Iraq. Hence, after the first eight weeks of the crisis, references to world opinion on the crisis and references to the threat of isolation against Iraq converge by date for the two newspapers. The Indian newspaper, displaying a self-consciousness regarding its nation's image in its stories, appears to fall in line with the emerging international consensus on the crisis.

Nations who fear for their world image are amenable to the threat of international isolation. For these nations, world opinion, as it was defined above, carries a great influence over public statements and actions. This interpretation allows one to observe the emerging process of world opinion, from divergence to consensus, as it is perceived in the two newspapers. It also allows one to perceive the United States acting the role of world opinion leader, stressing the moral component of international opinion that is intimately linked to the threat of isolation and world reputation. Indeed, Bush made this point explicit in his final letter to Saddam Hussein, in which he stated that compliance with the U.N. resolutions on Kuwait was necessary before Iraq could "rejoin the world community."

This conclusion raises serious questions about the emergence of a "New World Order," given the evidence gathered from these two newspapers. Some might argue that we are witnessing an "artificial" world opinion, "manufactured" for use by major nations like the United States to justify their actions. "World opinion" could merely be another means by which the major powers gain hegemony over other nations. In this interpretation, major nations would define world opinion, or deny its existence, in cases where it suits them. The "New World Order" would mimic past world orders, as the perspective of one or a few major powers dominated the discussion and conduct of international affairs.

If we are witnessing a process of world opinion into which all nations have inputs, however, a "New World Order" might truly be emerging. In this case, all nations' actions have the potential for being scrutinized according to some standards of international behavior, however loosely or fluidly defined. Nations would have to conform to the judgments of world opinion, or pay the price in terms of international isolation. This interpretation could explain why the embargo against Iraq was so much more successful than previous actions of this type. In the past, national interests have tended to preclude international collective actions such as embargoes; it was generally assumed that such cooperation among nations was impossible without some shared authority to enforce it (see Barry and Hardin 1982; Schelling 1958; Jervis, 1970; and Snidal 1985 for examples). If the threat of isolation is sufficient in certain cases to enforce (or at least support) cooperation, international relations might require reformulation.

A content analysis of references to world opinion on the Kuwaiti crisis in these two newspapers cannot prove the existence or power of world opinion in the emerging international order. However, the potential lessons for the United States and other nations raised by this analysis are critical. If a new order is emerging and all nations have at least some input into the process of world opinion, then all nations—major and Third World—must be aware of the dictates of the process. The leaders of major nations would be mistaken to assume that world opinion would always conform to their interests. Further analysis on subjects that do not conform to the interests of the major nations may be able to address this issue more directly. The analysis of the *Times of India* and the *New York Times* during the Kuwaiti crisis has shown that both papers' references converge to define a power for world opinion that nations ignore at their own risk. If this power also exists when the interests of major nations are challenged, and the moral imperative favors Third World or less prominent nations, a "New World Order" might indeed be taking shape.

NOTES

This research was supported by a Summer Research Fellowship and a Grant-in-Aid from Rider College. The author would like to thank his research assistants Robert Archibald and Kim Griffith, for their arduous work on the project. The author would also like to thank Roberta Fiske-Rusciano for her research and commentary on the manuscript, and Bosah Ebo, for his commentary. The author is, of course, responsible for all of the material contained herein.

1. The significance of Pearson's r and other statistics was greater than .10.

2. The chi-square value for the relationship is 24.3, with 11 degrees of freedom; the significance level of this value is .011.

3. The last two-week period includes three extra days added in from the remainder of the period.

4. The chi-square value for this relationship is 15.22, with 11 degrees of freedom, indicating a difference that is significant at less than the .17 level. The combination of dates into two-week periods is a convention from a previous work on world opinion (see Rusciano and Fiske-Rusciano 1990) adopted for ease of reporting the data. The finding also applies if one groups the data by weeks (chi-square value of 28.5, with 22 degrees of freedom, and a significance level of less than .16) or by individual days (chi-square value of 64.5, with 73 degrees of freedom, and a significance level of less than .75).

5. The relationship between the measure used for world opinion and the newspaper where the citation appeared is significant, with a symmetric lambda of .36.

6. The resulting value of r for this relationship was .516, with a significance level of .000.

7. The resulting r showed no difference between the newspapers.

8. By contrast, the *New York Times* did not tend to debate whether or not all nations of the world would benefit if it became necessary to go to war; instead, the debate centered on whether American interests justified bearing the major burden in such a conflict (see "The Larger Patriotism," *New York Times*, January 10, 1991).

9. Pearson's r equals only .135, with an unacceptable significance level of .394.

10. Pearson's r equals .530 with a significance level of .000.

11. The chi-square value for the relationship is 16.63 with 10 degrees of freedom; the significance level for the relationship is .083, failing to reach the acceptable .05 level for social science research.

12. These results thereby made the boycott two to three times more successful than the most successful past actions of this sort (Haubauer and Elliott 1991: A17).

13. Indeed, there have been studies conducted that have analyzed the effect

of public relations campaigns by Third World nations to affect their image in other nations, as reflected in the content of newspaper coverage of the countries involved (see Albritton and Manheim 1985: 43–59; and Manheim and Albritton, 1984: 641–57).

REFERENCES

Albritton, Robert B., and Jarol Manheim. "Public Relations Efforts for the Third World: Images in the News." *Journal of Communication* (Winter 1985): 43–59.

Barry, Brian, and Russell Hardin. *Rational Man and Irrational Society?* Beverly Hills: Sage, 1982.

Bogart, Leo. "Is There a World Public Opinion?" *Polls* 1 (1966): 1–9.

Davidson, W. Phillips. "International and World Public Opinion." In *Handbook of Communication*, ed. Ithiel de Sola Pool, et al., 871–86. Chicago, Ill.: Rand McNally, 1973.

Hufbauer, Gary C., and Kimberley Elliott. "Sanctions Will Bite—And Soon." *New York Times*. Section 1, January 14, 1991, A17.

Jervis, R. *The Logic of Images in International Relations*. Princeton, N.J.: Princeton University Press, 1970.

Manheim, Jarol, and Robert Albritton. "Changing National Images: International Public Relations and Media Agenda Setting." *American Political Science Review* 78 (1984): 641–57.

Morgenthau, Hans J. "Is World Public Opinion a Myth." *New York Times Magazine*. March 25, 1962, p. 23.

Rusciano, Frank Louis, and Roberta Fiske-Rusciano. "Towards a Notion of 'World Opinion.' " *International Journal of Public Opinion Research* 2 (1990): 305–22.

Schelling, Thomas. "The Strategy of Conflict: Prospectus for the Reorientation of Game Theory." *Journal of Conflict Resolution* 2 (1958): 203–64.

Snidal, Duncan. "Coordination Versus Prisoners' Dilemma: Implications for International Cooperation and Regimes." *American Political Science Review* 79 (1985): 923–42.

Ullman, Richard H. "Flunking World Order 101." *New York Times*. January 12, 1991, 21.

Unger, David C. "Ferment in the Think Tanks: Learning to Live with No Global Threat." *New York Times*. January 5, 1991, 20.

Chapter Five

Vox Populi: Talk Radio and TV Cover the Gulf War

Dan Nimmo and Mark Hovind

Few analytical commentaries on the character of American cultural, social, and political institutions and practices have survived the test of time as has Alexis de Tocqueville's classic, *Democracy in America*. Originally published in Jacksonian America, Tocqueville's analysis has reappeared in numerous editions. Midway through Volume I, the author turned to a theme that would occupy much of his trenchant analysis, namely the power and effects of popular majorities in American politics. Writing of the power of the majority exercised "over thought," Tocqueville commented that in Europe even the most absolute of sovereigns were not able to prevent thoughts hostile to their rule from circulating among the populace. "It is not like that in America," he observed. For, "while the majority is in doubt, one talks." And, "when it was irrevocably pronounced, everyone is silent, and friends and enemies alike seem to make for its bandwagon" (1969: 254). Critics with opposing thoughts seem to vanish.

The tyranny of the majority in democracies was a theme Tocqueville returned to often in *Democracy in America* and in the work undertaken shortly before his death, *The Old Regime and the French Revolution* (1955). Simply put, Tocqueville recognized that in democracies open discussion, free expression, and controversy are honored only in the breach. So long as individuals perceive no dominant view on a question to exist, they feel free to speak out. But once they sense a majority exists—even though they may be in doubt regarding its precise nature—they fear being cut off, isolated from perceived orthodoxy. Hence, they either fall silent or "make for its bandwagon." Thus were citizens in eighteenth-century France reluctant to express their allegiance to the Catholic Church in

what they perceived to be an anti-church environment: "Dreading isolation more than the stigma of heresy," they "professed to share the
sentiments of the majority" (1955: 155).

Tocqueville, of course, was not the first political analyst to fear majority
tyranny or to ponder the dampening effects of jumping on the opinion
bandwagon. For example, in the *Federalist* #49 James Madison had anticipated the potential threat of majorities in the newly created representative democracy of the United States:

If it be true that all governments rest on opinion, it is no less true that the
strength of opinion in each individual, and its practical influence on its conduct,
depends much on the number which he supposes to have entertained the same
opinion. The reason of man, like man himself, is timid and cautious when left
alone, and acquires firmness and confidence in proportion to the number with
which it is associated. (1937: 329)

And, almost two centuries later Elisabeth Noelle-Neumann founded her
widely acclaimed (and critiqued) theory of the "spiral of silence" (1984)
on much the same thought as that of Madison and Tocqueville before
her. Speaking of the willingness of persons to voice their views on issues
in public she theorized that it depended on one's assessments of the
climate and trend of majority opinion: "It is greater if he believes his
own view is, and will be, the dominating one" (1974: 45).

The purpose of this chapter is to explore the presence in one form of
coverage of the Gulf War of the phenomenon commented on by Tocqueville throughout much of his life, that is, that of "friends and enemies"
alike to "make for the bandwagon" of majority opinion, perhaps reinforcing the impression that a majority has "irrevocably" made up its
mind (1969: 254). The coverage under investigation is that provided by
the "talk" format of radio and television broadcasting stations during
the period of the Gulf War. We begin by exploring the nature of that
type of programming.

THE EGOISM OF TALK RADIO AND TELEVISION

Tocqueville argued that a pervasive egoism, that is, the widespread
tendency of individuals to withdraw from public concerns out of preferences for concentrating on material gain for themselves and families,
characterizes social democracies (Lively 1987). Caught up in the pursuit
of material possessions, citizens have little inclination to study, reflect
about, and articulate informed opinions on public issues. Yet, thought
Tocqueville, every society—including one bound to the material tenets
of democratic individualism such as America—required some form of
intellectual authority. Democracies find that authority in public opinion.

Having withdrawn from public matters out of egoism, individuals conform to majority opinion when public questions arise that citizens simply cannot avoid, for example, Operation Desert Storm.

In contemporary America a major forum that provides opportunities for the popular expression of both individual egoism and conformity to reigning opinion lies in the growing reach of talk radio and television formats. Consider first talk radio. Roberts (1991: 57) labels the reach of radio as a medium "awesome." On a daily basis radio reaches 80 percent of the population via approximately 10,000 stations. The competition for listeners is fierce, a point aptly depicted in "Shock Waves," a documentary on the oft-neglected influence of radio that aired on the CBS-TV series *48 Hours* (December 4, 1991). During the 1980s many radio stations, particularly AM stations fighting for survival, adopted "talk" formats to attract audiences. The talk format makes listeners participants in programs via telephone calls that air citizens' views, comments, gripes, and questions of talk show hosts and guests. Between 1988 and 1989 the number of radio stations employing talk formats increased from 308 to 405; at the beginning of the 1990s the number had risen to 500 (Roberts 1991). Granted this is but 5 percent of all stations; granted also that the percentage of radio listeners who actually call talk radio programs is only about 5 percent. Yet, in the industry the talk format has found a niche that, if not dominant, still claims to be highly influential on certain issues and most certainly is highly publicized.

Although claims that talk radio is "democracy in action" may be hyperbole, advocates of talk formats do point to notable examples wherein talk shows allegedly made differences in the outcome of public controversies (Roberts 1991). One of those most frequently cited involved the effort in 1989 by members of the U.S. Congress to vote themselves a pay increease of 51 percent. The opposition to the proposal voiced by callers to talk radio across the country was loud and unrelenting. Urged on by talk show hosts, callers innundated congressional offices with protesting calls and letters. For a variety of reasons Congress backed off the pay raise. (A year later the House of Representatives voted itself a much smaller increase as part of a reform package.)

Influential or not, talk radio, talk show hosts, and the talk format are heavily promoted. There is, for example, a talk industry newspaper, *Talkers*. There are talk radio networks—the Mutual Broadcasting System with its *Larry King Show*, NBC's Talknet, A.M. Talk, Daynet, Sun Network, and Newstalk Radio Network. Moreover, many talk show hosts have become national celebrities commanding impressive speaker's fees and national TV exposure. Larry King, for example, doubles in brass on Mutual Radio and on Cable News Network's (CNN) *Larry King Live*. Rush Limbaugh of WABC in New York is syndicated across the nation on 250 stations and reaches an audience of 4 million. Limbaugh received the ultimate in American TV exposure when CBS's *60 Minutes* profiled the avowed conservative drumbeater on its program of October 6, 1991.

The expansion of cable television in the 1980s brought with it a search for programming formats to lure viewers. Talk TV joined talk radio. By the close of the decade, for example, the Cable Satellite Public Affairs Network (C-SPAN) prided itself on its regular programming permitting viewers to call in and talk with guests—viewers not only from the United States but from Europe and other regions of the world. Other networks including CNN and CNBC, along with the over-the-air networks of ABC, CBS, and NBC, increasingly incorporated one or more featured programs relying on viewer call-ins. Moreover, syndicated TV shows—*Donahue* being the granddaddy of them all—incorporated call-in portions to their talk TV formats.

The crisis in the Persian Gulf and Operation Desert Storm enlarged the scope of talk broadcasting even more. On radio, for example, at the outbreak of the war National Public Radio (NPR) added a two-hour afternoon talk, call-in program featuring an NPR correspondent—frequently Daniel Shorr—as host backed up by panels of invited pundits. CBS added to its lineup a national radio call-in program. On television CNN developed a late night talk and call-in program to supplement its already existing *Larry King Live*.

Although not a major focus of scholarly interest by those who study the mass media, nonetheless the talk format of radio and television has been examined in systematic fashion. For example, well before the growth of the format in the 1980s, scholars explored the functions radio forums perform in democratic societies (Crittenden 1971); the interpersonal dimensions of talk radio (Turow 1974); the demographic characteristics of talk radio audiences (Avery, Ellis, and Glover 1976); the feature of talk formats that attract listeners and callers (Avery, Ellis, and Glover 1978); the uses and gratifications provided callers via talk formats (Tramer and Jeffres 1983); learning by listeners using call-in formats as background (Andreasen 1986); and the relationship of the talk format to rising levels of alienation and disaffection with politics in America (Levin 1987). Since we agree with Avery and his colleagues (1978: 17) that "talk radio must continue to receive serious scholarly attention" and cannot "be treated lightly," we hope to add to our understanding of the talk format by exploring the content of talk radio and TV across the time span of a single public event that penetrated the normal pervasive egoism (if Tocqueville be correct) of Americans in 1991, the Gulf War.

MAKING FOR THE OPINION BANDWAGON VIA TALK RADIO AND TV

This examination is based upon the analysis of the content of five nationally broadcast public affairs programs during the period of the

Gulf War that employed the talk/call-in format. Four of these programs were regularly scheduled radio talk shows—three aired by the Newstalk Radio Network and one by National Public Radio. The fifth was a week-night TV program, namely, CNN's *Larry King Live*. We sampled each of the five programs by recording one hour of each show's daily broadcasts and randomly constructing for each program a five-day week of broadcasts Monday through Friday, that is, selecting a Monday broadcast from one week, a Tuesday from another week, a Wednesday from another, and so forth.

The five programs certainly do not represent the diversity of all talk radio and TV formats aired by broadcast networks during the Gulf War. However, findings are illustrative of four typical formats: (1) a "host-guest format" with a host interviewing a guest and taking listeners' views and questions via telephone—two sampled programs employed this format; (2) a "panel format" with a host, a panel of experts, and calls from listeners; (3) an "open line" format involving a host, call-ins, but no guest; and (4) a "debate" format employing two hosts with conflicting points of view, a guest, and calls from listeners. Although the analysis of content involved both quantitative and qualitative techniques, the findings reported here derive primarily from qualitative methods that examine "texts as structured and interdependent wholes" (Carragee 1991: 2). Key to our analysis of the content of war coverage provided by talk radio/TV is our focus on variations in content associated with differences in program formats. Specifically we explore content that exhibits harmonious, confrontational, or instructional programming as related to formats that feature the roles and interactions of hosts, callers, and guests.

Vox Host and Vox Populi: A Format of Agreement

The configuration and pace of the opinion bandwagon portrayed by talk radio/TV owes a great deal to the program format employed. Avery, Ellis, and Glover (1978) found that most callers to talk shows are attracted to particular personalities. Consequently, interaction among callers, guests, and hosts varies with the host. A bond develops between callers and hosts when callers perceive a host as agreeable and not dogmatic. Of course, that perception itself may well depend on the host's point of view: Callers contact hosts with opinions sympathetic to listeners/viewers.

Of the radio/TV talk show formats as sampled during the Gulf War, the one most conducive to constructing agreement between host and caller found by Avery, Ellis, and Glover is that which excludes so-called experts and/or guests from the show and exploits what is called in the vernacular of talk show programming the "open line" design. It was rare during the sampled week of the single open line program that we examined to find any disagreement between callers and the host, a host who often announced, apparently with pride, that "I don't have guests on my show." During the sampled week, the self-styled "radio talk show host" took thirty-two calls in five hours of air time. In only three cases was there a hint of a confrontation between host and caller.

A few sampled exchanges illustrate the bonding that developed on perceptions of the war. "John" called in to declare, with reference to the Iraqis after the ground fight at Khafji, that coalition forces should simply "nuke 'em." The host agreed, pointing out the utility of the "neutron bomb" for tactical battles, concurring that in any event after what Iraq had tried to do with Scud missiles against Israel, the "bums" (Iraqis) can't be allowed to live. The same day "Tom," describing himself as a "hard core Democrat," called to say that he had been fearful about the prospect of war, but once it started he supported it. He believed that "75 percent" of other Democrats were like him on the issue, hence no one should get upset about "professional protesters." Caller and host then found common ground, rallying around the principles of patriotism, loyalty, and the American flag—while severely criticizing anti-war protestors. No sooner had "Tom" departed than "Susan" called to announce that she too was bothered by the protesters for they "hurt our POWs"; she, by contrast, had respect for the American flag and for God. The host agreed: "I talk to God; my country right or wrong; My Country."

Among the topics on which host and callers reached agreement in the sampled week of the open line format were support for the war and opposition to anti-war protests (protesters were "looney tunes" said the host, "peaceniks" said a caller); Vietnam veterans (called "boys") should be accorded hero status along with veterans of the Gulf War; the pro-Iraq stance of Jordan's King Hussein was shameful (he was a "little weasel" and "the tiny king" but a "survivor," said the host); a call for the use of tactical nuclear weapons in the conflict ("Should nuke the whole damn city" of Baghdad agreed caller "Greg"); criticism of both Japan and Germany for not increasing their support of the war effort ("I'm tired of the arrogance of Japan," said the host, the Japanese only "smile, bow, and stick a knife in our backs"); and invectives aimed at Saddam Hussein: "Butcher of Baghdad," a "mad man," and a "punk," urged the host, while callers invoked "murderer" and "creep."

However, the topic most frequently provoking solidarity between host and callers was not the war itself but news coverage of the war. Although the host expressed sympathy for the desire of Peter Arnett (of CNN) to "get the story" from Baghdad, saying "I would do so myself," that sympathy did not extend to the *content* of Arnett's reports, to CNN, or to other journalists involved in covering the war. Thus, when "Cheryl" criticized CNN for "making news rather than reporting it," she found the host's ear receptive to her plea. The host regarded CNN's owner, Ted Turner, as supportive of Saddam Hussein—there was between them, he urged, "a wink and a nod" that communicated Turner's message, that is, "Hey guys, I'm on your side." When "Richard" read a satire on CNN's (and Arnett's) coverage of the war, the host laughed approvingly and urged the caller to send it to Ted Turner.

CNN's Ted Turner was not the only media target of the program's criticism. Peter Jennings of ABC News raised the ire of both host and callers. The host labeled Jennings "a jerk" for an ABC report on the bombing of what coalition forces claimed was an Iraqi intelligence headquarters, but Iraq (and presumably ABC) claimed was a civilian bunker. "Fred" called in to concur with the host's assessment of Jennings. Both voiced the conviction that the news media would not be happy until there were "finally" body bags filled with U.S. troops. The host informed "Fred" that ABC's coverage was actually understandable: "Jennings isn't an American anyway." (Jennings is, in fact, Canadian.) At least, claimed the host, "talk shows tell the other side of the story." "Guy" called to agree that he too had "no use for news people." And, after a call from "Rick," who added his agreement with the critical view of the news media being expressed, the host closed the program with a final thrust: "I expect CNN to cut our throats," but why would the other networks do it? The answer: "They take stupid pills in the morning."

Vox Guest and Vox Populi: Formats of Confrontation

Just as the open line format proved a likely candidate for exemplifying the comfortable relationship between talk host and callers, the "debate" format offers a prime opportunity to investigate a confrontational relationship. The talk radio program with a debate format examined for this study involved co-hosts of differing political persuasions, on-air interviews with guests, and comments and/or questions from callers. Each segment of the program followed the same pattern. First, the co-hosts, both males, introduced themselves, one identifying himself as "on the left," the other "on the right." Then, one of the co-hosts introduced the topic for the program segment, such as the extent of Soviet assistance to Iraq during the Gulf War. This introduction always included the co-host's views on the topic, views frequently and often loudly interrupted by the co-host of the opposing persuasion. Such theatrics employ many of the rituals of Japanese *no theater*: Vocal recitative is indispensable, the co-hosts don masks to suit the topic of debate, and farcical interludes offer comic relief. The only difference is that *no theater* manifests restraint, the talk/debate format overacting. Once interruptions ceased, the co-host continued the introduction by presenting a guest expert "on the newsline," that is, on the telephone line. Co-hosts took turns firing questions at the guest with the co-host "on the right" or "on the left" taking issue with the guest, the other co-host siding with the guest. Phone lines were then opened to callers' questions; those questions provoked exchanges of more opposing views. The segment ended with an obligatory "Thank you" to the guest and a final, parting barbed exchange between the co-hosts before a commercial break.

Like the agreement format discussed above, the confrontational one aims at being entertaining, but at holding an audience not out of host/caller bonding but via co-hosts/guests/caller controversy. As debates raged over Soviet assistance to Iraq, the potential for a ground war, the fate of Saddam Hussein, the role of the French or Germans in the war, and other topics, listeners were treated to a verbal war disseminated via radio that, although not as lethal in its consequences, was waged with as much tenacity as the Gulf War itself. In the process overall coverage of the war via such talk radio programming took on a contrived quality. We illustrate this by considering but one segment of the debate format. It aired on February 25, 1991, following the opening of the much discussed, debated, and long-awaited ground offensive against Iraq forces in Kuwait by members of the allied coalition.

The co-host "on the right" introduced the topic, noting that what Saddam Hussein had pronounced the "mother of all battles" might well prove to be a "grandaddy of nightmares" for Iraq. The co-host "on the left," who had expressed skepticism about an easy coalition victory in a ground war during earlier programs, now stated that there was no doubt about a military victory, *for* "once again" the coalition forces had overestimated Iraq's capacity to wage war. As an example, the co-host "on the left" ridiculed published reports that Iraq possessed a "super-cannon" by uttering a loud "Ha!" The introductory debate between co-hosts continued in this vein. The rightist co-host noted that "83–84 percent" of Americans favored a ground war that would "thoroughly, utterly, destroy Saddam Hussein's war capacity." That very day "thousands" of Iraqis were surrendering. The leftist co-host dismissed the coalition thrust and success by again expressing doubts about the necessity for using such massive forces against Iraq's "tenth rate military."

On this day the guest expert was the director of a thinktank specializing in "defense journalism." This qualified him to discuss news media coverage of the war. That topic, however, was quickly passed over by both co-hosts (the guest thought Americans were mature people who did not need to be protected by government from seeing what was happening on the battlefield). Instead the co-hosts relied upon another area of the guest's expertise. The guest's father had fought for the Germans at Normandy. Moreover, the guest had "flown fighter aircraft" himself. These aspects of the guest's background presumably combined to permit him to assess the strength of the likely Iraqi response to the ground assault by coalition forces. Under questioning by the rightist co-host the guest said he anticipated "light losses" of coalition troops. This pleased the rightist co-host, a dogged supporter of the Gulf War. But, when the guest went on to say that the Iraqi air force had always been "third rate," the leftist co-host saw his chance to win debating points. He charged again that the Bush administration had overestimated the strength of the Iraqi military. The guest agreed but questioned why such an overestimation would have been made. "To make the military victory significant," responded the co-host "on the left."

At this point, apparently sensing a victory of his own, the leftist co-host gave no opportunity for his partner "on the right" to intervene, choosing instead to go to a caller, "Greg" in Kings Mountain, North Carolina. The caller announced that he was against the war, that war was always "morally wrong." Although the leftist co-host agreed with "Greg," the guest was not so sure. Some rulers simply must be moved out of power by force, the guest said. The leftist co-host disagreed for, as in Vietnam, there is always a "self-fulfilling prophesy about going to war." But the guest took issue with the Vietnam analogy. Coalition forces in the Gulf War had far superior air craft and munitions than in Vietnam. The co-host "on the right" pounced on the opportunity afforded by the guest: the Iraqis are "ducks in a shooting gallery." "Absolutely," responded the guest.

The debate continued in this manner throughout the program. Indeed, it had been conducted in this manner, and would remain so, throughout the program's coverage of the Gulf War. To the degree that vox populi derives from listeners' calls, the debate format of talk radio largely ignores it. Given the emphasis upon the confrontation between the co-hosts, with co-hosts using guests first as plaintiff and then as defense witnesses in the contrived proceedings, callers' questions and opinions receive short shrift. Rarely during the sampled period of the debate program we examined did any program segment contain more than one listener's call. There were only nine calls in the whole of the sampled week. The egoism of talk radio, at least with respect to the debate format, is not the egoism of the audience but the egoism of the sparring, and entertaining, co-hosts.

Whether the format of talk radio/TV provokes agreement or confrontation among audience members and between audiences and hosts frequently depends upon how a host exploits a particular format. In some instances a host may bond with audiences by minimizing conflict between host and guest during an interview; in others the host may maximize disagreement with an invited guest to provoke calls from viewers that join the host in bashing the guest. This was the case with one of the programs following a "host–guest" format examined in this study. In the host–guest format there is but one host (unlike the debate format that has co-hosts). The host introduces guests, interviews them, then invites calls from audience members.

To illustrate the host's exploitation of guests as a means of bonding with audience members, we consider two examples from the sampled week of the single host–guest talk radio format sampled for this study. In one the host's interview of the guest is sympathetic and supportive of the guest's views. In the other the host launches an attack on the guest, an attack joined by callers. In the first instance the topic for discussion was Soviet behavior during the Gulf War. The guest expert was a staff member of the U.S. Committee on Foreign Relations. Under minimal and gentle questioning by the host, the guest provided the following profile of Soviet conduct: the Soviets were "not on our side" as evidenced by the fact that they sold intelligence photos to the Iraqis, thus giving Iraq a war capability it did not have; Soviet military advisors were in Iraq; moreover, the Soviets might even be acting as tank commanders; the Soviets knew of Iraq's plans to invade Kuwait, for there was an "intimate" relationship between Soviet–Iraq intelligence services; finally, Mikhail Gorbachev warned Saddam Hussein in advance of when coalition forces would begin bombing Baghdad at the war's beginning. The guest charged Soviet "duplicity," and that there would be dead Americans "because of Soviet assistance." Why did not the United States protest, inquired the host as a rhetorical question? Because, the host continued, "We don't want to undercut Gorby!"

Callers bonded with both host and guest. "Bob" asked what had happened to the "one thousand Soviet advisors" in Iraq; they had not left, replied the guest. The press, thought Bob, was guilty of "treason" for not making this known. "Mike" called from Virginia to say he knew from personal experience that the Soviets "lie as normal behavior." He had lived in Moscow and he found "wonderful people" there, but the government officials "lie." This prompted the host to inquire of the guest, "Why is Bush following the Soviet lies?" The guest confided that he knew that Bush had said, "Forget you ever heard this," when the president had been informed of Soviet aid to Iraq. The White House, the guest opined, has simply "invested too much" in the Soviets. "Who," then, "is the enemy?" pondered the host.

"Kim" called to ask the guest about the Soviets' objectives. The guest pointed out that the United States was losing ground economically and politically in the world, but the Soviet Union was gaining, particularly as a large producer of oil. The Soviets "are playing both sides of the street," said the host; "I can't believe we are all this dumb!" "Tony" called to say he was not surprised at Soviet duplicity, thus joining the opinion bandwagon already boarded by other callers, driven by the guest, and on which the host was riding shotgun.

Contrasted with the sympathetic treatment given the guest in the preceding case, the host took a markedly different tact toward another guest on a different topic. Under discussion were anti-war protests. The guest was a coordinator for a group advocating peace in the Middle East through negotiations. The host began the interview by asking why anti-war protests were continuing now that the war was a month old and going well. Was not the country "tired" of protests? The guest responded that there was a "right to protest," that indeed the best way to "support troops" was to insist upon a peaceful resolution to the conflict not to commit them to a ground war. "Don't you want to win a victory?" demanded the host. Why were there no protests against Saddam Hussein? The guest ignored the thrust of such questioning, responding instead that the protest effort was merely to make "our government" responsive to citizens. But "why blame Bush, not Saddam Hussein?" the host persisted. Because it's "*our*" tax dollars that finance the war, the guest replied. No, protestors are "undermining American policy," the host went on. The guest took the bait and offered an argument roundly criticized by callers: What was at work were rival propaganda machines, one of the U.S. government, one of Saddam Hussein; one doesn't know which one to believe, but one can't believe the United States, for it may be lying. The vox populi that followed concurred with the host's observation that the guest certainly had a "strange idea" for peace.

The host–guest format provides more opportunities for calls from audience members than does the debate format. More calls, however, do not produce any greater likelihood that callers disagree with the host than in the open line format discussed earlier. Of twenty-five calls for the sampled week of the host–guest format in question, none took a position contrary to that advanced by the show's host. Callers joined the host in criticism of CNN's (and Peter Arnett's) coverage of the war; Soviet duplicity; anti-war protests; the likelihood of coalition victory; George McGovern's anti-war stance, praise for Colin Powell, chairman of the Joint Chiefs of Staff; and so forth. Thus did the bandwagon of opinion roll on.

Vox Host and Vox Guests: Formats of Instruction

The rhetoric need not be so heated nor the host as openly opinionated as in the case of the debate and guest–host formats illustrated above to provoke either agreement or confrontation between hosts and callers. Based upon our sample of talk radio/TV coverage of the Gulf War, we found that when voices are lowered and the hosts' opinions yield center stage to those of guests, programming content moves away from an urgent agitational tone to one with informational, integrational dimensions (Ellul 1965). Such was the case of both NPR's "call-in program to

answer your questions" carried each weekday afternoon during the period of the Gulf War, and of programs of *Larry King Live* sampled from
weeknights during the war.

In addition to having a panel of guests and the show's host respond
to callers, the NPR program differed in other respects from the call-in
format yielding the type of agreement or confrontation described above.
Typically the NPR host introduced the call-in program with a review of
the day's war events. There then followed a five-minute summary, by
an NPR correspondent, of war news, other items of national/interna-
tional interest, and of financial news from Wall Street. At that point the
call-in host introduced the day's "panel of experts" and the 1–800 call-
in number for listeners. The tone set by the lengthy series of reviews,
news, and introductions was calm, tepid, and dispassionate. In spite of
the time provided for panelists' opening remarks (thirteen panelists were
featured in the one week of one-hour programs in our sample), there
was sufficient air time for fifty-nine callers during the sampled week.
Although the host frequently reminded callers that they were to ask
questions of the experts rather than offer lengthy opinions, callers did
not always adhere to the rules. When they did not, rarely did either the
NPR host or the show's guest rise to the bait and declare either clear-
cut agreement or disagreement with the caller's views. More frequently
host and guests alike shifted the grounds of the discussion, ignored the
callers' questions and/or comments, or expressed a sense of shared ignorance that avoided either consensus or confrontation. Instruction,
although often befuddled, took precedence over either bonding or
debate.

A few examples from the sampled constructed week of NPR broadcasts typify the general tenor of the call-in format. NPR's guest panelists
during the sampled week fell into four categories of expertise: (1) defense, military, or Middle East analysts from leading think tanks; (2)
academics with published works on the Middle East region; (3) journalists; and (4) diplomats, former diplomats, or other policy officials.
Given the high levels of expertise represented by panelists callers might
well be justified in expecting that their questions would be answered
directly or their views vigorously debated, a perception reinforced by
the host's glowing appraisal of the qualifications of each panel member.
If so, callers were frequently disappointed.

By way of illustration, caller "Joel" of Butler, Pennsylvania, phoned
the program two weeks after the beginning of Desert Storm (February
1, 1991) to inquire what impact the upcoming religious period of Ramadan might have on the war's conduct; moreover, Joel asked why, if
the Arab states were so concerned about the Palestinians, did those
states not simply give the Palestinians land? The show's host dismissed
the second question as "making a point" and, as to the effect of Ra-

madan, confessed not to know. Neither panelist, a think tank analyst and a journalist, viewed the religious celebration as likely to have effect, but gave no reasons why. "Gary" from Miami sought confirmation regarding reports of an oil well set ablaze in Kuwait and about an oil slick in the desert. In response, the panelists ignored the question about well fires, spoke instead about a single reservoir fire; the host mentioned an oil slick drifting in the Persian Gulf but made no mention of any slick in the desert. Whereas Joel received an answer about Ramadan, but no reasons, and Gary's direct questions were ignored as panelists (in the convention of the TV game show "Jeopardy") framed their own questions, "Catherine" in California received a frank admission of ignorance. She asked why Iraqi prisoners of war captured by the coalition forces were blindfolded. The panelists simply said they did not know.

Finally, there were instances when callers' questions received a confused, ambiguous, or even contradictory response from the experts. Compare, for instance, panelists' responses to two calls, one on the eve (February 22, 1991) of the beginning of the ground war; the second after the success of coalition ground forces, February 27. In the first, "Silvia" of Cincinnati called to blame Saddam Hussein for the war and to suggest the United States, not the U.S.S.R., should set the terms whereby Iraq could avoid a ground war. (At the time the Soviet government was proposing terms to avert a ground war that included terms for Iraq to begin withdrawal from Kuwait in four days and be out entirely in three weeks.) The composition of the panel guaranteed that there would be no clear-cut response to the caller. The first panelist to respond was a Jordanian journalist; he claimed George Bush had "torpedoed" Jordan's effort to avert a crisis over Kuwait. Asked by the host whether Bush had sought to entrap Iraq into the invasion of Kuwait, the journalist replied that the "Americans did not give peace a chance." A second panelist representing a policy think tank thought the war aims of the coalition forces had changed over the weeks, but there had been no entrapment. A third panelist, a military analyst, said "Saddam Hussein is no longer what he used to be," and Iraq had now become a protectorate of Iran. Since at no point had Sylvia spoke of entrapment, Jordanian efforts, coalition aims, or Iranian involvement, she scarcely received a direct response from the partially contradictory, partially confusing exchange between the panelists.

In the second instance on February 27 the host was joined by two panelists, one a specialist on the Middle East and the other a representative of a foundation promoting peace. "Kirk" called from Seattle to ask what could be done to prevent atrocities in Kuwait as Iraq departed the country. The regional expert said he did not know, the host that Iraq was not "home free" if they committed atrocities, and the foundation spokesman opined that after war there were "always a lot of messy things to clean up." A few moments later "Andy" in Ohio asked what could be done to prevent future wars in the region. The regional expert thought the successful performance of coalition forces might deter conflict; the panelist from the foundation thought the performance sent a distinct message to radical regimes but was not a "paradigm" for future U.S. intervention; the host pondered, "Does making war become habit forming?" Perhaps such questions as "What about atrocities?" and "How to prevent future wars?" are, indeed, beyond answer, but for Kirk and Andy the responses received might well have left them more puzzled than informed.

This is not to say that NPR's "call-in show to answer your questions" always dismissed, begged, shifted, confused, or simply did not answer those questions. There were cases when questions received direct answers. When that was the case, however, it was frequently because the caller's question was the cue for the host or panelist to offer an extended statement on a favored subject. Especially prone to exploit callers' questions, but not always to provide responsive information, were academic scholars who took the opportunity to work in a plug for their recently published books. Thus a political scientist took a question as a cue to discuss a recently published theory on "cross-cutting cleavages" in the Middle East; another scholar responded to a question comparing Iraq's treatment of Kuwaitis with Israel's treatment of Palestinians to discuss the contents of her book on problems in the Middle East.

Whether they agreed or disagreed with the point of a caller's question, panelists when they so chose could seize the opportunity to voice a pet theory. For example, when on February 8, 1991, "Peter" of New York City called to ask if a "commercial orgy of arms sales" had led to the Gulf War, one panelist—a former British diplomat—responded eagerly that the "caller was a man after my own heart." He provided extended remarks on the "arms sale jamboree in the Middle East" that made it difficult to put the "genie back in the bottle," and advocated an arms embargo and "collective restraint," but closed by saying (apparently in contradiction to the causal relationship implied in Peter's question) that there must still be solutions to the "source of the conflict." On other occasions a caller's question could prompt a quick dismissal of a view if experts thought it counter to their own thinking. "John" in Pittsburgh, for instance, voiced a conspiracy theory of the war crisis. He thought that Saddam Hussein had been "lured" into Kuwait so that the United States could retaliate. John met with a resounding dismissal of his theory. No, came the panelist's response; Kuwait was a tempting "honey pot" and Iraq alone was responsible for the crisis.

Unless NPR's guest panelists were persons opposed to U.S. actions against Iraq (the Jordanian journalists being an example), the call-in panel format resulted in a consensus supportive of the war in general and of coalition aims in particular. This was the case in spite of the fact that, unlike the other radio talk shows examined, NPR's received calls opposed to the war and coalition aims. The proportion was not high, little more than 15 percent, yet more notable than for other talk shows. However, the panelists' responses that ignored, confused, or restated callers' questions and views effectively played down minority opposition. Hence, NPR's overall tone was similar to other talk formats and scarcely threw the opinion bandwagon of which Tocqueville spoke off track.

A parallel conclusion can be drawn from the sampled week of CNN's *Larry King Live*. As King's loyal fans know, the CNN weeknight production is a televised version of the host's highly successful late night radio talk show for the Mutual network. The format of *Larry King Live* is, on the surface, instructional and interactional. The show features a single guest per show (for example, White House Chief of Staff John Sununu on the telecast of February 28, 1991, at the end of the Gulf War), one guest per segment of a single hour, or a panel of guests. Regardless of the number or identity of guests, they share their expertise and experience with viewers. King's questions and comments, however, dictate what is and is not shared in the instructional format. Moreover, there may be several calls per show (there were forty-four calls during the sampled week of the war). Yet, with King as host each call is brief, the response by King or his guest(s) is terse, and the host places the question or comment of the caller within the context that King has established for the program. In short, guests are props for the host's instructional performance and callers are extras augmenting that performance.

During the sampled week constructed for this study, *Larry King Live* proved to be the most definitive of all talk shows surveyed as an example of the egoism of the electronic talk genre. Both King's guests and callers, at King's urging, were able to express the individuality of their private expertise and ambitions, while conforming to the bandwagon majority opinion supporting Operation Desert Storm. Of thirteen guests appearing during the week, only two took a negative stance toward U.S. and coalition actions. King served up to viewers a parade of defense, military, and Middle East analysts; journalists; Saudi businessmen and officials; White House officials; and members of coalition forces. To a person, they appraised the coalition cause as just and expressed optimism for the war's outcome and hope for the future of the region and for the United States in the war's aftermath. Callers' questions and comments, and the host's and guests' responses, reinforced the pro-war consensus.

The only exceptions to the consensus were expressed, predictably, by an editor of the *Arab News*, and by Iraq's ambassador to the United

Nations. King's questions to each were pointed, terse, and left little time for a detailed explanation of either guest's position. Thus, for example, King asked the Iraqi ambassador on February 13, 1991, "You don't believe the U.S. tried to kill innocent people?" (This was on the evening when Iraq claimed bombs had destroyed a civilian shelter, a structure labeled by U.S. forces as a "command and control center.") The ambassador replied in the affirmative to the question put in the negative: yes, the United States was attempting to break the civilian will. King immediately asked about Scud firings on Israel: Was it then all right to bomb civilians in Israel? Before the ambassador could spell out why one could not "equate" the two instances of civilian bombing, King was off to another series of questions. The adversarial posture taken with guests opposing the war, in effect, added to the force of the consensus.

A prime example of the nature of the popular consensus, and the pathos supporting it, came in King's telecast of February 19, 1991. King devoted a major portion of the program to an interview with a U.S. marine who had been wounded by, but who had "survived friendly fire" at the battle of Khafji. King opened the interview with a barrage of friendly questions, each establishing the credibility of the marine as a dedicated soldier doing a job he believed in: Why did he join the marines? Where did he do boot training? How long had he been a marine and how old was he? How long had he been in Saudi Arabia? What happened the day of Khafji? What happened in Khafji? What type vehicle was he in? Did he remember a sound of an attack or of being hit? Where was he evacuated to? What was the prognosis for recovery? To each question the marine responded in the fashion of a character in a Frank Capra film. What did it feel like to be a lone survivor? He owed it "all to God" was the reply. Would he stay in the marines? "Yes." Would he return to combat? "It's my job." How did he feel tonight? "Lucky," and with a sense of duty. Would he rather be back in Kuwait? "Yes," and again the marine expressed a sense of duty.

Following a commercial break King opened the phone lines to callers. Their questions and comments added to the pathos. The first caller's husband had been killed in the same vehicle carrying King's guest. Had her husband carried his Walkman player/recorder with him? Yes, but it had been lost. Had he said anything? No, was the reply. "You are a hero," the caller said. A second caller asked the marine about anti-war protestors. The soldier said he disagreed with them, but it was their right to protest. Two wives of the marine's fellow soldiers called to ask how their husbands were doing. "Real well," was the answer. "We will get back to this extraordinary human interest story," after the break, announced King. The return to the story continued the consensus theme as callers learned the Pentagon had *not* told the marine what to say, the Iraqis thought they had the upper hand at Khafji but were wrong, the marine had "no chance" to be scared, the vehicle in which he was hit was not "risky" (the caller's term) but had outstanding capabilities, his comrades who were victims of friendly fire had not died in vain, and the marine would "do what the president asks me to do." A final caller, from Camp Pendleton, California, expressed her thankfulness that the marine was still alive. Her husband was "over there" too. Did the marine happen to know the caller's husband, asked King. Yes, responded the marine, and the husband was "O.K." the last time that King's guest had seen him.

CONCLUSION: TALK HOSTS DRIVE THE BANDWAGON

We are unable, of course, to say that the guests and callers, in Tocqueville's phrase, actually perceived that a majority opinion of the Gulf War had spoken and, hence, as "friends and enemies alike" decided to "make for the bandwagon" (1969: 254) because of that perception. We can, however, conclude that regardless of the format of talk radio/TV employed in sampled programs, a consensus view in support of the war emerged via agreement, confrontational, and instructional programming. Playing a dominant role in the shaping of that consensus was the talk show host. One could certainly expect consensus to develop in the host–guest and open line formats, but consensus supporting the war proved to be the case in debate and panel formats as well. Panel and debate formats provided opportunities for voicing opinions opposing the war, but under the overall direction of hosts and via host–guest interaction, it was an opposition expressed within the context of a covering consensus rather than offering a serious threat to the consensus itself. Talk radio/TV coverage of the Gulf War thus produced a vox populi that was actually a vox host, one that afforded opportunity for friends and enemies alike to board the bandwagon.

BIBLIOGRAPHY

Andreasen, Margaret. "Listener Recall for Call-In versus Structured Interview Radio Formats." *Journal of Broadcasting and Electronic Media* 29 (Fall 1989): 421–30.

Avery, Robert K., Donald G. Ellis, and Thomas W. Glover. "A Demographic Profile of Talk Radio's Call-in Listener." Paper delivered at the Broadcast Education Association Annual Meeting, Chicago, Ill., 1976.

Avery, Robert K., Donald G. Ellis, and Thomas W. Glover. "Patterns of Communication on Talk Radio." *Journal of Broadcasting* 22 (Winter 1978): 5–17.

Carragee, Kevin M. "News and Ideology." *Journalism Monographs* 128 (August 1991): 1–30.

Crittenden, J. "Democratic Functions of the Open Mike Radio Forum." *Public Opinion Quarterly* 35 (Summer 1971): 200–10.

Ellul, Jacques. *Propaganda*. New York: Vintage Books, 1965.
Levin, Murray B. *Talk Radio and the American Dream*. Lexington, Mass.: Lexington Books, 1987.
Lively, Jack. "Alexis de Tocqueville." In *The Blackwell Encyclopedia of Political Thought*, David Miller, Janet Coleman, William Connolly, and Alan Ryan, eds. New York: Basil Blackwell, 1987.
Madison, James. "The Federalist No. 49." In *The Federalist*, Alexander Hamilton, John Jay, and James Madison, eds. New York: The Modern Library, 1937.
Noelle-Neumann, Elisabeth. "The Spiral of Silence: A Theory of Public Opinion." *Journal of Communication* 24 (Spring 1974): 43–51.
Noelle-Neumann, Elisabeth. *The Spiral of Silence*. Chicago: University of Chicago Press, 1984.
Roberts, James C. "The Power of Talk Radio." *The American Enterprise* 2 (May 1991): 56–61.
Tocqueville, Alexis de. *The Old Regime and the French Revolution*. New York: Doubleday & Co., 1955.
Tocqueville, Alexis de. *Democracy in America*. New York: Doubleday & Co., 1969.
Tramer, Harriet, and Leo W. Jeffres. "Talk Radio—Forum and Companion." *Journal of Broadcasting* 27 (Summer 1983): 297–300.
Turow, J. "Talk Show Radio as Interpersonal Communication." *Journal of Broadcasting* 18 (Spring 1974): 171–79.

Chapter Six

Constructing News Narratives: ABC and CNN Cover the Gulf War

Bethami A. Dobkin

As President Bush proclaimed the coming of a "New World Order" during the Persian Gulf War, media critics heralded a new world order of instant reporting. The continuous live reports provided by the Cable News Network (CNN) prompted some observers to call the conflict "The CNN War" (Laurence 1991). Academics have called the Gulf War a "critical incident" for television journalism (Zelizer 1992) because of the challenge CNN posed to the networks (ABC, CBS, NBC). But along with the praise and legitimacy conferred to CNN came ample criticism. The charges levied against CNN, and television news in general, included questions about media bias, the perceived inadequacy of information due to news management by the military, the manipulation of television news by political adversaries, and the potentially adverse effects of television news on public understanding of political events.

The magnitude of attention given to CNN suggests that its role in television journalism may go beyond providing the latest news during major crises. CNN has sought to expand its audience during periods of calm by making its evening newscasts a point of reference beyond opinion leaders (Waldman 1989). But these evening newscasts have eluded researchers who concentrate on CNN's live coverage or technological advantages (Walker, Wicks & Pyle 1991). An examination of CNN's *Headline News* reveals the extent to which conventions of television news presentation constrain CNN's packaging of events in ways similar to the three networks. Television news is known for its reliance on dramatic visual presentations, its need to captivate viewers, its condensation of information into brief segments, and its emphasis on immediate and technologically sophisticated coverage. Much contemporary research documents the existence of these constraints without assessing how they shape the telling of news stories. Television news formats shape the way news stories are told and the kinds of interpretations people make about those stories. Detailed analysis of the formats in television news can help explain public understanding of foreign conflicts and identify the kinds of policies viewers are likely to support (Altheide 1991; Dobkin 1992b).

Prior research has suggested that news formats among the networks—ABC, CBS, and NBC—are consistent. Although reporting styles may vary (Nimmo & Combs 1985), the three networks place similar emphasis on topic selection, use many of the same sources, devote comparable time to victims or families affected by crisis, and show the same video footage (Atwater 1989; Elliott 1988). CNN may not follow the same conventions: CNN's status as an international news service, with live reports and journalists behind enemy lines, has raised questions about its uniqueness. A central objective of analysis in this chapter is to assess the contributions of CNN and the degree to which its newscasts differ from that of the other networks.

A second concern raised by television coverage of the Gulf War underlies this comparison of newscasts. As Woodward notes in the first chapter of this book, media critics commend background reports in newscasts for offering journalistic freedom, providing much-needed context to events, and potentially countering the news management efforts of public and military officials. In fact, these background reports provide viewers with an interpretive framework by which they may understand ongoing events (Dobkin 1992a; Lewis 1985). Background reports, or reporter packages, also constitute a primary site of analysis in the newscasts. As Walker and colleagues (1991) note in their study of CNN's live coverage during the Gulf War, CNN presented accounts of action taking place without much simultaneous analysis. Viewers can find this contextual apparatus in the reporter packages that come before, during, and after cutaways to live events. These packages are consolidated each night in CNN's thirty-minute newscast, *Headline News*.

ABC's *World News Tonight* was chosen as a base of comparison for the thirty-minute format of *Headline News*. ABC *News* has consistently received top ratings among the networks; during the Persian Gulf War, ABC's anchor, Peter Jennings, was designated the most credible anchor by television viewers (Morin 1991). The volume of coverage given to the war also necessitates careful selection of data. Although the war was relatively short, key events punctuated the war and can be isolated with attention concentrated on those periods. The dates of coverage used here include ABC and CNN coverage between January 14 and March 1, but attention has been focused on the days immediately preceding the Allied air attacks and ground offensive: January 14 and 15, and

February 22, 1991. Television news began providing interpretive reports on U.S. military involvement in the Persian Gulf as early as August 1990, but by the final days before allied military intervention the narrative frame for interpreting impending events had become a standard feature of the newscasts. Understanding the nature and implication of this frame constitutes one means by which an assessment of CNN's contribution to coverage of the Gulf War can be made.

NEWS NARRATIVES AS STRUCTURAL FRAMES

Several researchers have noted journalists' reliance on frames, or interpretive categories, to handle the flow of news events (Gitlin 1980; Gameson 1989; Tuchman 1978). While the concept of news frames has been popular, the term remains somewhat ambiguous in its application to television news. As Tankard and his colleagues lament in their explication of the construct, "with some authors, the determination of what frames are being used in news stories about a certain event or situation seems to be done essentially by authority or by fiat" (Tankard et al. 1991: 1). They identify a list of prominent themes that serve as defining frames for interpreting a domain of news content. Frames certainly serve as organizing principles and set limits of discussion. But as I have argued elsewhere (1991; 1992b), news frames operate at two levels: First, semantic frames provide definitions, orientations, initial perceptions, or commonly accepted values by which the journalist apprehends an event; second, structural frames provide the formal conventions, or story forms, by which news is presented. These frames guide the explanations and contexts provided by journalists and constitute a standard format feature of television news.

Analysis of structural frames is critical to understanding the interpretations of news events that journalists advance. Through frames, journalists help define the political order and provide a field of reference for talking about events. Individual terms or characterizations make sense within the logic of these frames:

The articulation of individual signs . . . has a widereaching effect on a culture's understanding of a situation and the array of meanings and possible course of action which may be taken in the situation. Alternative descriptions of the situation thus tend to be systematically eliminated from the common sense understanding of what a problem is about. (Makus 1990: 504).

Journalists can establish or legitimize a situational logic for interpreting events, giving them the power to define political order (Cook 1991).

The power of news organizations to frame political events is constrained by both the demands of public and political audiences, and the economic imperative of news organizations. In summarizing research on audience comprehension of television news, Lewis (1991) argues that the structure of television news disengages audiences by failing to abide by the narrative codes that structure fictional programming. Two types of codes, sequential and hermeneutic, characterize structural news frames. Although Lewis argues that television news stories are structured "like newspaper stories with moving pictures" (1991: 130), this analysis demonstrates television journalism's much closer adherence to the fictional codes of narrative. An explication of sequential and hermeneutic codes identifies the frames most likely to meet audience demands and economic imperatives. The evaluation of CNN and ABC thus depends, in part, on the degree to which they adopt these frames.

The code of sequence, according to Lewis (1991), refers to a logic of appearances ordered by a theme or the passage of time. Although newscasts rarely proceed in chronological order, in the case of the Persian Gulf War events were marked by time rather than territory (Der Derian 1991), lending substantial significance to governmental deadlines and ultimatums as ordering features of the newscasts. Furthermore, in the serial news of continuing war coverage, scenes were more likely to be linked by ideas or themes rather than loosely associated by the transitions of anchors or reporters. The deadlines of January 16 and February 23 suggested a logic of impending conflict that prompted ABC *News* to spend 60 to 70 percent of its time on Gulf-related stories, with CNN *Headline News* following close behind. But time spent on a topic does not guarantee a sequential code, and Lewis stresses the relevance of story development in the sequence. Here lies the importance of the hermeneutic code, "the glue that fixes us to the screen, the device that tempts, teases, and rewards those of us who keep on watching" (Lewis 1991: 126). The hermeneutic code suggests a narrative structure by which news stories are told and interpreted.

The hermeneutic code consists of three stages: the enigma, which arouses audience curiosity by presenting a question or mystery; suspension of the enigma, in which resolutions are suggested and tensions heightened; and resolution of the enigma, or temporary satisfaction. Lewis (1991) contends that this hermeneutic code is present in popular television programming such as sports, quiz shows, soap operas, and advertisements, but is absent in television news. Although his analysis may hold true for many routine television news stories, the political and economic pressures shaping television journalism suggest that this enigmatic code may be apparent in news coverage of political crisis, particularly foreign ones. Journalists tend to report foreign policy initiatives uncritically and accept official storylines out of deference to policymakers and lack of information (Dorman & Farhang 1987). Additionally, television news storylines are likely to follow the structure of the romantic quest, a "universal structure" that "gives meaning to political practices and rituals" and which is "most evident in crisis situations or when attention is focused on the most exalted of political officers" (McGee 1985: 156–60). The romantic quest is a narrative structure that quickly establishes conflict and identifies a protagonist who, with the aid of a few supporting characters, takes action to resolve the conflict. This narrative structure meets both the political needs of high government officials who desire public support and attention and the economic needs of news organizations. Journalists cast presidents as heroes because "such dramatic and romantic themes attract larger audiences and thus maximize profits" (McGee 1985: 155).

The political expedience of using a quest narrative to frame the Persian Gulf War was recognized long before the first Allied air attacks. As Mann wrote:

Like other media stars, a successful politician seeks to play the leading role in a human drama with which the voters/viewers can psychologically identify. The gulf crisis provided President Bush with an obvious dramatic opportunity. Sophisticated politicians have long recognized that for purposes of psychological participation, traditional scenarios of good versus evil are highly effective, and Saddam Hussein was the perfect villain. (1990: 178)

The public reception of U.S. military intervention in the Persian Gulf depended partly on the degree to which this narrative frame was reproduced in television news coverage of the conflict.

Structural frames can reveal much about the interpretations of political crises that television news suggests to its viewers. Analysis of these frames requires attention to both introductions and transitions, or the code of sequence, and more fundamentally the hermeneutic code—or lack of one—evident in reporter packages and background reports. Such an inquiry can illuminate CNN and ABC's relative roles in building public support for U.S. military intervention in the Persian Gulf.

THE POLITICS OF SPECULATION

At the beginning of every newscast, anchors give an introduction that establishes the topic or question to lead the evenings news. Anchor introductions indicate the relative importance of news items and provide the terms or logic that will structure the forthcoming stories. During the week before the first Allied air strikes, and arguably for months prior to January 16, 1991, television news had been framed by the enigma, "Will the United States go to war with Iraq?" Variations on this theme emphasized the movement of time toward the United Nations deadline for Iraq's withdrawal from Kuwait. For instance, on January 15, Peter Jennings opened the ABC newscast: "Good evening. There is a fateful moment where one must act. This moment has, alas, arrived." Similarly, but perhaps with less drama, CNN's Lynne Russell began: "Time is running out, and there is no sign of compromise." The day before the start of the Allied ground offensive, Jennings specifically told viewers to mark time. He introduced the newscast with the instructions: "Remember the date and the time. Saturday, February the 23rd, at twelve o'clock noon, Eastern time" (February 22, 1991). These statements provided a chronological code of sequence, indicated the inevitability of Allied involvement, and set the stage for reports on war preparations and scenarios of war strategies.

The emphasis on deadlines and ultimatums is a predictable development in newscasts that operate on the narrative logic posed by enigmas. This structure leads viewers to emotionally expect the emotional satisfaction found in traditional narratives. As Lewis puts it, the enigma left unresolved is "a source of frustration and disappointment" (1991: 127). Background reports of troops in the Gulf training and waiting can build viewer frustration with the stalled narrative. One soldier identified this tension during the ABC *News* broadcast on January 14: "Ever since we've had this January deadline, line drawn in the sand, whatever you want to call it, our edge has been building as we get closer and closer to that date." Jim Hickey interviewed a pilot who, "like so many others have said so many times, is tired of waiting" (ABC *News*, January 15, 1991). Continual speculation about military involvement created a sense of urgency, because "the clock is ticking," "tensions [are] building," and American troops "simply want to get on with the job" (ABC *News*, January 14, 1991). Consistent portrayals of troop inaction threatened the movement of the narrative toward resolution.

The expectation of action was also bolstered by frequent speculations and scenarios about the probable course of warfare. With the "deadline for Iraq to leave Kuwait" only "two and a half hours away, the preparations for war" looked "ominous" (CNN, January 14, 1991). Both ABC and CNN gave detailed accounts of troop movements and combat readiness. For instance, Jennings told viewers: "The U.S. Navy has now moved two of its aircraft carriers in the region into the Persian Gulf itself so their planes are closer to targets in Iraq" (January 15, 1991). CNN confirmed "the Pentagon is moving about 20 B–52 bombers in an unnamed country closer to Iraq" (January 15, 1991). Given identifiable movement toward military action, negotiations were framed as outside the logic of the enigma. Correspondent Brit Hume seemed to recognize the force of this logic when he reported that the administration "has long been afraid of being drawn into some negotiating process in which it would never be able to get the outright victory and triumph in all of this . . . that it believes is necessary and available" (ABC *News*, February

22, 1991). CNN quoted British Prime Minister John Major echoing similar sentiments, as the "allied leaders won't be strung along by insincere negotiations" (February 22, 1991).

The "will we fight?" enigma posed war as imminent, so speculation about how the fighting might develop seemed natural. Some researchers have relegated speculation to a form of description rather than analysis (Walker et al. 1991), but suggesting possible courses of action and building scenarios establishes the assumptions by which events can be interpreted. Television newscasts suggested that the challenge for the United States was not primarily how to achieve peace, but how best to make war. Jennings stated: "As the deadline approaches, two challenges for the United States—to fight again with a generation of American troops, the vast majority of whom have never been in combat, and to fight with a new generation of American weapons which have never been tested in battle" (January 15, 1991). With the answer to "will we fight?" as an implied "yes," the logical extension became "who will win?"

Television newscasts answered that question through ample scenarios that showcased American troops and technology. ABC has long relied on background reports that detail American military might; for example, throughout the 1980s ABC used simulations, Defense Department file footage, and scenes from popular movies to depict possible U.S. military responses to international terrorism (Dobkin 1992). Military scenarios were a standard feature of ABC *News* during Persian Gulf War coverage as well. As ABC's Bob Zelnick reported over file footage of missile launches and explosions:

Tomahawk cruise missiles like these could be among the first weapons to be launched against Iraq. Navy sources say the U.S. has about 500 of the missiles aboard surface ships and submarines in the Gulf area. They would be launched against Iraqi command centers, air bases, fuel depots, and chemical weapons facilities. . . . Just as in the 1986 raid on Libya, the key early mission for U.S. aircraft will be to destroy Iraqi planes and surface-to-air missile batteries . . . only after the U.S. has achieved command of the skies would B–52 and FB–11 bombers begin to hit entrenched Iraqi ground forces. (January 14, 1991)

Lengthy scenarios such as this one primed viewers to accept a military frame for understanding foreign conflict, one that also privileged the antiseptic bombing footage to come later during the war.

Although CNN followed similar conventions in providing scenarios of military action, the news organization reflected its international orientation by offering scenarios that highlighted Allied military forces. For example, CNN's Richard Blystone built this scenario of Israel's possible response to an Iraqi assault:

A hilltop overlooking a Jordan valley. American-made HOG anti-aircraft missiles practice a deadly minuet. Israel is showing off one of the reasons it says on Iraqi mission over here would be a one-way trip. . . . If Israel decides the results of an Iraqi strike require retaliation, it will strike back. . . . The (Iraqi) Sukors and their escorts would come up against Israel's fighters and interceptors. . . . Israel has been readying two batteries of Patriot ground-to-air missiles, offspring of the Star Wars program, developed with the United States. (January 15, 1991)

CNN was less detailed in its predictions, using fewer graphics and military file footage. Blystone presented the Israeli scenario with frequent references to U.S. participation and equipment, but the American influence was less pronounced in CNN's newscasts than in ABC's reports and commentary. When Jennings asked correspondent Dean Reynolds if Israelis "sense that one of their most deeply felt adversaries is about to get it," Reynolds replied, "Behind all of the apprehension is a certain amount of satisfaction that the man they wanted to see go away is going to go away at the hands of the United States" (January 15, 1991). These comments were made after detailing Israeli preparations for attack, and they indicate the different emphases in ABC and CNN scenarios.

Both ABC and CNN had to temper confidence in U.S. military superiority with a note of apprehension for the enigma to remain suspended. The "Patriots have never been to war," but military officials remained confident; the Apache attack helicopter was "yet to be tested" but called "fit to fly," and "capable of showing the taxpayer[s] they got their money's worth" (ABC *News*, January 15, 1991). Despite potential problems, Jennings said, there was "a lot of talk about kicking the butt of the enemy with great ease" (January 15, 1991). The progression from "will we fight?" to "who will win?" and "how will the war develop?" simulated the enigmatic structure apparent in televised sports (Lewis 1991). In fact, in adopting a narrative frame that replicated the hermeneutic code of sports, television news added force to the ubiquitous sports metaphors and analogies that permeated Persian Gulf coverage. Rather than providing contextual knowledge or an analytical frame by which to evaluate U.S. policy in the Gulf, ABC and CNN used their background reports in a manner that implicitly supported U.S. military intervention. Even when CNN attempted to provide historical analysis for military intervention, explanation came in the form of comparisons to American military strategy in the Civil War and World War I (February 22, 1991). Lewis explains the significance of background reports in providing a frame for audience interpretation:

What is also particular about television news is that, unlike many other forms of television, it operates on a discursive level that most people find elusive. . . . the frameworks respondents used to make sense of a news item frequently originated from the news itself. (1991: 143)

Television news, particularly when reporting about foreign events, operated as a closed system, reinforcing its own presuppositions and frames. "Will we fight/will we win" became a common sense enigmatic code for television news and was supported by speculations and scenarios. It simultaneously served the economic interests of media organizations that needed to captivate viewers and the political goals of a government that desired public support for military intervention. Finally, this enigma provided an interpretive frame that suggested news viewers be politically passive but emotionally active, responding to events in the Gulf as spectators (Mann 1990).

DEVELOPING ENIGMA THROUGH THE QUEST NARRATIVE

The main characters in the narrative established by the "will we fight?" enigma were apparent as early as August 3, 1990, when President Bush verbally committed U.S. military support to Saudi Arabia. Iraq's invasion of Kuwait was quickly constructed in television and print news reports as a personalized showdown between George Bush and Saddam Hussein rather than an act of aggression by one Arab state toward another. The identification of heroes and villains forms the basis of the quest narrative, a structural frame on which television relies for both news and entertainment narratives. Sperry (1981) explains this standard narrative form:

The world at peace is disrupted by some event. . . . That event becomes the evil, is named and, if possible, analyzed and understood. It is then attacked by some leader, the hero figure, often a representative of the people. However, this leader, whether by choice or by the nature of his vocation, may not be able to meet the problem alone. So he gains allies, other leaders, and he also gains enemies—potential leaders who disagree with his plan of action, or rebels who align themselves with the evil. As these alignments become apparent, stories are then told of the effect of the problem on the average man [sic]. (301)

The elements of the quest narrative detailed by Sperry are easily identified in television news coverage of the Persian Gulf War. Coverage during the first month of Desert Shield improved Bush's popular standing, "hammered" Saddam and established the Hitler metaphor for him, and created a sense of urgency about the crisis (Dionne 1990). Television news organizations could depend on this quest structure to appeal to audiences and generate interest in the enigma. Politicians could use the quest narrative as an interpretive frame that justified military intervention in the Persian Gulf.

The key characteristics identified by Sperry are also evident in the newscasts analyzed here. ABC and CNN both emphasized Bush's leadership and his allies, described Hussein—and often by extension, the Iraqi people—as villainous, depicted protesters as rebels, and reported on the moods, beliefs, and reactions of "average" Americans. ABC began each day with reports on the president's moods, perhaps attending to Bush's earlier declaration "that he alone would decide for or against war, no matter what Congress or the public had to say" (Barber 1991: 28). ABC gauged Bush's attitudes with quotes from congressmen who said "he hasn't changed his view that force may well have to be used" and "he's still hopeful that we can have some peaceful resolution." Although Bush took little reported action that day beyond having "some public sport with a furry microphone," he remained the center of attention on ABC (January 14, 1991). The next day, ABC reporters described Bush as "at peace with himself," "resolute and confident," and with "a lot of thoughts about the American people" (January 15, 1991). Similarly, CNN described Bush as "reflective and resolute, and at peace with himself" (January 15, 1991). As the protagonist, Bush featured prominently in television newscasts regardless of his relative inaction.

CNN's coverage, though paralleling much of ABC's, provided a more tenuous link of Bush to the quest narrative. Although Russell eventually mentioned Bush and attributed a strong coalition to him, her January 14 newscast emphasized U.N. Secretary General Javier Perez de Cuellar's efforts to achieve peace. She began that evening with a story about the shooting of Palestine Liberation Organization members in Tunisia and then detailed both de Cuellar's activities and those of France in forwarding peace plans to the U.N. Security Council. Differences between CNN and ABC were also apparent in coverage of the impending ground offensive. Jennings introduced the first reporter package, labeled "The Ultimatum," by describing "a breathtaking twenty-four hours during which the Soviet/Iraqi plan for getting out of Kuwait has been completely eclipsed by the President's ultimatum" (February 22, 1991). During CNN newscasts, decisions were linked to those around Bush rather than isolating him as a leader. CNN reported that "members of Congress are backing President Bush's ultimatum to Iraq" and "allies want a tight time frame for the withdrawal" (February 22, 1991). ABC highlighted U.S. activities and goals, stating that negotiations were failing because they "would *fall short of what the Administration wanted*" (ABC News, February 22, 1991, emphasis added). The differences are subtle, but they indicate the varying degrees to which television news organizations abide by the strictures of the quest narrative. Both ABC and CNN depicted dueling sides, but ABC privileged the U.S. role as leader and Bush as hero, while CNN stressed the team working with the protagonist.

As the war progressed, the most important team players featured on both ABC and CNN were the American troops. Many media critics have charged that journalists were "cheerleaders" for the military, and, given the similarities of television's hermeneutic code to that of sports, the metaphor may be an apt one. For purposes of this analysis, however, it suffices to note that in addition to speculations about U.S. military actions, television news couched U.S. military aggression in defensive rather than offensive terms. So, when CNN reported that marines used napalm against Iraq, it prefaced the information with Pentagon reports that "a U.S. Marine has been killed in the ground combat along the Kuwaiti border" and followed it with the comment that napalm "is used only to burn off oil in trenches around fortifications" (February 22, 1991). Presumably, napalm was a necessary response to an Iraqi ground offensive. ABC also explained that napalm bombs were being used "to burn off oil," and noted that the "front lines are being warned that one of every four Iraqi missiles contains poisoned gas" (February 22, 1991). The phrase "chemical weapons" was never used in conjunction with Allied action but was assumed, without evidence, to be part of enemy attacks. Napalm bombs were shown as shiny metal canisters, without visual emphasis on their destructive capabilities. Pilots coming back from "stepped up" missions remarked not on the consequences of their attacks, but on the weather: "It's real nice up there today. The worst part is the oil smoke here" (ABC *News*, February 22, 1991).

Of course, American television journalism cannot (nor, perhaps, should) be expected to focus on the more gruesome and tragic aspects of U.S. military action. And as many critics of military censorship during the Gulf War have argued, potentially damaging information about the consequences and conduct of U.S. actions in the Gulf was carefully controlled during the conflict. Television journalists who wanted to depict the horrors as well as the triumphs of war were constrained in gathering the information and video footage they needed until after the resolution of the hermeneutic code. But, more fundamentally, the quest narrative also limited this kind of reporting. Quest narratives require clear heroes and enemies, and questioning the legitimacy of the hero and his team would have threatened not only the cohesion of the narrative but also the authority of the narrator.

While Bush and his troops clearly constituted the heroes of the narrative, the Iraqi citizens were depicted as complicit followers of an evil, brutal enemy dictator. Television news characterizations of the Iraqi people dehumanized and distanced them from American viewers. For instance, both CNN and ABC called Iraq's version of congressional authorization to use force a "rubber stamp" assembly meeting (January 14, 1991). But though both news organizations provided depictions of Iraqis, CNN spent much less time than ABC on these background reports. Russell, for example, merely referred to the "tens of thousands

of Iraqis rallied around their leader and denounced President Bush,"
while ABC covered the event with reporter Gary Sheppard's package
that included quotes from an Iraqi military leader and translations of
chanting crowd members. "With our spirit, with our blood, we are with
you, Saddam," Sheppard intoned, interpreting Iraqi slogans over footage of the parliament members clapping hands and raising fists (January
14, 1991). The next day, Sheppard continued his coverage of the Iraqi
masses chanting and parading, with close shots of individual Iraqis
reserved for soldiers and children in uniform (January 15, 1991). These
portraits of the enemy differed substantially from those of Americans
or their allies. Whereas Iraqi schools were closed so youngsters could
take part in the government-organized demonstrations, in Israel a far
more comfortable school setting was featured, where "school children
are getting into the act with play [gas] masks, as if to make the real thing
seem not so scary" (ABC *News*, January 15, 1991). One characterization
explains war by the fanaticism of Iraq, the other shows heroic bravery
in the face of danger. Both neatly fit the development of the quest
narrative.

Sperry outlines two final elements in the narrative: the emergence of
rebels who align themselves with the enemy and reports of how the
conflict is affecting the average person. In Gulf War television coverage,
these two elements in the quest narrative were dichotomized as war
protesters and supporters. "Average" Americans were assumed to be
war supporters. As Cokie Roberts commented, "The American people
support this war, and no one in Congress is going to even raise any
questions whatsoever about it. One Democratic strategist said 'only 7
percent of American men . . . are against this war. We're not crazy
enough to speak against it' " (ABC *News*, February 22, 1991). To raise
questions was to be a rebel.

Rebels were treated similarly in CNN and ABC news reports. Newscasts gave brief mention of protests around the country, frequently
showing activists as small groups rather than using close shots of individuals or depicting substantial gatherings. In an apparent search for
deviant behavior, Russell reported that Chicago and San Francisco
protesters "snarled traffic" (January 14, 1991). That same day, Jennings
noted that people "took to the streets" in those cities, and "some people
opposed to the war took over the State House in Olympia, Washington.
High school students opposed to the war walked out of class in Iowa
and Minnesota" (ABC *News*, January 14, 1991). Both sets of comments
were bracketed by longer stories about Americans showing support for
the troops. When CNN and ABC did devote considerable time to the
anti-war movement, packaged reports focused on protest as a form of
expression rather than on the potential questions about foreign policy
raised by the demonstrations. ABC's Ken Kashiwahara interviewed

protesters who "simply wanted to talk about their frustrations, their fears," grouping peace activists with people who called crisis hotlines "just to talk" and who shouted hysterically during talk shows such as *Oprah* (January 14, 1991). Arguably, CNN lent legitimacy to the "new peace movement" by describing its "accelerating activities" as "more in the mainstream" than Vietnam-era protests. Brian Jenkins reported on "a new generation grappling for the first time with the prospect of a major war and just warming up to protest" (CNN, January 15, 1991). But protest organizers were not asked for their views about the war or reasons for protesting; they were interviewed about the membership of peace movements and the social stigma of involvement. As the war progressed and support for it became equated with patriotism, protesters were increasingly portrayed as marginal and deviant. In television news, anti-war protesters became rebels without a cause.

Finally, average Americans were featured in the newscasts as small-town, predominantly white, middle-class, church-going war supporters. Gauging the mood of this group became a consistent preoccupation with television news organizations. For instance, CNN went to Glennville, Georgia, a rural town with "something special" that "makes it stand apart": a community support group for military families, where military wives feel "so good" and feel "so much love and affection." After all, "Glennville is good people" (January 14, 1991). ABC often used churches, church bells, and church services in its mood pieces:

In Sioux Falls, office workers bowed their heads at their desks. In a Spokane, Washington high school, students paused for a minute of silent prayer. Nowhere were feelings more evident than at Fort Bragg, North Carolina, home of the 82nd Airborne Division, where friends and relatives prayed for those serving in the Gulf. (January 14, 1991)

Frequent reports of Americans praying for peace, tying yellow ribbons, sending letters, and voicing their concerns all created a sense of community and defined normal American responses to the war.

Developing the enigma through a quest narrative seemed to come naturally to television news, particularly for the more traditional and sophisticated ABC newscasts. This structural frame was also conveniently suited to a president who wished to take on an heroic role in foreign conflict. Not only was the hero quest a foreseeable frame for television news, it was, as Barber argues, a predictable adventure for Bush. "As he declared in accepting the Republican presidential nomination," Barber writes, " 'I am a man who sees life in terms of missions'—missions that have tended to be driven less by specific goals than by a vague quest for adventure and self-reliance" (1991: 25–26). War afforded Bush the paradigmatic opportunity to embark on a hero's quest and revive sagging public ratings of his performance. The adoption of a quest frame by television journalists could only help Bush in his mission.

CONCLUSION: THE SIGNIFICANCE OF DIFFERENCE

This analysis indicates that both ABC and CNN adopted similar structural frames in their reporting of the Persian Gulf War. ABC's *World News Tonight* and CNN's *Headline News* posed the enigma, "Will the U.S. go to war with Iraq?"; marked time with deadlines and ultimatums; used the structural frame of romantic quest to develop heroes, villains, allies, and rebels; and focused audience concern on the outcome of the narrative. Television newscasts provided an interpretive framework through reporter packages that privileged military intervention and focused on war strategies. Before the first Allied air strikes, television news had established a structural frame that fit the emerging needs of the Pentagon and White House.

ABC and CNN's reliance on speculations and scenarios about military action also established legitimacy for the plethora of retired generals and military experts in subsequent Gulf War coverage. As Katz writes, "Their expertise framed the public's response from the first brainy bomb, tilting it away from human costs or political implications of war toward the payload of F153s and the trajectory of patriots" (1991: 93). But CNN, while focusing on tactical and strategic military analysis of the war, often presented the teamwork of Allied forces rather than highlight Bush's role as a solitary leader. CNN sometimes began newscasts with settings, such as Kuwaiti beaches and cities in Saudi Arabia, rather than the words or actions of key characters in the narrative. CNN thus showed less allegiance to the character development demanded by quest narratives while maintaining the structural frame with traditional us/them dualities and speculations of military action.

Additional differences between CNN and ABC news narratives can be identified. CNN's structure of *Headline News*, with Gulf coverage, economic reports, sports highlights, and regular "updates" as part of each newscast, more closely resembled the "shopping list" organization of print news identified by Lewis (1991) and makes the title, *Headline News*, particularly appropriate. The print-based mode of organization, Lewis argues, discourages viewers from making connections between ideas and limits their understanding of news events to "moments of discursive or ideological resonance" (1991: 143). Since television newscasts lack historic context for understanding action sequences, viewers either remember discrete moments of news that fit the interpretive frame provided by journalists, or viewers construct their own, alternative perspective based on knowledge they have acquired from other sources.

Viewer comprehension is aided when television adheres to the hermeneutic code, which emotionally engages the audience and carries them through the narrative to a satisfying resolution. ABC *News*, with its gifted narrator and solid reliance on narrative logic, is more apt to draw the audience into its stories and to exercise control over viewer responses.

Television journalism's reliance on enigmatic codes and quest narratives transcends issues of news bias and indicates the probable success of news management efforts that fit these structural logics. The framing devices of "will the U.S. go to war?" and "will we win?" inevitably focus on process and outcome, not deliberation and rationale. Larger issues, such as "why we fight," are subsumed under the enigmatic codes that best fit the logic of television. Similarly, the romantic quest is not necessarily contrived by politicians or journalists in a conscious attempt to use television news as propaganda. The quest narrative is culturally situated and is a pervasive part of popular American entertainment. Telling news stories with this structural frame might increase audience interest in and comprehension of television news. With this audience engagement, though, might also come an insidious form of ideological control that accompanies the quest narrative. The challenge for television journalism is to use structural frames that provide thematic continuity and aid audience comprehension without relying solely on those forms that implicitly support American military intervention.

BIBLIOGRAPHY

Altheide, David L. "The Impact of Television Formats on Social Policy." *Journal of Broadcasting and Electronic Media* 35 (Winter 1991): 3–21.

Atwater, Tony. "News Formats in Network Evening News Coverage of the TWA Hijacking." *Journal of Broadcasting and Electronic Media* 33 (Summer 1989): 293–304.

Barber, James David. "Empire of the Song." *The Washington Monthly* (October 1991): 25–29.

Cook, Timothy E. "Are the American News Media Governmental? Re-examining the 'Fourth Branch' Thesis." Paper presented at the International Communication Association Convention, Chicago, May 1991.

Der Derian, James. "Videographic War." Paper presented at the Iowa Symposium on the Rhetoric of Inquiry, Iowa City, April 1991.

Dionne, E. J. "Are the Media Beating the War Drums or Just Dancing to Them?" *The Washington Post National Weekly Edition*, September 10, 1990, 23.

Dobkin, Bethami A. "Framing the Enemy: The Construction and Use of 'Terrorism' in Public Discourse." Paper presented at the Iowa Symposium on the Rhetoric of Inquiry, Iowa City, April 1991.

Dobkin, Bethami A. "Paper Tigers and Video Postcards: The Rhetorical Dimensions of Narrative Form in ABC News Coverage of Terrorism." *Western Journal of Communication* (Spring 1992): 143–60. (a)

Dobkin, Bethami A. *Tales of Terror: Television News and the Construction of the Terrorist Threat.* New York: Praeger, 1992. (b)

Dorman, William and Mansour Farhang. *U.S. Press and Iran.* Berkeley: University of California Press, 1987.

Elliott, Deni. "Family Ties: A Case Study of Coverage of Families and Friends During the Hijacking of TWA Flight 847." *Political Communication and Persuasion* 5 (1988): 67–75.

Gameson, William A. "News as Framing: Comments on Graber." *American Behavioral Scientist* (1989): 157–61.

Gitlin, Todd. *The Whole World is Watching.* Berkeley, Calif.: Free Press, 1980.

Katz, Jon. "The Air War at Home." *Rolling Stone,* March 7, 1991, 93–100.

Laurence, Robert P. "So You Got Mad at the Tube." *San Diego Union,* March 1, 1991, A12.

Lewis, Justin. *The Ideological Octopus: An Exploration of Television and Its Audience.* New York: Routledge, 1991.

Lewis, Justin. "Decoding Television News." In *Television in Transition,* P. Drummond and R. Patterson eds., 205–34. London: British Film Institute, 1985.

Makus, Anne. "Stuart Hall's Theory of Ideology: A Frame For Rhetorical Criticism." *Western Journal of Speech Communication* (Fall 1990): 495–514.

Mann, Patricia S. "Representing the Viewer." *Social Text* 9 (1990): 177–84.

McGee, Michael C. "Some Issues in the Rhetorical Study of Political Communication." In *Political Communication Yearbook 1984,* Keith R. Sanders, Linda L. Kaid, and Dan Nimmo eds., 155–82. Carbondale: Southern Illinois University, 1985.

Morin, Richard. "The New War Cry: Stop the Press." *Washington Post National Weekly Edition,* February 11, 1991, 38.

Nimmo, Dan, and James E. Combs. *Nightly Horrors: Crisis Coverage by Television Network News.* Knoxville: University of Tennessee, 1985.

Sperry, Sharon. "Television News as Narrative." In *Understanding Television,* Richard P. Adler, ed. New York: Praeger, 1981.

Tankard, James W., Laura Hendrickson, Jackie Silberman, Kris Bliss, and Salma Ghanem. "Media Frames: Approaches to Conceptualization and Measurement." Paper presented at the Association for Journalism and Mass Communication Convention, Boston, August 1991.

Tuchman, Gaye. *Making News.* New York: Free Press, 1978.

Walker, Douglas C., Robert H. Wicks, and Robert Pyle. "Differences in Live Coverage Between CNN and the Broadcast Networks in the Persian Gulf War." Paper presented at the Association for Journalism and Mass Communication Convention, Boston, August 1991.

Wallis, Victor. "Media War in the Gulf." *Lies of Our Times* (February 1991): 3.

Waldman, Peter. "CNN Re-channels Efforts to Achieve Premier Status." *Wall Street Journal* (October 16, 1989): B1.

Zelizer, Barbie. "CNN, the Gulf War, and Journalistic Practice." *Journal of Communication* (Winter 1992): 66–81.

Chapter Seven

C-SPAN's Coverage of the Gulf War: Television as Town Square

Janette Kenner Muir

In his State of the Union Address on January 28, 1992, George Bush once again celebrated the victory of the Persian Gulf War and the triumphs it brought to the United States. Evoking images of sacrifice and dedication, Bush identified America's victory in the Gulf War as a turning point for his vision of a "New World Order," and a prelude to the dissolution of the Soviet empire, and the end of the Cold War.

Yet, as the president continued to proclaim victory even in the fragile world of 1992, historians, politicians, and average citizens continue to revise interpretations about the Gulf War success. Saddam Hussein still remains in power as the Iraqi dictator, Iraq and Kuwait have been declared environmental disaster areas, and a true count of the total number of civilian casualties has never quite been determined.

While polling results and congressional votes tended to support the president's decision to fight this war, a bewildered public debated the issue in classrooms, offices, local bars, and living rooms across the country. Everywhere people went, the Cable News Network (CNN) provided on-the-spot coverage of the fight between Scuds and Patriot Missiles. While the Vietnam War will be remembered as the first televised war, bringing powerful images of death and destruction into American living rooms, the Persian Gulf War will long be remembered as a highly controlled media event using the latest visual technology to capture the conflict and present it to the American people.

Despite the continuous reporting by CNN and the major television networks, nowhere was the Persian Gulf War covered with such depth and intensity as it was on C-SPAN, the Cable Satellite Public Affairs Network. As President Bush decried a ruthless enemy and pleaded a case for the helpless Kuwaiti people, and as political leaders debated the decision to go to war, C-SPAN served an important role for the world—it enabled the public to watch what was happening and make their own decisions about the right or the wrong of fighting the war. It also enabled the people to speak for themselves: world leaders, generals, soldiers, friends and relatives, everyday citizens, and even children. And, for the first time in history, the entire coverage of the war, the debates, the addresses, the briefings, and the public reaction, is available to any scholar through the Purdue University Public Affairs Archives that houses all C-SPAN programming.[1]

C-SPAN functions through the medium of television to watch, listen, and transmit vital information and opinions to its viewers. It also contributes an important forum, an electronic town square, for the public to voice opinions, ask questions and provide significant reactions to policy making. The focus of this chapter is to discuss C-SPAN's coverage of the Persian Gulf War with particular emphasis on the town square phenomenon. The nature of the network, the nature of the call-in shows, and specific ways people talked about the Persian Gulf War are central to this discussion.

THE C-SPAN NETWORK

C-SPAN was formed in 1979 as a non-profit cooperative of the cable industry, dedicated to providing the public with gavel-to-gavel coverage of the House of Representatives. In 1982, the service was expanded to twenty-four hours, with a continued commitment to covering the House, and expanded coverage of presidential addresses, National Press Club speeches, congressional hearings and daily happenings around Washington D.C. Following the 1986 Senate vote allowing television cameras into its chamber, C-SPAN added a second satellite channel, C-SPAN II. Funding for these channels primarily comes from cable television subscribers. Two cents of each cable bill goes to fund the network, providing an annual operating budget of approximately $12 million.

C-SPAN's goal is to provide "in-depth coverage of the American political system, its elected officials, and the journalists who cover it" (*C-SPAN Guide for Educators*: 2). Unlike the conventional network, C-SPAN does not edit events to make them interesting or entertaining; public events are covered in their entirety, absent commentary and analysis (Lamb et al.: xvi). The philosophy is to let the public watch and decide for themselves their positions on various issues. With this goal in mind, C-SPAN will air all White House speeches, House and Senate proceedings, various political events and rallies, a "Road to the White House" series, and numerous other programs. The intent is to have cameras present, covering what happens without the commentary and spin control that often follows on other networks. In addition, interviews with authors, journalists, and politicians will round out the perspectives presented on various issues. This makes, of course, for long, sometimes tedious talk about issues, but it also reveals the realities of daily policy making.

In following the philosophy and goal of the network, the call-in show play an important role by providing a vehicle through which the public voice can be heard. Call-ins are dispersed throughout C-SPAN's weekly programming format, often following major public addresses or critical events, and featuring special guests discussing the relevant issue of the day. For example, a senator may appear on a day when an important bill is being debated, a journalist may talk about coverage of an international issue, or a law professor might discuss the merits of a case before the Supreme Court. Following some discussion, time is provided for people to call the network and let their positions be heard, to ask questions of the guests, and to disagree or agree with previous callers.

Given its nature, many often wonder who watches C-SPAN. In a survey sponsored by the network, nearly 46 million people watched C-SPAN I or II during 1990 and 1991, representing a diverse audience, drawn from a variety of socioeconomic and educational backgrounds. While the C-SPAN viewership is varied, some generalities can be made regarding the typical viewer. Maura Clancy of Statistical Research, Inc., reveals that 40 percent of the audience are between eighteen and thirty-four years of age ("Survey," 1). Males constitute the majority of the audience, and minority viewership averages about 14 percent of the audience. Approximately 92 percent voted in the 1988 presidential election, and 74 percent in the 1990 state elections. Participants in the survey were evenly divided between the two major parties—34 percent were Democrats, 33 percent were Republicans, and 24 percent described themselves as Independents. The survey also notes that over 50 percent of the viewers are college educated.

More significant than the statistics about who watches C-SPAN are profiles about the kinds of people the network attracts. Public officials, the press, educators, voters, those involved in public policy making, those capable of affecting the nation's political process are the primary viewers (Lamb et al.: xvii). Georgia Representative Roy Allen describes the typical viewer:

The C-SPAN viewer is the true politico, the activist, the person who has in his or her blood a penchant for being on top of all key issues, national issues. Probably the one thing I've learned about America is that most people aren't into politics. A tiny few are heavily into it, but the average man would probably not know the names of his two U.S. senators. C-SPAN fills the appetite for that real zealot with political yearnings. (Lamb et al.: 2)

Those citizens willing to speak out in call-in shows tend to represent an active group of people who participate in the political process on an apparently regular basis. They are interested enough to place long distance calls at their own expense, both in terms of time and money. The network does not have a WATTS line, so viewers calling from across the nation, along with the international audience, call in and are placed on hold at their own expense. No time delay exists in the program, so a Californian who calls an 8:00 A.M. show is actually placing his or her call at 5:00 A.M. While viewers are predominately from the United States, there are also occasional international callers, particularly from Europe. Those who participate in C-SPAN call-in shows are people who watch C-SPAN and who are interested in voicing their opinions about significant issues. A 1987 study conducted by the University of Maryland Survey Research Center revealed that of those viewers who called in to the network, 63 percent called to voice an opinion, 25 percent wanted to respond to the issue discussed, and 12 percent called to respond to the featured guest (Lamb et al.: 379).

A test for any significant public affairs medium is its coverage of crisis events. The Persian Gulf War was like no other crisis because it was the first time in history that an entire war, from beginning to end, could be watched from one's living room. C-SPAN's coverage provided a complete video history of America's decision to go to war, the subsequent impact of that decision on the evolution of the Middle East conflict, and the role of the United States in its resolution.

THE GULF COVERAGE

According to Brian Lamb, founder and chief executive officer of C-SPAN, the network's purpose in covering the Persian Gulf War was to be a mirror, or a "video verité" on events as the conflict and eventual war evolved. To this end, C-SPAN cameras covered all White House announcements, they were present during the House debates over America's decision to go to war, they followed soldiers to the Gulf, and covered all military briefings.

Between August 2, 1990, the day Iraq invaded Kuwait, and February 28, 1991, following the president's announcement that the war had ended, the network aired over 1,100 hours of coverage, with 1,300 different programs (Browning: 1). These programs included over 100 hours of House and Senate proceedings, over 130 hours of news briefings, and over 50 hours of speeches. While CNN and the major networks carried much of the same news, C-SPAN's coverage was important for four reasons: The network covered the House debate in its entirety, showed all military briefings, provided an open pipeline to the Gulf, and encouraged call-in participation by citizens.

Debates About the War

C-SPAN provided the only complete coverage of the House debate over whether the United States should go to war to defend Kuwait. Statistical Research, Inc. (SRI) researchers found that 85 percent (an estimated 34.7 million adults) watched the January 11–12 congressional debate authorizing war in the Persian Gulf ("Survey," 3). Lamb noted that this was, by far, "the largest audience we've ever had" (Interview, January 6, 1992).

No other congressional debate is as important as America's decision to fight in a war, especially a war that carried such significant consequences for the world oil supply and for regional peace as the Persian Gulf conflict. America was faced with a momentous decision, one that could dramatically alter the world. In this debate, images of the failure of Vietnam, of alienated veterans returning home, and of needless death and destruction were recalled, evoking powerful emotions. House members claimed those who were against the war were unpatriotic and traitors to the president and to the country. Other members argued that America's involvement would be too costly, in terms of both money and lives.

It was a difficult decision for House members, one that could have had significant ramifications for their reelection prospects if opponents had chosen to use their decision as an issue in the next campaign. C-SPAN's coverage of this debate, and the public reaction to it, serve as important historical texts regarding America's decision to go to war, including the ways policy makers define the nation's role in the foreign policy arena, and the patriotic images called forth when lawmakers face decisions with life and death consequences. C-SPAN also provided an important service by airing debates over this decision from the British and Canadian Houses of Commons.

Military Briefings

Once America decided to go to war, a second valuable service C-SPAN provided was coverage of military briefings. While most networks focused on briefing highlights, C-SPAN covered all American, British, and Saudi Arabian military briefings. Additionally, the network re-aired the briefings so that viewers could watch them at night after work. Lamb remarks that "We carried every briefing that was held. We're the only ones I know of that carried every one . . . all of them, one way or another; and we were the only ones who put them on at night" (Interview, January 6, 1992).

While many American citizens had little interest in the tedious details of the war, the C-SPAN viewer interested in all facets of decision making

was able to watch and make his or her own judgments about the unfolding events. Viewers could then see how segments of briefings were
translated into the news coverage on major networks and in daily newspapers. Though the briefings were full of jargon, and sometimes misleading, they were important elements in the evolution of the war. Those
who wanted shorthand versions of what was happening in terms of
military strategies could tune into other networks, but C-SPAN's commitment to this coverage provided information that in its archival form
serves as an important resource in rounding out the story of the Gulf
War.

An Open Pipeline

While C-SPAN, like other networks, aired Gulf War video footage
from press pool arrangements,[2] an important service the network provided was live coverage of military activity. In particular, C-SPAN
showed the public the reactions of those directly involved in the war—
soldiers, journalists, and citizens. Lamb recalls the difficulty in getting
the Pentagon to take the network seriously, to realize that they did
indeed want to be part of the Middle East coverage: "We didn't have
reporters or correspondents, we just wanted to look and watch, and be
an open pipeline for the public" (Interview, January 6, 1992). As a result,
C-SPAN provided an insider's view of what was happening by interviewing those who participated in the war, whether it be journalists,
generals, or the soldiers themselves.

One network highlight was vice-president Susan Swain's travel with
a North Carolina national guard unit to Saudi Arabia. Following the unit
from the beginning of their trip allowed C-SPAN to personalize the war
by showing the real emotions of those who were to fight in it. As Swain
explains,

I believe that the whole process of being able to travel with the national guard
unit was important to do, because it put a personal face on a big story. We saw
real live people . . . not just those in the prime of their youth, but forty-year olds
with children for example . . . I remember sitting with them on Army cots talking
to them about their fears, with the camera running. (Interview, January 6, 1992)

With the cameras on, Swain talked to the men and women who made
up the unit about their fears and about commitment to American principles. Viewers were thus able to identify with the soldiers—to put a
personal face on the Gulf War crisis.

Those who made up the national guard unit were as varied as many
other units fighting in the Gulf. Those who watched the interviews found
two people in particular to be the most memorable. One was a sixty-

year-old man who cooked for the unit; the other was the youngest member of the group, who had never flown on an airplane before. These personal encounters heightened a sense of reality as Swain recalls: "In 1990 to be flying on an airplane for the first time was one thing, but to be going off to war was really quite another experience" (Interview, January 6, 1992).

C-SPAN's role in this coverage was to provide a mirror of what was happening, to let various personalities involved in the war tell their individual stories. With crews in Saudi Arabia and Israel, the network was able to provide interviews not only with soldiers, but with the journalists who covered the war, hence allowing viewers to better understand the process of media coverage in general.

Call-In Shows

A fourth important aspect of C-SPAN's coverage was the call-in show format. Three hundred hours of C-SPAN coverage, over one fourth of its overall war coverage, centered on the public's reaction to the war. While the C-SPAN audience is considered somewhat specialized and limited, this by no means undercut the importance of these calls in identifying concerns and perceptions about the Persian Gulf War. The anonymity that comes with a call, identified only in terms of geographic location, offered an unbridled way to express viewpoints without fear of repercussion or direct scorn.

With over three hundred hours in calls, at an average of fifteen to twenty calls per hour, C-SPAN received well over 6,000 calls from the United States and several other countries during the Gulf War. Lamb describes the wide variability of audience types following C-SPAN coverage:

The swing goes all the way from the morning that we got a call from a Jew in a small town in Israel, all the way to an Arab calling from San Rafael, California. So you had three hours the one way and seven hours the other, a time span of 10 hours. . . . For those here in this country watching, it is a global village because they hear voices from all over the world. (Interview, January 6, 1992)

This global village becomes even more meaningful in times of crisis and war. During the first week of the Persian Gulf War, C-SPAN's continual coverage of the happenings prompted over 1,600 calls from people around the country and around the world (Barton 1991: S–1). Frequently, C-SPAN had no guest, and just provided an open forum for citizens to call in, with only a moderator to identify incoming calls and to screen out anyone who had called within the past thirty days.[3] Over eight hundred cities and seven foreign nations were represented as the network kept its phone lines open nearly round-the-clock, allowing viewers to offer their positions on the war, hearing analysis from military experts, congressional representatives, journalists, and historians.

Susan Swain describes the "national catharsis" that went on during this continuous coverage:

People needed an outlet to call up and say "I'm scared," or "I just want to support the troops" or whatever. And to be in a place where other people were worried about the same thing. . . . everybody was talking . . . the other networks were unable to give words to those folks, and that's what I think is important, after all, that the average citizen who has a stake in it has a voice. (Interview, January 6, 1992)

These calls gave voice to a public that challenged America's right to be involved in the conflict, questioned tactical decisions made by military forces, supported the president's handling of the crisis, and celebrated America's quick and decisive victory. By analyzing a segment of the calls made during the Persian Gulf War, the remainder of this chapter looks at a sample of call-in shows during the war for patterns of talk which occur, the major topics mentioned, and the ways in which people talk about the war.

TALK ABOUT THE WAR

In an effort to understand the various citizen perceptions of war, and to move beyond polling reports provided by the various networks, this section looks at some of the general tendencies in the ways the public talked about the Persian Gulf War. Thirty-six hours of C-SPAN viewing time was recorded over a six-week period between January 16 and February 28, 1991. This period included major events such as the first announcement of the bombing of Baghdad, George Bush's State of the Union Address, and the decision to begin the ground war. Of the hours recorded and analyzed, 512 calls, approximately 15 percent of the call-ins during this period of time, were collected and evaluated for the ways citizens discussed the war, the role of the president, and specific issues surrounding U.S. involvement in the Gulf. Each call was coded by two trained evaluators who listened for the sex and location of each caller, the major topics discussed, and the styles of talk each caller used.[4]

Caller Profiles

Forty-eight states and three American territories were represented in the sample, and one call was coded from Switzerland. Each geopolitical region within the United States was represented, with the Pacific West having the greatest representation with 32 percent of the calls.[5] California had by far the greatest representation, with ninety calls to the network.

Of the eight geopolitical regions in the United States, the Pacific West led with 25 percent of 126 calls, followed next in line with 82 calls from the Deep South. The least represented regions were New England and West Central with 6 percent and 3 percent, respectively. Male callers dominated the sample by 64 percent, with eighty-one calls from the Pacific West, followed by the Mid-Atlantic region with sixty-two calls. The Pacific West also had the greatest number of female callers, followed by the East Central region.

Primary Themes

Coders identified three major topic areas for attitudes regarding the Persian Gulf War. These areas included attitudes about U.S. involvement in the war, about the president's role in leading the allies, and about the anti-war protesters who maintained daily vigilances outside the White House gates.

Attitudes about the War

Various polling results tended to reveal overwhelming support for U.S. involvement in the Persian Gulf. For example, one *Washington Post* survey indicated that by February 24, 1991, 84 percent approved U.S. actions in the Gulf.[6] C-SPAN callers in this sample, however, were slightly different. Of the 512 calls coded, 252 or 49 percent of those who called talked about their attitudes toward the war. Of those calls, 49 percent were in favor of U.S. involvement, and 51 percent were against it. Interestingly, the percentage of men and women for and against the war was roughly the same.

Those who supported the war based many of their arguments on the need for a U.S. presence in the Gulf and the necessity to thwart Middle East instability. Many who supported the war were clear to indicate that while war was not good, it was necessary in this situation to stop Saddam Hussein. Adopting much of the administration rhetoric, Saddam was compared to Hitler, an evil dictator who had to be stopped at any cost.

Many who took an anti-war stance argued that the United States should have given sanctions more time. A number of respondents identified oil profits as the key reason for our involvement in the gulf, and many saw Saddam in a much different light. A few argued that the United States created Saddam by supplying him with weapons, supporting him, and encouraging him over the years. Some called the United States hypocritical because of this earlier support. Others were concerned about who, ultimately, would pay for the costs of the war.

Attitudes toward the President

Support for the president was similar to polling results around the country, though not as dramatic as the 90 percent support identified by *The Washington Post* (Morin 1991: A14). Two hundred and eight calls (40 percent) focused specifically on George Bush and his role as president during the war. Interestingly, though more callers in this sample were against the war overall, more people (58 percent) supported the president's role in directing the war. Callers did not strongly support the war, but did seem to respect the competence of the president in carrying out an unpopular policy.

Callers referred to George Bush's presidential power in revealing ways. Whether they talked about the power he had to conquer Saddam, or to lead the nation in the right direction, those who supported Bush agreed that he was able to make the right decisions in leading the war effort. Appeals to nationalism and patriotic spirit were foremost in talk about the president. A number of callers remarked that it was up to the president and the country to uphold freedom around the world. One caller argued that "nobody else will fight like the United States" (C-SPAN Call-In, January 16, 1991). Another concluded that "we have no choice but to uphold freedom around the world" (C-SPAN Call-In, January 16, 1991). Recognizing that the U.S. role has always been to rescue the world from the clutches of tyranny, many callers observed that it was the United States's duty to defend the world, and that George Bush could heroically lead the nation in that effort.

Those who perceived the president's actions as unfavorable saw Bush as dictatorial and even villainous. One caller talked about the imperialistic presidency, remarking that the media should "uncover Bush's real reasons for going to war, and ask why the imperialist president is sacrificing the blood and bones of soldiers" (C-SPAN Call-In, January 18, 1991). Another caller drew an analogy between Ronald Reagan and George Bush. "Reagan," he argued, "was a dictator, and therefore, so is his predecessor" (C-SPAN Call-In, January 18, 1991).

A number of callers questioned Bush's motives in getting the United States into war in the first place. Some attributed his interest in Kuwait to foreign oil dependency. Others remarked that the president's excessive interest in the war blinded his ability to wait out the sanctions. His "moral outrage" was selective, ignoring the atrocities in China and Lithuania, hypocritically noting only what seemed to be in the nation's best interest.

Those who criticized Bush, especially following major addresses such as the State of the Union speech, argued that Bush's leadership in the Gulf was merely a distraction from the domestic agenda, especially the economy. Many citizens were concerned about the unemployment rate, the nation's inability to pay its debts, and the increasing costs of the war. They viewed presidential speechmaking as "empty rhetoric," and "phoney baloney" ploys that distracted the country from more pressing issues.

Attitudes about Protesters

Some networks, including C-SPAN, ran coverage of the ceaseless protesting outside the White House. To the beat of continuous drums, rallies were held in Lafayette Square, and signs proclaimed that the United States supported death and destruction. These protests sparked many responses from callers. One hundred and fifteen callers (22 percent) talked about the anti-war protesters in front of the White House. Almost two-thirds (64 percent) of the calls were against their actions, and 36 percent supported them. More women (71 percent) were against the protests than men (60 percent).

Those who talked against the protesters argued that the objectors were undermining the president's authority to appropriately handle the Middle East crisis. Equating protest against the war to protest against the soldiers, the United States, and George Bush himself, many callers claimed that the protesters were an affront to socially accepted uses of power. One caller actually thanked the protesters for "giving Hussein false hope that the president would weaken," arguing that they would mislead Saddam into thinking that the United States was against the president (C-SPAN Call-In, January 19, 1991).

As part of the appeals against anti-war beliefs, the protesters were identified as undemocratic, and the horror of burning or defacing the American flag became a focal point for discussion. Some argued that the war was an important enough issue to warrant support for Bush's efforts to ban the defamation of this national emblem, and called, once again, for a flag-burning amendment.

The major concern for many of the callers who objected to the protests was the effect the protestations could have on the soldiers' morales. Callers overwhelmingly supported the troops, and many reasoned that when morale suffered, lives would also be threatened. One caller argued that the protesters would actually increase the killings; another remarked that the protests were "full of liberals who never support war or the president."

On the other hand, those who supported the protests cited the Constitution as the ultimate arbiter for their right to protest. While many did not agree with the aim of the protests, they supported their Constitutional rights and expressed respect for the protesters' efforts.

Subordinate Themes

Beyond the dominant attitudes about the Persian Gulf conflict, subordinate themes existed, which also revealed interesting talk about the war.

Support for Veterans

Twenty-three callers (4 percent) identified themselves as veterans, retired military, or current military personnel and, of those who talked about the war, 58 percent supported the U.S. effort, 42 percent opposed it. Most military callers were against the protesters with the exception of one Vietnam veteran who was adamantly against U.S. involvement in the war.

In addition to military identification, many expressed concerns about all veterans, but especially those who had served in Vietnam. One caller remarked that the Persian Gulf War would "finally vindicate the Vietnam vets." Other callers expressed concern about how the veterans would be cared for after the war.

Media Coverage of the War

Thirty-five callers (7 percent) talked directly about the way media was covering the war. Of those who called, over half were critical of the coverage. Many callers agreed that the media should be censored, that too much information was being relayed to the public. Others argued that the media, especially CNN, was controlled by Saddam. Those who mentioned C-SPAN's coverage took both positions. Some liked the way the network covered the war, especially how the American people were allowed to present their perspectives; others claimed that the network was biased in coverage "just like all the other networks."

Many of those who were against the war were especially critical of media coverage, accusing the media of only showing one side of the story, and one caller accused CNN of faking newscasts (C-SPAN Call-In, January 20, 1991). Some were especially critical of CNN, arguing that the network was a tool of Saddam, and that the network was sending a wrong signal to the American public. One caller observed that "the coverage glamorized war, making it appear like a video game" (C-SPAN Call-In, January 20, 1991).

The Oil Industry

A smaller group of people (4 percent) talked specifically about the oil industry and its role in the Persian Gulf War. Motives for U.S. involvement, they argued, were couched in concerns for maintaining oil interests. One caller accused Bush of being "an oil-profit motivated imperialist president" (C-SPAN Call-In, January 24, 1991). Several argued that the United States was exchanging "blood for oil" as their justification for not supporting U.S. efforts.

STYLES OF DISCOURSE

In addition to the specific talk about the war, coders also considered the styles of discourse, the ways people put forward their arguments about the war. Three areas were considered in this analysis: whether a caller asked a question or just made a statement, the dominant language used to make a point, and the types of proof (stories, analogies, examples, identification, and supporting evidence) used to support his or her arguments. The following sections summarize the findings:

Questions versus Statements

Far more statements were made than questions asked by the callers, yet, it is interesting to note that men tended to ask more questions than women. Of the total sample, 28 percent of the male callers asked questions, compared to 19 percent of the female callers. This finding is statistically significant, based upon a .005 level of confidence.[7]

This result is intriguing because it begins to address some of the ways men and women may differ when they participate in call-in shows. Studies regarding the differences between men and women's communication patterns, for example, have generally found that women tend to ask more tag questions than men (Pearson et al. 1985: 113). Tag questions, statements followed by questions such as "the movie was good, don't you think?", are often used when more information is needed, or when trying to keep conversations going (Pearson et al. 1985: 114). Additionally, the use of questions by women, often perceived as an indirect form of request, may indicate sensitivity and politeness (Tannen 1990: 225). For the anonymous C-SPAN caller, the use of questions, and the types of questions asked, can provide rich data for gender comparisons. In the case of talk about the Persian Gulf War, for example, the comfort provided in the anonymity of the phone call may have enabled women to express ideas with greater confidence. At the very least, for a highly emotional issue such as war, the different patterns of response, and the ways women specifically talk about the war, could be significant study in itself.

The Language of War

It is interesting to note how the language of war tends to permeate the public psyche, especially the words of the presidency. Kathleen Jamieson talks about those memorable phrases that become an important part of what citizens remember about various presidencies, those "epit-omizing phrases and sentences . . . most generative of collective assent" (1988: 91). These synecdochic phrases are evident in citizen talk about the war as some C-SPAN callers adopt the president's rhetoric for their own. The phrase "New World Order," while not statistically significant, is mentioned enough times to be noteworthy. As a synecdoche for Bush's vision of the post-war world, a world respectful of international law, kept in line by high-tech weaponry and ballistic defense systems, this phrase was recognized by a number of callers who supported the president. Discussion about patriot missiles and Scud attacks also became a natural part of the vocabulary as people praised the war effort and Bush's responsibility as commander-in-chief.

Some synecdochic phrases also tended to backfire for the president. For example, phrases such as "a kinder, gentler nation" and "New World Order" reverse their impact with citizens concerned about the president's show of too much power, especially as the incessant Allied bombing continued to devastate Iraq. Some callers asked "what has happened to our kinder, gentler nation" while others appeared to be skeptical about the nature of Bush's "New World Order," wondering what the new order really entailed for the future.

Types of Proof

Several types of proof or support for arguments was evident in this sample of citizen talk about the war. Specific argument types such as examples, analogies, and story-telling, were used as well as identification and supporting evidence.

Argument by Example

By far the most popular way of presenting a position during a phone call, representative examples often guided the viewer's opinion of the president and his Persian Gulf policy, framing positions about U.S. involvement. Whether one discussed an example of Saddam's show of force, or identified an instance of American supremacy, a significant example could shape one's entire perspective about the war, focusing attention on a single incident that guided perceptions, and therefore conclusions about the war's legitimacy.

Argument by Analogy

Whether a caller drew a comparison between Vietnam and the Persian Gulf, or between the leadership tactics of Bush and Saddam, analogies often represented bipolar extremes. They tended to set up dichotomies where one side of the equation represented all that was good and worth fighting for, and the other side depicted the evil that must be conquered, or eliminated. Sometimes the analogies were not representative—there were far too many differences than similarities in the comparisons being made. Nevertheless, Richard Weaver recognized this type of argumentation as one of the strongest and most ethical that can be presented (1953: 17), and 7 percent of those who called used this reasoning process to make arguments about the war.

Story-telling

Another type of argument occurs in the stories callers provide for the listening audience. Story-telling is an important way people express their opinions and values. This was evidenced by the former soldier who relayed his experience of war in an effort to criticize anti-war protests against the president, or the wife of a marine who told of her young children who couldn't understand why their father was not home anymore. The stories of war identified heroes and villains and isolated important morals for future decision making. They provided emotional narratives with which many callers could identify—stories that tended to bind a culture and provide a coherent vision of America's role in the world, and the leaders who guide that role in a time of war.

Identification Strategies

For some callers, identification was an important aspect of this form of public participation. While names are rarely mentioned, vocations and affiliations are. Callers identified themselves as war veterans, members of military families, teachers and professors, high school and college students. Using identification strategies as a starting point, by either defining an affiliation or recognizing a mutual scapegoat, callers shared their individual perceptions about Bush and the war, providing an important frame of reference for their statements.

Supporting Evidence

A final strategy worth noting is the use of evidence to support arguments. Evidence usually took the form of quotations provided from various sources. A number of callers quoted letters from soldiers, the Bible, and their ministers to make arguments about the justification of war. One woman read part of a letter from her husband to support her claim that the soldiers were being hurt by the anti-war protesters. Another caller quoted the Bible as evidence that the United States should not be fighting in the war.

These styles of discourse, while only briefly discussed in this context, are worth considering because they reveal important patterns in the ways people express concerns about the war. Each style apparent in this sample is worthy of an entire essay on language and reasoning patterns, but for purposes of this chapter, they serve as useful starting points for further analysis.

CONCLUSION

The public voice supplied through the call-ins provides a rich area of research for scholars interested in how the average citizen talked about America's involvement in the war and the implications of that involvement. The electronic town square, couched in an anonymity that encourages free expression of ideas, provides a resource that goes beyond the polls and the public approval ratings, to the heart of how Americans talk. The evidence in this study suggests that call-in shows can provide a meaningful way for people to express viewpoints and ask questions, in essence, to engage in public debate about the political process.

Sustaining Meaning in a Crisis

C-SPAN's coverage of the Persian Gulf War, the emotional debates, the endless military briefings, the on-the-spot interviews with those involved in the war provided an element of coverage that few networks could match. Providing an outlet for people to express their views, for the average citizen to voice outrage over what was happening to the world, was perhaps the most important service the cable industry could provide.

Lamb describes the powerful emotions communicated by many of the callers during the first week after the air war had begun:

It's pretty hard to explain it unless you hear people's voices, but you could tell as you went through that period where people were coming from . . . what you're struck by is that the voices were so sincere. Whether it was a World War II veteran who might have been disabled talking about his own commitment, or whether it was a young person saying the war was a dumb idea, or the opposite, or whether it was a mother with a son, there were a lot of tears. You could hear a lot of tears through the sounds of their voices, about people who were afraid, who were sad. You heard a lot of people who were macho "America go for it, clean it up, get over Vietnam." It's just very real. (Interview, January 6, 1992)

The call-in format was an important outlet for average citizens to discuss how the war was evolving and express concern about its outcome.

Given the fragmented and isolated world that we live in, the call-in program provided an important means of identification for viewers, enabling the public to realize that in times of war there were others who shared similar hopes and fears. Kenneth Burke's writings about identification as a significant part of rhetorical action is useful to this discussion. With regard to the identification process he explains:

A is not identical with his colleague, B. But insofar as their interests are joined, A is *identified* with B. Or he may *identify himself* with B even when their interests are not joined, if he assumes that they are, or is persuaded to believe so. . . . In being identified with B, A is "substantially one" with a person other than himself. Yet at the same time he remains unique. . . . Thus he is both joined and separate, at once a distinct substance and consubstantial with another.[8] (1989: 180)

Disparate voices blending together, voicing similar concerns and common enemies is indeed one of the most powerful aspects of the C-SPAN call-in show. In times of war, when individuals who watch from the sidelines may feel powerless and frustrated, the ability to identify together provides a powerful connection for thousands of people.

Certainly another important aspect of sustaining meaning in times of crisis is the puissant characteristic of story-telling. Walter Fisher recognizes the importance of stories in the building of his narrative paradigm, noting that humans are essentially storytellers and that "the world is a set of stories which must be chosen among to live the good life in a process of continual recreation" (1984: 8). The concepts of narrative probability—that which constitutes a coherent storyline, and narrative fidelity—those stories that ring true with individual experiences, summarize the way story-telling is a central part of the natural socialization process (1988: 8).

Callers contributed powerful narratives about war and about their reactions to unfolding events in the Persian Gulf. As people told their own stories, a coherent sense of rationality was maintained during the extremely chaotic and disordered wartime situation. Hence, the totality of the call-ins moved beyond catharsis, a mere venting of hostilities, to linking the people to some sense of reality, enabling those who listened to maintain a small grip on the escalating chaos. In this sense, the network provided a true "town square" phenomenon, letting people identify together, tell their stories, and attempt to make some sense of the chaotic atmosphere of war.

Moving Beyond Military Control

For years to come scholars will undoubtedly address the problems with media pools and the military control of information presented to the American public. To a great degree, military control of information was enhanced by the soundbite phenomenon so prevalent during election years. Journalists who watched and reported on military briefings, or who tried to summarize footage from the media pool, provided the public with only a limited understanding of the war. C-SPAN, on the other hand, moved beyond the fragmentation of controlled information by enabling the public to watch and determine for themselves the meaning behind the various actions of war.

Additionally, C-SPAN's focus on the *process* of coverage was important because it contextualized the information provided to the public. Allowing journalists, soldiers, and military leaders to talk to the public about the evolving strategies enabled viewers to better understand, and gain a context for, various decision making. For example, Deborah Amos of National Public Radio talked about the use of the media pools in covering the war:

We work off a media pool, and that makes it like a giant jigsaw puzzle . . . one tag team of reporters is out in the field . . . and what we have to do is try to piece it all together and sort out details, facts, and find out what happened. (Barton 1991: S4)

By providing a forum for journalists, soldiers, strategists, and scholars to share their opinions about the war, C-SPAN contributed to the flow of information by focusing on the process of war rather than just providing the storyline. Though much of the public may not be interested in the details of policy making and journalistic reporting, this kind of coverage provided a self-reflexive form of contextualizing—enabling the public to see that there are always more questions than answers in wartime.

Providing a Rich Resource for Investigation

It seems clear from this discussion that C-SPAN coverage provides a rich resource for scholars wishing to explore the unfolding of the war and the public debate that became part of its evolution. By furnishing alternate aspects of coverage, full military briefings, debates, and public talk, researchers have a wealth of information to explore about America's role in the Persian Gulf War.

Availability of material through C-SPAN is significant. The Purdue Archives houses all the networks' Gulf War coverage, and it is available for anyone to purchase. Additionally C-SPAN's liberal copyright policy encourages viewers to tape programs off the air and use them for research and teaching. In the event of future wars, as debate unfolds about American involvement around the world, C-SPAN should be considered a valuable resource for investigation.

By creating a system that allowed the people of the world to communicate with each other in a time of war, and by providing features different from the major networks, C-SPAN has reinvigorated the notion of the town square, and established a significant place in the annals of the television history. Its potential has only begun to be tapped, and in that lies its potency and power for the future.

NOTES

The author wishes to express appreciation to Claire C. Smith for the significant time she spent processing caller data into a workable computer analysis, to Star A. Muir for helpful suggestions and providing the right word at the right time, and to Edward Lang, Robyn McKibbin, Camille Schmidt, and Monica Wiley for their endless hours of commitment in analyzing and coding C-SPAN call-in shows.

1. The Purdue University Public Affairs Video Archives was founded in 1987 and houses all C-SPAN programming from that time. Catalogs are available that describe each program C-SPAN has done, in addition to the time and key people involved. For more information about the archives, contact Robert Browning, Director, Public Affairs Video Archives, Purdue University, 1025 Stewart Center, West Lafayette, IN 47907.

2. Press pool arrangements have been discussed in varying degrees throughout this book. The concept of the press pool was developed following the exclusion of the press during the 1983 invasion of Grenada, and has been the subject of debate between the Pentagon and media since its inception. From the Pentagon's perspective, press pools can limit access, control coverage and minimize the burden of having too many reporters around during a war crisis. On the other hand, many journalists view the press pool concept as limiting, disorganized, and as a central form of military censorship. During the Gulf War, the press pool served as one of the most significant methods for gathering information about the war. A press pool would cover the latest military maneuver and feed this footage to all the networks. C-SPAN carried a great deal of this press pool coverage. For more information about the relationship between the press and the military consult Richard Halloran's "Soldiers and Scribblers Revisited: Working with the Media," in *Newsmen and National Defense*, Lloyd J. Matthews, ed. (New York: Brassey's Inc., 1991), 131–41.

3. The thirty-day policy was established to allow as many people as possible opportunities to express their opinions on the network. Moderators of typical programs try to enforce this policy on a regular basis. For example, should a moderator recognize the voice of a caller, especially one from a familiar geographic location, then discretion may be used and the caller disconnected. The network maintains that only a few callers violate this policy.

4. Coders were trained in methods of rhetorical criticism, content analysis, and political communication. The results were instrumental in providing useful analysis and discussion in this chapter.

5. Geopolitical regions include the following breakdown: *New England*—Connecticut, Maine, Massachusetts, New Hampshire, Rhode Island, Vermont; *Middle Atlantic*—Delaware, District of Columbia, Maryland, New Jersey, New York, Pennsylvania; *East Central*—Illinois, Indiana, Michigan, Ohio, Wisconsin; *West Central*—Iowa, Kansas, Minnesota, Montana, Nebraska, North Dakota, South Dakota; *Border South*—Arkansas, Kentucky, North Carolina, Oklahoma, Ten-

nessee, Virginia, West Virginia; *Deep South*—Alabama, Georgia, Louisiana, Mississippi, South Carolina, Texas; *Mountain West*—Arizona, Colorado, Idaho, Montana, New Mexico, Utah, Wyoming; and *Pacific West*—Alaska, California, Hawaii, Nevada, Oregon, Washington (*The '88 Vote* [New York: Capital Cities/ABC, Inc., 1989], 831).

6. Polling results were based on a nationwide *Washington Post*/ABC *News* telephone poll of 514 randomly selected adults, 18 years of age and older (Richard Morin, "Public Support for War Surges with Start of Ground Assault," *The Washington Post*, February 26, 1991, A14).

7. Statistical testing was used to determine whether gender was an important factor in asking questions or making statements in telephone calls. A single-sample, chi-square test was used to assess the difference. The results showed that at a .005 significance level the research hypothesis, that men asked more questions than women, was accepted.

8. Emphases and gender use in original text.

BIBLIOGRAPHY

ABC News. *The '88 Vote*. New York: Capital Cities/ABC, Inc., 1989.

Barton, Mary Ann. "On the Phone with the War: Journalists Covering Desert Storm Talk with Viewers During Live Call-ins." *C-SPAN Update* 9 (February 3, 1991): S1–S4.

Browning, Robert. "Public Affairs Video Archives, Persian Gulf Programming." Unpublished report.

Burke, Kenneth. *On Symbols and Society*, Joseph R. Gusfield, ed. Chicago: University of Chicago Press, 1989.

C-SPAN. *C-SPAN in the Classroom: An Educator's Guide*. Washington, D.C. No date provided.

C-SPAN Call-In Programming, January 16, 1991, through January 22, 1991.

Fisher, Walter. "Narration as a Human Communication Paradigm: The Case of Public Moral Argument." *Communication Monographs* 51 (March 1984): 1–22.

Halloran, Richard. "Soldiers and Scribblers Revisited: Working with the Media." In *Newsmen and National Defense: Is Conflict Inevitable?*, Lloyd J. Matthews, ed. New York: Brassey's, Inc., 1991.

Jamieson, Kathleen. *Eloquence in an Electronic Age*. New York: Oxford University Press, 1988.

Lamb, Brian, et al. *C-SPAN: America's Town Hall*. Washington, D.C.: Acropolis Books Ltd., 1988.

Lamb, Brian. Interview with author. Washington, D.C. January 6, 1992.

Morin, Richard. "Public Support for War Surges with Start of Ground Assault." *The Washington Post* February 26, 1991, A6, A14.

Pearson, Judy C., Lynn H. Turner, and William Todd-Mancillas. *Gender and Communication*. Dubuque, Iowa: William C. Brown, 1985.

"Survey: More Young Viewers are Tuning in C-SPAN." *C-SPAN Update* 9 (March 3, 1991): 1, 3.

Swain, Susan. Interview with author. Washington, D.C., January 6, 1992.
Tannen, Deborah. *You Just Don't Understand: Women and Men in Conversation.*
    New York: William Morrow, 1990.
Weaver, Richard. *Ethics of Rhetoric.* Chicago: Henry Regnery, 1953.

Chapter Eight

News Viewing, Authoritarianism, and Attitudes Toward the Gulf War

Mary Beth Oliver, Marie-Louise Mares, and
Joanne Cantor

One of the most striking features of the war in the Persian Gulf was the level of support among Americans for U.S. military involvement. Throughout the war, various polls of public attitudes toward the conflict indicated that approval of America "having gone to war with Iraq" ranged from 75 percent to 84 percent (Roper 1991, reported in *The Public Perspective*). A CBS poll taken in early February found that 83 percent of respondents reported feeling "proud about what the United States is doing in the Persian Gulf" (also reported in *The Public Perspective* 1991).

The purpose of this chapter is to explore two questions. First, what variables predicted support for the war? And second, how did support for the war affect interpretations of media coverage of the conflict? In answering the first question, two possible predictors of war attitudes were considered. The first was a personality variable, authoritarianism; the second was a media variable, exposure to mass media coverage of the war.

Two studies were conducted to examine these relationships. The first study was an exploratory survey conducted on high school students, in which measures of news viewing and authoritarian punitiveness were correlated with support for the war. The second study was a replication and extension of the first survey. The sample consisted of college students rather than adolescents; an additional, more direct measure of authoritarianism was employed; and an experimental manipulation was utilized to test for the effects of support for the war on information interpretation.

AUTHORITARIANISM AND SUPPORT FOR THE GULF WAR

When Adorno, Frenkel-Brunswick, Levinson, and Sanford (1950) first described authoritarianism, they argued that it was a personality type indicated by nine major characteristics.[1] There has been subsequent debate about the number of characteristics that distinguish authoritarianism, and even whether measures of authoritarianism do more than reflect extreme conservatism (Duckitt 1985; Ray 1973, 1985). However, authoritarianism has consistently been found to be associated with attitudes that seem highly relevant to an individual's judgments about war, particularly when the war is against members of a different race or culture.

For example, Raden (1981) found that authoritarianism was positively correlated with support for the Vietnam War. There is also some suggestion that Vietnam veterans who were high in authoritarianism were more strongly in favor of the war, and tended to suffer from less guilt and depression upon their return, than individuals high in intraception (Strayer & Ellenhorn 1975).

The relationship between support for war and authoritarianism is not surprising when one considers some of the characteristics that are associated with authoritarianism. First, ethnocentrism has repeatedly been found to correlate positively with authoritarianism (Meloen et al. 1988). Van Ijzendoorn (1989), reporting on several studies conducted in The Netherlands, found that authoritarianism explained up to 67 percent of variance in ethnocentrism scores.

Second, authoritarianism is associated with aggression and punitive treatment of those with less power. Moghaddam and Vuksanovic (1990) found that authoritarianism was consistently negatively correlated with support for human rights (correlations ranged from $-.42$ to $-.66$). In addition, Ryckman, Burns, and Robbins (1986) found that authoritarians were more punitive when giving sentences to people committing serious crimes (though no more punitive toward people who committed less serious crimes). Finally, Altemeyer (1981) reported that authoritarianism was positively associated with longer recommendations of prison sentences for a person convicted of mugging or rape, but was negatively associated with recommendations of prison sentences for a person convicted of police brutality.

Third, although authoritarians tend to be aggressive toward those with less power, they simultaneously tend to be unquestioningly submissive to those in authority. McCann (1990) found that authoritarians indicated stronger preferences for presidential candidates they judged to be powerful, and Altemeyer (1981) reported that authoritarianism was positively correlated with acceptance of illegal acts committed by government officials such as censorship and illegal drug raids.

Given this pattern of ethnocentrism, punitiveness, and submission to strong authority figures, we predicted that:

H_1: There would be a positive correlation between authoritarianism and support for the war.

Several researchers have suggested that in times of threat, people become more authoritarian in their attitudes (Doty, Peterson, & Winter 1991; McCann & Stewin 1987). Therefore, one could argue that a correlation between authoritarianism and pro-war attitudes could indicate that popular support for the war led to increases in authoritarianism. In our first study, however, authoritarian punitiveness was measured before the outbreak of the war, and therefore could not have been *caused* by the conflict.

TELEVISION NEWS VIEWING AND SUPPORT FOR THE GULF WAR

The second predictor of war attitudes examined in this study was exposure to television coverage of the war. The outbreak of the war led to increased exposure to news coverage and, in particular, to increased television news viewing (Greenberg 1991; Greenberg, Cohen, & Li 1991). While there are few empirical analyses of media coverage of the war, anecdotal evidence suggests that the mass media presented U.S. involvement in a positive light, and encouraged identification among viewers with U.S. military in the Gulf (see Lee & Devitt 1991; McMasters 1991; O'Heffernan 1991).

For example, Naureckas (1991) noted that journalists covering the war typically used "we" when talking about the U.S. military, which implied that the journalists, the audience, and the military were one allied group. Naureckas also argued that there was a lack of media emphasis on opposition to U.S. involvement in the war. He cited a study done by Fairness and Accuracy in Reporting (FAIR) that examined the types of war-related sources used by ABC, CBS, and NBC nightly news. Of 878 on-air war-related sources, only one was a representative of a national peace organization, and less than 2 percent of the sources were protesters—about the same number of sources who were asked about how the war had affected their travel plans.

Naureckas further argued that journalists not only implied cohesion in America, but also tended to depict the war as a fight against one clearly identifiable villain, Saddam Hussein, rather than as a war against a nation of people. In addition, consequences of U.S. actions were discussed primarily in terms of the damage done to Saddam Hussein rather than in terms of damage done to soldiers and civilians in Iraq. Hallin (1991) also argued that as during the Vietnam War, the media's military analyses of the Gulf War were presented in language that removed any sense of the political meaning or human cost of the war.

Several studies support the idea that the media's coverage of the war was misleading or was misunderstood by some viewers. A survey conducted by Times Mirror Center for People and the Press (1991) found that the term "collateral damage" (a phrase frequently used to refer to civilian casualties and unintended damage from bombing) was misunderstood by 79 percent of respondents. The center then compared the level of concern reported when respondents were asked about "collateral damage caused by Allied bombing" to the amount of concern reported when respondents were asked about "the number of civilian casualties and other unintended damage." The results indicated that when the question referred to civilian casualties, twice as many people reported being very concerned as when the question asked about collateral damage.

Lewis, Jhally, and Morgan (1991) found that although 81 percent of their respondents knew the names of the missile used to shoot down Iraqi Scuds, very few knew information about the Middle East or U.S. foreign policy. The more the respondents reported watching television coverage of the war, the less they knew about the reasons for the war, and the less they knew of information that may have suggested inconsistencies in U.S. foreign policy.

Lewis et al. (1991) also found that heavy viewers were more likely than light viewers to report "strongly" supporting President Bush's decision to use military force against Iraq. These authors interpreted this finding as supportive of the idea that the media were engaging in selective misinformation, with less emphasis given to information that would make it more difficult to support the war. Furthermore, they argued that this pattern of news coverage was partly attributable to the economic structure of the major media organizations. These authors suggested that the fear of being accused of being "anti-American" and the need to supply advertisers with audiences in the "proper mindset" led media organizations to cover the war in a positive light.

Given that news coverage of the war seems to have presented the conflict in a favorable manner, we predicted that:

H_2: Exposure to news coverage of the war would be positively correlated with more favorable attitudes toward the war.

INTERPRETATIONS OF MEDIA COVERAGE OF THE GULF WAR

Unlike authoritarianism, which was measured before the war began (and hence could not have been caused by the war), news viewing co-occurred with attitude formation, making the direction of causality unclear. It is possible, as Lewis et al. (1991) strongly suggest, that exposure to biases in news coverage led to support for the war. On the other hand, it is also possible that people who held positive attitudes toward the war were motivated to attend to news about the conflict, particularly if the news coverage was relatively uncritical.

The substantial body of literature on the effects of group membership suggests that those who strongly identify with a group (in this case, the United States and, in particular, the U.S. military) are motivated to attend to positive information and screen out negative information about their group. Group members may even engage in selective interpretation of information in order to maintain the perception of their own group's superior performance (Park & Rothbart 1982; Rothbart, Dawes, & Park 1984; Sherif 1966; Sherif et al. 1961).

There is some evidence that this type of selective exposure and interpretation occurs in the political domain. Sweeney and Gruber (1984) reported on a survey conducted during the U.S. Senate Watergate hearings of 1973. They found that Nixon supporters reported less interest in, and paid less attention to Watergate-related matters than did McGovern supporters or people who were undecided. Nixon supporters also appeared to know less about the committee proceedings than the other two groups (*see also* Chaffee & Miyo 1983; Conover 1984; Cotton & Hieser 1980; Rhine 1967).

Other studies concerning perceptions of political debates have revealed similar patterns in terms of selective interpretation. For example, a New York Times/CBS poll conducted after the Carter–Ford debates showed very different interpretations of the event depending upon the respondents' political orientation (Apple 1976). Of the respondents supporting Ford, 66 percent thought that Ford had won the debate while only 14 percent thought that Carter had won. The reverse pattern was obtained for Carter supporters; 40 percent believed that Carter had won, while only 14 percent believed that Ford had won. Similar patterns of selective interpretation were also revealed in response to the Kennedy-Nixon debate (Kraus 1962).

Not surprisingly, group members report liking and trusting a source of information that favors their group more than a source of negative information. For example, Fulero and Fischhoff (1976) found that respondents who were satisfied with election results reported in the mass media rated the media more positively than respondents who were dissatisfied with the election results.

It is interesting to look at public perceptions of the mass media's performance during the Gulf War in the light of these findings. First, as surveys from the Times Mirror Center for the People and the Press (1991) indicate, Americans were largely pleased with media coverage of the war—over eight in ten Americans rated the coverage as good, with 45 percent rating it as excellent (for similar results see polls reported in *Roper* 1991, and Dennis et al. 1991). This strength of public support for the media may suggest that the media were saying things that the public wanted to hear (as in Fulero & Fischhoff 1976).

In addition, there is some indication that although the public may have been selectively misinformed as Lewis et al. (1991) suggest, the public were both aware of and in support of this misinformation. McLeod et al. (1991) reported that "many respondents seemed to want a 'sanitized' account of the war" (18). The majority of respondents preferred that the media not show wounded (69.6 percent) or dead soldiers (79.1 percent). In addition, 57.6 percent felt that the media should not show anti-war protests, nearly half felt that the government should be trusted to decide what information the people should hear (47.5 percent), and 40 percent of the respondents agreed that the media should only show information that "helps the war effort." (For similar results of national polls, see the report of Times Mirror Center for the People & the Press 1991, and Dennis et al. 1991.)

In order to examine the effects of attitudes toward the war on satisfaction with media coverage of the war, both studies reported in this chapter examined associations between attitudes toward the war and perceptions of television news coverage. In addition, the second study contained a manipulated magazine story about the war which subjects read and rated. In one condition the magazine article criticized Iraq, and in the other condition the magazine article was identical except that the target of criticism was the United States. Given prior research on selective exposure and interpretation, it was predicted that:

H_3: Positive attitudes toward the war would be positively associated with more favorable attitudes toward media coverage of the war.

H_4: There would be an interaction between support for the war and the manipulated news-story versions, with pro-war attitudes positively associated with favorable ratings of the story critical of Iraq, but negatively associated with ratings of the story critical of the United States.

In summary, the two studies reported in this chapter examined the relationship between authoritarianism and news viewing in war attitudes. In addition, an experimental manipulation of a news story was employed in the second study to examine selective perception of news coverage of the Gulf War as a function of war attitudes.

Study 1

Method

RESPONDENTS AND PROCEDURES

The participants in this study were selected from a group of ninety-three high school students who had participated in a previous study conducted in the fall of 1990. In the present study, telephone interviews were conducted with the high school students on February 27, 1991, one day before the cease fire was declared. Because interviewing was terminated after the war ended, only forty-seven of the ninety-three students were contacted. Of the forty-seven students contacted, thirty-six students (76.6 percent) agreed to participate in the interview. These thirty-six students consisted of sixteen males and twenty females, with a mean age of 15.7 ($SD = 0.99$).

The telephone interviews were conducted by trained undergraduate students. The interviewer first spoke with the student's parent and explained that the purpose of the interview was to gather information about high school students' attitudes toward the Gulf War. Subsequently, the interviewer explained the purpose of the interview to the student. Interviews were conducted only if the parent gave permission for his or her child to participate and if the student also agreed. No respondents in the present study were aware of the connection between the telephone interview and the previous study conducted in the fall of 1990.

MEASURES

Punitiveness

During their participation in the study conducted in the fall of 1990, respondents completed Altemeyer's (1988) Mean-Spiritedness scale. The Mean-Spiritedness scale includes eight scenarios that describe a person who breaks a social norm (e.g., uses drugs, lies to his or her parents, etc.) and subsequently suffers a misfortune or punishment as a consequence. The subscale of punitiveness employed in the present study is composed of items concerning how much the respondents agree or disagree that the people in the scenarios "got exactly what they deserve" when they suffered or were punished.[2] Altemeyer (1988) reported that the Mean-

Spiritedness scale was positively correlated with measures of authoritarianism, with measures of racial prejudice, with recommendations of longer prison sentences for a gay-rights activist described as being involved in a scuffle at a public demonstration, and with greater assignment of blame to a female prostitute who was murdered.

Because the Mean-Spiritedness scale was originally designed for use with college students, several minor revisions were employed to make the scale appropriate for the high school students in this sample. For example, several scenarios in the original scale describe individuals that the subject "may have *known* in high school or university." These scenarios were altered so that they would apply to students *currently* enrolled in high school. Respondents indicated their agreement or disagreement that the punished person in each scenario "got exactly what he/she deserved" by circling a number on a scale ranging from 1 (*not at all*) to 7 (*very, very much*). The mean of the responses across all scenarios was calculated to form the measure of punitiveness ($M = 4.71$, $SD = 1.22$, Cronbach's alpha $= .87$).

A one-way analysis of variance was conducted on the punitiveness scale to examine possible differences between the respondents who agreed to participate in the telephone interview, the respondents who declined to participate, and the respondents who were not contacted. No differences were revealed between the three groups ($F(2,90) = 0.91$, $p = .41$).

Media Use

During the telephone interview, respondents were first asked to report their normal amount of television viewing on a given weekday and weekend. Subsequently, respondents were asked to report the amount of time per day they had been viewing television news during the Gulf War. Respondents were also asked to report their attitudes toward news coverage of the war on a scale ranging from 1 (*very negative*) to 5 (*very positive*).

Gulf War Attitudes

To assess attitudes toward the Gulf War, respondents were presented with a list of people and topics associated with the war in the Gulf and were asked to report how positively or negatively they felt about each one. This list included six items: America's use of military force, American soldiers, Saddam Hussein, war protesters, George Bush, and U.S. patriotism. Responses were recorded on scales ranging from 1 (*very negative*) to 5 (*very positive*).

Results

ATTITUDES TOWARD THE GULF WAR

An examination of each of the items used to assess attitudes toward the war revealed that most respondents were supportive of U.S. actions. Sixty-seven percent reported positive attitudes toward America's use of military force ($M=3.86$, $SD=0.87$), 83 percent reported positive attitudes toward U.S. soldiers ($M=4.25$, $SD=0.73$), 100 percent reported negative attitudes toward Saddam Hussein ($M=1.36$, $SD=0.49$), 61 percent reported negative attitudes toward war protesters ($M=2.28$, $SD=0.74$), 75 percent reported positive attitudes toward George Bush ($M=3.92$, $SD=0.65$), and 83 percent reported positive attitudes toward U.S. patriotism ($M=4.19$, $SD=0.71$). Two items, attitudes toward war protesters and attitudes toward Saddam Hussein, were inverted, and the mean of the six responses was calculated to form a war-attitudes scale. Higher scores on this scale reflected more positive attitudes toward the war in the Gulf. The mean of this scale was 4.10 ($SD=0.45$), with a reliability of .70 (Cronbach's alpha).

PREDICTORS OF GULF WAR ATTITUDES

Regression analyses were used to examine variations in scores on the war-attitudes scale. The first analysis used punitiveness as a predictor, with gender of respondent entered on the first step of the analysis as a control variable.[3] The results showed that punitiveness was significantly positively associated with favorable attitudes toward the war (R^2 change $= .21$, $\beta = .46$, $F(1,33) = 9.91$, $p<.01$).

The second analysis used the amount of news viewing as a predictor of war attitudes. Gender of respondent and time spent viewing television per weekday and weekend were entered into the equation on the first step as control variables. The results showed that time spent viewing television per weekday and weekend were unrelated to scores on the war-attitudes scale (weekday: $\beta = -.10$, $t = -0.45$, $p=.66$; weekend: $\beta = .12$, $t = .51$, $p=.61$). However, news viewing was significantly positively associated with more favorable attitudes toward the war (R^2 change $= .13$, $\beta = .40$, $F(1,31) = 5.44$, $p<.05$). Together, punitiveness and news viewing accounted for 25.4 percent of the variance in attitudes toward the Gulf War ($F(2,32) = 6.40$, $p<.01$).

Although the former analysis used news viewing as a predictor of war attitudes, it is possible that the news coverage of the war was more appealing to viewers who were supportive of U.S. actions. In other words, attitudes toward the war may be seen as a predictor of news viewing rather than (or in addition to) news viewing as a predictive of attitudes, particularly if news coverage was perceived as especially favorable among those who supported the war. Therefore, a regression analysis was employed using the war-attitudes scale as a predictor of attitudes toward television coverage of the war. As in the previous two analyses, gender of respondent was entered on the first step of the regression equation. The results showed that positive attitudes toward the Gulf War were significantly related to more favorable attitudes toward news coverage (R^2 = change = .21, β = .48, $F(1,33)$ = 8.56, p < .01).

Study 2

Method

SUBJECTS AND PROCEDURES

The subjects in the second study were sixty-five undergraduate students enrolled in communication arts classes during the summer session of 1991. The sample included thirty-four males and thirty-one females with a mean age of 21.45 (SD = 2.92).

Subjects were told that their participation would involve completing two different questionnaires for two separate studies, one study concerning attitudes about social issues and the other concerning attitudes about television and news coverage of the Gulf War. Subjects completed the two sets of questionnaires in random order. In order to convince the subjects that the two studies were unrelated, the questionnaires were printed on different color paper, each questionnaire contained duplicate items concerning the subjects' gender, academic year, and age, and subjects were instructed to complete the questionnaires in the order that they were presented to insure that "answers on one questionnaire would not affect answers on the second questionnaire."

MEASURES

Punitiveness and Authoritarianism

As in the first study, subjects completed Altemeyer's (1988) Mean-Spiritedness scale from which a measure of punitiveness was computed. Scores could range from 1 to 7, with higher scores reflecting higher levels of punitiveness (M = 4.40, SD = 1.12; Cronbach's alpha = .82).

In addition to completing the punitiveness scale, subjects also completed a modified version of Altemeyer's (1988) Right-wing Authoritarianism (RWA) scale. This scale has been shown to correlate positively with punitiveness, prejudice, negative attitudes toward homosexuality, and self-righteousness (Altemeyer 1988). In the present study, items on the RWA scale that pertained directly to attitudes toward protesters were dropped from this scale because one of the measures of Gulf War attitudes pertained to war protesters. The final authoritarianism scale used in this study consisted of twenty-five items pertaining to attitudes toward authority, obedience, religion, sexuality, crime, punishment, and discipline, with subjects indicating their agreement or disagreement with each item on a scale ranging from 1 (*strongly disagree*) to 7 (*strongly agree*). Responses were coded such that higher scores reflected greater endorsement of authoritarian attitudes ($M = 3.91$, $SD = 0.82$; Cronbach's alpha = .87).

News Viewing and Gulf War Attitudes

In the questionnaire concerning news viewing and Gulf War attitudes, subjects were first asked to indicate the average amount of time per day that they normally spent watching television news. Subsequently, subjects were asked to report the average amount of time per day that they spent watching television news during the Gulf War. Subjects were then asked to rate their perceptions of television news reporting of the Gulf War by three adjectives: accurate, fair, and interesting. Subjects rated their perceptions on scales ranging from 1 (*not at all*) to 7 (*very much*). The mean score on these ratings was calculated to form a news-perception scale, with higher scores reflecting more favorable perceptions of news coverage of the Gulf War. The mean score on this scale was 4.73 ($SD = 0.95$), with a reliability of .69 (Cronbach's alpha).

To assess attitudes toward the Gulf War, subjects in this study were presented with the same list of people and topics used to assess war attitudes in the first study, with subjects indicating how positive or negative they felt about each one on scales ranging from 1 (*very negative*) to 7 (*very positive*). In addition, subjects were asked to indicate how positive or negative they felt about U.S. involvement in the Gulf War, and to indicate how justified or unjustified the United States was in bombing targets that were close to civilian populations. Responses to these items were recorded on seven-point scales ranging from 1 (*very negative/not at all justified*) to 7 (*very positive/very justified*).

In the final portion of the questionnaire, subjects were presented with a photocopy of a news story and were told that the story had been published in a national magazine during the Gulf War. In actuality, the news story was composed of excerpts from two news commentaries published in *Newsweek* and *The Progressive* (Cronkite 1991; "Propaganda" 1991), both of which were critical of U.S. military censorship during the Gulf War. However, two versions of the news story were created: one version critical of U.S. war propaganda, and one version critical of Iraqi war propaganda. A desk-top publishing program and laser printer were used in the format of the news stories to increase the appearance of authenticity. (Figure 8.1 contains photocopies of both versions of the news story used in this portion of the study.) After reading the bogus news story, subjects rated their perceptions of the stories using the same three adjectives used to rate their perceptions of television news coverage of the war: accurate, fair, and interesting. Responses were recorded on seven-point scales ranging from 1 (*not at all*) to 7 (*very much*), and the mean of the responses was calculated to form a story-perception scale ($M = 3.97$, $SD = 0.97$, Cronbach's alpha = .71).

Results

ATTITUDES TOWARD THE GULF WAR

Although attitudes toward U.S. involvement in the Gulf War did not appear to be quite as positive as in the first study, the majority of subjects in the second study did express positive attitudes on most items. Fifty-five percent of the subjects reported positive attitudes toward U.S. involvement in the war ($M = 4.46$, $SD = 1.85$), 86 percent reported positive attitudes toward U.S. soldiers ($M = 6.12$, $SD = 1.16$), 97 percent reported negative attitudes toward Saddam Hussein ($M = 1.52$, $SD = 0.81$), 43 percent reported negative attitudes toward war protesters ($M = 3.88$, SD-1.93), 51 percent reported positive attitudes toward George Bush ($M = 4.34$, $SD = 1.74$), 60 percent reported positive attitudes toward U.S. use of military force ($M = 4.52$, $SD = 1.89$), and 68 percent reported positive attitudes toward patriotism ($M = 5.02$, $SD = 1.65$). One item for which the majority of respondents did not report favorable responses concerned U.S. bombing of targets near civilian populations; 52 percent reported that the United States was unjustified in such actions ($M = 3.82$, $SD = 2.08$). Items were recoded so that higher scores reflected positive attitudes toward U.S. involvement in the war, and the mean of the scores was calculated to form a war-attitudes scale. The mean of the war-attitudes scale was 4.86 ($SD = 1.31$), with a reliability of .90 (Cronbach's alpha).

Predictors of Gulf War Attitudes

The first analysis of the war-attitudes scale used punitiveness and authoritarianism as predictors in a regression analysis, with gender of subject entered on the first step of the equation as a control variable. The results showed that punitiveness and authoritarianism together accounted for a significant amount of the variance in the war-attitudes scale (R^2 change = .32, $F(2,61) = 14.10$, $p < .0001$), with both predictor variables positively related to favorable attitudes toward the war (pu-

Figure 8.1
News Stories Used in the Experimental Portion of the Second Study

Critical of the U.S.

Propaganda War
by Pat Snyder

In preparation for the now eminent ground war, the Bush administration has launched a massive propaganda offensive designed to revive faltering public enthusiasm and win support for the unsupportable. The U.S. military is trampling on the civilians' right to know.

President Bush and other officials are deploying every conceivable deception and distortion: that's the time-honored tactic governments use when they are determined to lead their people into war. But this type of propaganda is doing a disservice—not only to the American people, but also to history and to our country's own best interests.

After World War II most Germans protested that they did not know what went on in the heinous Nazi concentration camps. It is just possible that they did not. But this claim of ignorance did not absolve them from blame: they had complacently permitted Hitler to do his dirty business in the dark. They raised little objection, most even applauded, when he closed their newspapers and clamped down on free speech. Certainly our leaders are not to be compared with Hitler, but today, Americans are not being permitted to see and hear the full story of what our military forces are doing in an action that will reverberate long into our nations' future.

Critical of Iraq

Propaganda War
by Pat Snyder

In preparation for the now eminent ground war, Iraqi officials have launched a massive propaganda offensive designed to revive faltering public enthusiasm and win support for the unsupportable. The Iraqi military is trampling on the civilians' right to know.

Saddam Hussein is deploying every conceivable deception and distortion: that's the time-honored tactic governments use when they are determined to lead their people into war. But this type of propaganda is doing a disservice—not only to the Iraqi people, but also to history and its own best interests.

After World War II most Germans protested that they did not know what went on in the heinous Nazi concentration camps. It is just possible that they did not. But this claim of ignorance did not absolve them from blame: they had complacently permitted Hitler to do his dirty business in the dark. They raised little objection, most even applauded, when he closed their newspapers and clamped down on free speech. Certainly Iraq is not to be compared with Hitler, but today, Iraqi civilians are not being permitted to see and hear the full story of what their military forces are doing in an action that will reverberate long into their nations' future.

nitiveness: $\beta = .21$, $t = 1.95$, $p = .06$; authoritarianism: $\beta = .50$, $t = 4.63$, $p < .0001$).

The second analysis of war attitudes used time spent viewing news during the Gulf War as a predictor variable in a regression analysis, using both gender of subject and normal news viewing as control variables. Although normal news viewing was not significantly associated with attitudes toward the Gulf War ($\beta = -.009$, $t = -.07$, $p = .94$), news viewing during the Gulf War was significantly associated with higher scores on the war-attitudes scale (R^2 change $= .13$, $\beta = .50$, $F(1,61) = 9.13$, $p < .01$). Together, punitiveness, authoritarianism, and news viewing accounted for 36.7 percent of the variance in attitudes toward the Gulf War ($F(3,60) = 11.62$, $p < .0001$).

Perceptions of News of the Gulf War

Perceptions of Television News

A regression analysis was conducted to examine attitudes toward the Gulf War as a predictor of perceptions of television news coverage of the war. Gender of subject was entered on the first step of the analysis as a covariate. As in the first study, the results showed that favorable attitudes toward the war were significantly associated with more positive perceptions of news coverage of the conflict ($R^2 = .13$, $\beta = .37$, $F(1,62) = 9.61$, $p < .01$).

Perceptions of News Stories

To examine perceptions of the bogus news story as a function of both the story version (critical of the United States, critical of Iraq) and attitudes toward the war, a regression analysis was conducted on the news-perception scale. Gender of subject was entered on the first step of the equation as covariate, the war-attitudes scale and the story version on the second step to test for main effects, and the product of the war-attitudes scale and the story version on the third step as a test for the interaction between these two variables (Cohen 1978). The story version was dummy coded as 0 for the version that was critical of the United States, and 1 for the version that was critical of Iraq.

As Table 8.1 shows, the regression analysis revealed no main effects for war attitudes or story version on perceptions of the news story. However, a significant War Attitudes × Story Version interaction was revealed. In order to further illustrate this interaction, two separate regression analyses examining the relationship between war attitudes and story perceptions were conducted for each of the story versions. Figure 8.2 illustrates the regression slopes of war attitudes on story

Table 8.1
Regression Analysis of Perceptions of the News Story as a Function of War Attitudes and Story Version

	ß	R^2 change	F
Step 1		.00	.09
Gender of Subject	-.04		
Step 2		.05	1.44
War Attitudes	.04		
Story Version	-.20		
Step 3		.14	10.30**
War Attitudes x Story Version Interaction	1.46**		

*$p<.05$ **$p<.01$

perceptions for each version of the story, and further illustrates that favorable attitudes toward the Gulf War were positively related to favorable perceptions toward the news story if the story was critical of Iraq ($p<.05$), but were negatively related to perceptions of the news story if the story was critical of the United States ($p=.07$).

Discussion

The results of the first study showed that both punitiveness and news viewing were significantly associated with positive attitudes toward the Gulf War. In the case of punitiveness, it seems safe to conclude that punitive attitudes *affected* attitudes toward the war given that punitiveness was measured before the war began. In the case of news viewing, however, the causal direction is less clear. While it may be that news viewing caused positive attitudes toward the war, it is equally possible that people with positive attitudes elected to watch the news more frequently. This interpretation seems particularly plausible given that positive attitudes toward the Gulf War were significantly associated with positive attitudes toward news coverage of the conflict. Therefore, the second study was conducted to replicate the results revealed in the first study, and to further explore the association between attitudes toward the war and perceptions of news coverage.

The results of the second study also showed that punitiveness and news viewing of television coverage of the Gulf War were positively related to favorable attitudes toward the conflict. This study also showed

Figure 8.2
Separate Regression Slopes of War Attitudes on Story Perceptions as a
Function of Story Version

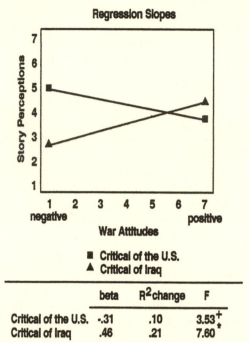

Regression Slopes

	beta	R^2change	F
Critical of the U.S.	-.31	.10	3.53[+]
Critical of Iraq	.46	.21	7.60[*]

$+p<.10$ $*p<.05$

that a more direct measure of authoritarianism was a particularly strong
predictor of positive attitudes toward U.S. involvement in the conflict.

The results of the second study also showed (as did the first study)
that positive attitudes toward the Gulf War were associated with more
favorable attitudes toward news coverage of the conflict. However, ratings of the bogus news story showed that positive attitudes toward the
Gulf War were associated with positive attitudes toward the news story
provided that the news story was critical of Iraq and/or not critical of the United
States.

Although the results of these two studies show strong and consistent
associations between authoritarian tendencies, news viewing, and positive attitudes toward the Gulf War, there are several limitations that
should not be overlooked. The first study had relatively few subjects
because it was limited to measuring attitudes of people who had previously been assessed for punitiveness. Despite the limited statistical
power created by the low sample size, however, significance of predic-
tion was revealed.

A second limitation involves the use of adolescents and college students as participants. Clearly, caution should be used in generalizing the results obtained in these two studies to other populations with wider variations in age and educational levels. However, Pan et al. (1991) large-scale random survey of adults in central New York showed findings similar to those reported in this study: supporters of the war were generally less critical of media coverage than were non-supporters. In addition, supporters were more likely to believe that the media gave too much attention to Iraq's point of view, and non-supporters were more likely to believe that the media gave too much attention to Bush's point of view. Given the consistency between the results obtained in the present studies and those reported by Pan et al. (1991), the limitations involved with the samples employed in the present research do not appear to have strongly distorted the findings.

A final limitation of the present research involves the timing of the two studies; the first study was conducted on the last day of the war, and the second study was conducted retrospectively. One might argue that attitudes toward U.S. involvement may have been more favorable once it was clear that the war had been won by the United States and allies. However, results of national polls suggest that once the war began, pro-war attitudes prevailed and were relatively consistent throughout the war, even toward the end and immediately afterwards. Therefore, although the timing of the two studies reported in this chapter is a limitation, it seems unlikely that the findings revealed were the result of interview scheduling.

To summarize, the results of these studies replicate previous work that suggests a link between authoritarianism and support for war, and they also provide evidence of a link between news viewing and supportive attitudes. While Lewis et al. (1991) suggest the latter correlation is largely attributable to pro-war coverage *creating* positive attitudes among viewers, we would suggest that the direction of causality could go the other way, and that ultimately the relationship is probably circular. Those who initially saw coverage of the war and developed pro-war attitudes may have then become selective in their exposure to, and interpretations of subsequent coverage. While this is not to deny that news coverage may have been biased in reporting the war in a positive light, it does suggest (as does McLeod et al.'s 1991 study of support for censorship) that this bias met with the approval of a substantial proportion of the audience.

NOTES

1. These nine characteristics include authoritarian submission, authoritarian aggression and punitiveness, conventionalism, anti-intraception, superstition

and stereotype, power and "tough-mindedness," destructiveness and cynicism, projectivity, and an exaggerated concern with sexual "goings-on."

2. Although punitiveness is only one characteristic of authoritarianism, this measure was used in the first study because this variable was measured as part of a previous study conducted before the war began. In the second study reported in this chapter, the punitiveness measure as well as a more direct measure of authoritarianism were employed.

3. Gender was used as a control variable in all analyses reported in this chapter because numerous studies and polls have shown that females consistently report less favorable attitudes toward the use of force than males (see Fite, Genest, and Wilcox 1990). In a review of national opinion polls conducted by the Roper Organization, NORC, Gallup, Louis Harris, and the Survey Research Center, Smith (1984) reported:

Women and men differ both in their use of violence and in the approval of violence across a wide range of social conditions including foreign affairs, social control and law enforcement, and interpersonal relations, and the difference is reasonably stable across time. (384)

BIBLIOGRAPHY

Adorno, T. W., E. Frenkel-Brunswick, D. J. Levinson, and R. N. Sanford. *The Authoritarian Personality*. New York: Harper, 1950.

Altemeyer, B. *Right-wing Authoritarianism*. Winnipeg, Canada: University of Manitoba Press, 1981.

Altemeyer, B. *Enemies of Freedom: Understanding Right-wing Authoritarianism*. San Francisco: Jossey-Bass, 1988.

Apple, R. W. "Voter Poll Finds Debate Aided Ford and Cut Carter Lead." *The New York Times*, Sept. 27, 1976, 1.

Chaffee, S. H., and Y. Miyo. "Selective Exposure and the Reinforcement Hypothesis: An Intergenerational Panel Study of the 1980 Presidential Campaign." *Communication Research* 10 (1983): 3–36.

Cohen, J. "Partialed Products *Are* Interactions; Partialed Powers *Are* Curve Components." *Psychological Bulletin* 85 (1978): 858–66.

Conover, P. J. "The Influence of Group Identifications on Political Perception and Evaluation." *The Journal of Politics* 46 (1984): 760–85.

Cotton, J. L., and R. A. Heiser. "Selective Exposure to Information and Cognitive Dissonance." *Journal of Research in Personality* 14 (1980): 518–27.

Cronkite, W. "What Is There to Hide?' Military Arrogance Keeps the Public in the Dark." *Newsweek*, Feb. 25, 1991, 43.

Dennis, E. E., D. Stebenne, J. Pavlik, M. Thalhimer, C. LaMay, D. Smillie, M. FitzSimon, S. Gazsi, and S. Rachlin. *The Media at War: The Press and the Persian Gulf Conflict*. New York: Gannett Foundation Media Center, 1991.

Doty, R. M., B. E. Peterson, and D. G. Winter. "Threat and Authoritarianism in the United States, 1978–1987." *Journal of Personality and Social Psychology* 61 (1991): 629–40.

Duckitt, J. "Social Class and F Scale Authoritarianism: A Reconsideration." *High School Journal* 68 (1985): 279–85.

Fite, D., M. Genest, and C. Wilcox. "Gender Differences in Foreign Policy Attitudes: A Longitudinal Analysis." *American Politics Quarterly* 18 (1990): 492–513.

Fulero, S. M., and B. Fischhoff. "Differential Media Evaluation and Satisfaction with Election Results: The Bearers of Good and Bad Tidings." *Communication Research* 3 (1976): 22–36.

Greenberg, B. S. *The Role of Personal Salience in Response to Media Coverage of Desert Storm.* Paper presented at the meeting of International Association of Mass Communication Research, Istanbul, Turkey, November 1991.

Greenberg, B. S., E. Cohen, and H. Li. *How the United States Found Out About the War.* Unpublished manuscript, Michigan State University, Department of Communications, East Lansing, Mich., 1991.

Hallin, D. C. "Living Room War: Then and Now." *Extra* (May 1991): 21.

Kraus, S. *The Great Debates: Background, Perspective, Effects.* Bloomington: Indiana University Press, 1962.

Lee, M. A., and T. Devitt. "Gulf War Coverage: Censorship Begins at Home." *Newspaper Research Journal* 12 (1991): 14–22.

Lewis, J., S. Jhally, and M. Morgan. *The Gulf War: A Study of the Media, Public Opinion & Public Knowledge* (Document No. P–8). University of Massachusetts, Amherst, Mass.: The Center for the Study of Communication Research Archives, 1991.

McCann, S.J.H. "Authoritarianism and Preference for the Presidential Candidate Perceived to Be Higher on the Power Motive." *Perceptual and Motor Skills* 70 (1990): 577–78.

McCann, S.J.H., and L. L. Stewin. "Threat, Authoritarianism, and the Power of U.S. Presidents." *The Journal of Psychology* 121 (1987): 149–57.

McLeod, D. M., E. M. Perse, N. Signorielli, and J. A. Courtright. *Public Opinion toward Censorship and Press Performance During the Persian Gulf War.* Paper presented at the meeting of Speech Communication Association, Atlanta, Georgia, 1991.

McMasters, P. "The Pentagon and the Press: The War Continues." *Newspaper Research Journal* 12 (1991): 2–9.

Meloen, J. D., L. Jagendoorn, Q. Raaijmakers, and L. Visser. "Authoritarianism and the Revival of Political Racism: Reassessments in The Netherlands of the Reliability and Validity of the Concept of Authoritarianism by Adorno et al." *Political Psychology* 9 (1988): 413–29.

Moghaddam, F. M., and V. Vuksanovic. "Attitudes and Behavior toward Human Rights across Different Contexts: The Role of Right-wing Authoritarianism, Political Ideology, and Religiosity." *International Journal of Psychology* 25 (1990): 455–74.

Naureckas, J. "Gulf War Coverage: The Worst Censorship Was at Home." *Extra* (May 1991): 3–10.

O'Heffernan, P. "Television and the Security of Nations: Learning from the Gulf War." *Television Quarterly* 25 (1991): 5–10.

Pan, Z., R. E. Ostman, P. Moy, and P. Reynolds. *Audience Evaluations of U.S. News Media Performance in the Persian Gulf War.* Paper presented at the annual meeting of the International Communication Association, Chicago, Ill., May 1991.

Park, B., and M. Rothbart. "Perception of Out-group Homogeneity and Levels of Social Categorization: Memory for the Subordinate Attributes of In-group and Out-group Members." *Journal of Personality and Social Psychology* 42 (1982): 1051–1068.

"The Propaganda War." *The Progressive* (January 1991): 8–9.

Raden, D. "Authoritarianism Revisited: Evidence for an Aggression Factor." *Social Behavior and Personality* 9 (1981): 147–53.

Ray, J. J. "Conservatism, Authoritarianism and Related Variables: A Review and Empirical Study. In *The Psychology of Conservatism*, G. D. Wilson (ed.). London: Academic Press, 1973.

Ray, J. J. "Defective Validity in the Altemeyer Authoritarianism Scale." *The Journal of Social Psychology* 125 (1985): 271–72.

Rhine, R. J. "The 1964 Presidential Election and Curves of Information Seeking and Avoiding." *Journal of Personality and Social Psychology* 5 (1967): 416–23.

Roper Center Review of Public Opinion and Polling. "The American Enterprise." *The Public Perspective* (March/April 1991): 74–77.

Rothbart, M., R. Dawes, and B. Park. "Stereotyping and Sampling Biases in Intergroup Perception." In *Attitudinal Judgment*, J. R. Eiser (ed.), 109–34. New York: Springer-Verlag, 1984.

Ryckman, R. M., M. J. Burns, and M. A. Robbins. "Authoritarianism and Sentencing Strategies for Low and High Severity Crimes." *Personality and Social Psychology Bulletin* 12 (1986): 227–35.

Sherif, M. *Group Conflict and Cooperation: Their Social Psychology*. London: Routledge & Kegan Paul, 1966.

Sherif, M., O. J. Harvey, B. J. White, W. R. Hood, and M. Sherif. *Intergroup Conflict and Cooperation: The Robbers' Cave Experiment*. Norman: University of Oklahoma Book Exchange, 1961.

Smith, T. W. (ed.). "The Polls: Gender and Attitudes toward Violence." *Public Opinion Quarterly* 48 (1984): 384–96.

Strayer, R., and L. Ellenhorn. "Vietnam Veterans: A Study Exploring Adjustment Patterns and Attitudes." *Journal of Social Issues* 31 (1975): 81–93.

Sweeney, P. D., and K. L. Gruber. "Selective Exposure: Voter Information Preferences and the Watergate Affair." *Journal of Personality and Social Psychology* 46 (1984): 1208–1221.

Times Mirror Center for the People and the Press. *The People, the Press and the War in the Gulf: Part II. A Special Times Mirror News Interest Index*. Washington, D.C., 1991.

Van Ijzendoorn, M. H. "Moral Judgment, Authoritarianism, and Ethnocentrism." *The Journal of Social Psychology* 129 (1989): 37–45.

Chapter Nine

War in the Global Village: A Seven-Country Comparison of Television News Coverage of the Beginning of the Gulf War

David L. Swanson and Larry David Smith

Although the term was often used with reference to Vietnam, in many respects the Gulf War was the first television war. Viewers in many countries were transfixed by the drama unfolding on the screen as coverage dominated television news virtually worldwide. The critical role of television news as a source of information during crises, a role that had been seen earlier during such episodes as the Kennedy assassination and its aftermath in the United States (see Greenberg and Parker 1965) and the 1973 Yom Kippur War in the Middle East (see Peled and Katz 1974), was demonstrated again in surveys of viewership of televised war coverage in a number of countries (for example, Blood 1991; FitzSimon 1991; Gantz 1991; McLeod et al. 1991; and Shaw and Carr-Hill, 1991).

Several aspects of television's coverage of the Gulf War were remarkable. The immediacy of the coverage was striking. The 1973 Arab-Israeli war was the first to receive same-day television news coverage. Later, same-day or even occasional live coverage was transmitted from the conflicts in Nicaragua, El Salvador, and Lebanon (Larson 1984), and more recently from Panama and Grenada. But the Gulf War marked the debut of live coverage from the combat zone as a routine feature of daily reporting by many television services. Indeed, competitive pressures on U.S. television networks to be first to report new developments led to a number of inaccurate live reports and generated a debate about whether live reporting from a war zone should be allowed.[1]

Coverage also was notable for the extensive efforts of leaders on both sides to use television as a vehicle for conducting diplomacy and manipulating public opinion. Of course, political leaders had endeavored to use television for these purposes before (see O'Heffernan 1991 for examples), but coverage, especially during the extended run-up to the war and in the days immediately following the outbreak of hostilities, featured the leaders of the belligerent countries exchanging messages and orchestrating coverage on a new and larger scale (for examples, see Alter et al. 1991; Heiberg 1991; and O'Heffernan 1990).

Our interest in this chapter centers on a third remarkable feature of television coverage, its global character. In a sense, the war was a global undertaking as the multinational coalition acted with the sanction of the United Nations and consisted of, depending on how one counts, forces from thirty nations with another eighteen countries providing financial, humanitarian, or other assistance. And the war was the lead story virtually everywhere, the subject of the most extensive television reporting in the history of warfare. Compared to World War II, the number of reporters sent to cover the Gulf War was vast.[2] The official media rosters for the multinational coalition's Joint Information Bureaus in Riyadh and Dhahran, Saudi Arabia, for February 23, 1991, list 1,563 journalists, including crews representing 52 different television services in 31 countries as well as international television news services (e.g., WTN, Visnews) (U.S. Congress 1991: 195–235).[3] These figures do not include journalists who were covering events related to the war from elsewhere in the region: Israel, Jordan, some of the Gulf states, and other locations.

The large number of television services represented by crews in the Gulf does not convey the full extent to which the outbreak of the war dominated television news worldwide, however. In an informal survey of the evening news programs of nearly thirty television services around the world during the week following the beginning of the bombing, we noted that war coverage seemed to be nearly as prominent on services that had no crews in the Gulf as on those that were represented. Moreover, there were numerous instances in which the same pictures produced by the same crews showed up on service after service. It was as though every television service had shopped for war video in the same supermarket. This phenomenon reflects the steady advance of what has been called the globalization of television news.

"Globalization" refers to a set of technological and organizational developments in recent years that have strengthened and accelerated the international dimension of mass communication. In the world of television news, these developments have enabled a growing number of services to receive video material from international suppliers and to share material with each other at the same time that international television news broadcasts have become available to rapidly expanding audiences. The result is that television news is becoming "a truly global product" that is "increasingly oblivious of national boundaries," to borrow Gurevitch's (1989: 222) description.

The concept of globalization provides a useful frame of reference for examining differences in reporting between countries, what they represent, and how they can be accounted for. With virtually every service covering the same story for an extended period of time, it is possible by comparing coverage to assess the extent to which globalization has advanced and to consider some of its social and political implications. In order to do so, we must first describe in a bit more detail the international environment of television news.

THE INTERNATIONAL ENVIRONMENT OF TELEVISION NEWS

Insofar as the production and distribution of news stories are concerned, the international environment of television news consists of several interrelated elements.[4] Of these, perhaps the best known are the twenty-four-hour international news services such as the U.S.-based CNN (Cable News Network) and British-based Sky News that broadcast to multinational audiences primarily by satellite. At last report, CNN's signal was being broadcast to over eighty countries and "pirated by government agencies and private distributors in virtually every nation" (O'Heffernan 1991: 71; see also Hester 1991). CNN in particular played an especially important and visible role in covering the Gulf War, from providing live coverage of the first bombing raids on Baghdad to the controversial reports of correspondent Peter Arnett who remained in Baghdad after the ouster of other journalists, and was the subject of numerous commentaries on television's role in the war (for example, Corry 1991; Mott 1991; and Rosenberg 1991).

A second element of the international environment consists of the international television news agencies, Visnews and Worldwide Television News (WTN). Both based in Britain, these "news wholesalers" supply television news video and stories to subscribing television services in something like the way the wire services provide print news stories and photographs. Whereas the wire services distribute primarily material prepared by their own staffs supplemented as needed by local stringers, however, the video agencies distribute not only material produced by their own personnel (at least in the case of Visnews) but also, and primarily, video material provided by other services. Visnews distributes material from NBC (in the United States), the BBC (in Britain), and other services; WTN, which succeeded the UPITN service, distributes material provided by ITN (in Britain), ABC (in the U.S.), and other services.[5]

The reach and importance of Visnews and WTN as suppliers of international television news are very great. Visnews, for example, distributes material to more than 200 subscribers in 98 countries (Hester 1991: 40) and has been described as "perhaps the closest thing" to

McLuhan's concept of the "global village" (King 1981: 283). The agencies also provide material to the international television news broadcasters, such as CNN (Wallis and Baran 1990: 105, 113). Most television services depend quite heavily on the agencies for their international news (Nasser 1983), so much so that Richstad (1981: 242) has described the agencies as even more predominant than the wire services.

The third element of the international television news environment consists of exchanges that have been established in several regions of the world through which member television services can share material with each other. Of these, perhaps the best known is the Eurovision News Exchange, organized within the European Broadcasting Union. Other active exchanges include Asiavision, by which the Asian Broadcasting Union provides exchange of material between services in East Asia through a zone center in Tokyo and in West Asia through a second zone center in Kuala Lumpur, and Intervision, which links Eastern European television services (for a description of these exchanges, see Wallis and Baran 1990).

Connections between the three elements of the international television news environment are complex. Asiavision receives a daily satellite feed of material from the Eurovision service; CNN is affiliated with both Eurovision and Intervision; Sky News' international material primarily comes from Visnews and WTN; and so on. For our purposes, however, it is sufficient to note the result of these connections: The international television news environment is organized in such a way that, in addition to whatever material they produced for their own use, most television services around the world had access to what was essentially a common stock of video material concerning the Gulf War.

The interconnected global environment of television news is regarded with both optimism and alarm. On the optimistic side, as Gurevitch, Levy, and Roeh (in press) have pointed out, globalization provides resources that ought to enable us to move ever closer to a global community in which, regardless of national boundaries, people share the same information about world events. We are far from a global community, of course, but an impressive number of studies have documented similarities in the practices of television news around the world (e.g., Cohen, Adoni, and Bantz 1990; Golding and Elliott 1979; Gurevitch, Levy, and Roeh in press; Straubhaar et al. in press). In most cases, the similarities have been attributed to Western practices coming to serve as a model for the rest of the world (Nasser 1983: 54–55; Straubhaar et al. in press). As a result, scholars increasingly are speculating about a "transnational news-value culture" (Cohen, Adoni, and Bantz 1990: 44) in which, regardless of their location, persons working in television news share a common professional culture. Although there remain many differences between countries' newscasts, the standards of news value and judgment and the conventions for producing news stories seem to be similar (Gurevitch 1989; Gurevitch, Levy, and Roeh in press; Head 1985: 1–2; Servaes 1991; Straubhaar et al. in press).

On the other side of the globalization coin, concern arises from a tradition of press theory and comparative media studies that seeks to connect economic, cultural, and political differences between countries to corresponding differences in national approaches to journalism (e.g., Martin and Chaudhary 1983; Siebert, Peterson, and Schramm 1956). Out of this tradition emerged, for example, the concept of "development journalism" as a distinct, non-Western approach to serving the needs of developing nations. Seen in light of traditional media theory, it is disturbing to note with Wallis and Baran (1990: 161) and Nasser (1983: 55) that heavy dependence on material provided by a handful of Western suppliers is a necessity for most of the world's television services because they lack the resources to produce their own coverage of international events. The degree of dependence on "borrowed news" can be quite high. For instance, Hudson and Swindel (1988) found that borrowed news comprised on average over 60 percent of Saudi newscasts. A by-product of dependence may be to spread throughout the world news that "is inevitably slanted to mesh with the worldview as seen through the Western lens" (Fisher 1987: 64). Thus, the charge of "media imperialism" is the obverse of media globalization's optimistic face (see Tunstall 1977).

Of course, things are a bit more complicated. In many countries, official gatekeepers sit astride the flow of news from abroad. Officials monitor the inflow of material from wire and television news agencies and, in some countries, frequently censor stories, delete offending portions of stories, or provide their own interpretations of events (Hudson and Swindel 1988; Nasser 1983; Ogan 1991). In addition, several (variously successful) Third World regional news exchanges and satellite services have been established explicitly for the purpose of providing alternatives to dependence on Western sources and agencies (Hester 1991; Nasser 1983; Stephens 1991). Moreover, we should note that the television news agencies are latecomers to an industry that was established by Western-owned wire services long ago, that news from foreign sources is available by shortwave in every country of the world (Hester 1991; Stephens 1991), and that as a result of signal overspill viewers in many locations in Eastern and Western Europe, the Middle East, North Africa, and elsewhere have long been able to watch television news from neighboring countries having quite different political systems and cultural orientations (Ogan 1991; Paraschos 1991).

Even so, the globalization of television news is more than just the newest phase in a process that began with the development of the wire services. Rather, some argue, we are seeing "a qualitatively new stage in the globalization of news" (Gurevitch, Levy, and Roeh in press). The special concern with television news probably reflects a widespread belief that television has unique influence by virtue of its "ability to bring the world and its events visually into the living room," so that in the advance of television news globalization, "the nation with the greatest resources holds the communication advantage: it selects the subject material and the nuance of its presentation" (Fisher 1987: 73).

TELEVISION COVERAGE OF THE GULF WAR AS A CASE STUDY IN GLOBALIZATION

Recent research on the globalization of television news, particularly the work of Cohen, Adoni, and Bantz (1990), Gurevitch, Levy, and Roeh (in press), and Straubhaar et al. (in press), suggests a focus for the present study: The content of television news reflects a variety of influences that, in complex ways, shape the transformation of reality into "stories." Some of these influences are occupational and professional. Television news is created by persons socialized within a professional culture that, among other things, prescribes and directs what is accepted as the competent practice of the craft. Elements of this culture are shared worldwide and reflect the global diffusion of a grammar of practice. On another level, however, every newscast reflects in both obvious and subtle ways the indigenous context of its production. In each country, the professional culture of television journalism has developed over time within particular organizations and institutions, so that the resident professional culture reflects local agendas and interests. In turn, local institutions of mass communication operate within a nexus of interrelationships with other political, economic, and social institutions in society, all of which are shaped by and mold the culture in which they exist. Thus, an adequate understanding of the content of television news must recognize both its cultural specificity and its participation in a global grammar of practice.

In order to reveal the tug and pull of national versus transnational influences in war coverage, we employ narrative analysis to examine the content of television news coverage of the war. Narrative analysis is a macroanalytic method designed to describe in a holistic way entire stories or series of stories. It identifies the larger features of news content, such as the overall meaning and interpretation that are conveyed, the structure that unites the various elements into a coherent whole, and the general valence of the treatment. Narrative analysis accomplishes this by focusing on the fundamental narrative elements of characterization, plot, action, and resolution as these form the materials of news stories. The dramatic unity of these elements gives a news story its coherence as a readily understood "story" rather than a melange of chronologically arranged but otherwise unconnected "facts." As researchers who have approached the news from a variety of theoretical viewpoints have demonstrated, across media, time, topic, and national boundaries, the essential structure and components of news stories are those of story-telling or narrative (e.g., Altheide 1976; Altheide and Snow 1979; Hallin 1986; Mander 1987; Roeh 1989; Schudson 1982; Sperry 1981).

Narrative analysis is well suited to comparative study of coverage of the first days of the Gulf War. During the first week of the war, the essential task facing television newsworkers was how to construct and sustain over time an intelligible interpretation of what was happening, why it happened, what it meant, and where it would lead. In other words, the essential task was to construct narratives. Because narrative analysis exposes the essential interpretive logic through which television news stories construct the overall meaning of events, it provides a useful framework for comparing how a given story is reported by multiple news organizations (e.g., Entman 1991; Nimmo and Combs 1985, 1990; Smith 1988; Smith and Nimmo 1991).

In the analysis that follows, we describe the narratives of the beginning of the Gulf War that were offered to viewers in nightly newscasts of television services in seven different countries: BBC (United Kingdom), CBS (United States), Doordarshan (India), Jordan Television (Jordan), TV3 (Malaysia), Televisión Nacional (Chile), and ZDF (Germany). The newscasts were aired during the period January 17–25, 1991, the week immediately following the first air attacks on Iraq and Kuwait. Because the outbreak of hostilities had long been anticipated, newscasts from this period may be expected to represent the second stage in crisis coverage described by Graber (1984: 291–95). That is, the initial period of confusion and uncoordinated messages had by this time given way to coherent narratives about the conflict in the Gulf. In addition to characterizing the fundamental structure of each narrative (e.g., story genre, major characters, action) as recommended by Roeh (1989) and other narrative analysts, we highlight some of the aspects of the narratives that similar studies (e.g., Cohen, Adoni, and Bantz 1990; Gurevitch, Levy, and Roeh in press; Straubhaar et al. in press) have found to bear directly on globalization issues: extent and form of the use of borrowed material, sources of information offered as authoritative, slant toward one side in the conflict, and provision of local frames of reference for interpreting the conflict.

The seven television services examined vary along dimensions that can be expected to produce some diversity in their reporting of the war's beginning. The United States and Great Britain were, of course, the leader and second-most militarily involved participant in the multinational coalition, respectively. Germany was a perhaps reluctant member of the coalition, having sent a squadron of aircraft to the NATO base at

Incirlik, Turkey, but seeking to avoid being drawn into the conflict as a military participant. Instead, Germany provided financial support to the coalition and aid to Israel to assist in repairing damage caused by Iraq's Scud missile attacks. Chile did not participate in the conflict, although it supported the U.N. effort and, at the time of these newscasts, was considering sending medical teams to support the coalition. Malaysia provided humanitarian assistance to the coalition and, as a temporary member of the Security Council, voted in favor of U.N. Resolution 678 authorizing the use of military force. At the same time, Malaysia has a large Muslim population and a government committed to Islamic sensibilities. During the 1973 Yom Kippur War, TV3 provided what was described as extensive pro-Arab coverage (Central Intelligence Agency 1989). India also had an ambivalent position on the war. India supported the United Nations and allowed U.S. aircraft to use Indian refueling facilities (Public Affairs Guidance 1991), while Indian government officials made a number of gestures of support for the Iraqi cause and for PLO Chairman Yassir Arafat during the opening days of the war. Finally, Jordan's official position of opposition to the war and support for the Iraqis was well publicized.

The seven television services all rank as "developed press systems" (Kurian 1982) and have more or less extensive connections to the global television news distribution system (Central Intelligence Agency 1989). Two of the systems are privately owned (CBS and TV3); one is operated by a semi-autonomous public corporation (the BBC), one is operated by the states comprising the German federal union (ZDF), and three are operated by national governments (Doordarshan, Jordan Radio and Television, and TVN in Chile). Most operate in competitive television environments. Considering their degree of autonomy from government control as rated by the Freedom House comparative ranking system, four systems rank in the "most free" category (the United States, the United Kingdom, Germany, and India), two are rated "moderately free" (Chile and Malaysia), and Jordan ranks in the "least free" category (Stephens 1991: 55–58). Thus, the services display the kinds of divergence that should allow a useful if limited exploration of similarities and differences in narratives about the beginning of the Gulf War.

SEVEN NARRATIVES OF THE FIRST WEEK OF WAR

Jordan—Jordan Radio and Television

"News at Ten" is the nightly English-language newscast of Jordan Radio and Television's second channel. While the first channel broadcasts in Arabic, the second channel broadcasts primarily in French and English, with lesser amounts of time devoted to programming in Hebrew and Arabic (*World Radio TV Handbook 1992:* 403). The government-operated service has a significant viewership in Israel, where the daily Hebrew press regularly prints the schedule for Jordan television (Cohen, Adoni, and Bantz 1990: 206). "News at Ten" employs a simple anchor-controlled style within a presentation that, while more sophisticated than Doordarshan's, seems a bit outmoded judged by current Western presentational conventions. Internal and external video were used, along with remote commentary and, in one notable instance discussed below, a live feed from CNN.

For "News at Ten," the beginning of the war was, of course, a local story with global impact. The convention of reporting the actions of both sides in the conflict was observed, but Jordanian affinity with the Iraqi position was communicated clearly in several ways. Patterns of sources showed relatively little attention to statements by coalition leaders and more attention to sources whose views supported the Iraqi position (e.g., the Iraqi ambassador to Japan who predicted that the Americans will find the "Vietnam war will be just like a picnic compared to this" and the Pakistani Prime Minister who claimed that the war "benefits only Israel").

Reports of events in the war depicted the coalition as powerful but somewhat inept and the Iraqis as outgunned but clever and dangerous. For example, the lead story on January 22 painted the massive coalition air campaign as militarily ineffective but causing massive civilian casualties and destroying holy sites. According to various sources: "90 percent of the allied strikes against Iraq have missed their targets"; "only 30 Iraqi combat aircraft were known to have been destroyed out of a total of 800"; "Forty Iraqi air bases are still able to operate"; and "all of Iraq's planes and missiles were hidden and protected in underground shelters." The coalition has, however, caused widespread destruction: "Allied plane and missile raids had killed women and children and destroyed civilian shelters, including places of worship"; "air raids also targeted religious shrines." The Iraqis were described as fighting back, having shot down twenty-three aerial targets (both planes and missiles) on January 22 alone. At the same time, a U.S. Defense Department spokesman was quoted as praising the Iraqi's use of decoys—"plastic dummies of planes"—and Scud missiles—"to cheat incoming attacking missiles."

The Jordanian position also was reflected in considerable attention given to expressions of opposition to the war, which were framed as opposition to the United States. Massive anti-American demonstrations were described as taking place throughout Pakistan. A representative of the French government was reported to be "trying to explain France's position in the Gulf War" in a tour of Morocco, Algeria, and Tunisia, where "popular feelings were running high" against the French participation in the coalition. Local video showed a protest march in Amman in which a group of women "demand an end of attacks on Iraq" and "cursed the United States as the enemy of God and George Bush as a butcher of children." Reports from Australia, Bangladesh, Indonesia, the United States, and Japan provide evidence that, in the anchor's narration, "allied operations against Iraq continued to ignite an anti-war sentiment around the world."

Although the war was a local story in Jordan, the story nevertheless was domesticated in the development of several themes. Jordan's official position of neutrality and opposition to both sides' choice of "the war option" was explained by the Jordanian Crown Prince in a lengthy (7:45) interview conducted by ABC News and shown on "News at Ten." The plight of refugees arriving from Iraq and the difficulties of caring for them were examined. Possible environmental consequences of the Iraqis' setting fire to Kuwaiti oil wells were described.

Standard "signature pictures" from external video sources were used (e.g., cruise missiles being fired from warships, coalition aircraft taxiing and taking off at Saudi Arabian bases), but the most interesting use of external video by "News at Ten" occurred on January 22 when, at roughly twenty-three minutes into the broadcast, the anchor cut to a live feed from CNN for nearly two minutes of coverage of a new Scud attack on Israel, "just to confirm," the anchor said, "that at least one Scud missile landed in Israel."

Overall, "News at Ten" constructed the war as a tragedy for all sides that, as the Crown Prince explained, was "in God's hands" to play itself out while Jordan, caught in the middle, was left to cope with some of the disastrous consequences. Both sides of the conflict were condemned for having selected "the war option" rather than peaceful resolution of differences. The multinational coalition, and especially the United States, were portrayed as having outraged public opinion worldwide by attacking Iraq. The considerable military might of the coalition was showing itself to be relatively ineffective against the Iraqi military but intentionally destroying religious sites and inflicting death and injury on innocent civilians. The Iraqis, in turn, remained resolute and, through cleverness and careful preparation, were still a formidable adversary even in the face of the massive air campaign against them.

India—Doordarshan

From its establishment in the 1950s as a U.N.-funded experiment, Indian television grew to become a significant force in the 1980s. It assumed its present configuration in 1976, when the television service was removed from All India Radio and established as a free-standing unit, Doordarshan ("Distant Vision"), under the Ministry of Information and Broadcasting (Chen and Chaudhary 1991: 233). The service combines national broadcasts from New Delhi with broadcasts from regional centers throughout the country and accepts both advertising and sponsored programs. Estimates of the size of the viewing audience vary from 25 percent (Pendakur 1991: 246) to 70 percent of the population (Chen and Chaudhary 1991: 233).

We examined both national English-language and regional Hindi-language evening newscasts ("The News") broadcast from New Delhi for the period in question. The newscasts were technologically unsophisticated by current Western standards, and the English-language newscasts, especially, contained various video and audio "glitches." "The News" employed anchor-dominated formats with dual anchors supported by locally produced video, considerable externally produced video, and occasional remote telephone interviews. War news dominated the newscasts, consuming at least two-thirds of each program.

In reporting the war's first days, Doordarshan followed the journalistic convention of presenting both sides but strongly favored the Iraqi viewpoint. This was evident in the order of headlines, where news favorable to the Iraqis (e.g., "Second consecutive and serious attack on Saudi Arabia by the Iraqis") always was bannered before news of the coalition (e.g., "Heavy bombardment of the cities of Baghdad and Basra by coalition forces") just as, within stories, news from the Iraqi viewpoint typically preceded reports of coalition activities (for example, Iraqi claims of downed coalition aircraft usually preceded coalition claims). Similarly, the texts of stories often were written in ways that reinforced Iraqi military capabilities and called coalition performance into question. On January 19, for example, the anchor narrated the lead story about the second Scud attack on Israel by saying, "Iraqi missiles have slammed into Tel Aviv . . . and sent the Israelis scurrying into sealed rooms to dawn gas masks." This proves, she noted, "that the American bombing missions have not been fully successful." The story continued with a Palestinian spokesman on video describing the event as a "message for the Israelis."

In the same vein, coalition statements and claims frequently received a scrutiny that was not applied to Iraqi claims. In the lead story on January 22, for example, the Doordarshan narrator explained, "American sources claim that coalition forces are attacking only military bases and not civilian areas. But a cruise missile fell in front of the Al Rashid Hotel . . . creating much destruction. . . . the Iraqis . . . also report that one of their oldest churches was destroyed by American missiles." And later, in the same story: "American sources claim that . . . coalition soldiers . . . are being used by the Iraqis as human shields. . . . In France, however, the Iraqi ambassador said that the reason why the POWs were shown on television was to challenge American sources who denied Iraq's claim that it had captured several POWs." In contrast, Iraqi statements, such as Baghdad radio's claim that Scud missiles fired at Israel and Saudi Arabia "were aimed at selected targets," were not disputed.

The focus of Doordarshan's narrative, however, was at home, not abroad. The local story developed two themes, both treated at length. One theme throughout the newscasts depicted Indian officials as leading efforts for a diplomatic solution that were earning praise from around the world. The Chinese government applauded "India's role as one of the strongest advocates for a peaceful resolution to the conflict." The Indian ambassador to the U.N. was continuously involved in the search for peace as, at home, the prime minister maintained "close ties" with PLO leader Yassir Arafat during the crisis. A second–home-front theme depicted the Indian people as united in their opposition to the war and determined, under government leadership, to manage whatever difficulties the war might create. Attention focused on supplies of food and oil and, in numerous lengthy statements, officials stressed that there were no shortages as yet and that prompt action was being taken to forestall or at least minimize future difficulties. Unity and leadership, it was suggested, would allow India to minimize at home the widespread suffering that the war was causing elsewhere (Sri Lanka, Bangladesh, the Philippines, and Pakistan were mentioned as particular sites of war-caused suffering).

Doordarshan was entirely dependent on external sources for video of events abroad. Considerable external video was used, mostly from sources that were not identified. The exception was CNN, whose "graphic bug" logo appeared frequently on Doordarshan. The English-language version of "The News" occasionally included the original audio commentary in CNN stories that it used. Not surprisingly, the external video was selected to fit the narrative Doordarshan was developing. Coalition leaders were shown less often than on other services; sources favorable to the Iraqi view appeared somewhat more often than on other services (e.g., Palestinian spokesmen, Iraqi ambassadors, the North Yemen ambassador to the U.N.). A telephone interview with an All India Radio reporter stationed in Dubai provided the only live coverage from the war zone in the newscasts we examined.

Overall, Doordarshan constructed a narrative of the war as a tragedy fraught with the potential for causing suffering in India, but a tragedy that, to the applause of the world, Indian leaders were acting boldly to halt. Both coalition and Iraqi perspectives were represented, but there was a decided and systematic preference for the Iraqi side in the conflict.

Malaysia—TV3

TV3, located in Kuala Lumpur, was privatized in 1983 but is owned primarily by members of the political party in power and thus is closely tied to the government (Lent 1991: 169). Islam is the official religion and, like all Malaysian media, TV3 is closely monitored by a government that is concerned about Islamic sensibilities and the influence of "Zionist control" of the foreign press. Under a revision of the Broadcast Act made in 1967, the minister of information is authorized "to monitor all radio and television programming to ensure that they are 'consistent with government policy' " (Lent 1991: 169, 195). Kuala Lumpur has become an important regional financial and media center and is one of two zone centers of the Asiavision television news exchange. Hence, TV3 is well connected to the international television environment. TV3 has fifteen repeater stations throughout Malaysia and competes with two govern- ment-operated channels in both Peninsular and East Malaysia (*World Radio TV Handbook 1992*: 408).

Malaysia offers a case study of the conflicting sentiments about the war felt in a number of Islamic societies: support for the U.N. effort, loyalty to Arab interests, and antipathy to Israel. "7:00 News," TV3's English-language evening newscast, concentrated almost entirely on the war and its local effects in the days immediately following the outbreak of hostilities. Events in the Gulf and elsewhere outside Malaysia were presented through externally produced video obtained from a variety of Western sources. Material from the BBC, NBC, and CNN was iden- tified and used extensively, both audio and video. In addition, TV3 produced its own narration to accompany video montages assembled from unidentified sources depicting events in the war and created in- house video for stories about the war's local consequences. The anchor's role primarily consisted of providing brief lead-ins.

From the beginning, in its January 17 newscast aired only eleven hours after the first bombs were dropped, the shape of TV3's narrative of the war was clear: World opinion opposes the coalition's action but the Iraqis' position is desperate and a quick cease-fire should be sought. The lead story on January 17 devoted slightly more than ten minutes to reports of initial coalition successes, told largely by coalition sources in Western video. After the anchor's lead-in ("U.S.-led air forces appear to control the skies over Baghdad, attacking targets with apparent im- punity"), a video montage of the "signature pictures" of war's beginning followed, accompanied by locally produced narration: "the most pow- erful air capability mounted in history . . . successfully disabled major Iraqi targets." Next, stories from the BBC including both audio and video showed the jubilation of Kuwaitis in Saudi Arabia ("I am very happy. I am waiting for this news long time") and returning coalition flyers ("Tremendous. Baghdad was lit up like a Christmas tree"). Finally, sto- ries (both audio and video) from CNN and NBC presented U.S. leaders' views of the initial successes. After a brief story on the Malaysian gov- ernment's position (sad at the outbreak of war; appealing to Iraq to pull out of Kuwait and "avoid further catastrophe"; monitoring the welfare of Malaysians in the Gulf), a three-minute story depicted opposition to the coalition's action from world leaders (of Iran, Libya, China, Cuba, and Yemen) and world opinion. The newscast ended with four minutes on the war's effects on world, regional, and local financial markets, introduced with the observation that "persons in the Far East are taking the war in the Gulf in their stride."

The "7:00 News" on January 18 devoted attention to the first Scud missile attacks on Israel and, in the process, made clear antipathy to the Israelis. Consistently, the government of Israel was referred to as "the Tel Aviv regime." While many in Tel Aviv were "forced . . . to hide in basements" as "Baghdad unleashed its missiles," TV3 pointed out that Palestinians in the occupied territories had not been issued gas masks by the regime. Purporting to show "how foreign correspondents in Tel Aviv fared during the Iraqi attack," the program actually showed a video of NBC correspondent Arthur Kent in his room at the Intercontinental Hotel during a Scud attack on Dhahran. The down side of the attack on Israel was concern that the "Tel Aviv regime" would retaliate with "the most sophisticated and largest military force in West Asia." On the Iraqi side, a 1:30 story showed the Iraqi "signature video" of Saddam Hussein's defiance on the day after the bombing began, noting that Saddam's "popularity seems to have not been affected by the war at all," "his call to rally all Arabs and Muslims to his cause is appealing," and he may still have "surprises for the allied forces," including "the terrible biological and chemical weapons" that he "has no qualms of unleashing."

Several themes tried to overcome distance and develop local angles. One theme explained the government's efforts to monitor the condition of Malaysians in the Gulf and plans for their evacuation if necessary. A second, more dominant, theme followed the war's effects on local, regional, and world financial markets on a daily basis. In addition to these recurring themes, a story on January 18 described the anxieties and conflicting emotions felt by Iraqis and other Arabs living in the United States as the war got underway. The war's regional relevance was reinforced by referring to its location as West Asia.

In sum, the "7:00 News" offered the most fragmented, least integrated narrative of the services we examined, perhaps reflecting the conflicting sentiments felt in Malaysia. On the one hand, TV3 broadcast intact Western reports featuring coalition spokespersons and military personnel explaining their initial success and suggesting an optimistic prospect for coalition victory. On the other hand, antipathy to Israel and recognition of the appeal of Saddam Hussein's cause were also evident. The local story of the war mirrored these same contradictions: Coalition success was good news for the financial markets but offset by worries about the safety of Malaysians in the Gulf.

Chile—TVN

Televisión Nacional (TVN), the government-operated service based in Santiago, is one of five Chilean television stations that function as networks in the sense of being broadcast in various regions of the country (TVN has 108 repeater transmitters). TVN is the only station with "near-national" coverage (International Centre on Censorship 1991); the other four stations are owned by universities (a system found in several Latin American countries) (Salwen, Garrison, and Buckman 1991). The history of Chilean broadcasting's freedom from government control is mixed and marked alternately by periods of repression and autonomy in a press system characterized as "moderately free."

TVN's resources were well displayed in the technologically sophisticated coverage of the beginning of the Gulf War offered on the evening news program, *24 Horas* (24 Hours), broadcast at 8:00 P.M. The programs employed two female anchors (alternating between programs) supported by domestic and foreign correspondents, in-house video, a studio commentator, live satellite interviews, telephone interviews, and video obtained from external sources. Presentationally, as in the U.S. model, the anchor dominated each newscast. Substantively, war news dominated each newscast. Programs opened with long (5–7 minutes) anchor-narrated montages of video assembled from various sources that described the day's war-related events; the remainder of each program was devoted to various aspects of the war described in more detail.

TVN offered a balanced narrative of the war inflected toward the coalition viewpoint. Care was taken to present both sides of the conflict, but coalition spokespersons nearly always were presented before Iraqi statements and spokespersons. Reports of the coalition's daily activities typically preceded reports of Iraqi activities as when, on January 19, the story of the second Iraqi Scud attack on Israel was preceded by the announcement that Patriot anti-missile systems that had "proved their effectiveness in Saudi Arabia" had just been assembled "in record time" in Israel. The pattern of "coalition first" may reflect only the availability of video concerning the coalition and the scarcity of comparable material representing the Iraqis, but it had the effect of structurally supporting the coalition viewpoint as coalition speakers and actions set the stage, followed by Iraqi responses. U.S. media were presented as believable; viewers were reminded that some information broadcast by the BBC during the Falklands War had turned out to be unreliable; Iraqi statements sometimes were characterized as "propaganda" and Iraqi press releases as "clearly slanted." However, both sides were allowed to speak for themselves on *24 Horas*.

Successes and failures on both sides were reported, but in a context that left no doubt about the inevitability of a swift coalition victory, a matter in the words of TVN's commentator of "a Third World country" trying to "confront a world power." Coalition power and technological sophistication were stressed repeatedly, and both government officials and TVN's commentator expressed relief that the war would be brief so that its consequences in human injuries and destruction would be minimized.

TVN generated a considerable amount of its own war coverage. Correspondents in Jordan and Washington filed video material and took part in live telephone interviews with the anchor. Live telephone interviews also were conducted with Chile's ambassadors in Amman and Riyadh concerning events in each location and the plight of Chileans there. Nevertheless, TVN relied on a great deal of externally produced video, particularly for its coverage of coalition and Iraqi activities. External video included the "signature pictures" from both sides, shots of coalition missile launches and aircraft taking off to begin the war as well as video of Saddam Hussein's January 17 appearance in a Baghdad street and meetings with his officers and advisers. Most of this video represented coalition activities and speakers, however. Much of TVN's external video came from sources that were not identified. Among identified video sources, Spanish-language sources such as Spain's TVE were used more by the Chileans than by the other services in our sample.

TVN took great pains to "domesticate" the story of the war by offering local frames of reference in each newscast. Government officials explained Chile's official position—support for the coalition but no military participation in the conflict—and reassured viewers that steps had been taken to ensure that the war would not harm the nation's economy. Reflecting Chile's Catholic tradition, TVN gave more attention than the other services to a statement issued by Pope John Paul II concerning the war. An unusual domestic frame took the form of a four-minute story on a U.S. Latino family in which both the father and a son were serving with U.S. forces in the Gulf. The story was introduced with the observation that "about 30 percent to 60 percent of the soldiers in the Gulf are Latinos." Interviewed in their Brooklyn home, family members described their sadness and concern for their loved ones along with support for the war. Another domestic frame was offered in a story sent by TVN's correspondent in Amman. "We have to explain we are Chilean, South American," the correspondent said. "But the people hear 'America,' and that is directly related to Bush, and obviously the people reject us . . . now we say we are Spanish."

Overall, TVN offered a non-participant's narrative that carefully presented both sides of the conflict but, consistent with the government's position, reinforced the coalition view and portrayed the inevitability of a swift coalition victory. Extensive use of externally produced video was supplemented with substantial locally generated material, the better to develop the most distinctive feature of TVN's narrative, namely, the domestication of the distant conflict in terms of local concerns and frames of reference.

Germany—ZDF

ZDF (Zweites Deutsches Fernsehen), the second German national television network, operates in a highly competitive environment combining multiple broadcast networks and a growing number of satellite-delivered services. ZDF is a public service network created by an agreement among the German Federal states and accepts advertising to supplement revenue produced by license fees (Smith 1991: 48). *Heute* ("Today"), ZDF's evening newscast, is broadcast at 7:00 P.M. from network headquarters in Mainz. The broadcast's presenter is described as an "editor" rather than an "anchor" because the editor writes his or her own copy (Cohen, Adoni, and Bantz 1990: 203).

The outbreak of war was, of course, the major story on *Heute* during the period we examined, although not to the complete exclusion of other matters. Roughly the first eighteen minutes of the twenty-six and a half-minute newscasts were devoted to war-related events abroad and at home on January 18 and 19, diminishing to about ten to twelve minutes on January 22, 23, and 24. In each newscast, time was reserved for events unrelated to the war including sports, weather reports, and nightly "lifestyle" segments. ZDF deployed impressive resources to cover the war, with correspondents and crews in Saudi Arabia, Israel, Jordan, Washington, London, and various European sites. Despite *Heute*'s conception of its "editor," the presenter in these newscasts was an "anchor" who took a back seat to the on-location correspondents. The anchor provided brief lead-ins to lengthy correspondent reports and, in several cases, conducted live satellite interviews with ZDF correspondents whose expert opinions were solicited.

ZDF's narrative of the first days of the war reflected the coalition viewpoint. Coalition leaders and spokespersons were the primary sources of information as correspondents translated their remarks into German: George Bush, Dick Cheney, Brent Scowcroft, and others in Washington; Prime Minister John Major, Defence Secretary Tom King, and various political leaders in London; CENTCOM briefers in Riyadh; the British commander in Bahrain; President François Mitterrand of France; and U.N. Secretary-General Javier Perez de Cuellar. Iraqi spokespersons were absent except for video taken from Iraqi television showing Saddam Hussein's activities after the first raid on Baghdad. Correspondent reports from Washington were a daily feature of coverage. Interviews with British and American fliers conveyed the pride and concerns of coalition fighters. The story of a daring rescue of an American pilot downed in Iraq added human interest. World outrage at the Iraqi missile attacks on Israel was covered in detail. Generally, coverage of public opinion about the war outside of Germany was limited to the United States and United Kingdom, where reports of anti-war demonstrations were placed in the context of overwhelming majority support for the war. Coalition disappointments (e.g., that eradicating Iraq's Scud capability was proving more difficult than had been expected) and the continuing threat posed by surviving Iraqi military capabilities were duly noted, but within a framework that stressed coalition power, unity, resolve, and technology.

Approximately one-fourth of *Heute*'s early war coverage was domestically oriented. Large daily anti-war demonstrations were staged throughout Germany during this period, and ZDF's cameras recorded them for nightly viewing. However, every story about the German demonstrations closed with comments by German government and political leaders condemning the protests. A second story building throughout the week concerned the possibility that Iraq might attack Turkey in retaliation for U.S. sorties being flown from NATO's base at Incirlik, and that Germany might be drawn into the conflict through its treaty obligation to a fellow NATO country. *Heute* scrupulously reported the views of government officials and leaders of each of the major political parties about this possibility, carefully fulfilling its legal and political obligation to balance representation of opposing views (Cohen, Adoni, and Bantz 1990: 204). The amount and financing of Germany's share of the cost of the coalition campaign received attention, as did the visit to Israel of a delegation of government officials and other political leaders to pledge solidarity and assistance in the wake of the Scud attacks.

Overall, *Heute* supplemented its own extensive international video coverage with externally produced material (such as CNN's pictures of the first raid on Baghdad) to create a coalition-focused narrative dominated by official sources whose statements were taken at face value. Local war-related themes also were developed within official frameworks and, in general, reflected German concern about how to support the coalition effort without being drawn into the conflict as a participant.

United Kingdom—BBC

From London, the BBC's early evening newscast, "The Six O'Clock News," capitalized on substantial resources deployed to cover the war: satellite-based live interviews with correspondents in Washington and the Gulf; relatively long, fast-paced video stories produced by BBC crews at far-flung sites (as well as pool video from Saudi Arabia and material from CNN); sophisticated graphics. The dual anchors provided lead-ins and continuity to a presentation in which the field correspondents were the stars.

The BBC's coverage of the Falklands War in 1982 was criticized by the British prime minister and foreign secretary for being " 'unacceptably evenhanded' in its treatment of Argentina" (Head 1985: 75). In contrast, the "Six O'Clock News" covered the beginning of the Gulf War in a romantic style reminiscent of the early days of World War II when the organization declared the "maintenance of public morale" to be the "principal aim" of its programming (Marwick 1982: 149). On January 17, with vivid pictures and evocative language, BBC correspondents described how "Iraq trembled under the hammer blows of Tomahawk cruise missiles, . . . precision weapons of the twenty-first century." "The lethal aerial armada" with its "vastly superior technology" achieved "stunning results" so overpowering that "there is more than a glimmer of hope tonight that the allies could triumph without a war of attrition between the massed armies in the desert." From the RAF's base in Bahrain with accompanying video, a correspondent described how "the [RAF] Tornados . . . glided out of the dawn sky. . . . telling physical evidence of Britain's commitment to the war effort."

Concerning the courage of the fliers and the rightness of their cause, there were no doubts. Interviews with five U.S. airmen and three RAF fliers made clear the determination with which they faced their dangerous tasks. A correspondent summarized, "Ahead lay the unknown capabilities of the Arab world's most powerful military machine. But the Americans seemed raring to go." "For the young [RAF] airmen" returning from their first mission, "a taste of fear and exhilaration. . . . They're pleased with what they've done so far, but there's a long way to go before their difficult work is over." Asked "what is your message to the pilots," a Kuwaiti replied, "God bless them." The Kuwait Crown Prince was shown announcing to his people in a televised address that "the sunshine of liberation is near." The coda came from Riyadh where, at British headquarters, the chief of staff quoted from Shakespeare's speech of Henry V before the battle of Agincourt: "Gentlemen in England now abed should think themselves accursed they were not here."

Opposing the coalition forces was a villain of morality play dimensions in the BBC's construction of Saddam Hussein. The issue of Iraq's treatment of downed coalition fliers led to perhaps the BBC's most sharply drawn portrait of the Iraqi president, offered in the newscasts of January 21 and 22. Responding to statements by the POWs' broadcast on Iraqi television and an Iraqi threat to use the fliers as "human shields" at strategic targets, British, coalition, and Red Cross officials agreed that the Iraqis were committing a war crime. Defence Secretary Tom King declared, "We have the gravest suspicion of the means that may have been used to achieve [the POWs' televised] statements for [the Iraqis'] own political purposes." A BBC correspondent noted, "Some of the captives looked battered; all spoke woodenly. There were long pauses while the haunting conversation was translated into Arabic." The Iraqi ambassador "shilly-shallied" in response to the Foreign Office's demand that the Geneva Conventions be observed. Labour leader Neil Kinnock observed in the House of Commons: "Mr. Saddam Hussein may wear the uniform of a soldier; he certainly doesn't take the risks of a soldier or follow any soldier's code that I know of." Prime Minister John Major proclaimed of Saddam: "He may yet become a target of his own people. This man is amoral. He takes hostages. He attacks population centers. He's a man without pity. Whatever his fate may be, I, for one, will not weep for him."

Saddam Hussein's villainy was only amplified by his amateurish propaganda, according to the BBC. Concerning the much-publicized Iraqi video of Saddam being greeted by civilians in a Baghdad street on the day after the bombing began, the "Six O'Clock News" correspondent observed that "it's impossible to know when the pictures were taken. There's no sign of damage, and only a few people are shown greeting him." Saddam's "long and rambling" televised speech to the Iraqi people received the same critical scrutiny: "The videotape fault showed that his speech certainly was recorded." And the speech was pronounced ineffective: "Although he castigates America for attacking him, the general reaction around the world has been to blame Saddam Hussein personally for forcing an unwanted war."

Within the BBC's morality play, care was taken to represent the respective roles of the British and the Americans. The war was an American-led enterprise, but the British played the leading supporting role. This relationship was communicated structurally through the organization of reports from the war zone, where stories about the Americans' activities typically preceded stories of British activities, as well as daily reports about the actions of national leaders, where stories from Washington usually preceded stories from Downing Street. The importance of British participation was developed substantively through the theme of continuing Bush–Major consultation. It was reported that "the key decision" to begin the air assault "had been taken by Mr. Major and Mr. Bush when they met before Christmas," and it was stressed repeatedly that British officials were "in continuous touch with the White House." Anti-war protests in the United States and Britain were noted but contrasted to the unity and determination of officialdom in both countries. Thus, the BBC "localized" the war story primarily through its construction of the importance of British participation founded on national unity.

In sum, "The Six O'Clock News" offered a partisan view of the early days of the war structured as a morality play, a conflict between coalition virtue and villainy personified in Saddam Hussein. British participation in the war was stressed, though carefully subordinated to the American role.[6] Iraqi spokespersons were shown only rarely, and their claims were reported with skepticism and, sometimes, disdain.

United States—CBS

As the American representative we selected CBS's coverage of the first days of the war. With the first reports of the raid on Baghdad on January 16, CBS abandoned regular programming and went to continuous war coverage that lasted into January 18. In order to obtain material comparable to the newscasts of the other six countries examined, we selected from January 17 a one-hour segment that was designated a "special hour-long edition of the CBS Evening News." The first half-hour of this program occupied the normal "CBS Evening News" time slot. The other CBS newscasts examined were regular editions of the program, occasionally expanded from thirty minutes (on January 19, 21, 22, and 23) to one hour (on January 18 and 24).

CBS deployed substantial technological and human resources in the United States, Europe, and the Middle East to cover the war during the period of interest. Coverage was organized into a series of standard topics, each assigned to a lead correspondent, that were presented on every newscast (the order of the topics varied depending on events of each day): latest information from the Pentagon; events in Saudi Arabia reported from Dhahran; events in Israel reported from Tel Aviv; actions of U.S. government officials, particularly President Bush; effects of the war on the U.S. economy and financial markets; and, the American "home front," stories about demonstrations and how ordinary Americans were responding to the war. These topics were supplemented by daily reports from correspondents with U.S. ground troops in Saudi Arabia and by reports on other war-related subjects that varied from day to day. CBS star anchorman Dan Rather moderated each of the newscasts except January 19, when Bob Schieffer was substitute anchor. With the exception of Iraqi and Israeli television, no video was identified as the product of another television service, although a fair amount of pool video from Saudi Arabia was used.

Of the services we examined, CBS offered the most complex narrative of the war. One theme of the first week's coverage made clear that the war was decidedly an American undertaking. Care was taken to include references to "the United States and other nations" in the initial newscast on January 17, but these references became increasingly rare as the first week wore on. The leaders of the coalition were Bush, Cheney, Powell, and Schwartzkopf; the technology was American; the troops were American; and the costs would be borne by Americans. On January

17, for example, the "Evening News" carried comments by nine American officials and political leaders, seven American soldiers and airmen serving in Saudi Arabia, thirty American civilians at home, and two Palestinians living in Jordan. Representing other members of the multinational coalition was one sentence from British Prime Minister Major, comments from two British civilians interviewed in a London railway station, and a report that after "dithering" the Italian Parliament voted to commit forces to combat. In general, although American public opinion was monitored daily in the "home front" segment, opinions elsewhere received relatively little notice.

Motifs of technology, danger, and strategy dominated the story of the American war in the Gulf, told in a lean, matter-of-fact style. U.S. technology and weaponry were stars of Desert Storm on CBS from the beginning. The story of the first air assaults was told by Pentagon correspondent David Martin in terms of the individual roles played by twelve different types of aircraft plus the Tomahawk cruise missile. A stream of facts and figures from the Pentagon and Riyadh assessing the technology's success was reported throughout the week, along with additional stories describing the capabilities of the Patriot anti-missile system, the M1A1 Abrams tank, the Apache helicopter, spy satellites, reconnaissance missiles, and other systems. Video of the success of "smart," laser-guided missiles and bombs was shown almost nightly as a particular highlight.

The motif of danger was ever-present as CBS balanced American successes with disappointments and failures. Optimistic first-day predictions of quick and easy victory gave way to daily reports of problems and concerns. On January 18, "There is great fear [in Dhahran] of Iraq's missiles"; "increasingly, some pilots are not returning." From the Kuwaiti border, "The Iraqis are proving difficult to displace, a harbinger, perhaps, of things to come." On January 19, "The air war is now being concentrated on Iraq's ground forces . . . but it's not being done without costs." On January 21, "Only a small fraction of Saddam Hussein's air force has been destroyed"; "for those who have suffered losses, war is painful already." On January 22, after the most damaging Scud attack on Israel, "Saddam Hussein has cracked a U.S. defensive shield and struck his heaviest blow so far" as U.S. Patriots "failed to hit anything"; Iraqi command and control remains intact despite being the "principal aim of the air campaign." As seen from the Pentagon, "not everything is going according to plan." For the first time since World War II, U.S. troops will be led into battle by non-commissioned officers who mostly have never been in combat themselves; "Before they can conquer the Iraqis, they must conquer their own fear."

Military and political strategy was the frame in which information about the war's progress was interpreted and evaluated. Each night, the

"Evening News" offered assessments and predictions by its military consultants, retired U.S. Marine General George Crist and retired U.S. Air Force General Michael Dugan: "We're going to have to take Kuwait; . . . when we go, it's going to be violent, Patton-like armored thrusts, perhaps an amphibious end run." "We've had some successes, but clearly we've had some losses." We're up "against the fifth largest military power in the world as of twenty-four hours ago." Consultant Fouad Ajami, professor at Johns Hopkins University, speculated about the Iraqis' reactions and motivations. Coverage of President Bush's actions focused on strategies for prosecuting the war, preparing the American public to accept the casualties that were expected, dissuading the Israelis from retaliating against the Iraqis, keeping the Arab members of the coalition in line if the Israelis did retaliate, and laying political groundwork to manage the war's aftermath in the Middle East.

Interviews with Americans serving in the Gulf provided counterpoint to the war's strategy and technology. From the exuberance ("ran our first play and it worked great, scored a touchdown, and there was nobody home") and sober realism ("scary to think what damage we're going to be doing and how many lives we're going to be taking") of those taking part in the first air attacks to the determination, preparedness, and high morale of those moving into position for the ground invasion, the experiences and emotions of those facing combat were related day by day.

The enemy was personified in the ruthless, iniquitous Saddam Hussein, a leader "hunkered down in Baghdad" but still dangerous and in control. His speech to the Iraqi people on January 17 was "taunting" and "defiant," although his propaganda was crudely staged, made "ridiculous" claims, and was generally ineffective. Missile attacks on Israeli cities and mistreatment of coalition POWs were represented through comments by U.S. officials as particular manifestations of Hussein's villainy.

The final element of the "Evening News" narrative was the American public's reaction to the war. Hallin (1986: 19) has described U.S. television news as distinctive in its populist concern "with ordinary people and ordinary life," and this concern was a major component of war coverage. Daily "home front" stories monitored the tides of public sentiment through such indicators as demonstrations for and against the government's policy, support for the war as measured by the latest polls, and demand for U.S. flags outstripping the supply. The most common story, however, revealed the emotions of people touched by the war: a group of Vietnam veterans for whom the war triggered recurrent post-traumatic stress disorder; a proud Texas father who had seen his pilot son return from a sortie on television; children expressing fears for their mothers and fathers serving in the Gulf; two little girls watching a home video sent by their mother from Saudi Arabia. With the exception of January 17, every newscast during the period of interest ended with "home front" stories attempting to describe the mood of the country.

In sum, the complex narrative of CBS described an American war in a series of juxtapositions: the strategist's language of battle management versus the soldier's language of confidence and preparedness; the overwhelming might and technology of American forces versus the cleverness and evil of Saddam Hussein; American pride versus fear, confidence versus doubt. The story's structure was that of the morality play, but it was a play in which both adversaries had their successes and their failures and the costs of resolution would be keenly felt by victims on both sides.

HOW MUCH GLOBAL, HOW MUCH VILLAGE?

The results of our brief look at a limited sample of newscasts accord, by and large, with findings of similar comparative studies of television news that have examined other countries, other topics, and other periods (e.g., Cohen, Adoni, and Bantz 1990; Gurevitch, Levy, and Roeh in press; Servaes 1991; Straubhaar et al. in press). The simplest gloss from our sample is that there were considerable variations in the story of the war's first week told by our seven services, and this despite the reliance of most of the services on the same sources of information and video material and coverage of generally the same events. Insofar as our sample is concerned, there was no global television news story of the war; there were seven different village stories. At the same time, there were many similarities between the services' stories. The kinds of similarities and differences we observed, and the way in which they relate to each other, may tell us something about influences on television coverage of the war and about television news globalization more generally.

Similarities in the newscasts were, perhaps, as striking as the differences. All the newscasts were organized in a similar format—anchor(s), correspondent reports, mixture of internal and external video, use of narrative montages, preference for live reports when possible, organized with most important stories first, and so on. In every newscast we found the narrative story form, reliance on officials as the authoritative sources of information and interpretive frames, the roles of anchors and reporters constructed as "observers" and "interpreters" whose credibility derives from command of the facts, representations of the statements and actions of both sides of the conflict, and attention to domestic angles connecting viewers to the war. These similarities appear to reflect a shared professional television news culture that prescribes conventions by which news is produced and presented. Such shared conventions have been observed in several recent comparative cross-national studies (e.g., Cohen, Adoni, and Bantz 1990; Gurevitch, Levy, and Roeh in press).

From our point of view, the most important differences between the newscasts were those content elements that contributed directly to each service's overall narrative construction of the meaning of the war and the abilities and motivations of the antagonists. As we have seen, these constructions varied widely. In form, the narratives of five services featured the essential elements of the morality play, a confrontation between good and evil. CBS, in a complex narrative, and the BBC, in a somewhat simpler narrative, both personified the enemy in Saddam Hussein, a figure whose villainous qualities were highlighted as a major theme of coverage, and contrasted him to the coalition, which had exhausted all peaceful means of putting things to right and been forced to wage war only with the greatest reluctance. Jordan Television, Malaysia's TV3, and India's Doordarshan constructed some of the elements of a morality play as seen from the other side of the confrontation. None of the three services explicitly represented Saddam Hussein as a virtuous figure, although his rallying call to Arabs was described as appealing, but all three made it clear that the coalition's actions were producing villainous consequences—such as the death and injury of innocent women and children and wanton destruction of religious sites—that outraged world opinion. Chile's Televisión Nacional and Germany's ZDF offered narratives that focused less on virtue and vice than on the inevitability of coalition victory and the determination of both countries to stay out of the conflict, even though each narrative was inflected toward the coalition viewpoint.

Differences in the services' overall narrative constructions were displayed perhaps most clearly in a few key elements of the newscasts. Organizationally, although all services covered the actions and public statements of both sides of the conflict, the choice of which side typically was covered first in each story related strongly to the inflection of the narrative. Narratives favorable to the coalition generally reported coalition news first, as narratives more favorable to the Iraqis reported news from that side first. Also important were the time and credibility accorded to spokespersons for each side. Every service reported statements from both sides, but statements by spokespersons for the favored side were reported more frequently, at greater length, and typically were taken at face value. Statements from the disfavored side not only were reported less often but also frequently were bracketed by "disdaining" commentary from reporters that undercut the credibility of the statements (the phenomenon of disdainful commentary is described in detail by Semetko et al. 1991: 129–32). The Chilean and German services, whose narratives were less framed in moral terms than the other services, tended to report the combatants' statements with little or no comment.

The construction of each side's military competence and power was another theme that related strongly to differences in the overall narratives. Every narrative acknowledged the overwhelming superiority of coalition might, but pro-coalition morality plays stressed the high-tech effectiveness of coalition air strikes and feeble nature of Iraq's response while anti-coalition morality plays stressed coalition ineffectiveness and the ability of Iraqi cunning to even the odds a bit. Similarly, attention given to civilian casualties of coalition bombing differentiated narratives, with relatively more attention being given by anti-coalition narratives. Finally, treatment of the theme of official and public opinion was an important feature distinguishing the narratives. Anti-coalition narratives constructed "world opinion," both from government leaders and civilian populations, as virtually unified in opposition to the coalition's actions. Anti-war demonstrations around the world were covered at length and given much significance. Pro-coalition narratives gave less attention to "world opinion," concentrating more on expressions of opinion in the combatant countries. Anti-war demonstrations were reported, but typically in a context that made clear majority support for coalition policy.

As the foregoing suggests, each service created a more or less distinct narrative by following a common protocol of journalistic conventions but applying the conventions differently. For example, each service reported statements by both sides of the conflict, but the more partisan narratives took care to distinguish credible statements from statements that were not believable. In different ways, each service reported the themes of "public opinion," "military effectiveness," and "consequences of the bombing," but there were important differences in how each narrative constructed these themes. Thus, every service we examined constructed a distinctive story of the war not only by exploring the domestic relevance of the war to each country but also by interpreting events of the war in different ways. The effect of the differences was to produce narratives that reflected the national culture and sentiment in each country. In the case of early war coverage, participation (or not) in the conflict, differences in media ownership, degree of media competition, and the like were less helpful in explaining differences in narratives than were national sentiment and affinities.

As a way of describing analytically the relationship between national and transnational influences on early news about the war, the metaphor of a grammar may be helpful. Our observations may be read as suggesting that the transnational professional television news culture operates something like a syntax, indicating to television journalists around the world the appropriate elements of reporting and the forms in which these elements may be combined to create stories. Within this syntax, there is considerable lexical variation. Stories are event-centered, but which aspects of events should be highlighted may be a matter of lexical choice. Authoritative information comes from officials, but decisions about which officials may be taken at face value introduce lexical variation. Events are important when they affect large numbers of people, but which people are most affected and what form the most newsworthy effects take offer lexical choice. And so on.

In terms of the grammar metaphor, the interconnected international television news environment might be seen as consisting of both a shared code of professional practice, or syntactic rules, and a steady supply of information from transnational wire and video news agencies. The competent practice of television news allows considerable room for lexical variation between countries, and these variations produce the result that, in early coverage of the Gulf War, television services produced narratives that were professionally competent in terms of syntactic rules but nationally distinctive in terms of lexical choices. In the first week of the war, every television service we examined made use of externally prepared video, but no service used all the external video that was on offer, and each service made somewhat different choices of which material to use. In the great majority of cases, services provided their own narration to accompany external video, a practice which allowed for variation in interpretation and may reflect the "open" nature of video text (Gurevitch, Levy and Roeh in press), particularly when video is fragmented into bits and pieces that are selectively woven into montages by recipient services.

In the services we examined, media globalization did not produce a global narrative. On the contrary, the global television environment provided ample resources by which nationally relevant and distinctive narratives were produced. Viewers of each service saw a coherent narrative of the beginning of the Gulf War, what was happening, why, and what it had to do with them. From the odd perspective that researchers take on such things, we saw seven narratives and seven wars.

NOTES

The authors would like to acknowledge the assistance of Rebecca A. Carrier, project research assistant and a doctoral student in Speech Communication at the University of Illinois at Urbana-Champaign, who compiled videotapes of the newscasts examined in this study. Translation costs and other expenses were funded by an Arnold O. Beckman Research Award to the first author from the Research Board of the University of Illinois at Urbana-Champaign.

1. See Rosenberg (1991: 19); see also the exchange between U.S. Senator John Glenn and former CBS Evening News Anchor Walter Cronkite during the U.S. Senate hearing on media coverage of the Gulf War (U.S. Congress 1991: 24–25).

2. In World War II, 461 journalists were accredited by Supreme Headquarters, Allied Expeditionary Force to cover the Normandy invasion (and 27 reporters actually went ashore with the troops) (Williams 1991: 11). In Vietnam, an average

of 400 journalists were in the country on any given day, swelling to a high of 648 journalists accredited in March 1968, following the Tet offensive (Sidle 1991: 52). Following Iraq's invasion of Kuwait in August, the Iraqis allowed more than 1,800 journalists from around the world into Baghdad to cover the story (Hieberg 1991: 113). In Saudi Arabia, the U.S. and international press corps grew from 0 at the time of the invasion of Kuwait to 17 when the first U.S. Department of Defense press pool arrived on August 13, to 800 in mid-December, one month before the war began, to 1,400 in mid-February, 1991 (Williams 1991: 8, 10).

3. Personnel representing television services in the following countries were registered with the Joint Information Bureaus in Riyadh and Dhahran on February 23, 1991 (some countries, such as the United States, United Kingdom, France, and Germany, were represented by multiple television services): Australia, Austria, Belgium, Brazil, Canada, Denmark, Egypt, Fiji, Finland, France, Germany, Greece, Holland, Indonesia, Italy, Japan, Korea, Kuwait, Malaysia, Mexico, Monte Carlo, New Zealand, Norway, Portugal, Spain, Sweden, Taiwan, Thailand, Turkey, United States, United Kingdom.

4. For the most part, studies of media globalization have focused on patterns of ownership in the media industries (e.g., Negrine and Papathanassopoulos 1990; U.S. Congress 1990). Here, however, we are interested primarily in the content of television news. Thus, media ownership is relevant to the present study only insofar as it is reflected in features of news content.

5. In part, these arrangements reflect ownership of the two agencies. The BBC, NBC, and Reuters own shares in Visnews; the British ITN network, Bond Media, and ABC own shares in WTN. For a detailed discussion of the organization of the international television news distribution system, see Wallis and Baran (1990).

6. Nevertheless, in survey taken in England in February, 1991, 97 percent of the respondents overestimated the proportion of the coalition air sorties that had been flown by RAF fliers (Shaw and Carr-Hill 1991).

BIBLIOGRAPHY

Alter, J., E. E. Dennis, L. Grossman, D. Hallin, and J. Nelson. "The First Casualty Revisited: A Roundtable Discussion." In *The Media at War: The Press and the Persian Gulf Conflict*, ed. C. LaMay, M. FitzSimon, and J. Sahadi, 65–76. New York: Gannett Foundation Media Center, 1991.
Altheide, D. L. *Creating Reality: How TV News Distorts Events*. Beverly Hills, Calif.: Sage, 1976.
Altheide, D. L., and R. P. Snow. *Media Logic*. Beverly Hills, Calif.: Sage, 1979.
Blood, R. W. "Public Reaction in Australia to the Media and the War." Paper presented at the annual meeting of the International Communication Association, Chicago. May 1991.
Central Intelligence Agency. *The World Factbook 1989*. Washington, D.C.: Central Intelligence Agency, 1989.
Chen, A. C., and A. G. Chaudhary. "Asia and the Pacific." In *Global Journalism: Survey of International Communication*, ed. J. C. Merrill, 2d ed., 205–66. New York: Longman, 1991.

Cohen, A. A., H. Adoni, and C. R. Bantz. *Social Conflict and Television News.* Newbury Park, Calif.: Sage, 1990.

Corry, J. "TV News & the Neutrality Principle." *Commentary* 91(5)(1991): 24–27.

Entman, R. M. "Framing U.S. Coverage of International News: Contrasts in Narratives of the KAL and Iran Air Incidents." *Journal of Communication* 41(4)(1991): 6–27.

Fisher, G. *American Communication in a Global Society,* rev. ed. Norwood, N.J.: Ablex, 1987.

FitzSimon, M. "Public Perception of War Coverage: A Survey Analysis." In *The Media at War: The Press and the Persian Gulf Conflict,* ed. C. LaMay, M. FitzSimon, and J. Sahadi, 86–95. New York: Gannett Foundation Media Center, 1991.

Gantz, W. "Watching the War: Patterns of Information Seeking During a Crisis." Paper presented at the annual meeting of the International Communication Association, Chicago. May 1991.

Golding, P., and P. Elliott. *Making the News.* London: Longman, 1979.

Graber, D. A. *Mass Media and American Politics,* 2d ed. Washington, D.C.: Congressional Quarterly Press, 1984.

Greenberg, B. S., and E. B. Parker, eds. *The Kennedy Assassination and the American Public: Social Communication in Crisis.* Stanford, Calif.: Stanford University Press, 1965.

Gurevitch, M. "Comparative Research on Television News: Problems and Challenges." *American Behavioral Scientist* 33(1989): 221–29.

Gurevitch, M., M. R. Levy, and I. Roeh. "The Global Newsroom: Convergence and Diversities in the Globalization of Television News." In *Communication and Citizenship: Journalism and the Public Sphere in the Media Age,* ed. P. Dahlgren and C. Sparks. London: Routledge, in press.

Hallin, D. C. "Network News. We Keep America on Top of the World." In *Watching Television,* ed. T. Gitlin, 9–41. New York: Pantheon, 1986.

Head, S. W. *World Broadcasting Systems: A Comparative Analysis.* Belmont, Calif.: Wadsworth, 1985.

Heiberg, R. E. "Public Relations as a Weapon of Modern Warfare." *Public Relations Review* 17(2)(1991): 107–16.

Hester, A. "The Collection and Flow of World News." In *Global Journalism: Survey of International Communication,* ed. J. C. Merrill, 2d ed., 29–50. New York: Longman, 1991.

Hudson, J. C., and S. Swindel. "TV News in Saudi Arabia." *Journalism Quarterly* 65(1988): 1003–6.

International Centre on Censorship. *International Freedom and Censorship: World Report 1991.* Chicago: American Library Association, 1991.

King, J. "Visnews and UPITN: News Film Supermarkets in the Sky." In *Crisis in International News,* ed. J. Richstad and M. E. Anderson, 283–98. New York: Columbia University Press, 1981.

Kurian, G. T. (ed.). *World Press Encyclopedia* (2 vols.). New York: Facts on File, 1982.

Larson, J. F. *Television's Window on the World: International Affairs Coverage on the U.S. Networks.* Norwood, N.J.: Ablex, 1984.

Lent, J. A. "Telematics in Malaysia: Room at the Top for a Selected Few." In

Transnational Communications: Wiring the Third World, ed. G. Sussman and J. A. Lent, 165–99. Newbury Park, Calif.: Sage, 1991.

Mander, M. S. "Narrative Dimensions of the News: Omniscience, Prophecy, and Morality." *Communication* 10(1987): 51–70.

Martin, L. A., and A. G. Chaudhary. "Goals and Roles of Media Systems." In *Comparative Mass Media Systems*, ed. L. J. Martin and A. G. Chaudhary, 1–31. New York: Longman, 1983.

Marwick, A. "Print, Pictures, and Sound: The Second World War and the British Experience." *Daedalus* 111(4)(1982): 135–55.

McLeod, D., E. Perse, N. Signorielli, and J. A. Courtright. "Public Perceptions and Evaluations of the Role of the Media in the Persian Gulf War." Paper presented at the Conference on Media and the Gulf War, Media Studies Project, Woodrow Wilson International Center for Scholars. Washington, D.C., September 19, 1991.

Mott, P. "New King of the Hill." *The Quill* (March 1991): 14–16.

Nasser, M. K. "News Values versus Ideology: A Third World Perspective." In *Comparative Mass Media Systems*, ed. L. J. Martin and A. G. Chaudhary, 44–66. New York: Longman, 1983.

Negrine, R., and S. Papathanassopoulos. *The Internationalisation of Television*. London: Pinter, 1990.

Nimmo, D., and J. E. Combs. *Nightly Horrors: Crisis Coverage in Television Network News*. Knoxville: University of Tennessee Press, 1985.

Nimmo, D., and J. E. Combs. *Mediated Political Realities*, 2d ed. New York: Longman, 1990.

Ogan, C. "The Middle East and North Africa." In *Global Journalism: A Survey of International Communication*, ed. J. C. Merrill, 2d ed., 129–153. New York: Longman, 1991.

O'Heffernan, P. "Television and Crisis: Sobering Thoughts on Sound Bites Seen 'Round the World." *Television Quarterly* 25(1)(1990): 9–14.

O'Heffernan, P. *Mass Media and American Foreign Policy: Insider Perspectives on Global Journalism and the Foreign Policy Process*. Norwood, N.J.: Ablex, 1991.

Paraschos, M. "Europe." In *Global Journalism: Survey of International Communication*, ed. J. C. Merrill, 2d ed., 93–128. New York: Longman, 1991.

Peled, T., and E. Katz. "Media Functions in Wartime: The Israeli Homefront in October, 1973." In *The Uses of Mass Communication: Current Perspectives on Gratifications Research*, ed. J. G. Blumler and E. Katz, 46–69. Beverly Hills, Calif.: Sage, 1974.

Pendakur, M. "A Political Economy of Television: State, Class, and Corporate Confluence in India." In *Transnational Communications: Wiring the Third World*, ed. G. Sussman and J. T. Lent, 234–62. Newbury Park, Calif.: Sage, 1991.

"Public Affairs Guidance on Refueling of C–141 Aircraft in India." U.S. Department of Defense. January 31, 1991.

Richstad, J. "Transnational News Agencies: Issues and Politics." In *Crisis in International News*, ed. J. Richstad and M. E. Anderson, 242–57. New York: Columbia University Press, 1981.

Roeh, I. "Journalism as Storytelling, Coverage as Narrative." *American Behavioral Scientist* 33(1989): 162–68.

Rosenberg, E. "TV and the Gulf War." *The Quill* (March 1991): 17–19.

Salwen, M. B., B. Garrison, and R. T. Buckman. "Latin America and the Caribbean." In *Global Journalism: Survey of International Communication*, ed. J. C. Merrill, 2d ed., 267–310. New York: Longman, 1991.

Schudson, M. "The Politics of Narrative Form: The Emergence of News Conventions in Print and Television." *Daedalus*, 111(1982): 97–112.

Semetko, H. A., J. G. Blumler, M. Gurevitch, and D. H. Weaver, with S. Barkin and G. C. Wilhoit. *The Formation of Campaign Agendas: A Comparative Analysis of Party and Media Roles in Recent American and British Elections*. Hillsdale, N.J.: Erlbaum, 1991.

Servaes, J. "European Press Coverage of the Grenada Crisis."*Journal of Communication* 41(4)(1991): 28–41.

Shaw, M., and R. Carr-Hill. "Mass Media and Attitudes to the Gulf War in Britain." *Electronic Journal of Communication* 2 (November 1991).

Sidle, W. Testimony of Major General Winant Sidle (U.S. Army Ret.), Chairman, Joint Chiefs of Staff investigation of U.S. news policy during invasion of Grenada. Hearing on *Pentagon Rules on Media Access to the Persian Gulf War*, 52–54. U.S. Congress, Senate, Committee on Governmental Affairs, 102nd Congress, 1st sess., February 20, 1991.

Siebert, F., T. Peterson, and W. Schramm. *Four Theories of the Press*. Urbana: University of Illinois Press, 1956.

Smith, A. *The Age of Behemoths: The Globalization of Mass Media Firms*, a Twentieth Century Fund report. New York: Priority Press, 1991.

Smith, L. D. "Narrative Styles in Network Coverage of the 1984 Nominating Conventions." *Western Journal of Speech Communication* 52(1988): 63–74.

Smith, L. D., and D. Nimmo. *Cordial Concurrence: Orchestrating National Party Conventions in the Telepolitical Age*. New York: Praeger, 1991.

Sperry, S. L. "Television News as Narrative." In *Understanding Television: Essays on Television as a Social and Cultural Force*, ed. R. P. Adler, 295–312. New York: Praeger, 1981.

Stephens, L. F. "The World's Media Systems: An Overview." In *Global Journalism: Survey of International Communication*, ed. J. C. Merrill, 2d ed., 51–71. New York: Longman, 1991.

Straubhaar, J. D., C. Heeter, B. S. Greenberg, L. Ferreira, R. H. Wicks, and T. Y. Lau. "What Makes News: Western, Socialist, and Third World Television Newscasts Compared in Eight Countries." In *International and Intercultural Communication Annual*, vol. 16, ed. F. Korzenny and E. Schiff. Newbury Park, Calif.: Sage, in press.

Tunstall, J. *The Media are American: Anglo-American Media in the World*. London: Constable, 1977.

U.S. Congress. 1990. House of Representatives. Subcommittee on Telecommunications and Finance, Committee on Energy and Commerce. Hearing on *Globalization of the Media*. 101st Congress, 1st sess., November 15, 1989. Serial No. 101–98.

U.S. Congress. 1991. Senate. Committee on Governmental Affairs. Hearing on *Pentagon Rules on Media Access to the Persian Gulf War*. 102nd Congress, 1st sess., February 20, 1991.

Wallis, R., and S. J. Baran. *The Known World of Broadcast News: International News and the Electronic Media*. London: Routledge, 1990.

Williams, P. Testimony of Pete Williams, Assistant Secretary for Public Affairs, U.S. Department of Defense. Hearing on *Pentagon Rules on Media Access to the Persian Gulf War*, 6–11. U.S. Congress, Senate, Committee on Governmental Affairs, 102nd Congress, 1st sess., February 20, 1991.

World Radio TV Handbook, 1992 edition. London: Billboard Limited, 1992.

Chapter Ten

Media Coverage of Women in the Gulf War

Anne Johnston

In many analysts' eyes, the Gulf War and the victory of the U.S. and Allied forces against Iraq was a salve on the American public's wound from the Vietnam War. The war was mercifully short (lasting from mid-January 1991 until early March 1991) and received widespread support from the American public. Public opinion was generally positive for both the military and the media, and it appeared as if there was approval of the job being done by both. But the Gulf War may also serve as the point where a smaller battle was taking place. That battle was one of the acceptance of women in combat roles and the destruction of stereotypes about the mission that women have in the military. Although it certainly was not the first time that women had been close to combat zones and in danger from enemy fire, the Gulf War and media coverage of it did provide Americans with a close-up view of the roles that women played in the military. The coverage of women in the Gulf before, during, and after Desert Storm featured stories of individual hero(ine)s, of the personal and professional triumph of women soldiers and pilots, of female POWs and those killed in action, and of a nation's concern with the children left behind. Following Desert Storm, media featured national debates about the expansion of military women into previously off-limit jobs and discussions about the images that had come into the American public's mind through newspapers, magazines and television. As Ellen Goodman wrote, "In the aftermath of Desert Storm, it's all begun to seem like a mirage. Women manning Patriot missile launchers? A ponytail sticking out of the cap of a helicopter pilot? Americans had believed there was a law against women in combat" (1991: 11A).

Americans were right to believe that women were not allowed in combat. There was legislation passed in 1948 excluding women from combat missions. These exclusion laws forbid air force and navy women from flying combat missions and prohibited women from serving aboard ships or aircraft of navy and marines involved in combat missions. The army was not covered by the exclusion laws but had its own regulations preventing women from flying in combat and from frontline infantry and armor units ("Senate Repeals Ban" 1991; Smith 1991). But women had, since the Revolutionary War, been a part of combat, serving in support positions and coming under fire in battles. Folklore and history had attributed the first action seen by a woman to a woman who stepped into her husband's position to fire a cannon when he collapsed from wounds during the Revolutionary War (Campbell 1990; Enloe 1983). Since that time, women have been a part of every American battle, serving in support or secondary roles. In the Gulf War, however, women served in a wider array of assignments than they had in any other battle; because of the long-range technology, there were no hard lines between front and rear positions, so women were closer to combat than originally thought (Priest 1991e).

The media, by covering the debates that developed because of the expanded role of women in the Gulf War, helped to redefine the issues surrounding women in combat. The Gulf War and the media's depiction and discussion of women in non-traditional roles may have helped shape the perspective of the American public on the ability of women to serve in these roles. Certainly, the media coverage of certain aspects of women in the Gulf gave female soldiers and pilots the opportunity to bring the debates to light and to attempt to reform the rules excluding them from combat. There were certain categories of coverage that developed from the coverage of women in the Gulf, and this chapter is an attempt to discuss how these issues were framed by print (generally) media coverage.

WOMEN AND THE MILITARY

The importance of women and their role in the military can first be understood by looking at their place in military life and at what serving in the military means to women who have chosen that as a lifestyle. In her 1983 book, *Does Khaki Become You?*, Cynthia Enloe argues that women in the military have traditionally been seen as "camp followers," that they have been kept ideologically marginal to the essential combat function of the military. She suggests that this marginality in military life reflects culture's view of women in general, "she is financially dependent on men; her labour is used but she does not control it or reap its rewards; she is expected to be nurturing and self-sacrificing; but if she steps out of line, she can be labelled a 'common whore' and marginalised even further" (6).

Women have always had an interest in military life, but have been restricted in their advancements because of the regulations that exclude them from certain positions. The inability to pursue these positions (about 60 percent of military's total jobs are open to women) has meant that women officers and others cannot reach the top unless they have combat experience, but because they cannot be in combat these top tiers of the military are closed to them (Nordheimer 1991). Although women appear to report more "dovish" attitudes than men in opinion polls, studies have shown that they cite certain benefits because of their service in the military (Campbell 1990). In a study of women who served in World War II, Campbell found that increased self-esteem and independence were the two most frequently cited positive effects of having served in the military during wartime, in addition to other rewards that the women cite, such as the development of lifelong friends, development of a broader perspective on life, and rewarding memories and independence.

During the coverage of women in the Gulf, the media seemed to frame the issues around three main areas. The issues covered can be grouped into (1) a focus on how children were affected by parents serving in the Gulf, (2) a description of how women serving in the Gulf were doing jobs and put into situations not normally thought they would be in, and (3) a discussion of the debates about how their performance spilled into issues of equality in the work force.

"WHEN DAD AND MOM GO TO WAR"*

One of the issues covered by the media during the Gulf War dealt with how children in the United States were dealing with the images of war in general. Fred Rogers of "Mr. Rogers' Neighborhood" created several public service spots, talking with children and adults about the war. ABC News produced a Saturday morning special news report specifically geared toward children and their concerns about the war (Blau 1991). The purpose of most of this resulted from the concern that children might be adversely affected by coverage of a war. Articles and programs in the media dealt with how parents and teachers could allay children's fears about the impact of the war on them. Among the concerns that children had were fears about how close bombs were to them, how directly they were threatened by the war and their worries about the possibility of terrorist activities ("When Little Children" 1991). The attempt of the media to assist in helping the country's children deal with fears and nightmares also featured interviews with the nation's counselors and pediatricians who offered advice to adults on how children

*The headline used as the title for this section is from *Time* (February 18, 1991): 69.

might best be helped in talking out these fears ("First Aid" 1991; "What Parents Need" 1991). Even the first lady, Barbara Bush, advised parents to be careful about what they were allowing their children to watch on TV and to help them talk through their fears and nightmares (Radcliffe 1991).

Although most of these stories and programs dealt with the images that might scare children as they watched stories of the war on television, others dealt more directly with the plight of children who had relatives in the war. "For American children, especially those with relatives in the military, war no longer seems remote or abstract. Television has made it as vivid as a bomb-blasted building or a rubble-choked street" ("When Little Children" 1991: 40). In an article headlined with "The Gulf: When Father is at the Front," the media interviewed children who had been affected more directly because a parent was in the war. The story detailed how the children dealt with increased security on their military bases, their fears about terrorism on their base, and the increased responsibilities they had now that their dads were gone (Gross 1991).

The American public quickly learned, however, that mothers too were at the front, and in fact many children had been left stateside with both parents serving in the Gulf War. The second concern, then, following general concern about how children were viewing the war, was a more specific concern about the well-being of children "abandoned" because mom and dad were at war. This new understanding was perhaps best illustrated by a cartoon in an issue of the *Washington Post Weekly*. In the first frame of the cartoon, three soldiers with rifles are positioned in a foxhole (a man and a woman on one side and a man on the opposite side) with a caption above the solitary soldier reading "In times of war you want to tell your mom and dad you love them." In the second frame, the same soldier says, "I love you, mom and dad" and the two other soldiers respond, "We love you too, son." ("Drawing Board" 1991: 30). The concern about children during the Gulf War crisis quickly changed from a concern about all children to a concern about those left behind when mom and dad went to war.

Many of the stories dealt with how children were dealing with having been left with grandparents or other relatives so quickly when their parents were called into Desert Storm service (Pressley 1991). As more stories appeared of infants and toddlers left without parents during the war, and of the stress this was causing to families, the nation reacted with concern and the Pentagon began to investigate just how many children had been left in the care of relatives because of Desert Storm. "As parents with infants as young as a few weeks old face leaving their youngsters with grandparents, friends and babysitters, a campaign in favor of exempting one parent from the combat zone has gained support among military parents, legislators and children's advocacy groups" (Priest 1991b, A1). In mid-February, the Pentagon released figures that children from 17,500 families (16,300 single parents and 1,200 couples) had been left without both parents or their custodial single parent because of Desert Storm (Priest 1991a).

The debate heated up as child advocacy groups suggested that exemptions needed to be made because children left without their parents for very long would suffer from fears of abandonment, mental trauma, and grief (Priest 1991b; Sanders 1991). The idea of exempting a parent in military families or the custodial parent in single-parent families continued to gain attention because of the media reports of their plight (Priest 1991c). Caution was expressed that the debate not be framed in terms of women only being exempted so as not to hinder women's career advancements (Priest 1991c).

In fact, there appeared to be "little support for a government policy that would automatically designate military women as the parent primarily responsible for caring for children" (Priest 1991c, A10). Some women expressed concern over the featuring of military mothers as the responsible parties in this debate. In a February column, Judy Mann suggested that the debate over mothers at war mirrored the debate that "has occurred over the last 25 years in American society, namely should mothers work outside the home. . . . Working mothers do not need any more guilt trips. . . . any debate over how these military mothers mediate the conflicting demands of work and family ought to (be) framed in gratitude, not guilt" (Mann 1991b, B3). In an interview after the war, Brig. Gen. Evelyn "Pat" Foote expressed the same concern that mothers returning from the Gulf might be criticized and not applauded for their role in the Gulf War (Mann 1991a). Other groups entered the debate by calling for policies to exclude women from combat. Phyllis Schlafly argued that women should be exempt from war and called upon men to "show their manhood. The military should make a judgment that mothers are just like men with disabilities" (Priest 1991c, A10).

Sen. John Heinz' (R-PA) introduction of the measure to exempt one parent from the combat zone received support from military families and child advocacy groups, but little support from Pentagon officials. The arguments from military personnel, including Defense Secretary Dick Cheney and Colin Powell were that it would weaken combat capability and be unfair to enlistees who were not parents (Priest 1991b). The Pentagon argued that the difficulties of caring for children had been exaggerated, and were the exceptions, not the rule (Clymer 1991). They emphasized that military or reserve parents had always been required to make childcare arrangements for their children in case of an emergency and were supposed to have appointed a guardian for them. They also said that the military offered families a support network that featured counseling and other services and, therefore, they stood by their "no-exception policy" (Sanders 1991).

Even with some public support evident for an exemption rule, the Senate voted in late February 1991 against allowing some Desert Storm parents to return home. Media editorials following the decision advocated attention to these issues at a later date ("Support the Families" 1991). After the war, there was no real debate on this issue in the media; no reintroduction of measures to limit the service of parents during war. In one case, an article in the *Washington Post Weekly* framed the issue in terms of work equality for women and suggested that, "The separation of a child from a parent is no trivial matter. But neither is war or, for that matter, a career. If we are to bar the single mother from serving abroad with the troops, then what are we to say to the scientist who has the opportunity to spend several months in space? In the name of her child, should we say no?" (Cohen 1991).

WOMEN WORE BOOTS TOO*

The majority of images that Americans saw of the Gulf War were masculine; images of male soldiers writing home to loved ones or a photo essay of soldiers "At the front of the storm" featuring only men ("At the Front" 1991; "I Don't Want" 1991). But interspersed with these images, Americans saw women working alongside men, performing the same jobs as men, and soon the media were reporting on individual female pilots and patriot missile commanders and their accomplishments. In an interview after the war, Elizabeth Fox-Genovese, director of women's studies at Emory University, said, "One of the most important things to happen since August has been the ease with which our country has adjusted to women in the Gulf. To see women performing well, with no drama or fanfare, seems to me to be more striking than anything else women have done lately." ("The Military's New Image" 1991: 51). Without a doubt, the media coverage of women in the Gulf helped put the image of women performing well into the minds of the American public.

Women faced, as media coverage demonstrated, battles that the men faced. As early articles on the Gulf began to appear, it was reported that servicewomen were serving with air defense units that were deployed close enough to the Kuwaiti border to fall under Iraqi fire. Though prohibited from serving on warships, on attack planes, or in ground combat units, women served in other jobs supporting those fighting forces putting them in danger (Schmitt 1991). "From the infantry women

*The headline used as the title for this section is from *Parade Magazine* (June 6, 1991): 6.

who operated deep inside Iraq to the flashy airwomen who flew supply and refueling missions over the battlefield, Operation Desert Storm put an end to the illusion that women serve only behind the lines" (Copetas 1991: 26).

The media presented images and stories of women working alongside men doing their job as competently as the men. It also covered the accomplishments and plights of specific women whose actions and circumstances seemed unique to the American public and illustrated how much a part of the Gulf War women were.

Women, in general, during the Gulf War, faced a battle to prove themselves, not so much to the American public but to the men serving alongside them. Initially, women faced sexist comments and attitudes about their roles in the war. In some cases, military women talked about the need to prove themselves to the men and to deal with snide remarks and wolf whistles. There were, according to media reports, times during the early days of the war when women had to deal not only with come-ons but also with concerns from male soldiers about whether or not a woman would carry her load, but eventually the novelty of women in the Gulf wore off (Gugliotta 1991). In an article following the war on the contribution of African-American women to the Gulf War, the female soldiers discussed how they sometimes dealt with racism and sexism from the men they were serving beside. "Ironically, many Black servicewomen say there were times when the punishing conditions of the desert paled in comparison to the punishment they endured from some fellow soldiers who opposed their very presence in the Gulf and made no secret of their deep-rooted belief that war is man's business" ("The Untold Story" 1991: 106). Other women interviewed said they resented comments from their fellow male soldiers that "women should be women and get to the rear." Others said that although several men seemed overly protective of the women, most of the men eventually treated them equally and did not offer them any special consideration just because they were women. As Alabama National Guard Specialist Foy Harris said, "You're no longer a female here—you're a soldier, like everyone else" (Schmitt 1991: A12).

Female soldiers expressed similar attitudes toward the war effort as did their male counterparts. They talked about their fears, loneliness, and concern for their families. But they also reported on their pride in what they were doing and the unity they felt with fellow soldiers. Some wished they could serve in combat units or wished they could have been fighter pilots, but said the reasons they were not were sometimes expressed by men who feared they (the men) would be in trouble if they put women in harm's way. According to the women, the men feared that media would "splash pictures of blown up females across the front page, and the United States can't handle that" (Kifner 1991: 15). There were some women who were not sure about the role of women in combat and expressed similar attitudes and concerns as the men, saying that they believed that America was not "ready to see women coming home in body bags" or, as one female soldier put it, "it's always been a man's army. I'm sure [women are] capable of killing, but I'm not sure they should be" (Gugliotta 1991: A19).

Media also reported on the pride women took in being able to defuse strains and tensions in battle, by joking or by offering a sympathetic ear or a shoulder to cry on. Female soldiers expressed the feeling that women had proven themselves equal to men in their ability to handle Desert Storm and function well in their jobs. As army sergeant Kay Likely said, "The only difference between us and the men is that we hold hands whenever there's a Scud attack or incoming artillery" (Copetas 1991: 33).

In addition to having to prove themselves to male soldiers that they served alongside, American military women faced other types of sexism, sometimes in the form of hostility toward their presence and other times in more subtle forms that trivialized their role in the Gulf War. Female soldiers were subjected to upbraiding by Saudi men who criticized them for not veiling their faces or for leaving their arms bare or hair uncovered when they walked through Riyadh's streets (Talbott 1991). Before the war began, a California company offered an "Operation Desert Shield Calendar" that featured (according to the company) "young women in military-like settings and garb" ("Skimpy Shield" 1990: 2A). The calendar was not a tribute to military women but rather a typical calendar of female models. And although men in the Gulf could not put up "more traditional locker decorations" because of Muslim sensibilities (not sensitivity to the female soldiers), a favorite pinup was a Wrangler jeans ad featuring a female police officer leaning against her patrol car with a shotgun. According to a February 15 *New York Times* article, her picture was posted in every American military police and criminal investigation office in Saudi Arabia. The police officer, Jacqueline Phillips Guibord, said that she was gratified by the response from male troops and that "I've gotten a lot of positive feedback from females who were delighted that a fully clothed woman could be considered beautiful" (Reinhold 1991: A16).

However, it was not the "calendar girls" who received the most attention during the war. The women who received the most (individualized) press coverage during the war included the first female POW of the war, the first woman to shoot down a Scud missile, the first women to die, and the last woman to die in the war. In covering the circumstances of these women, the media focused on the uniqueness of their plight or mission. The press raised questions about how women close to the front would handle being taken prisoner, and it spent a lot of time trying to dig into the background and family of these women. In the interviews, the media asked how these women would hold up under the pressure they would encounter and found in these interviews with friends and family that these women were usually described as tough, ambitious, and qualified.

The first female listed as missing in action and later assumed to be a prisoner-of-war was Melissa A. Rathbun-Nealy. The media reported in early February 1991 that the jeep (later it was reported to be a truck) she had been in had become lost, then stuck, and military personnel said she and the person accompanying her came under small arms fire. When her vehicle was discovered, she was missing as was her partner ("2 Missing Soldiers" 1991; Terry 1991). Interviews with friends, parents, and military personnel suggested that she was a tough soldier and a patriot, but that being taken prisoner could not be easy for her (Terry 1991). The speculation about her capture and assumptions that she would be treated horribly seemed to reflect a broader concern expressed in the media of how Americans would view women being captured and of how women over in the Gulf would deal with captivity. *Newsweek* reported that "Throughout history America has had fewer than 100 women POW's, including 88 in WWII and two in Vietnam" but that the risk to women in the Gulf had increased that likelihood because of the blurring of lines between combat and noncombat lines. "The question is how the public will react to seeing women held captive—and possibly tortured—by the enemy. For women in the military, attaining equality may carry a terrible price" ("Women in the Military" 1991: 20).

When Rathbun-Nealy was released, Americans discovered that she had not been treated cruelly, but in fact her Iraqi captors had done everything to make her comfortable. She had held up well under captivity, crying only three times, she reported, once when her wounds were dressed and twice when she thought of her parents (Powell 1991). She had survived by trying to remember every detail of her life and sing every song she could think of. Her greatest fear had been that Allied bombing would hit the place where she was being held. She was told by her Iraqi captors that she was a hero, as brave as Sylvester Stallone and as beautiful as Brooke Shields (Walsh 1991). Her capture, according to an interview with her father, had not changed his view about women in the military or in combat, "I don't see any reason why women can't be wherever men are, . . . That's Melissa's feeling too . . . if a woman wants to be there, let her" (Walsh 1991: A23).

The second female POW was a helicopter pilot, Army Maj. Rhonda L. Cornum. The media reported that Major Cornum's helicopter had been shot down on February 27. She did not reveal any information about her capture, except that both of her arms had been broken during the crash, but the media reported on her record and accomplishments once she was released. Her bravery was also emphasized during the media reports; media-reported friends described her as tough as nails (Hanley 1991; "Iraq Frees Second" 1991). One friend commented that Major Cornum was "a definite over-achiever in everything she does. Somehow I think the war ended sooner because she was over there" ("Iraq Frees Second" 1991: A21). Major Cornum's position as a helicopter pilot and the story about her being shot down and then captured gave Americans a more in-depth look at the type of women in the Gulf that the media had alluded to: women who were doing jobs traditionally reserved for men and were doing them under the same circumstances as men—not in safe, behind the lines positions, but in combat zones where they were in the same type of danger as the men. Media reports about Major Cornum, in addition to featuring statements from friends and family about her character, provided a litany of her qualifications as an army doctor, a Ph.D. in biochemistry from Cornell, a paratrooper, pilot, flight surgeon, and one of one hundred finalists in NASA's search for future astronauts (Hanley 1991; "Iraq Frees Second" 1991).

On the evening of January 21, 1991, Lt. Phoebe Jeter, commander of a Patriot missile battery, became the first soldier to shoot down a Scud missile aimed at Riyadh. Lieutenant Jeter was one of the black women serving in the Gulf. Estimates were made that 40 percent of the female soldiers who went to war in the Gulf were black ("The Untold Story" 1991). Little information was given about Lieutenant Jeter's accomplishment until after the war. In an interview published almost six months after the war, Lieutenant Jeter revealed she had practiced destroying missiles before actually shooting one down, but was afraid she would choke when it came time to take charge of shooting down the missile. But she was comfortable with her command of an all-male platoon and with taking charge of the mission: "I was the commander inside that van. I was in charge of everything that happened inside that van. It was my responsibility" ("The Untold Story" 1991: 101). Lieutenant Jeter received a medal for her role in destroying the Scud missile and made history as the first and only woman to shoot down a Scud. Her experiences in the Gulf and her pride in her job mirrored those of her female colleagues in the Gulf. She also had to deal with sexism about her role in the Gulf and had to call a meeting with her fellow lieutenants to put an end to the ugly and sexist comments they made about her ("The Untold Story" 1991).

In late February 1991, it was reported that among the victims of a recent Scud missile attack were the first two women to die during the war (Priest 1991d). The American public now knew that what once had been speculation on the part of media that technology had blurred combat and non-combat zones in this war was indeed fact. Scud missiles could, in fact, reach any position once assumed to be safe and behind the lines. Women were and had been since the war's beginning on the front line. Also killed in a helicopter crash the day after the cease-fire was Army pilot, Maj. Marie T. Rossi. Before the ground assault had begun, Major Rossi had been interviewed on CNN about her duty as a helicopter pilot flying supplies to troops in the combat zone. Her national visibility had spurred calls to her parents about their daughter's role in the Gulf War and about their feelings on the role of women in combat. The media reported that she had made the war personal for many people in her interview and had during the interview expressed her belief in her ability to contribute to the war effort: "as an aviator and a soldier, this is the moment that everybody trains for—that I've trained for—so I feel ready to meet the challenge" (Sullivan 1991: B4).

Final media reports said that approximately 35,000 women went to the Gulf and 13 died. Interviews with women suggested that women felt they had done as well as men in the Gulf War and were hoping this carried over for them in the future. Shortly following the war, armed with the knowledge of their successes during Desert Storm, many women argued that change was needed in the military to give women full equality. Many women felt they had proven themselves in combat and were anxious to change the rules preventing them from achieving top positions.

A WOMAN'S PLACE IN A TIME OF WAR*

Before the war ended, women were already arguing that military rules needed to be redefined so that women could have a legal equality in the military that would match the equality they had shown in combat. After the war, a campaign began in earnest to try to change the type of jobs available to military women.

In an interview with Judy Mann in March, Brig. Gen. Evelyn "Pat" Foote talked about how in earlier skirmishes women weren't armed or trained and were sent into areas without the training to defend themselves. As women received training in defense skills, their confidence grew and their belief grew in their ability to help defend their units, according to Foote (Mann 1991a).

Others echoed the belief that women had been better trained and that their presence had seeped into the public's mind and into public discourse about the war (Priest 1991e). A January 1991 *New York Times*/CBS poll reported that 72 percent of Americans said women should be allowed to serve in combat units, and a *Newsweek* poll released July 29

*The headline used as the title for this section is from *Washington Post Weekly* (March 25–31, 1991):1 35.

had shown that four out of five Americans believed that military women should be eligible to fight (Priest 1991e; Smith 1991).

With what appeared to be an approval by the American people about the function they had served during Desert Storm, military women took their battle to Congress to change the ban on women in combat. Arguments were made that "The lines dividing combat missions from noncombat missions exist largely on paper and in the imagination," and Capt. Carol Barkalow, who served in a support unit for the infantry during the war suggested, "For our generation of women, Desert Storm is going to bust the glass ceiling" (Goodman 1991: 11A).

In May 1991, the House of Representatives voted 268–161 to approve a military budget authorization bill that included a provision repealing restrictions on women flying combat aircraft. Pat Schroeder, D-Colo., a sponsor of the bill said, "The Persian Gulf helped collapse the whole chivalrous notion that women could be kept out of danger in a war. We saw that the theater of operations had no strict combat zone, that Scud missiles were not gender-specific—they could hit both sexes and, unfortunately, did" (Nordheimer 1991).

The argument from military women was that they had always been exposed to risk and that to advance in the military they needed to be able to serve in combat. Although opponents of changing the rules argued that combat readiness would be affected by the long deployment of women to a combat zone, military women said they had begun to change some of the "old guard's" mind about women in combat by showing them how well women handled their jobs during the Gulf War (Nordheimer 1991).

In the summer following the war, a formal congressional hearing was held to discuss allowing women to fly combat aircraft. As media reported, female officers pleaded for a repeal of the ban, saying they would have more opportunities in the military by serving in combat roles. They argued that because women go through the identical training that men go through in pilot training, there was no reason to ban them from combat. However, testimony from male officers clearly illuminated the long-held biases against allowing women in combat. A former top marine warned that allowing women into combat roles would cripple military morale and would destroy and make a combat unit ineffective. Combat, according to Robert H. Barrow, former commandant of the Marine Corps, was "uncivilized, and women can't do it" ("Senior Pentagon Officers" 1991: 13A).

On the last day of July following the Gulf War, the Senate voted to overturn a law prohibiting air force and navy women from flying combat missions. The two services were given the authority to develop their own regulations concerning women pilots ("Senate Repeals Ban" 1991). Military women had won the victory of repealing the ban, but knew that they still faced a reluctance from male military officers to send women pilots to battle. In addition, the army still had its own regulations excluding women from combat units. For military women, they had helped win a war, but their battle for equality was not yet over.

CONCLUSION

The first media reports and images coming back from Desert Storm that showed women serving alongside men may indeed have seemed like a mirage (as Ellen Goodman said) to the American public. Women were not supposed to be in combat; in fact, there were arguments that had been around for a long time about why they were not allowed to fight: women needed to be protected from harm's way, their presence in combat units would destroy unit cohesion and make men act inappropriately to show off or to protect them, they lacked the necessary physical strength and training to serve in the same capacity as men, they would suffer greatly if captured and held prisoner, and, besides, the country was not ready to see women come home in body bags.

The country, in fact, accepted the images from the Gulf War of women serving, being captured, and dying along with men. In addition, Americans heard about the heroic deeds of men and women during the war and of the issues that had surfaced because of the expanded roles that women had during Desert Storm.

Americans were told that one of the results of women being deployed in record numbers to the Gulf was that children were left without both military parents or without their custodial single parent. Although there was concern, and media covered this debate in some detail, the debate was not cast in terms of guilt that could be dumped on military moms but rather in terms of how changing new roles in society necessitated discussion and rethinking of old procedures and guidelines. The debate, though dropped somewhat after the war, seemed to be framed in terms of: now that women are playing a larger role in the military, perhaps the rules concerning military parents need to be rethought and restructured.

Americans also learned that women performed well in combat and had served their country with equal valor as the men had. The ability of military women to convince the public, the men they served beside, and (sometimes) top military officials about their competencies in combat may have been their finest long-range accomplishment. Many women after the war used this accomplishment to change old laws about restrictions on their military service. Though the American public was convinced that women should be allowed in combat, military women fought to convince lawmakers that the rules excluding them from combat were really rules that allowed for institutionalized sex discrimination in the military. The rules excluding navy and air force women from combat were repealed as a direct result of military women who had served in the Gulf taking their case to Congress.

In 1983, Cynthia Enloe argued that women have always been at the front of war, experiencing violent confrontation, but the military has tried to categorize women as being peripheral and at the rear. "The military has to constantly redefine 'the front' and 'combat' as wherever 'women' are not. Women may serve the military, but they can never be permitted to be the military. They must remain 'camp followers' " (Enloe 1983: 15).

The Gulf War may serve as the event where women were no longer viewed as camp followers by the American public but rather were viewed as being (at least a part of) the military. Through media coverage of Desert Storm, the public learned only too clearly that combat was a great equalizer; that a helicopter pilot flying supplies to front line units or flying rescue missions was in equal danger from enemy fire whether the pilot was a man or a woman. Because of technology and long-range missiles now available in modern wars and because of the ability of the Desert Storm women to convince others of their achievements, the experiences from the Gulf War have made it impossible to redraw combat lines so that one can say: combat is wherever women are not.

BIBLIOGRAPHY

"2 Missing Soldiers Identified by U.S." *New York Times*, February 2, 1991, Section 1, 15.

"At the Front of the Storm." *Newsweek* (March 4, 1991): 42–43.

Blau, Eleanor. "TV Tries to Help Children Deal With the War." *New York Times*, January 23, 1991, C11, C18.

Campbell, D'Ann. "Servicewomen of World War II." *Armed Forces and Society* 16, 2 (Winter 1990): 251–70.

Clymer, Adam. "In Capitol, Debate on Parent in Gulf." *New York Times*, February 16, 1991, Section 1, 10.

Cohen, Richard. "Tougher the Little Children." *Washington Post National Weekly Edition*, March 25–31, 1991, 27.

Copetas, A. Craig. "Conquering Heroines." *Mirabella* (June 1991): 26–35.

"Drawing Board." *Washington Post National Weekly Edition*, March 4–10, 1991, 30.

Enloe, Cynthia. *Does Khaki Become You? The Militarisation of Women's Lives*. London: Pluto Press Limited, 1983.

"First Aid for Kids' Fears." *Newsweek* (March 4, 1991): 68.

Goodman, Ellen. "Desert Storm Women Could Be First to Bust Military Glass Ceiling." *The News and Observer*, Raleigh, N.C. April 25, 1991, 11A.

Gross, Jane. "Early Lessons in Wounds of the Spirit." *New York Times*, February 19, 1991, A8.

Gugliotta, Guy. "Scuds Put U.S. Women on Front Line." *Washington Post*, January 28, 1991, A1, A19.

Hanley, Robert. "Freedom for Missing Soldier Is a 'Miracle' for Her Family."
    New York Times, March 7, 1991, B4.

Harp, Chadwick Allen. "U.S. Women Have Long Battle Tradition." *The News
    and Observer*, Raleigh, N.C. May 26, 1991, 7J.

"I Don't Want Any Tears." *Newsweek* (March 4, 1991): 30–31.

"Iraq Frees Second U.S. Female POW." *Washington Post*, March 6, 1991, A21,
    A23.

Kifner, John. "This Time, 'Good to Go' is American Battle Cry." *New York Times*,
    February 3, 1991, Section 1, 15.

Mann, Judy. "War Reveals Women's Advances." *Washington Post*, March 1, 1991,
    D3. (a)

Mann, Judy. "Women at War, Women at Work." *Washington Post*, February 20,
    1991, B3. (b)

"The Military's New Image." *Newsweek* (March 11, 1991): 50–51.

Nordheimer, Jon. "Debate on Women in Combat Heats Up." *The News and
    Observer*, Raleigh, N.C. May 26, 1991, 2A.

Powell, JoAnne. "At Last, a Happy Ending." *Life: In Time of War*, March 18,
    1991, 38–39.

Pressley, Sue Anne. "Army Child Longs for 'Someday'." *Washington Post*, Feb-
    ruary 9, 1991, A1, A14.

Priest, Dana. "17,500 Families Divided." *Washington Post*, February 15, 1991, A1.
    A30. (a)

Priest, Dana. "Military Reluctant to Alter Its Rules." *Washington Post*, February
    9, 1991, A1, A14. (b)

Priest, Dana. "Parent Debate Goes Beyond Sex of GI." *Washington Post*, February
    19, 1991, A10. (c)

Priest, Dana. "Pennsylvania Mourns 15 Scud Victims." *Washington Post*, Feb-
    ruary 28, 1991, A33. (d)

Priest, Dana. "A Woman's Place in a Time of War." *Washington Post National
    Weekly Edition*, March 25–31, 1991, 35. (e)

Radcliffe, Donnie. "First Lady Rates the War: PG." *Washington Post*, January 24,
    1991, B1, B4.

Reinhold, Robert. "Policewoman in Denim Is Betty Grable of Gulf." *New York
    Times*, February 15, 1991, A16.

Sanders, Alain L. "When Dad and Mom Go to War." *Time* (February 18, 1991):
    69.

Schmitt, Eric. "War Puts U.S. Servicewomen Closer Than Ever to Combat." *New
    York Times*, January 22, 1991, A1, A12.

"Senate Repeals Ban on Women as Combat Pilots." *The News and Observer*,
    Raleigh, N.C. August 1, 1991, 3A.

"Senior Pentagon Officers Balk at Allowing Women in Combat." *The News and
    Observer*, Raleigh, N.C. June 19, 1991, 1A, 13A.

"Skimpy Shield." *The News and Observer*, Raleigh, N.C. December 28, 1990, 2A.

Smith, Rick. "Fighting for the Right." *The News and Observer*, Raleigh, N.C.
    August 4, 1991, 1J, 3J.

Sullivan, Joseph F. "Army Pilot's Death Stuns Her New Jersey Neighbors." *New
    York Times*, March 7, 1991, B1, B4.

"Support the Families, Too." *New York Times*, February 26, 1991, A22.

Talbott, Strobe. "Mosque vs. Palace." *Time* (January 21, 1991): 43.

Terry, Don. "Her Strength Is Theirs, Family of Casualty Says." *New York Times*, February 3, 1991, Section 1, 16.

"The Untold Story of Black Women in the Gulf War." *Ebony* (September 1991): 100–102, 104, 106.

Walsh, Edward. " 'As Brave as Stallone . . . Beautiful as Brooke Shields'." *Washington Post*, March 6, 1991, A23.

"What Parents Need to Say." *Newsweek* (February 25, 1991): 52.

"When Little Children Have Big Worries." *Newsweek* (January 28, 1991): 40.

"Women in the Military: The First POW?" *Newsweek* (February 11, 1991): 20.

"Women Wore Boots Too." *Parade Magazine*, June 9, 1991, 6.

Chapter Eleven

"What Did You Advertise with the War, Daddy?": Using the Persian Gulf War as a Referent System in Advertising

Matthew P. McAllister

World War I was the first war to involve the systematic use of the mass media to spread war propaganda. Great Britain and the United States were especially successful in using government influenced or subsidized mass communication to effectively influence popular images of the enemy and keep motivation and morale high on the domestic front. This first modern, global conflict produced such famous war propaganda messages as the patriotic "We Want You" and the guilt-inspired "Daddy, what did *YOU* do in the Great War?", written to encourage enlistment.

During the Persian Gulf War, government-produced propaganda was less prevalent than during the world wars. Nevertheless many of the same pro-war messages were conveyed, but this time they came from another source. During and after the Persian Gulf conflict, one found in the mass media messages like:

An Anheuser-Busch television commercial, using slow motion images of waving American flags dissolving over images of celebrations in Kuwait, told returning soldiers through song that "You took a stand for all we stand for. You gave your hand when it was asked for. . . . We hear the children singing loud for every hero."

A Lord & Taylor's print ad, appearing in early February 1991, announced that "We salute the brave American men and women of Desert Storm. Our hearts and prayers are with you."

A Specialties, Inc. advertisement that appeared in the *New York Times* in early 1991 offered golf balls with the image of Saddam Hussein: "Enjoy Driving That Face 300 Yards."

A newspaper ad for an Atlanta Honda dealer "DECLARES 100 HOUR GROUND WAR ON PRICES! EVERYTHING ON THE GROUND IS A TARGET!"

An advertisement appearing in the *Columbus* (Ohio) *Dispatch*, for the Club Tahoe Nude Dancing Night Club, featured the drawing of a woman in a stars-and-stripes bikini with the copy, "$2.00 Off W/This Ad. Proceeds Go To Troops Families."

The above are just a few of the advertisements that appeared in the United States during 1991 that mentioned or strongly implied the Persian Gulf War. Although many in the advertising industry claimed that advertising would stay away from war themes and images, hundreds of different companies, locally and nationally, attempted to link their company or product with the Persian Gulf. This chapter will explore the use of the Gulf War as a "referent system" in advertising, including the historical precedence for such linkages and the implications for our understanding of the role of advertising and of what is an appropriate purview for advertising. As such, the chapter will be divided into four sections: (1) a discussion of what advertising does when it attempts to associate itself with things of value in a culture, (2) a brief history of the relationship between war and advertising, (3) the quantity and categories of advertising that mentioned the Persian Gulf crisis, and finally (4) the social and cultural implications of advertising using war as an associative device.

ADVERTISING AND REFERENT SYSTEMS

Scholars who focus on advertising rightly point out that advertising is very rarely about the product alone. Factual information about a product in advertising, as a sole strategy, is not perceived as successful for several reasons. First, many mass-produced products (toothpaste, soap) are not significantly different from their competitors: stressing product information may highlight the similarities between products rather than differences. Also, advertising addressing factual information is often viewed as boring: other techniques are more useful for grabbing and keeping consumer attention. Finally, there is a legal incentive for not including much factual information about a product in an ad: the regulatory body of advertising, the Federal Trade Commission, looks primarily at how misleading factual claims in advertising are to consumers. Because there is no requirement to include factual claims, the easiest way for advertisers to avoid legal hassles is to have no factual claims at all in the advertisement. What, then, do advertisements do? Most advertisements work by association and metaphor. They try to link their product strongly with socially and culturally desirable objects and values of the product's consumer market.

This process has been discussed by many critics of advertising. S. I. Hayakawa (1972), for example, labels this process the "poeticizing of consumer goods." Hayakawa argued that poeticizing is so pervasive in advertising that "Almost all the symbols of daily living—especially those symbols that have any connotations of happiness and joy—have been appropriated by the advertisers" (225). Similarly, Leiss, Kline, and Jhally (1990) created the term "Product-Image Format" to describe advertising that argues that products have a "more abstract and less pragmatic domain of significance than mere utility" (244). Andren, Ericsson, Ohlsson, and Tannsjo (1978) discuss this same process as "value transference." Williams (1980) notes that the linkage property of advertising makes it a modern "magic system."

But the scholar who has written most extensively on this advertising technique is Judith Williamson (1978), in her book *Decoding Advertisements*. She describes the associative process that advertisers use as a linkage with "referent systems." A referent system is the social and cultural significance that is claimed by a product in its advertisement. The idea in ads is to create a firm linkage in our mind with a product and something "outside" the product, something that we value in our daily lives and may have actually nothing inherently to do with the product. This latter "symbolic significance," then, is a referent system. Referent systems can be any number of things: social acceptance, social mobility, nature, wealth, sexual allure, fine quality, even history. Things that symbolize these qualities in our society (for example, a racehorse for power or a Ming vase for quality) often are used in an advertisement to associate a product with these values. At the most superficial level, advertisers hope that some of the positive attributes of the referent system will "rub off" on the product (we see a Ming vase as positive, it is placed next to a Lincoln Continental, so we see the car as positive). Yet, as Williamson points out, this process is much more complicated.

For advertisers, the associative "rubbing off" process is not enough. Williamson argues that advertisers want the product-referent system link to be so strong that consumers believe the product generates the referent system, not just merely symbolizes it. As Williamson notes, "It is one thing for a product to *mean* happiness, it is another for it to *be*, or create, happiness" (36). The establishment of the "Product as Generator" is the ultimate association, especially if the advertisement can convince the consumer, through images, through narrative analogy, that this product is the *best* generator of the referent system. A perfume ad may tell, through a story, that the perfume does not just symbolize sexuality, it causes sexuality to a degree unlike any other perfume.

Successful advertising that uses this technique does more than simply associate the product with a desirable referent system: it also alters the referent system. When advertisers associate something with their product, they want to be sure that the association is as positive as possible. It is antithetical to their cause (selling the product) if the referent system has some negative baggage for the consumer.[1] Advertising is, in this sense, demagogic; it gives consumers exactly what they want. It spoon-feeds completely desirable referent systems back to the consumer. Thus, advertising does not simply adopt a referent system, it adapts it as well. Advertising purifies the referent system, removing any negative connotations the referent system may have and stressing only the positive elements for the consumer. This goes along with Hale and Mansfield's (1990: 94) conclusion that when advertising does deal with social and political issues, it simplifies and trivializes them.

Finally, one last point about the use of referent systems in advertising is that the quantity of cultural referent systems available to advertising is almost infinite. Advertising has shown a remarkable ability to incorporate anything, whether it is religion (Hayakawa 1972: 224), social movements like environmentalism (called in the trade journals "Green Marketing"), or even systems traditionally critical of advertising, like feminism (Williamson 1978: 170). Advertising is able to do this, in part, because of its ability to decontextualize the referent system: to purify the system so that only the pro-advertising elements remain.

During the Persian Gulf War, the war itself became a referent system of much advertising. Such usage, however, is not new. Historically, advertising has used war as a referent system, especially in the United States. The next section reviews the relationship between advertising and war.

A BRIEF HISTORY OF THE RELATIONSHIP BETWEEN ADVERTISING AND WAR

Although it may seem odd to explore the relationship between advertising and war, the two institutions actually share a rich history of interaction. In fact, traditionally the American advertising industry has almost always benefited from war.

For example, the mass advertising industry grew from infancy to at least adolescence during and immediately after the Civil War, and the war itself had much to do with that growth. According to Goodrum and Dalrymple (1990), technologically the advertising industry gained from the development of newsprint from wood, a development sparked by wartime shortages that made paper cheaper than it had ever been. Likewise, the demand for newspapers to print war illustrations increased the application of printing technology that advertising could exploit for its purposes. More importantly, the Civil War created the supply of mass-produced goods like clothes (improved because of uniform needs), and legitimized the purchase of mass-produced commodities by women, who often worked long hours in factories producing war goods. Related to this, the War Between the States illustrated to advertisers the importance of women as an important market. Finally, the government's own innovative use of advertising to promote enlistment, donations, and rationing highlighted how effective and visible large print advertising can be (Goodrum and Dalrymple 1990: 22–37).

World War I emphasized even more how the government can use advertising during wartime, and how the advertising industry can benefit from war. As Taylor (1990) points out, World War I was a totally different type of war: It was a "Total War." In total war the entire populace is directly involved, with every member of a society being actively urged to pitch into the war effort. Failure to do so, it was believed, could lead to the collapse of the modern society. Thus, the U.S. government during World War I, as noted at the beginning of the chapter, systematically used every means of mass communication (and interpersonal influence) to promote the legitimacy of the war and the importance of individual effort. One of these means was advertising. Within one week after war was declared, President Wilson created the Committee on Public Information (CPI), essentially the official propaganda arm of the United States. The CPI utilized elements of advertising as war propaganda in two ways: (1) advertising personnel (such as William H. Johns, president of the American Association of Advertising Agencies) played an important part, creating government-sponsored ads that encouraged the war effort, either by presenting the nobility of the Allies and their effort, or the atrocities of the "Huns" (Mock and Larson 1939); and (2) it encouraged commercial advertising likewise to promote the war, to use war as a referent system. Companies such as Owl Cigars ("bullets and bayonets are the only kind of lingo that a Hun can *understand*!," reproduced in Atwan, McQuade and Wright 1979: 55) and Goodyear, carrying the CPI's symbol as a seal of approval, promoted patriotic (and, by extension, jingoistic) ideas and behaviors (Hollihan 1984).

U.S. advertising gained important advantages from World War I. Because shortages often dictated rationing of goods, specific product advertising was seen as useless or even harmful during the war. So institutional advertising was developed during this time, promoting the good name of an entire company rather than an individual product (Rowsome 1959: 165). The specific techniques of product advertising may also have been refined by the war. Williams (1980) implies that war propaganda techniques helped to shift advertising away from a product-centered utility perspective ("Buy Ivory soap because of its purity") to a consumer-centered anxiety perspective ("Buy Ivory because if you don't you will have B.O."), which was a prime tactic of war propaganda. Another advantage was the further legitimation of advertising as a social institution. Rowsome (1959: 162) argues that the focus and success of war advertising during World War I helped win over conservative business holdouts who scoffed at advertising. Lastly, the war also helped the advertising industry by undermining its critics. The Progressive Reform Movement, turning its attention increasingly to the abuse and power of advertising in the twentieth century, was effectively killed by the country's focus on World War I (Fox 1984).

During World War II, the advertising industry undertook many of the same responsibilities, conducted many of the same activities, and benefited in the same ways as during World War I, but to a larger degree. World War II was even more of a "Total War" than the first one, both in terms of scale and total civilian involvement (Taylor 1990: 191). As such, advertising perhaps played a more important role in legitimizing the war effort, especially since a new, more pervasive (and commercially funded) medium, radio, had been implemented between the war years. Rationing was more extensive, and advertisers often may have pushed patriotic themes in part because they had no inventory to promote, or because they felt it important to explain shortages to consumers. Illustrating this latter need, one of the most famous ads produced during World War II was "The Kid in Upper 4," an ad for New Haven Railroad. The "kid," as depicted in the ad, was a young soldier going overseas to fight for his country. Essentially, the ad was meant to invoke guilt in those who complained about railroad tardiness, a tardiness often caused by the company's contribution to the war effort: As the copywriter for the ad explained, "I vowed I would write an ad that would make *everybody* who read it *feel ashamed* to complain about train service" (Metcalf 1959: 149). Literally hundreds of other World War II–era commercial advertisements used the war as a referent system, in addition to the scores of government-produced ads. Lucky Strike had indeed gone to war, as had Phillip's Milk of Magnesia, Chesterfield, Maxwell House Coffee ("When you've done your bit for Uncle Sam, It's Maxwell House Coffee Time"), Smith Corona, and countless others.

Once the smoke had cleared, American advertising found itself in a stronger social position than when the war began, just as it had during the Civil War and World War I. Similar to post–World War I, advertisers in the late 1940s found themselves with a new legitimacy. Anti-advertising movements (this time in the form of consumer organizations like the Consumers Union rather than Progressive Reform Organizations of the turn of the century) were seriously derailed by the war (Fox 1984). Added to this was the creation of the War Advertising Council, the World War II equivalent of the CPI's Advertising Division. Unlike World War I, however, the Advertising Council continued to exist after the war, donating advertisers' time and talent for charitable causes, thus improving the public image of advertising (Morgens 1990).

Not surprisingly, the use of current wars and militarism as referent systems decreased significantly since the 1940s, especially during the 1960s through the 1980s, and did not increase again until the Persian

Gulf conflict. Vietnam as a referent system was especially taboo for advertisers. As one advertising executive explained, "With Vietnam, we were in denial" (cited in Brown 1990: 36).

However, war themes did not disappear entirely in advertising. Through the 1970s and 1980s, for example, military recruitment ads could be found on television and other advertising media. Also, perhaps one legacy of advertising in wars previous to the 1950s was the use of generic American patriotism in ads, an ad referent system that increased in popularity during the 1980s. As Schudson (1986: 219) points out, reference to "America" in U.S. advertising is more often found than reference to the home nation in other countries' advertising. Commercials such as one for Chrysler LeBaron during the 1980s included strong "America is Better" messages (Hale and Mansfield 1990).

But the Persian Gulf War renewed advertisers' inclination for patriotism and for using war as a referent system. The next section details the reaction of the advertising industry to the Persian Gulf situation, including an exploration of the quantity, and the themes, of war advertising in 1991.

HOW ADVERTISING REACTED TO THE PERSIAN GULF WAR

A cursory look at the articles in advertising and entertainment industry trade publications like *Advertising Age* and *Electronic Media* seems to indicate that the most significant effect of the Persian Gulf War upon the advertising industry was anxiety, especially over the revenue implications of the war. Already in the midst of a recession, many trade articles implied that the advertising industry wanted to distance itself, culturally, as far away from the Gulf as possible. In August 1990 *Advertising Age* ran an article about the impact of the Iraqi invasion of Kuwait and the subsequent U.S. military build up upon retail businesses and their plans for Christmas selling. Indeed, some advertisers did disassociate their products from the Gulf crisis during this early stage. Chips Ahoy!, for example, cancelled an ad that promoted the abundance of chocolate chips in its cookies with the headline "Richer than an OPEC Nation" ("Saddam Scrooges Retailer's Plans" 1990: 38).

When the January 15, 1991, deadline approached and passed, it seemed that the disassociation strategy was even more firm. *Advertising Age* announced that "Marketers are distancing their brands from the Persian Gulf crisis as quickly as they can" ("Marketers Slash Ads as War Erupts" 1991: 1). There was even talk (for a very short time) that the Super Bowl, television advertising's largest showcase, would be cancelled (Donaton and Walley 1991). The networks announced that advertising would be suspended if war broke out; CNN, for example, said before the deadline that no commercials would run for twenty-four hours if war developed (Donaton and Walley 1991: 42). Once the bombing started, many advertisers did temporarily pull their television commercials, such as United Airlines; many others, like Proctor and Gamble and Pizza Hut, refused to run commercials during the actual war coverage ("Marketers Slash Ads as War Erupts" 1991). A few entire industries, such as the travel industry, had to re-think their marketing strategy during the conflict, downsizing their advertising and promoting their products through more subtle means, like public relations (Teinowitz 1991).

As far as using the war in advertising itself, most industry analysts and insiders publicly stated that it was a bad idea, and predicted that the advertising industry would generally not use the Persian Gulf War as a cultural text. An article in *Adweek* noted that several West Coast advertising agencies "were looking at all their advertising, scrutinizing for anything inappropriate" (Sharkey 1991: 4). *Advertising Age*, in a late February editorial, congratulated the industry on using constraint and prudence in its use of war images ("Ads and the War" 1991: 18). *Marketing News* reported that manufacturers were worried about being labeled a profiteer if they promoted war products (Associated Press 1991). Likewise, in the very visible forum of the *New York Times*, one advertising executive stated that "Trying to benefit overtly from the war doesn't make sense. . . . Any advertiser who tried that strategy would be courting disaster" (Foltz 1991a: C16). Even after the conflict had ended, in mid-March, the "Newspaper of Record" reported that executives of advertising agencies still insisted that "trying to capitalize on the victory in the Persian Gulf war was a mistake" (Foltz 1991b: C1).

But in this case the newspaper of record was wrong. Many, many advertisers did try to capitalize on the war and to use the situation to their best economic (and symbolic) advantage. In fact, a clue that advertisers were going to link themselves to the war may be found on the very same page as the above mentioned March 11 article in the *New York Times*. Immediately adjacent to the headline, "Agencies Caution Clients on Using Patriotic Themes," was a large ad for *Time* magazine ("MAKE TIME FOR TIME") that produced a cover featuring a woman, holding a small U.S. flag, hugging a soldier who had just come home, with the superimposed headlines, "A Moment To Savor," and "And the Lessons of Victory." The advertising of the newspaper betrayed its content.

Although some advertisers did try to position themselves away from the conflict in the Gulf, other companies alternatively attempted to get a piece of the symbolic action right from the beginning. In fact, many advertisers took advantage of the war situation in other ways besides incorporating war reference systems in their advertising.

First, several companies, even as early as August 1990, used the situation as fodder for public relations. When companies began to see the free publicity that Quaker Oats received from shipping 20,000 cases of Gatorade (despite the U.S. Surgeon General's disapproval), many also began shipping merchandise to troops in the area, hoping to cash in on the heavy media scrutiny of the situation ("PR Offensive Hits Persian Gulf" 1990: 53). Coca-Cola, *The National*, Circus Circus Enterprises (a producer of playing cards), and Nintendo all sent items to the troops, presumably along with press releases to the media trumpeting their generosity. The president of Artesia Waters sent over 5,500 gallons of his company's bottled water to the Middle East when he saw U.S. soldiers drinking a competitor's water on television ("PR Offensive Hits Persian Gulf" 1990: 53). In December and January, Nabisco initiated "Operation Oreo," sending gift boxes of Nabisco products to military personnel and their families (Dagnoli 1991: 42).

Companies also illustrated their willingness to associate with images of the Persian Gulf War through their media buying. As noted above, there was anxiety about whether advertisers would pull their ads over a long period of time from media that carried war images. So serious was this anxiety that *Electronic Media*, *Adweek*, *Broadcasting* and the *Wall Street Journal* all reported on a study done by a media consulting organization reassuring the industry that viewers are not turned off by advertising during war news coverage (see, for example, Granger 1991: 4). CBS and the advertising agency Foote, Cone, and Belding also conducted viewer surveys with similar results (King 1991: B4).

But much of the anxiety was unfounded. In fact, some media benefited from increased advertising before and immediately after the January 15 deadline. Advertising pages in the weekly *Army Times* significantly increased from the comparable period the year before ("Troops Spur Ad Maneuvers" 1990: 36). And even after the initial backoff by some companies during the early stages of war coverage, many companies embraced sponsorship of war information and images, especially when it was obvious that the conflict was so one-sided, with the United States on top. CNN's popularity as an advertising vehicle because of the popularity of its war coverage was obvious within the first week of the conflict. Although the network had earlier announced that the first twenty-four hours of the conflict would be commercial free, within eleven hours it began to run advertising (Crain News Service 1991: 52). Despite the fact that CNN increased its advertising rates as much as 400 percent after the war began, advertising sales organizations reported increased interest in buying time on CNN by both national and regional advertisers (Oberlander 1991: 3).

But the most obtrusive and pervasive way that many U.S. advertisers attempted to link themselves to the Persian Gulf conflict was through the use of the war as a referent system in the advertising itself.[2] The Persian Gulf situation was mentioned specifically, or strongly implied, in hundreds of advertisements. It is important to stress that this cultural linkage occurred both during the conflict and after the conflict was over.

Even as the United States began bombing, a few advertisers immediately incorporated the situation into their public image construction. For example, less than twelve hours after the U.S. attack started, in the middle of the night, one Los Angeles advertising agency executive received a phone call from a client "wanting to do something that showed the world and community that they care." The agency had begun work on this ad by the next working day ("An Ad Strategy Unfolds in the Dead of Night" 1991: 30). Boeing, on CNN, ran what *Adweek* called the "First Troop Salute" by a U.S. advertiser (featuring "a soulful rendition of *America the Beautiful*") in the latter weeks of January (Brown 1991). Although the defense contractor Northrop Corporation pulled an ad from an issue of *The National Journal* distributed on January 18, another contractor, BDM International, filled the space by placing an ad supporting and congratulating the military in its actions ("Marketers Slash Ads as War Erupts" 1991: 54).

How many advertisers created ads with the Persian Gulf War as a referent system during the war itself?[3] In the national arena, the numbers were significant but not overly large. At least twenty-one different advertisements could be found from January 16 to February 28, 1991. These companies included A & P Supermarkets ("OUR THOUGHTS & PRAYERS ARE WITH OUR ARMED FORCES OVER SEAS"), CNN, Phar-Mor, Naturalizer Shoes ("We Support Operation Desert Storm"), CompuAdd ("When the U.S. Central Command needed hundreds of the latest technology personal computers to handle logistical and administrative tasks for Operation Desert Storm—*delivered in three weeks*—COMPUADD MET THE CHALLENGE!"), McDonnell Douglas, and Lorillard Inc. (which featured yellow ribbons in the corners of its cigarette ads) (Collins 1991).

However, even though many national advertisers may have avoided using the war in their ads, local advertising throughout the country was loaded with references to the Persian Gulf situation in January and February, especially in local newspapers (which makes sense, because newspapers are the most popular medium for local advertisers). Choosing one newspaper at random, *The Atlanta Constitution* (and the jointly published weekend and holiday editions of *The Atlanta Journal-Constitution*), and going through it page by page, sixty-five different ads (many of which were published more than once during the war) were found that mentioned or implied the war in some capacity. Of course, a few of these ads were for Persian Gulf-related merchandise, such as Operation Desert Storm and Shield T-Shirts ("Display your support for our dedicated troops") and Gas Masks ("Survival in the 90's!"). But many war references were included in such diverse merchandise ads as pet stores ("OPERATION TROPICAL FISH STORM"), office equipment ("We Support Our Troops in the Gulf. Meeting the office equipment needs of Atlanta Businesses for over 30 years!"), stereo equipment ("SIGN THE RIBBON FEB. 23RD AT ANY SOUND WAREHOUSE"), crafts ("Patriotic Values All Over The Store This Week!"), butchers, and car dealers. Based upon this collection and a more informal survey of two other geographical areas (Columbus, Ohio, and Roanoke, Virginia), it is logical to assume that several hundred local advertisers in this country referred to the Gulf situation in their advertising and promotion.

Once the U.S. victory was established, advertisers incorporated war imagery and references even more frequently. As a writer for the *Wall Street Journal* argued, "The Gulf war spawned a trickle of patriotic ads. The Gulf peace is unleashing a flood" (Lipman 1991: B4). At least forty-five different national advertisements mentioning the Gulf appeared in a variety of media after February 28, 1991. Persian Gulf references could be found in ads until at least mid-November; Hills Department Store, for example, in its November 10 Sunday newspaper supplement, featured "Hills Desert Storm Veterans" wearing discounted clothing. Radio Shack, Gordon's Jewelers ("NOW IS THE TIME TO SHOW YOUR SUPPORT. RESERVE YOUR SPECIAL EDITION DESERT STORM WATCH $99.99"), Firestone ("FREE OIL CHANGE FOR OUR TROOPS!"), Macy's, Best Department Stores, AT&T, Moët & Chandon Champagne, the U.S. Council for Energy Awareness ("Nuclear-generated electricity saves more oil each day than we used to import from Iraq and Kuwait"), Mobil Oil, NBC, CBS, ABC, CNN, Coca-Cola, Amway, and Miller Lite Beer (in a television spot featuring their ex-athlete endorsers) were among the national advertisers to salute the U.S. victory. In addition to this, over twenty national companies provided special discount offers to returning troops and their families, and several others sponsored "Welcome Home" parades (Colford 1991a; Lipman 1991; "Marketers Welcome Home Troops" 1991). Local advertisers were equally willing to congratulate the victory. Again, a survey of ads in the *Atlanta Constitution* finds forty-three different local advertisers (nearly all of them different from those who placed ads before the war ended) connecting with the Gulf in their ads from March 1 to March 12; no doubt this number would be substantially larger if the search had been extended or had included other local newspapers.

Overall, what generalizations may be made about these advertisements? Most striking about these ads were the characteristics that they shared with government created or sanctioned war propaganda, especially that used in the two world wars. These shared characteristics were the use of patriotism, emotionalism, claims of wide support among the populace, and portrayals of the enemy as evil (for a complete list of the techniques of propaganda, see Roucek 1971: 30).

By far the most obvious characteristic of Persian Gulf War advertisements was the use of patriotism. The U.S. flag was probably the most frequently used visual icon of the ads. Rich's department stores, for example, created a full page newspaper ad with the flag's stripes on the background of the ad. In the foreground were the words, "Rich's salutes the men and women who served this country during Operation Desert Storm. With courage and commitment, they brought peace to Kuwait and pride to America." Likewise, a two-page magazine advertisement by Boeing was filled with a picture of the American flag, taking up most of the two pages. Next to the flag, in small print, was the copy, "MILLIONS OF MEN AND WOMEN HONOR THIS FLAG BY SERVING UNDER IT." A pet-supply store urged readers of a central Ohio newspaper to "Help welcome our troops home, we have American Flag Bandannas for your pet!" Pushing all troublesome subtlety aside, an ad for an Ohio pizza and beer drive-thru stated that "We have the bravest fighting men & women, we have the finest planes & military equipment, we have the world's best leader ALL AMERICAN MADE!"

Television ads were not shy about superimposing slow-motion images of flag waving while music or dialogue reinforced the nationalistic visuals. Big Bear, a supermarket chain in Ohio, cooperating General Motors/United Auto Workers, Anheuser-Busch, and Coca-Cola essentially produced carbon copy television advertising with generous use of flags and patriotic copy.

Of course, many other advertisers who did not mention or imply the Persian Gulf situation nevertheless promoted American patriotism in their commercial promotions. Bloomingdale's, Jordan Marsh, and Neiman Marcus set up special patriotic, red, white and blue merchandise "boutiques" in their stores (Ward and Fahey 1991). Consumers may also have bought Ralph Lauren robes, bathing trunks, and duffle bags with the U.S. flag (Vigoda 1991: D1). And because advertisers are always in search of the unique "niche," a patriotic shopper could also have bought merchandise that signified a special type of patriotism, such as "Rugged Patriotism" (as announced in Britches ads) and "Fashionable Patriotism" (described in Ross-Simons ads).

Similarly, the pervasive use of emotional appeal was a strong commonality of many war ads. In fact, next to flag images, yellow ribbons were probably seen most often in war ads, urging U.S. troops to "Come Home Soon" (logically enough, many ads, like the one appearing for Northwest Airlines in a late April issue of the *Wall Street Journal*, featured both flags and ribbons). Along these emotional lines, many advertisers appealed to a higher power to protect U.S. troops. A local hair parlor in the South let the troops know in their ads (despite the fact that most of the troops referred to would not see the ad), "GOD LOVES YOU & WE SUPPORT YOU." Carson Pirie Scott said in their mid-February ad, "God bless our troops abroad and their families here at home." Several advertisers declared their willingness to pray for the U.S. troops. Television ads exploited their ability to convey emotion with the use of slow motion techniques and the use of emotional music filled with the sounds of pianos, violins, and choruses.

A third characteristic of the Persian Gulf ads that was also common with more traditional war propaganda was the implied shared consensus of the discourse. Modern war propagandists learned early on that the use of the word "you" in propaganda is generally not effective. In the early stages of World War II, the British war propaganda office noted the failure of the slogan, "*Your* Courage, *Your* Cheerfulness, *Your* Resolution Will Bring Us Victory." They later successfully altered their slogans to imply group consensus and identification: "Let Us Go Forward Together" and "We're Going to See It Through" (Taylor 1990: 194). Such use of the first person plural in persuasive discourse is effective in building identification and creating consensus largely because it goes unnoticed (Cheney 1983: 148–49).

Alternatively, commercial advertising usually tends to be a more "you"-oriented discourse. As Williamson (1978: 53) points out, advertising draws on mostly an individualistic appeal. "You" are an individual who, given a free choice, will buy this product. The product will improve (or reinforce or fit in with) "your" most desired characteristics. Examples of the use of "You" in commercial advertising include the slogans "This Bud's for You" and "You've Come a Long Way, Baby."

So the fact that war advertisers forsook "you" for "our" is particularly noticeable. War advertisements were not individually oriented but rather were group oriented: the first person plural helped establish this. "Our" was used in war advertising to build implied group consensus in at least two different ways. First, "our" and "we" was used to refer to the entire company being advertised. Every employee of this company, these ads implied, support the U.S. military actions in the Persian Gulf. For example, Graphic Engraving Co. announced that "We Support Our Troops in the Middle East." A sandwich shop similarly declared, "We are behind our Troops."

More broadly, though, the use of the first person plural also was often meant to signify the nation in general. We are all part of one group, this grammatical construction implied, and as this one group we all support the war effort. Scores of ads did not just talk about "U.S." troops or "the" troops, but rather "our" troops. An AT&T ad appearing in an April issue of *Time* accentuates this strategy: "Saturday is Armed Forces Day. And this year, Americans have something very special to celebrate. We can all feel proud. And united." The observation that "We came

together in an outpouring of pride, patriotism and purpose to support
this United Nations effort" is offered by a Mobil ad.

Finally, one last characteristic of Persian Gulf advertising that is shared
by war propaganda in general is the portrayal of the non-Allied side of
the conflict as evil or someone to be ridiculed. Although this characteristic was not found as frequently as the others mentioned above, it
nevertheless was evident in several ads, both before and during the war.
In this case, of course, the personification of evil, the object to be vilified,
was Saddam Hussein. Many of the ads that mentioned Saddam Hussein
were Persian Gulf War merchandise ads, such as the Saddam Hussein
golf ball ad described earlier. Similarly, one advertisement for a T-shirt
shop presented a T-shirt with a drawing of Hussein being chased by a
missile, with the caption, "YOU CAN RUN BUT YOU CAN'T HIDE."
Another ad, for an "adult toy store," promoted Persian Gulf sexual
commodities like the Saddam Condom ("DIRECTIONS: USE THIS CON-
DOM TO HELP PREVENT UNWANTED MISTAKES LIKE SADDAM
HUSSEIN"). A trade advertisement for "Damn Saddam" commemorative trading cards advised retailers to "GET 'EM WHILE HE'S STILL
WARM! GET 'EM WHILE THEY'RE HOT!!" Some advertising copy was
reminiscent of World War I propaganda that constructed images of des-
poiled Belgium as evidence for German brutality. For example, in an ad
for Heroes of Desert Storm $5 Commemorative Coin appearing in *Parade*,
the national newspaper Sunday magazine, readers were informed how
U.S. troops "took *only 45 days* to lift the yoke of tyranny from the tiny,
ravaged nation of Kuwait." Not all ads referring to Saddam, however,
were for war merchandise. An ad, appearing in a December 1990 issue
of *Time* magazine, for the *Time* television special "Images of 1990," labeled Saddam Hussein as a "villain."

IMPLICATIONS OF PERSIAN GULF WAR ADVERTISING

Although there may be several conclusions drawn about the role of
advertising in society based upon how ads used the Persian Gulf War
as a referent system, this last section will focus on two of the most
significant implications: the "expansion" of advertising into different
arenas of life and society, and the "purification" of the Gulf War as
portrayed in the advertising.

It was described earlier in the chapter how advertising traditionally
has taken values and objects that are considered cherished and valuable
in society, and co-opts them for promotional and sales purposes. Ads
that used the Persian Gulf War as a referent system illustrate this trend
and perhaps even expand it.

It is true that in previous wars, specifically World War I and World
War II, advertising promoted the war effort. However, these wars were

"Total Wars," where the entire nation was threatened, the entire civilian population was involved, a large percentage of the population was sent as soldiers to fight, and advertisers were restricted in their direct promotion of products because of rationing and wartime manufacturing efforts. No such rationales existed for Persian Gulf War advertisers. Our nation was not at risk. Most civilians were not directly affected by the war. No products were rationed because of the war. But many advertisers referenced and even celebrated the war anyway. Why? No doubt because it was perceived, especially after the first week of Allied bombing, that this war was going very well for the United States, that this war would end fairly quickly, and that opinion polls showed that the majority (but not the entirety) of American people supported the war effort. In short, the war had become cherished and valuable, at least for the purposes of the advertisers. The war had become fair game.[4]

Earlier it was mentioned that the first goal of advertisers of the use of referent systems was a "rubbing off" effect: that consumers would see the valued referent system portrayed in the advertisement and the value would "rub off" to the product. Clearly, many advertisers using the Persian Gulf War hoped this would happen. Products and companies having nothing to do with war would nevertheless have, as part of their ad, some patriotic icon along with the declaration that "We Support Operation Desert Storm." The pride of the war would bleed over as good feeling for the company, it was believed.

But many ads went beyond this. Symbolic techniques were used that maximized the ties between the product being advertised and the war referent system. Many ads implied that the products were not just symbolically associated with war pride, but in fact were necessary *generators* of war pride.[5] Much of the advertising for war merchandise fell into this category. Buying the anti-Saddam Hussein products mentioned above, for example, would display—would generate—the consumer's hatred for America's enemy. More obvious was the appeal found in many pro– United States war product ads. Buyers are urged to buy and wear an Operation Desert Storm T-shirt to "Display your support for our dedicated troops." Another T-shirt company ad, appearing after conflict was over, more desperately appealed to the need to generate patriotism through their products: "Now that the ground war has begun and the troops will be coming home soon, it is more important than ever to show support for our troops fighting for world peace in the Gulf." Equally shrill was the ad for "Desert Storm Voice Mail," exclaiming, "DON'T LEAVE THEM ALONE . . . THEY NEED YOU *NOW!*" One ad for a commemorative coin (different from one described earlier) stressed how the product was needed for the American heritage. The ad ordered readers to buy this coin to "Preserve the heroism for generations to come of the historic Desert Storm victory."

It was argued earlier that the advertising industry has traditionally benefited from war. The most significant long-term benefit that advertising will gain from the Persian Gulf War could be that the boundary for what is considered permissible for an ad to co-opt has been expanded. The ubiquitous nature of war ads, as well as the strong connection made between product and war in these ads, further expand the purview of what is a legitimate referent system by advertisers. If even *war* is fair game, is there anything that is not?

One last implication of the use of war imagery in advertising is the "purification" of the Persian Gulf War. When advertising uses something as a referent system, it often changes it. Unwilling to accept any negative connotation, advertising will alter the referent system so that it is optimal in its advantage to the advertised product. This purification process was quite evident in war advertising.

One element that purified the war in advertising was the implied group consensus mentioned above. In many ads, the entire company ("We Support the Troops!"), as well as the entire country ("Show Our Support!"), was behind the war effort. In the world of war advertising, there is no war dissent and no war protests. The country is completely united in its support. The many war protesters that voiced their outrage in this country before and during the war, including the tens of thousands that met in Washington, D.C., on January 26, did not exist in the purified advertising consensus.

Also, the narrative descriptions of the war in many of the advertisements helped to remove bothersome impurities by symbolically or stylistically aligning the ads with two other types of discourse: the U.S. administration's descriptions of the war, and military recruitment ads. Illustrating the parallelism between war ads and the official justification for the war, one local advertisement in the *Atlanta Constitution* for the "United We Stand Lapel Pin" described the war in this way:

On January 16, 1991, after many months of futile diplomatic negotiations, the United States of America initiated the use of force in Operation Desert Storm, for the purpose of liberating the people of Kuwait. . . . Now is the time for all Americans to stand up and be counted. Our soldiers are on the front lines for America and everything She stands for.

In this discourse, the Persian Gulf War does indeed come close to being a "Total War," like World War II. It is not oil at stake, nor Middle East control, but rather it is the very ideals of America that are on the line in the Gulf. Likewise, the purity of the war effort was confirmed in a self-congratulatory ad by the military contractor BDM International, which labeled the war in its ad headline, "A Cleansing Storm," and went on to declare that "Desert Storm is a triumph and vindication of

American technology and world resolve." This, of course, fits in perfectly with the agenda and language of the Bush administration. Sometimes ads highlighted this fit explicitly, using the exact terminology of the president. The same BDM ad quotes George Bush: "The liberation of Kuwait has begun." After the war, one retailer wonders in its ad, "What if all America lit not thousands, but millions of points of light to promise a warm welcome home, to tell them we love them."

The purification of the war in much of the Persian Gulf advertising can also be illustrated by the concordance of the ads with another type of advertising overtly designed to promote militarism: military recruiting ads. Crass militarism in war ads was sometimes found. The copy for a Corner Cupboard Crafts ad barked, " 'Stand at Attention!' We have handmade Desert Storm Wooden Pens. All Weather Red, White and Blue Bows. Desert Gear for Children (Overnight Bags)." But in many other ads, the similarity between recruitment ads for the military and Persian Gulf ads created by non-military ads was more subtle, but nevertheless striking.

During and after the war, the U.S. Department of Defense released new campaigns for recruitment, designed to incorporate the country's view of the Persian Gulf conflict (Colford 1991b). Stressing the slogans, "Count on Me" and "Freedom Isn't Free," the television spots feature a slow motion visual style with patriotic imagery such as U.S. flags and boy scouts. Without knowing the specific product being sold, these ads are virtually indistinguishable, stylistically and thematically, from postwar ads created by Big Bear, GM/UAW, Coca-Cola and Anheuser-Busch. Sometimes, the exact same visual images are shared in common. Both the "Freedom Isn't Free" U.S. Army television spot and a Nynex *Newsweek* print ad feature a picture of a little girl solemnly and patriotically raising her hand to her heart.

One television ad for Delta Airlines, which was shown long before the war, was altered for airing after the war was over, with the result being a symbolic correspondence to military ads. In the "before" version, the scenario was a military camp, where leave was about to begin. A tough-looking drill sergeant, holding the soldiers at attention, yells "Company, Dismissed!" and the soldiers all shout for joy as they rush to a pay phone to arrange air flights home. As the soldiers scramble toward the phone, the drill sergeant frowns and shakes his head at them. The operator at Delta takes all of the flight information from the scores of soldiers; at the end of the commercial, the operator's supervisor asks, "How many phone calls did you take today, Gail?" and the operator answers, ironically, "One." The frame freezes on the operator's tired and bemused face. In the post-war version, the drill sergeant's shaking head is edited out (any sign of military disapproval, even a light-hearted one, would be inappropriate for the commercial), and the ad ends much more sentimentally. The last words of the commercial come from a soldier still talking to Gail, the operator: "I'm goin' home." The last frame is the operator, smiling at the soldier's words. The ad was purified to fit the more celebratory post-war environment.

Critics of news, including some in this volume, pointed to the control of the press by the "news management" techniques of the government. Critics were concerned about the subtle "pro-war" spin put on the news during the Persian Gulf War. Yet much of the advertising during the war was even more blatant and ubiquitous in its celebration of the official U.S. position on the Persian Gulf conflict. If news can be criticized for giving viewers only "snapshots" of the war, then surely advertising is guilty of providing, to adopt a term used by Schudson (1986: 211), a "postcard" of the war. In ads, the war was heroic and apolitical. The nation was grand in its united support. In advertising's version, there were no 200-plus U.S. casualties, no 100,000-plus Iraqi casualties, no Iraqi civilian casualties, no "Highway of Death," no burning, maiming, or disfigurement.

And the United States itself was purified in the ads. In a time when recession seemed relentless, when international competition was challenging U.S. domination in the marketplace, when anti-U.S. sentiment abroad appeared deep, ads featuring the Persian Gulf War put America squarely on top. Many people wanted to hear during the war that "Our soldiers are on the front lines for America and everything She stands for," as a lapel pin manufacturer reassured us. America's ability to get the job done was reaffirmed and the stigma of Vietnam removed, when ads told us afterwards that the war was "the swiftest, most decisive victory in military history."

Advertising during the Persian Gulf War became a modern propaganda, not just for the war, nor for the country, but also for itself. One wonders how such a purification of events affected popular sentiment of the war, will affect popular memory about the war, and will affect what is now considered socially acceptable for advertising to co-opt and adapt in its service.

NOTES

The author wishes to thank Professor Ross Wolin for his thoughtful comments on an earlier version of this chapter.

1. This is not to say that advertising never deals with anything negative. Negative referent systems (failure, nerdiness) can be used in advertising to explain what happens if the consumer does not use the product, or if the consumer uses the competitive brand.

2. The use of war references in U.S. advertising contrasts with the situation in other countries. In Italy, for example, self-regulatory organizations searched for "distasteful" ads in light of the war situation (McCarter 1991), while in Britain

the BBC banned ads that "raised the specter of war." When told of American advertisers' use of patriotism and war references in their ads, one British advertising executive exclaimed, "That's amazing and, I have to say, typically American" (Emmrich 1991).

3. This analysis did not include non-product advocacy advertising placed by different special interest groups, like Sane/Freeze (anti-military intervention) and The Coalition for America at Risk (pro-military intervention). Many local community groups sponsored print advertising and even billboards addressing the war during and after the conflict. In Zanesville, Ohio, for example, a noncommercial billboard featured a cartoon drawing of Saddam Hussein being kicked back to Baghdad by a boot draped in an American flag. See Battaglio (1991: 9) for a discussion of the possible role of advocacy advertising during the Persian Gulf Conflict.

4. Another difference between the advertising situation in the world wars versus the Persian Gulf War is simply the level of commercialism of the wars itself. This chapter lists numerous instances of war-related merchandise produced to exploit the popularity of the Persian Gulf War. One of the most outrageous examples of this is the creation of Persian Gulf War Trading Cards for children. Jay Mariotti, a writer for the now-defunct sports paper *The National*, pointed out that World War II trading cards were produced, but nearly ten years after the war was over. He concludes that "never has a company been so bold as to publish them during wartime" (Mariotti 1991: 5). Perhaps equally bold was a March 4, 1991 article in *Advertising Age*, which wondered aloud, "Iraq as Hot Ad Market?" (Crumley 1991). See Shuger (1991) for other examples of Persian Gulf War merchandising efforts.

5. One obvious instance of product as war generator, of course, was many of the ads for media organizations. Often these ads would trumpet the organization's quality, and necessary, coverage of the war. One ad for CNN appearing at the end of January in *Time* argued, "Now more than ever. CNN delivers the most complete coverage on television. The network more Americans say is doing the best job of reporting in the Gulf." Synergistically, a local cable system advised readers that "You need CNN on cable TV for the latest developments in the Gulf."

BIBLIOGRAPHY

"Ads and the War." *Advertising Age*, February 25, 1991, 18.
"An Ad Strategy Unfolds in the Dead of Night." *Adweek*, January 21, 1991, 30.
Andren, Gunnar, Lars O. Ericsson, Ragnar Ohlsson, and Torbjorn Tannsjo. *Rhetoric and Ideology in Advertising: A Content Analytical Study of American Advertising*. Stockholm: LiberForlag, 1978.
Associated Press. "War-related Products Face 'Profiteering' Tag." *Marketing News*, March 18, 1991, 1–2.
Atwan, Robert, Donald McQuade, and John W. Wright. *Edsels, Luckies, and Frigidaires: Advertising the American Way*. New York: Delta, 1979.
Battaglio, Steven. "Gulf Crisis Triggers Ad Assault." *Adweek*, January 21, 1991, 9.

Brown, Kathy. "Ads Talk Softly as Recession, War Fears Mount." *Adweek*, November 12, 1990, 36.

Brown, Kathy. "First Troop Salute Marches onto Air." *Adweek*, January 28, 1991, 1, 4.

Cheney, George. "The Rhetoric of Identification and the Study of Organizational Communication." *Quarterly Journal of Speech* 69 (1983): 143–58.

Colford, Steven W. "Hopping onto Parade Bandwagon." *Advertising Age*, April 22, 1991, 10. (a)

Colford, Steven W. "Military Launches Ads." *Advertising Age*, March 4, 1991, 1, 47. (b)

Collins, Ronald K. L. "Media Images Pitch War for Profits," *Media and Values* 56 (1991): 7.

Crain News Service. "CNN Gulf Coverage Shines." *Advertising Age*, January 21, 1991, 1, 52.

Crumley, Bruce. "Iraq as Hot Ad Market?" *Advertising Age*, March 4, 1991, 48.

Dagnoli, Judann. "Nabisco Brands Is Touched by War." *Advertising Age*, January 28, 1991, 42.

Donaton, Scott, and Wayne Walley. "Gulf War Could Delay Super Bowl." *Advertising Age*, January 14, 1991, 1, 42.

Emmrich, Stuart. "Britannia Rules Wartime Airwaves; BBC Bans Songs, TV." *Adweek*, February 25, 1991, 12.

Foltz, Kim. "Agencies and Clients Plan Strategies If War Occurs." *The New York Times*, January 16, 1991, C16. (a)

Foltz, Kim. "Agencies Caution Clients on Using Patriotic Themes." *The New York Times*, March 11, 1991, C1, C3. (b)

Fox, Stephen. *The Mirror Makers: A History of American Advertising and Its Creators.* New York: William Morrow and Company, 1984.

Goodrum, Charles, and Helen Dalrymple. *Advertising in America: The First 200 Years.* New York: Harry N. Abrams, 1990.

Granger, Rod. "Ads in War News Don't Upset Viewers, Study Says." *Electronic Media*, February 25, 1991, 4.

Hale, Katherine, and Michael W. Mansfield. "Politics: Tastes Great or Less Filling." In *Politics in Familiar Contexts*, Robert L. Savage and Dan Nimmo, eds. 75–95. Norwood, N.J.: Ablex, 1990.

Hayakawa, S. I. *Language in Thought and Action.* New York: Harcourt, Brace, Jovanovich, 1972.

Hollihan, Thomas A. "Propagandizing in the Interests of War: A Rhetorical Study of the Committee of Public Information." *Southern Speech Communication Journal* 49 (1984): 241–57.

King, Thomas R. "Agencies Scramble to Prove Ads Aren't Hurt by TV War Coverage." *The Wall Street Journal*, February 21, 1991, B4.

Leiss, William, Stephen Kline, and Sut Jhally. *Social Communication in Advertising: Persons, Products and Images of Well-Being.* New York: Routledge, 1990.

Lipman, Joanne. "Gulf Peace Unleashes Campaigns Draped in Red, White and Blue." *The Wall Street Journal*, March 5, 1991, B4.

"Marketers Slash Ads as War Erupts." *Advertising Age*, January 21, 1991, 1, 54.

"Marketers Welcome Home Troops." *Advertising Age*, March 11, 1991, 4, 8.

Mariotti, Jay. "Topps Hits Bottom with War Cards." *The National Sports Daily*, February 13, 1991, 5.

McCarter, Michelle. "Italians Screen Ads." *Advertising Age*, January 28, 1991, 8.

Metcalf, Jr., Nelson C. "The Story Behind 'The Kid in Upper 4.' " In *The 100 Greatest Advertisements*, Julian Lewis Watkins, ed., 149. New York: Dover Publications, 1959.

Mock, James R., and Cedrick Larson. *Words that Won the War: The Story of The Committee on Public Information, 1917–1919*. Princeton, N.J.: Princeton University Press, 1939.

Morgens, Howard J. "War and Peace." *Advertising Age*, June 18, 1990, 58.

Oberlander, Kate. "Advertisers Snap Up CNN's Pricier Ads." *Electronic Media*, February 25, 1991, 3, 37.

"PR Offensive Hits Persian Gulf." *Advertising Age*, September 3, 1990, 53.

Roucek, Joseph S. "Advertising as a Means of Social Control." *International Behavioural Scientist* 3:4 (1971): 1–34.

Rowsome, Jr., Frank. *They Laughed When I Sat Down: An Informal History of Advertising in Words and Pictures*. New York: Bonanza Books, 1959.

"Saddam Scrooges Retailer's Plans." *Advertising Age*, August 27, 1990, 38.

Schudson, Michael. *Advertising, The Uneasy Persuasion: Its Dubious Impact on American Society*. New York: Basic Books, 1986.

Sharkey, Betsy. "Advertising in Wartime: Sober Times Call for Somber Ads." *Adweek*, January 21, 1991, 4.

Shuger, Scott. "Operation Desert Store." *Los Angeles Times Magazine*, September 29, 1991, 18, 20, 21, 44.

Taylor, Philip M. *Munitions of the Mind: War Propaganda from the Ancient World to the Nuclear Age*. Northhamptonshire, England: Patrick Stephens, 1990.

Teinowitz, Ira. "Travel Ads on Hold." *Advertising Age*, February 4, 1991, 3, 41.

"Troops Spur Ad Maneuvers." *Advertising Age*, October 1, 1990, 36.

Vigoda, Arlene. "Red, White and Blue Add Up to Green." *USA Today*, March 11, 1991, D1.

Ward, Adrienne, and Alison Fahey. "Retailers Rallying 'Round the Flag." *Advertising Age*, February 11, 1991, 4.

Williams, Raymond. "Advertising: the Magic System." In *Problems in Materialism and Culture*, Raymond Williams, ed., 170–95. London: NLB, 1980.

Williamson, Judith. *Decoding Advertisements: Ideology and Meaning in Advertising*. Boston: Marion Boyars, 1978.

Chapter Twelve

Celluloid Heroes and Smart Bombs: Hollywood at War in the Middle East

Stephen Prince

Unlike the years of World War II when Hollywood studios joined in support of the war effort by producing films to bolster spirits on the home front, the recent Persian Gulf War had scarcely begun before it was over, leaving the studios no opportunity of producing films during the span of the conflict. In previous years, however, Hollywood routinely employed the Middle East and its regional conflicts as settings for exotic melodramas and action-adventure tales. By the time of the Gulf War, a tradition of Arabic representation was well established in the American cinema. These conventions of representation, pre-dating the Gulf War, shared a number of similarities with the terms and images used in political discourse to explain and interpret the war itself. This chapter explores the nature of this similarity and tries to suggest some reasons for it.

In each case—the images and narratives of Hollywood films and the footage and rhetoric of the war—the visual constructions of information and entertainment media have intervened between real-world referents and the audience. In each case, the media–audience relationship has helped influence the impact of depictions of regional conflicts in the Middle East. We will begin our discussion by briefly considering the nature of this relationship. Ball-Rokeach and DeFleur (1976) have suggested that the degree to which an audience is dependent upon media information resources is a key variable in understanding the amount of influence which the media may exert upon the beliefs, behavior, or feelings of its public. They have suggested that when audience dependency is high, media information sources may achieve a credibility and degree of conviction which they might not otherwise possess. The concept of information dependency helps explain the degree of the media's impact upon public perception of the war. For many viewers, the events in the Gulf War were experienced primarily via the information media. Because the war was so brief, direct personal accounts did not have time to circulate through the culture in ways that might have reframed the official portraits. In addition, the war was fought in a remote land and involved a culture that traditionally has been very poorly understood by Americans. Furthermore, the Arabic world has virtually no organized presence inside American politics, culture, or the media. Without such representatives, the Arab perspective—indeed, virtually any contesting non–Western view of the conflict—was nearly absent from the debate and discourse that surrounded the war. Finally, the extraordinary information control policies of the U.S. military acted to further reduce and homogenize the range of debate and discourse.

When a mass audience is dependent on media information for its portraits of the world, the potential exists for selectively skewing those portraits in political or ideological directions. A disparity now exists between the mythology of the war in the popular consciousness and the realities which that mythology tends to obscure. The war was portrayed by the U.S. military, and it was soon understood by the public, as an essentially bloodless affair. In part, this was a function of the surprisingly low rate of U.S. casualties compared to the number of Iraqi dead, but, more fundamentally, it was due to the policies of censorship enforced by the military to which the media readily acquiesced. Reporters were denied free access to the troops and to the battlefield and were specifically kept away from combat scenes that the government did not want the public at home to view. Furthermore, there were virtually no images of human death carried by the media. Instead, coverage tended to emphasize property damage—bridges blowing up, military bunkers exploding—and other forms of non-human destruction. Shortly

after the air war began, General Schwarzkopf declared that he was not going to get into the body count business. During and immediately after the war, the U.S. military avoided providing a comprehensive and reliable accounting of Iraqi casualties. Initial estimates, however, placed them above 100,000 with an additional 100,000–200,000 civilian deaths (Arkin, Durrant, and Cherni 1991). For an 1,100-hour war, these are extraordinarily high figures. The selectivity of media coverage, however, and the decision by the U.S. military to minimize popular recognition of the scale of the killing helped generate the alternative impression of a relatively bloodless war. (This impression holds for the war itself, if not for its aftermath. Following the war, news reports did detail the uprisings in northern and southern Iraq and their bloody end.)

The impression of a bloodless war was partly due to the emphasis placed upon so-called smart weapons technology in Pentagon briefings and media coverage. Images of smart bombs going through the doorway of bunkers or finding their way through air ventilation shafts to their targets inside were among the most spectacular pictures of the war. While the performance of the smart weapons was apparently as reliable and accurate as military reports indicated, their overall importance in the war (in terms of total tonnage of weapons dropped) was not nearly as great as their symbolic function in helping generate a folklore of high-tech warfare. Smart bombs were, in fact, a very small portion of the total range of weapons employed. Approximately 90 percent of the individual weapons delivered were unguided or dumb bombs which missed their targets more than 50 percent of the time (Arkin et al. 1991: 80–82). But the symbolic function of the smart weapon was integral to the mythology of a low casualty war. These weapons were presented to the public as an essential means for achieving the military's stated objective of avoiding civilian targets. Except for the Amiriya air raid shelter bombing, the available evidence indicates that U.S. forces were fairly successful in avoiding direct civilian casualties. This is not, however, the same thing as avoiding civilian targets. Designated targets in the air war included not just war-making facilities but also points in the civilian infrastructure such as railroad and highway bridges, electrical power production centers, telephone and telecommunications stations, oil production, refining and distribution centers, and various government headquarters. As Greenpeace noted in its analysis of the Gulf War, targeting the civil infrastructure, while not resulting in direct civilian casualties, does have "a profound effect on the population's ability to sustain modern life. The targeting of these life support functions of the civilian population, even for military effect, disabled the very objects that are otherwise restricted from attack: medical care, safe water supplies, food" (Arkin et al. 1991: 147). Greenpeace concluded that while the old-fashioned definition of collateral damage entails that civilians be injured as a direct result of bombing, either through shrapnel damage or buildings collapsing on them, the Gulf War effectively inaugurated a new application and understanding of the term. "The new definition is that water, electricity, and fuel are taken away from civil society. People who live in cities, in modern societies, are dependent for their lives, not just their comfort, on such support systems. Thus their destruction is as much defacto terror bombing, as destruction of oil wells is environmental terrorism" (Arkin et al. 1991: 149).

In these ways—the beliefs that the war was a low casualty affair marked by a preponderance of smart bombs and an avoidance of civilian targets—popular perception and recognition of the war departed in fundamental ways from the methods by which it was actually conducted and their results. During the war and immediately afterward, the information control policies of the U.S. military ensured that there were a minimum of contesting or competing perspectives offering alternative accounts. The discourse surrounding the war was not subject to the kind of splintering and antagonisms that, as the Pentagon well knew, came to characterize the Vietnam War and that it sought to prevent by controlling information and emphasizing strategies (e.g., massive aerial bombardment) designed to ensure a brief conflict. (The shorter the war and the fewer the apparent casualties, the less likely it is for political controversy to consume its prosecution.) The discourse generated to explain the war, and the popular imagery by which it was understood, however, had roots far deeper and more complex than the fairly straightforward media control policies of the Pentagon. The images, mythologies, and cultural constructions surrounding the Gulf War did not spring full formed from the speeches of President Bush or the position papers of Pentagon spokespersons. The sinister characterizations of Saddam Hussein and the Iraqi attack on Kuwait were responses to more than just the crisis of August 2, 1990, and the imagery employed relied upon an established tradition of stereotyping Muslim and Arabic cultures. We will want to look more closely at this tradition, a legacy that is part of what Edward Said has termed an Orientalist perspective.

Before we do that, however, it should be stressed that the images and cultural constructions of the Gulf War—in the absence of reliable data and competing sources of information, and in the willful shaping of information toward foreign policy objectives that guided the military-press interaction during the war—assumed patently ideological functions. If we inquire into the sources of this ideology, we must look in part at its Orientialist underpinnings. If we inquire into the sources of the images themselves, we may profitably look to another tradition of imagery, that of Hollywood films set in the Middle East. During the war, a number of commentators noted that the aerial footage released by the Pentagon reminded them of a video game or a Hollywood movie. Indeed, it is the contention of this chapter that Hollywood films collectively elaborated over a period of decades an internally coherent picture of the Arab world that, in its stereotypical reductions, was consistent with much of the rhetoric that surrounded the Gulf War and the picture of Arab sneakiness and incompetence which emerged in the popular imagination from Saddam Hussein's unannounced aggression against Kuwait and quick defeat thereafter. Obviously, it was not Hollywood films that influenced the war. Instead, a particular cultural agenda and political universe lay behind both. But if we look, in particular, at Hollywood productions during the 1980s, especially during the few years preceding the war, a political discourse and set of images is revealed in those films that is quite compatible with the cultural and political imperatives voiced during the war. Furthermore, as the war itself became a matter of Pentagon briefings and selected video images, it became, in other words, strictly a media event for people who did not have a friend or relative in the armed forces in the Gulf. The question then arises of the extent to which a prior tradition of imagery—in this case one furnished by Hollywood films—may have helped create a set of cognitive and emotional coordinates that could be applied by viewers seeking to understand and respond to the video images of the war on their television screens. This chapter is suggesting that, under conditions of media dependency, in the video footage of the Gulf War and the imagery of recent Hollywood war films set in the Middle East, two sets of separate but ideologically interlocking cultural images are operating, acting in synergy and themselves existing within and reinforced by an Orientalist framework. To examine this relationship, we now need to turn to those visions of Hollywood at war in the Middle East that immediately preceded the Gulf War.

Major Hollywood war films focusing on the Middle East during the five years preceding the Persian Gulf War include *Iron Eagle* (1986), *The Delta Force* (1986), *Death Before Dishonor* (1987), *Steal the Sky* (1988), *Iron Eagle II* (1988), and *Navy Seals* (1990). In addition, although it was not a war film, the Sally Field vehicle *Not Without My Daughter* (1991) clearly belongs to the same ideological framework as these other films and, as we shall see, represents, in a way, their climax. These productions were part of a larger cycle of Hollywood films during the 1980s that dramatized the need for resurgent American military power. Other members of this cycle include *Red Dawn* (1984), *Rocky IV* (1985), *Invasion USA* (1985), *Rambo: First Blood Part 2* (1985), *Top Gun* (1986), and *Rambo III* (1988). This cycle of films, focusing on brave homelands and evil empires, dealt most frequently with an invasion-and-rescue scenario, whereby a brave American warrior either defends the U.S. homeland or invades a Third World adversary in order to defeat a renegade terrorist army and/or rescue American hostages (Prince 1992). A little background information is necessary here. In order to understand the political values operative in Hollywood's recent Middle East films, it will be helpful to describe in more detail the political orientation of this larger cycle of resurgent America films and the social context to which that cycle responded. This discussion, in turn, raises the issue of the interconnections between commercially produced film narratives and ideology, of the relationship of Hollywood production and political representation, and we should briefly characterize this relationship. This short background discussion will help sharpen our understanding of the cinematic and cultural context in which Hollywood's Middle East productions are situated.

The resurgent America cycle was part of the newly intensified Cold War of the Reagan years and the accompanying currents in political and popular culture that argued for a reawakening of the American military power that was perceived to have been restricted and hobbled during

the Carter years. The political culture of the Reagan period was formulated in explicit reaction against Carter's emphasis upon human
rights, which seemed to many in the new administration to be a symp-
tom of a weakened America, a nation no longer able to forcibly defend
its needs and friends throughout the globe. The right, furthermore, was
offended by the "loss" of Nicaragua and Iran, and the Soviet invasion
of Afghanistan seemed like a deliberately calculated move in light of the
apparent erosion of the U.S. position as a world leader and military
force. Jeane Kirkpatrick's *Commentary* article, "Dictatorships and Double
Standards," was a key document of the period, produced at the end of
the Carter years as a criticism of what she saw as a demeaning U.S.
posture of "continuous self-abasement and apology vis-à-vis the Third
World" (Kirkpatrick 1979: 45). Kirkpatrick ended her article with a call
for a renewed global projection of U.S. power that would not unneces-
sarily avoid the use of military force. The Reagan administration followed
suit, placing the CIA back on a more active footing, following the cut-
backs in personnel and data gathering capabilities of the 1970s, and
pledging itself to stop perceived Soviet aggression throughout the world.

A resurgent America (to borrow a term from Robert Tucker's [1980/
81] important *Foreign Affairs* article) became one of the major foreign
policy themes of the Reagan years and a major component of domestic
political culture. Hollywood responded to this more aggressive international posture and to this explicit reawakening of traditional patriotism
by producing the cycle of invasion-and-rescue films that collectively
argued for the need to project strong American military power overseas.
Films like *Top Gun* and *Rambo* dramatized the heroic ideals of empire,
and the aggressive heroes of these narratives functioned as personifi-
cations of a national will and warrior spirit encoded by the foreign policy
rhetoric of the Reagan period. As noted, the most recent group of films
in this resurgent America cycle focused upon conflicts in the Middle
East, and it is those films that will concern us here. It is important,
however, to situate those films as part of a much larger cycle of productions that had a consistent ideological aim and function. Acknowledgment of this function, however, must be coupled with a caveat. In
arguing that the cycle of resurgent America films was affiliated with the
anti-Communist, anti-terrorist rhetoric of the Reagan period and, subsequently, in exploring the interconnections of Hollywood's recent Middle East films and the war itself, I am by no means suggesting that the
Hollywood industry is necessarily supportive of state policy or must
inevitably express what cultural theorists (Britton 1986) have referred to
as a dominant ideology, taken to be an expression of the world view
and interests of dominant social groups or classes. As I have suggested
elsewhere (Prince 1992), Hollywood film production in the 1980s was
multi-voiced, polyvalent in its ideological and political content, and ca-

pable of responding in ways consistent with the foreign policy and domestic political objectives of the Reagan (and later the Bush) administration (e.g., the resurgent America films) and in ways that contest and criticize those policies (e.g., a cycle of films—*Missing* (1982), *Under Fire* (1983), *Salvador* (1986), and others—dealing with the conflicts in Latin America from a standpoint that is both liberal and critical of official policy in that region).

In analyzing the political content of Hollywood films, then, it is important to emphasize that they do not speak with one voice, nor are they reflective of a unified and dominant political outlook. Some film scholars (Rosen 1986) have suggested that the linearity of Hollywood narratives, the "invisible" editing style of the films, or the projection environment itself (called "the apparatus") may express or embody political relationships or ideologies based on the ways these styles or environments may call forth a certain kind of viewing and viewer. Other scholars (Ray 1985) have maintained that Hollywood films, whether superficially informed by right-wing or left-wing perspectives, actually collapse these political distinctions by elaborating a core set of traditional American myths (revolving around such attributes as the frontier, marriage, home, and family) whose function it is to resolve and reconcile political alternatives and differences. While we will have occasion to note the clear myth-making functions of Hollywood films, it is important to emphasize, as Douglas Kellner (1991) recently has, that popular films reproduce on a cultural level the basic conflicts within society and that, in doing so, as there are contending perspectives within the social arena, so too are there contending social and political perspectives within and among Hollywood films.

Exploring in these terms the political content and function of Hollywood films entails a recognition of the degree to which, and the special manner in which, film may function as a vehicle for social or political ideologies. Film is an especially potent and sensitive medium for the expression of ideologies, in part, as Ian Jarvie (1978) has suggested, because of the collaborative nature of its production. As a group effort and product, the result of negotiated decisions and the synthesis of different perspectives and creative emphases, film may be better able to exhibit sets of socially resonant dynamics and values than other forms or mediums that are less collaborative: "in film making we see society in a microcosm [in and through the group that makes the film]. . . . This perhaps explains why the mass media can sometimes develop an extraordinary resonance with a contemporary mood—quite different from that ever achieved by a single creative artist working by himself" (Jarvie 1978: 105). Recognition of the political function of popular film and, indeed, of film's special sensitivity to political culture (topicality has traditionally been essential for popular success and continued profitability in the Hollywood industry) entails a reciprocal recognition of the basically semiotic nature of ideology, the coexistence of the domain of ideology and the domain of communicational signs (Volosinov 1986). The range of meaning that is encoded into a communicational sign, in our case into the cinematic image and narrative, and that may be extracted by the reader or viewer, depends in turn upon the affective or cognitive frames that the sign producer, reader, or viewer brings to the material and the social or historical frames in which they, in turn, are situated. While we have questioned the application of the concept of a dominant ideology to the range of Hollywood film productions, it may nevertheless be true that the viewer's conditioning by historical frames of understanding can elicit a preferred set of meanings (Hall 1980) from the films. Control over the message at the encoding end, as well, can operate to enforce a preferred meaning upon the message or the event. As we have seen, Pentagon policies regarding press coverage of the war operated in this fashion to help create some of the popular misunderstandings discussed at the opening of this chapter.

If the Hollywood productions about commando raids and air strikes in the Middle East enforce a set of preferred meanings for their audiences, as I believe they do, then this may be a result of conditioning by historical frames of understanding shared by viewer and filmmaker alike (Zavarzadeh 1991). In order, then, to explore the affinities that prevail between Hollywood's images of conflict in the Middle East and the political rhetoric and discourse surrounding the Gulf War, we need to consider briefly the historical frames of understanding that have helped to influence both.

Edward Said has examined the roots of a singular, engrained mode of understanding deployed by the West upon the East and has called it Orientalism, a term denoting the manner in which complex and varied geographic and cultural regions are transformed into a more simplified construction. Said (1983: 223) points out that the discourse of Orientalism, developing initially as a means of seeing to the maintenance of European empires, constituted both its own object of study (by creating "a geographical entity called the Orient") and the terms by which that study was to proceed, namely, via "a set of institutions, a latent vocabulary (or a set of enunciative possibilities), a subject matter, and finally—as it emerges in Hobson's and Cromer's writing at the end of the nineteenth century—subject races." The Orientalist framework was a bipolar one in which the fundamental premise was "the ineradicable distinction between Western superiority and Oriental inferiority" (Said 1978: 42). The West was viewed as being rational, civilized, developed, humane, and superior while the Orient was viewed as undeveloped, inferior, irrational, and a source of crime, chaos, violence, and corruption—all differences, Said suggests, that point to a fundamental perception of distinctions between master and subject races.

Film and television images of Arabs and the Middle East have drawn from the assumptions of this tradition in creating stereotypical portraits in which Arabs stood in for a variety of categories of evil, disorder, and corruption. Moreover, as several scholars (Ghareeb 1983; Shaheen 1982; Woll and Miller 1987) have noted in surveys of ethnic and racial images in American film and television, stereotypic perceptions of Arabs have also been reinforced by more recent conflicts in the Middle East and the oil crisis to generate images of greedy Arab sheiks or brutal terrorists. Said has described the generally debased terms by which Arabic characters are portrayed: "In the films and television the Arab is associated either with lechery or bloodthirsty dishonesty. He appears as an over-sexed degenerate, capable, it is true, of cleverly devious intrigues, but essentially sadistic, treacherous, low. Slave trader, camel driver, money changer, colorful scoundrel: these are some traditional Arab roles in the cinema" (Said 1978: 286–87). Hollywood films have a long tradition of exploiting the terms of these images, frequently including Arab characters and Middle Eastern settings as threatening figures and exotic locales for melodramatic stories. Rudolph Valentino in the 1920s, for example, built a career around his portrayal of the leering, seductive, faintly sinister sheik who was invariably attracted to English women. In the 1930s, ancient Middle Eastern cultures rose from the dead to challenge the West in a series of horror films about vengeful mummies. Throughout decades of American filmmaking, Middle Eastern characters functioned as symbols for greed, primitive behavior, and violence in films as disparate as *Casablanca* (1942), *The Wind and The Lion* (1975), *Black Sunday* (1977), *Rollover* (1981), and *The Little Drummer Girl* (1984).

To the extent that an Orientalist outlook existed within the culture, furnishing an interpretive framework to orient film production, it could also function to situate the meaning of real-world historical events, such as the Persian Gulf War. Passage through the filters of such a frame, however, transmits the raw historical event into politically and culturally encoded and constructed discourse. It is in this sense that the visual and verbal rhetoric of the war, and the rhetoric inside recent Hollywood films dealing with military conflicts in the Middle East, may be understood as sets of mutually interrelated cultural images operating in synergy. They both draw from a common political, cultural, and epistemological orientation. To indicate this commonality, we now need to explore some of the affinities between the discourse of Hollywood film productions and the public political rhetoric connected with the Persian Gulf War.

We will examine four major points of similarity, of shared assumptions and logic: the view that the Middle East and Arabic cultures exist outside of time and history as part of an essentially unchanging and timeless landscape; the view that the struggle between the West and Arabic nations is a struggle between the forces of civilization and savagery; the use of stereotypical images of Arab backwardness and incompetence, guile and brutality to account for more complex political motives; and, finally, the creation of a visual and verbal iconography of East–West conflict to celebrate the use of high-tech weaponry and to urge investments in the future development of such technology.

In examining the first of these four areas, we will see that both Hollywood films and explanations of the Gulf War rely upon anti-historical projections that work to remove regional conflicts from their past and their roots and, thereby, to reduce their comprehensibility for an otherwise-uninformed audience. Anti-historicism is, of course, a very effective persuasive ploy, and it is a key component in the narrative logic Hollywood imposes upon the Middle East and in the Bush administration's explanations of the reasons for the invasion of Kuwait. Beyond issues of persuasive efficacy, however, this anti-historicism is part of a deeper tradition of viewing the East. Basic to Orientalism has been a kind of essentialism in which Arabs, Persians, and other Eastern peoples are seen in undifferentiated terms, possessing neither a history of their own nor a tradition of cultural achievement. Suleiman (1983), for example, has noted that Americans tend to perceive Arabs as a people who live outside of history.

George Bush's explanations of the reasons for war frequently made use of anti-historical projections and images. Bush (1991c: 259), for example, explained the war to the American people as a contest of good versus evil, congratulating Americans for their ability to "selflessly confront evil for the sake of good in a land so far away." In addition to Iraq being a place of evil in a remote land, Bush (1990a: 3) characterized its behavior, its aggression against Kuwait, as "a throwback to another era, a dark relic from a dark time," and he noted the historical abyss that separated Iraq from the civilized world, charging that the Iraqi regime "stands isolated and out of step with the times, separated from the civilized world, not by space but by centuries." Iraq was thereby exiled from the modern world and the twentieth century, banished to a nameless, pre-civilized period, effectively distanced in spatial, temporal, and moral terms from the West. Specifically, in the rhetoric of the war, this period is that of the jungle, defined by animal codes of behavior, by pre-civilized methods for dealing with conflict. Bush explained that the Gulf War was necessary to demonstrate that the law of the jungle could have no place in the twentieth century. The war was fought to ensure the triumph of a "world where the rule of law supplants the rule of the jungle" (Bush 1990c: 739). This construction of an enemy existing outside of history and culture was facilitated by avoiding discussion of the historical roots of the conflict between Iraq and Kuwait (Khalidi 1991). Since the late 1930s, for example, Iraq has claimed that Kuwait is an administrative sub-district of the Iraqi province of Basra, and it has historically sought access to the Persian Gulf for its oil exports. By omitting discussion of these and other claims and grievances that formed the historical roots of the conflict, the Iraqi invasion of Kuwait could be portrayed as an inexplicable and completely irrational undertaking, as an act that itself existed outside of time, history, and culture, an expression simply of violence and aggression.

Throughout the cycle of Hollywood films in which an American hero or a team of commandos launches a raid into the Middle East to break up a terrorist gang or rescue an American hostage, a variety of cinematic strategies are employed to de-historicize the regional conflicts. As a corollary of this, Western political perspectives and the premises of U.S. foreign policy are generally affirmed. Alternative political perspectives are often absent from the films, and the recognition of Arabic grievances is rare. Very few of the films present an articulate Arabic character capable of giving voice to an alternative political position. Political opposition to the West is frequently caricatured, embodied by characters typified by the brutal, sneering Colonel Nakesh in *Iron Eagle*. He kidnaps the young hero's father, holds him hostage, and tortures him while proclaiming that, in his country, his people make the rules, not the Americans or "your ridiculous Western alliances." A similar mode of framing oppositional political discourse occurs in *The Delta Force*. A swarthy terrorist hijacks a plane, declares "war against the American imperialists," and then proceeds to torture and execute an American passenger. In *Navy Seals*, which deals with the efforts of a group of American commandos to infiltrate the Middle East and recover a stolen cache of Stinger missiles, the leader of the terrorists calmly tells a Lebanese reporter that his people are at war with America because of the shelling of their homes by American warships during the Israeli invasion of Lebanon. Superficially, it might appear that the film permits this character to explain rationally the basis of his commitment to a struggle against the U.S. role in the Middle East. He justifies his position with reference to historical events (the invasion and the shelling) that helped mobilize, in the real world, the very opposition the fictional character symbolizes. But the visual and narrative design of the film effectively limits and subverts this appeal because the character is presented as a ruthless, brutal, and treacherous adversary. His brutality and treachery undermine whatever appeal might have accrued from the rational statement of his politics.

More interesting, from a cinematic and political standpoint, than the virtual absence of a credible non-Western political perspective in these films is the general tendency of the narratives to avoid locating the story in clear geographic terms. The country that kidnaps Doug Master's father in *Iron Eagle* remains mysterious and unidentified. In the sequel, *Iron Eagle II*, another unnamed Middle Eastern country acquires nuclear weapons and threatens the world in a kind of global hostage drama, prompting the U.S. and Soviet air forces to launch a joint strike against the unidentified renegade nation. The beginning of *Navy Seals*, in which a group of terrorists holds hostage and tortures several U.S. servicemen, is set in a location identified only as an "Eastern Mediterranean seaport." *Death Before Dishonor*, dealing with the kidnapping of a Marine colonel by a gang of Middle Eastern terrorists and his rescue by an elite Marine team, is set in the wholly fabricated nation of Jemal. The vague geographical and political specifications accruing to the national and cultural conflicts dramatized in these films operates to render them in strongly ideological terms, in which the enemy occupies no terrain specifiable on a map's coordinates but is rather a hazy, nebulous, threatening Other, a projection of political and cultural anxieties that are stripped of their historical basis and are assigned to regions of the world in generalized, superficial and essentially mythological terms. This is a geopolitics of the collective mind, of national fantasy that, like the president's rhetoric during and after the war, serves to remove the terrain of the Middle East from history and from a knowable politics.

Anti-historicism thus functions as a mode of propaganda construction, and the geographically unlocatable nature of the Hollywood enemy has its counterpart in political rhetoric in the geographically more specified but no less non-historicized nature of the Hussein regime and Iraqi invasion. Stripping one's adversary of history, geography, and culture is, of course, a very efficient means of dehumanizing that enemy. Such a process of dehumanization is evident throughout the cycle of films, as it was in the rhetoric that characterized the Iraqi regime during the war. A bipolar set of moral oppositions prevails in the films and the war's rhetoric, in which contemporary conflicts between the West and Arabic nations are portrayed as modern manifestations of a timeless, mythic struggle between civilization and primitive, prehistorical modes of life. The demonization of Saddam Hussein in public discourse was of the most extraordinary kind. George Bush (1991d: 354) proclaimed that Saddam Hussein was an expression of the "darker side of human nature." Bush (1991b: 312) also proclaimed that Saddam had "subjected the people of Kuwait to unspeakable atrocities, and among those maimed and murdered, innocent children." He went on to announce that "The terrible crimes and tortures committed by Saddam's henchmen against the innocent people of Kuwait are an affront to mankind and a challenge to the freedom of all" (1991b: 314). The issue here, of course, is not the question of whether Saddam is a brutal dictator or whether his invasion of Kuwait was unjust, but is, rather, to describe and understand the rhetorical functions of such descriptions. (Such rhetoric serves an obviously realpolitik function in mobilizing public opinion behind the war effort. In the years preceding the war, Amnesty International repeatedly issued documentation revealing the torture of children and adults by the Iraqi regime, but George Bush made no public comments about these reports. On the contrary, until August 2, 1990, the United States was committed to extending and broadening its relationship with Iraq. The issue, then, is not whether Saddam was brutal or practiced torture but when it became politic to comment upon it.) One of the most vivid metaphors for expressing the demonization of Saddam Hussein was, of course, the Hitler analogy. Several commentators proclaimed that Saddam was the Hitler of the 1990s. Charles Krauthammer (1991: 134), for example, called Saddam "a tyrant who is truly a nightmare out of the 1930s." Bush (1990b: 675) invoked the analogy in a White House speech on August 8. A. M. Rosenthal (1991: 202), while not employing the Hitler analogy, joined the general chorus in calling Saddam an "evil dreamer of death" and his henchmen "the unholy killers of the Middle East."

The brutal Arab terrorist, who does not flinch from practicing violence but welcomes it enthusiastically, is a characteristic fixture of Hollywood war films set in the Middle East. *Navy Seals*, *The Delta Force*, and *Death Before Dishonor* feature prolonged scenes of intense torture during which terrorists taunt, beat, mutilate, and execute their American kidnap victims. In *Iron Eagle*, Colonel Nakesh pays the terrorist's ultimate compliment to his victim, the father of the film's hero, Doug Masters: "I must say I admire the way you can handle pain. I'm looking forward to seeing you handle death." In several films, this implied contrast between the civilized virtues of the West and the extreme violence of the Middle East is developed via an explicit attention to the Western rituals of dining, marriage, and burial. In the opening of *Navy Seals*, a U.S. Navy helicopter is shot down in an unprovoked sneak attack by a gunship belonging to unidentified Middle Eastern terrorists. The film cuts from this attack and its deadly results to a wedding in which the black member of the Navy Seals team is about to marry his sweetheart. The intercutting of these two sequences develops an explicit contrast between polarized ideological constructions: the violence of the Middle East with its accompanying disrespect for life and the civilizing, family-oriented rituals of America that symbolically celebrate such life. Later in the film, the black team member is killed while on a commando mission to retrieve the Stinger missiles, and a long, ritualized funeral sequence replete with the folding of the flag, a gun salute, and taps is dwelt on by the film as a loving affirmation of the importance of human life in American culture, in contrast to the apparent fact that life counts for little in the Middle East. In *Death Before Dishonor*, this point is made most explicitly. After a terrorist bombs the U.S. embassy in Jemal, the American ambassador asks why there must be so much killing, and the Marine hero of the film (played by Fred Dryer) replies, "Maybe it's because it's [life] so cheap here." Earlier, in the opening sequence, two terrorists storm the residence of the Israeli ambassador in Cyprus (Israel, of course, functioning symbolically as a surrogate for the West). They assassinate the ambassador, his wife, and their two children at their dinner table. Before the assault, the family chats amiably about school and jobs, and the parents speak lovingly with their children. After the slaughter, the film cuts to a closeup of an upended wine bottle leaking its dark contents across the tablecloth and onto the floor, providing a synecdochic image for the bloodshed and the violation of civilized ritual by the agents of political chaos and nihilism.

Underlying this antagonism between the West and the Arabic world, projected in political rhetoric and film imagery, is the historical contest between Christianity and Islam. Recall George Bush's charge that Iraqi behavior represents a savage force that is centuries old and A. M. Rosenthal's reference to Saddam Hussein's "unholy killers." As Soheir Morsy (1983: 92) has pointed out, "A quick glance at the historical encounter between the Arabs and the West indicates that the Christian West has traditionally viewed Islam with suspicion and fear. Indeed, for centuries, Islamic ideology and Islamic institutions presented a serious threat to Christianity. This threat and its resulting fear, while no longer a reality, has nevertheless continued to influence Western attitudes toward Muslims, including Arabs." These religious anxieties, which formed a distant backdrop to the Persian Gulf conflict (and partly explain why it was so important that the United States secure some Middle Eastern partners in its alliance) are apparent in the films as well. In symbolically charged narratives, political anxieties are often conjoined with religious ones. The climax of *Navy Seals* takes place in Beirut as the team of commandos goes into the city under cover of darkness to recover the Stinger missiles. Beirut is visualized in extraordinarily expressionistic terms so that it becomes a charged political and religious symbol. In the film, it is a hell of rubble and gunfire, of gutted, crumbling buildings behind which faceless snipers lurk. All signs of civilized, indeed, of recognizably human, life have been extinguished from the twisted, blasted, ruined landscape. It is a city of death. The Navy Seals describe it as "the dark side of the moon" and "the asshole of misery." This visualization of a dark, violent city is a potent symbol for the film's view of the Middle East as a center of chaos and mindless violence. In this gutted, lightless city the Stinger weapons have been secreted, to assault the West's airlines and civilian populations, the city thereby functioning in the film as a visualization of hell, as a Godless force of destruction— a great nothingness—poised to strike at the social, political, and religious infrastructure of the West (the Stinger missiles are going to be used by terrorists to shoot down Western airlines). Fittingly and symbolically, one of the Navy Seals is a character referred to by his teammates as "God" because he takes the high ground during their raids and with super-sophisticated weapons picks off enemy snipers. During the dark evening in Beirut, however, God is shot and killed by a shadowy guerrilla who appears from nowhere. As God dies in Beirut, this expressionistic, symbolic sequence dramatizes the religious roots of the political anxieties that inform these resurgent American films.

From a propaganda standpoint, the most sophisticated expression of these politico-religious anxieties is found in the Sally Field vehicle *Not Without My Daughter*. Although this is not a rescue-and-invasion war film, the fears that it expresses clearly place it within the same ideological frame as the other productions. *Not Without My Daughter* deals with the experiences of Betty Mahmoody (Sally Field) and her family when they return to Iran so that her Iranian husband, Moody (Alfred Molina), may visit his relatives and introduce their daughter, Mahtob, to her grand-parents. *Not Without My Daughter* is a Jekyll-and-Hyde story emphasizing the radical transformation in Moody as he turns from being a loving and liberal American husband to a raving, frothing embodiment of West-ern perceptions of Islamic intolerance, intent on subjugating Betty to his power as the male head of the household and turning her into a sub-ordinate member of society. When we first meet Moody, he is very progressive, teaching Mahtob all the vitamins there are in fruits and encouraging her to be a doctor rather than a nurse when she grows up. He proclaims that he is as American as apple pie, but, once they are in Iran and he falls under the influence of Islam, he reverts to fanaticism and discards his progressive trappings. In the West, he was a physician practicing Western medicine and a man who enjoyed opera. In Iran, he repeatedly beats Betty (and even beats his daughter) and threatens her life unless she submits to traditional Islamic custom. As the film studies in melodramatic detail Moody's transformation, the horrified reaction of Betty, and the very real threat that he comes to pose to her life, the film constructs a symbolic drama about Islam's threat to subvert the West (symbolized in the film as the American family). In these terms, it is fundamentally akin to the ideological operations of films like *Death Before Dishonor* and *Navy Seals*. In those films, American commandos mount an armed military response to defeat the threat of Middle Eastern violence directed at the West, whereas in *Not Without My Daughter* Betty and Mahtob mount a heroic escape from Iran, finding deliverance across the border at an American embassy.

By way of stressing the dangers of Islam, the scenes in Iran are a virtual catalog of frenzy, cultural horrors and abuse. The idyllic family interludes of the early scenes in America, filmed in soft, diffused light and stable compositions, are succeeded by the Iranian scenes that are cut very rapidly and are shot using telephoto lenses in order to create a visual clutter of bodies, cars, rifles, flags, loud speakers, posters of Khomeini and anti-Western caricatures of Uncle Sam, and thronging, chattering, screaming crowds. Upon arriving at the home of Moody's relatives, Betty and Mahtob get out of the car and stumble across a twitching lamb dying before their eyes, its throat cut, its blood streaming across the pavement. As the lamb whimpers, Moody explains that its death is an honor intended as a greeting for them. Mahtob cries hysterically and clings to her mother, and they have to step over the dying animal to get indoors.

Not Without My Daughter is one of the most intense and extreme anti-Iran, anti-Islam films to find its way to American movie screens, and, in one of those mysteriously coincident acts of timing, its national release coincided with the onset of the Gulf War. The timing of the film's release potentially positioned its anti-Islamic politics to capitalize upon the legacy of American antagonism toward Iran and the prejudices about the Middle East evoked by the war itself. To the extent that the West perceives the Middle East as a geographically and culturally homogenous region, an anti-Iranian film might potentially serve the war effort just as effectively as an anti-Iraqi film, despite the evident fact that those two countries had been at war for years. Despite this timing, however (or perhaps because of it) *Not Without My Daughter* failed to perform well at the box-office. Its propaganda may have been too explicit and intense. In this, the film was at variance with a more normative Hollywood tradition in which the entertainment functions of a film generally take precedence over whatever social and political points a director or producer wishes to score. Being so intensely ideological may have worked against the popular success of this film.

While political and religious distinctions between the West and the Arabic world are frequently cast in terms of moral oppositions, an additional set of polarities constructs the opposition of Western technological superiority with perceived Arab backwardness and incompetence. As Edward Said (1978: 285) has shown in his work, this set of distinctions possesses a long historical legacy, giving rise to the image of a camel-riding nomad that functioned as "an accepted caricature as the embodiment of incompetence and easy defeat." The conduct and outcome of the Gulf War seemed to confirm and reinforce this image of easy defeat for the general public. Despite the size of his military, for example, Saddam Hussein failed to mount a sustained or credible defense. The rapid collapse of his army helped ensure the brief duration of the war, but this collapse was due less to Arab incompetence than the unprecedented intensity of the Allied air strikes. The amazing scale of the destruction and the efficiency of U.S. high-tech weaponry in crushing the opposition has led some in the U.S. military to label the Gulf conflict a "hyperwar" (Arkin 1991: 23). While for some segments of

the popular imagination, Saddam Hussein's quick defeat seemed to c̲____
firm stereotypes of Arabic technological inferiority, the Iraqi loss was
more consistent with the projected outcomes of what Pentagon officials
are now referring to as "mid-intensity conflicts" (Klare 1991), wars in
which highly sophisticated weapons designed for use in superpower
conflict with the Soviet Union are deployed against emerging powers
in the Third World. Although the Iraqi loss hinged less on matters of
racial or national capabilities than on the projected outcomes of a new
generation of Pentagon war scenarios, the interpretation of this loss in
popular culture will generally be in terms that are consistent with pre-
vailing cultural stereotypes.

Popular culture has traditionally embodied perceptions of Arabic technological and managerial incompetence. These have been conjoined to
an imperial disdain for the political and cultural capabilities of Middle
Eastern nations. In *Iron Eagle*, for example, the hero, Doug Masters,
plots a rescue mission to retrieve his father from the unnamed Arabic
nation where he is held captive. With a maverick pilot named Chapy
Sinclair (Louis Gossett), he plans to borrow two air force jet fighters, fly
them into the enemy country's air space, knock out its air and ground-
launched defense systems, locate his father, and forcibly extract him.
The odds—two intrepid American pilots against an entire nation's defense systems—do not inhibit Masters at all. On the contrary, he con-
temptuously asks Chappy Sinclair, "How tough could they be? They're
just a shitty little country." Earlier in the film, one of Doug's friends
describes the enemy nation as "a gimpy little country." When Doug and
Chappy plan their rescue mission, they do it between a lot of other
activities. They design their commando raid while jogging, taking show-
ers, and dining out. Clearly, this is a training exercise for spare-time
commandos, a presentation that implicitly affirms the power of the
United States relative to the outlaw Middle Eastern nation in the film.
The heroes succeed with a plan that they have put together swiftly and
sandwiched between other recreational activities. In *Death Before Dishonor*, the marine hero Sergeant Burns is chastised by his Jemalese counterpart, who tells Burns that he has the voice and manner of one who
thinks he is speaking to backward people. Burns replies "What I know
of your army is that you've had a lot of wars over the last twenty years.
You never seem to win any." At the film's climax, Burns responds like
Doug Masters in *Iron Eagle* when he is told that his eight-man rescue
team will be fighting forty terrorists. Burns replies, "I like the odds."
In *Steal The Sky*, about an Israeli attempt to steal a Soviet MIG from Iraq,
perhaps the most blatant and racist denigration of Arab abilities occurs.
A Soviet officer angrily tells a group of Iraqi pilots that, out of twenty-
four MIGs sold to Iraq, only three still work. He adds, "I would hate to
think that you were only capable of flying carpets."

This enduring image of Arab incompetence helps motivate the related portrait of Arabic guile and brutality. These latter character traits are seen as being used to compensate for poor technological, political and cultural achievements and abilities. The prevalence of torture scenes in films like *Death Before Dishonor, Iron Eagle, The Delta Force* and *Navy Seals* has already been mentioned. This brutality is coupled with the character traits of deceit and sneakiness. In *Navy Seals*, for example, a Middle Eastern gunboat hides behind a crippled, flaming oil tanker and pops out suddenly to shoot down a U.S. navy helicopter that is attempting to rescue the tanker's crew. Later in the film, the leader of the terrorists manages to escape capture by the Navy Seals by beating himself up and posing as a tortured Egyptian soldier. As in the other area of homology between Hollywood's wars in the Middle East and the real thing, the terms of these imaginary cultural projections were also used to interpret and explain real world events. President Bush, for example, stressed the sneakiness of Saddam Hussein when he wished to emphasize the unjustness of the invasion of Kuwait. In a speech at the White House on August 8, 1990, Bush announced the deployment of U. S. forces in what were then described as strictly defensive positions in Saudi Arabia. He stressed that the aggression against Kuwait "came just hours after Saddam Hussein specifically assured numerous countries in the area that there would be no invasion" (1990b: 674). After then invoking the Hitler analogy, Bush (675) went on to say, "twice we have seen what his promises mean. His promises mean nothing." Discussing the prevalence in Western discourse and the media of such popular conceptions as "the Arab mind," Edmund Ghareeb notes that, along with irrationality, extremism, aggression, and fantasy, composite portraits of the Arab mind typically also include prevarication. "The Arab means what he says at the moment he is saying it. He is neither a vicious nor, usually, a calculating liar but a natural one" (Ghareeb 1983: 161). President Bush merely had to say that Saddam Hussein's promises are inevitably a form of lying in order to implicitly evoke the terms of this composite portrait. In films as in the discourse on real historical events, the legacy of Arabic stereotyping furnishes a convenient and, on its own terms, quite coherent mode of interpretation and explanation, one which simultaneously guarantees the inherent moral, political, technological, and social pre-eminence of the West.

A final clear area of affinity between Hollywood's visions of war in the Middle East and the recent war against Iraq has been the use of video and film imagery, and the commentary that surrounds it, to familiarize the public with the newest generations of high-tech smart weaponry and to advertise and promote these weapons. As noted earlier, the spectacular media showcasing of the smart weaponry worked to confirm the relative weakness of the Iraqi army when confronting the military machinery of a global superpower. One result of this stark contrast was to reinforce stereotypes of Arabic incompetence. But the high-tech weaponry also helped promote the war itself, just as the war helped promote a forum for selling (in a figurative and literal sense) these weapons. The appeal of the Gulf War for the American public, evident in polls that showed overwhelming support for the war once it had gotten underway, was due to the brevity of the conflict, the low number of U.S. casualties, and the romance accruing to the use of precision-guided, smart weapons, munitions which helped give the war a more sanitized appearance than in past conflicts. Anti-radiation weapons, anti-tank missiles, laser-guided bombs, and the striking video imagery of missiles seeking out their targets with the intelligence of a living predator—coupled with the apparent absence of real human death—helped make the war a thrilling, aesthetically appealing, sexy, and morally unproblematic spectacle for audiences viewing it in the comfort of their living rooms. In a similar fashion during the years leading up to the Gulf War, the cycle of Hollywood commando films set in the Middle East had been modeling and displaying in the most striking of terms the weaponry of electronic warfare and intelligent mass destruction. In *Navy Seals*, for example, the character the team calls God uses thermal sights on his long-range weapon to locate enemy snipers by their body heat. He can then blast them through the walls of the building where they are hiding. The other team members, proud of their weaponry and its effects on less developed nations, display the attitudes appropriate to the conduct of hyperwar. In a debriefing following a raid, one of the Seals is asked if he engaged hostiles, and he replies smugly, "I vaporized hostiles."

The use of real-world news footage and the fictional imagery of popular culture to model and display advanced generations of weaponry not only helps the public prepare for and adjust to the use of this technology but also furnished a basis for arguing for future investment in research and development. President Bush (1991a: 515), for example, delivered a speech at the Air Force Academy commencement in Colorado in which he announced the refocusing of strategic defense toward protection from limited strikes, that is, the defense of U.S. forces from "the missile attacks of international renegades." The label of international renegade is clearly a synonym for Iraq and for other countries that are not part of the new world order. Furthermore, as this chapter has been suggesting, the legacy of Arabic stereotyping operates to secure the attachment of this label to Iraq and to validate it as an accurate description of the Iraqi status. In the same speech, Bush then called on the Senate to restore his administration's missile defense program. In a similar vein, Anthony Harrigan (1990), president of the United States Industrial Education Foundation, in a speech at the University of Colorado, announced that even though U.S.–Soviet tensions had abated, renegade powers in the Third World would remain to threaten world peace, and, given the dangerousness of the present world, he doubted that people alive today would ever see a peace dividend. In a world where mid-intensity conflicts are viewed as the emerging norm, the use of film and television to model new generations of smart weapons can possess obvious policy benefits.

These similarities in the visual and verbal rhetoric characterizing Hollywood's Middle East productions and the Pentagon's war against Iraq—the location of Arabic culture in a timeless anti-historical realm, the polarized moral, political, and religious distinctions between the West and Arabic nations, and the romanticization of new generations of weapons of mass destruction—are evidence of a common frame of historical perception and understanding that envelops both Hollywood film productions and the popular perception and comprehension of the Persian Gulf War. Situated inside this frame, cinematic images and narratives, on the one hand, and raw historical data on the other, may become interlinked as part of the same chain of signification, as film images and the real-world war are positioned by the assumptions and projections of an Orientalist framework and generate messages that in turn reinforce it. Encoded by the mass media and the rhetoric of politicians, the war thus becomes discourse in ways not fundamentally dissimilar from the more explicitly imaginary constructions and operations of Hollywood narratives.

Given the common ideological and conceptual discourse that informs both the war and Hollywood film products, and given the popularity and the longevity of the resurgent America film cycle, it does not seem unwarranted to speculate that the imagery provided by films like *Iron Eagle*, *The Delta Force*, *Death Before Dishonor*, *Navy Seals* and others, may have helped furnish the public with an experiential basis for responding to and evaluating the war in the Persian Gulf. The accompanying pre-censored news footage had the same clean, thrilling, bloodless qualities of the aerial dogfights and bombings in these films. Under conditions of media dependency, when a crisis involves a war in a foreign land with a poorly understood culture, one obvious media source to which the public might have recourse in seeking to understand a present crisis may be the imagery furnished by Hollywood about that distant region, especially if the ideological projections and stereotyping apparent in the political rhetoric and documentation surrounding the war are consistent with Hollywood's fictionalized counterparts. In this sense, the war and its outcome, and the legacy of Hollywood's images of Middle Eastern violence and conflict, seemed to operate to close down understanding and block comprehension of international relationships and foreign cultures. This, in turn, can help ensure a reproduction of the conditions of media dependency which helped produce the initial occlusions of understanding. Bound by the terms of ideologically closed discourse, viewers of media and movie imagery dealing with conflict in the Middle East can be led to reproduce that region in imaginary terms despite the challenge of war.

BIBLIOGRAPHY

Arkin, William. "The Gulf 'Hyperwar'—An Interim Tally." *The New York Times*, June 22, 1991, 23.

Arkin, William M., Damian Durrant, and Marianne Cherni. *On Impact: Modern Warfare and the Environment, A Case Study of the Gulf War*. Washington, D.C.: Greenpeace USA, 1991.

Ball-Rokeach, S. J., and M. L. DeFleur. "A Dependency Model of Mass-Media Effects." *Communication Research* 3, 1 (January 1976): 3–21.

✓ Britton, Andrew. "Blissing Out: The Politics of Reaganite Entertainment." *Movie* 31/32 (Winter 1986): 1–42.

Bush, George. "Aggression in the Gulf, Oct. 1, 1990." *Vital Speeches of the Day* 57, 1 (October 1990a): 2–4.

Bush, George. "Iraq Invasion of Kuwait, the Defense of Saudi Arabia, Aug. 8, 1990." *Vital Speeches of the Day* 56, 22 (September 1990b): 674–75.

Bush, George. "The Persian Gulf, The Deficit Problem, Sept. 11, 1990." *Vital Speeches of the Day* 56, 24 (October 1990c): 738–41.

Bush, George. "The Lessons of the Gulf War, Middle East Arms Control Initiative, May 29, 1991." *Vital Speeches of the Day* 57, 17 (June 1991a): 514–16.

Bush, George. "The Liberation of Kuwait Has Begun, Jan. 16, 1991." In *The Gulf War Reader*, ed. Micah L. Sifry and Christopher Cerf, 311–14. New York: Random House, 1991b.

Bush, George. "State of the Union Address, Jan. 29, 1991." *Vital Speeches of the Day* 57, 9 (February 1991c): 258–61.

Bush, George. "The War is Over, A Framework for Peace, March 6, 1991." *Vital Speeches of the Day* 57, 12 (April 1991d): 354–56.

Ghareeb, Edmund. "A Renewed Look at American Coverage of the Arabs: Toward a Better Understanding." In *Split Vision: The Portrayal of Arabs in the American Media*, ed. Edmund Ghareeb, 157–94. Washington, D.C.: American-Arab Affairs Council, 1983.

Ghareeb, Edmund, ed. *Split Vision: The Portrayal of Arabs in the American Media*. Washington, D.C.: American-Arab Affairs Council, 1983.

Hall, Stuart. "Encoding/Decoding." In *Culture, Media, Language*, 128–38. London: Hutchinson and Co., 1980.

Harrigan, Anthony. "Confrontation in the Middle East, Oct. 3, 1990." *Vital Speeches of the Day* 57, 5 (December 1990): 139–143.

Jarvie, Ian. *Movies as Social Criticism: Aspects of Their Social Psychology*. Metuchen, N.J.: Scarecrow Press, 1978.

✓ Kellner, Douglas. "Film, Politics, and Ideology: Reflections on Hollywood Film in the Age of Reagan." *The Velvet Light Trap*, no. 27 (Spring 1991): 9–24.

Khalidi, Walid. "Iraq vs. Kuwait: Claims and Counterclaims." In *The Gulf War Reader*, ed. Micah L. Sifry and Christopher Cerf, 57–65. New York: Random House, 1991.

Kirkpatrick, Jeane. "Dictatorships and Double Standards." *Commentary* 68, 5 (November 1979): 34–45.

Klare, Michael T. "The Pentagon's New Paradigm." In *The Gulf War Reader*, ed. Micah L. Sifry and Christopher Cerf, 466–76. New York: Random House, 1991.

Krauthammer, Charles. "Nightmare from the Thirties." In *The Gulf War Reader*, ed. Micah L. Sifry and Christopher Cerf, 134–36. New York: Random House, 1991.

Morsy, Soheir. "Politicization Through the Mass Information Media: American Images of Arabs." *Journal of Popular Culture* 17, 3 (Winter 1983): 91–97.

Prince, Stephen. *Visions of Empire: Political Imagery in Contemporary Hollywood Film*. New York: Praeger, 1992.

Ray, Robert B. *A Certain Tendency of the Hollywood Cinema, 1930–1980*. Princeton, N.J.: Princeton University Press, 1985.

Rosen, Phillip, ed. *Narrative, Apparatus, Ideology*. New York: Columbia University Press, 1986.

Rosenthal, A. M. "Saddam's Next Target." In *The Gulf War Reader*, ed. Micah L. Sifry and Christopher Cerf, 200–202. New York: Random House, 1991.

Said, Edward W. *Orientalism*. New York: Pantheon Books, 1978.

Said, Edward W. *The World, the Text, and the Critic*. Cambridge, Mass.: Harvard University Press, 1983.

Shaheen, Jack G. "The Arab Image in American Mass Media." *American-Arab Affairs*, no. 2 (Fall 1982): 89–96.

Suleiman, Michael W. "The Effect of American Perceptions of Arabs on Middle East Issues." In *Split Vision: The Portrayal of Arabs in the American Media*, ed. Edmund Ghareeb, 337–44. Washington, D.C.: American-Arab Affairs Council, 1983.

Tucker, Robert W. "The Purposes of American Foreign Power." *Foreign Affairs* 59, 2 (Winter 1980/81): 241–74.

Volosinov, V. N. *Marxism and the Philosophy of Language*. Trans. Ladislav Matejka and I. R. Titunik. Cambridge, Mass.: Harvard University Press, 1986.

Woll, Allen L., and Randall M. Miller. *Ethnic and Racial Images in American Film and Television*. New York: Garland, 1987.

Zavarzadeh, Mas'ud. *Seeing Films Politically*. Albany, N.Y.: State University of New York Press, 1991.

Chapter Thirteen

From the Great War to the Gulf War: Popular Entertainment and the Legitimation of Warfare

James Combs

In the motion picture *Patton*, at one point General Patton stands in his jeep and points to the convoy of military trucks and tanks on the Italian road before him. "Look at that, gentlemen," he remarks to his aides. "Compared to war, all other forms of human endeavor shrink into insignificance." It is one of the melancholy facts of human history that so much valuable time, effort, and energy has been devoted to the conduct of the significant enterprise of war. It can indeed be argued that humankind has not yet found a moral or political equivalent to war, nor any exit from the ultimate appeal to and use of organized violence as a means of conflict resolution. The felt necessity of the recourse to warfare still leads established elites to arm for that necessity, often at great cost and neglect of domestic problems. At the same time, however, political and military leaders are faced with the considerable problem of the *legitimation* of warfare. The populace of a country may be reluctant to go to war for a wide variety of reasons, not the least of which is that warfare entails the deaths of one's own countrymen (and now, countrywomen) and the possibility of defeat and destruction. The popular constraints against going to war have to be overcome in order to successfully conduct organized violence against another country. Thus popular support for at least the potential for fighting has to be courted, and public opinion shaped to make the populace willing to fight. American entry into both world wars was preceded by a long and bitter national debate over going to war, with "pro-war" forces finally dominating through the adroit use of propaganda and persuasion, and the occurrence of shocking events such as the sinking of the *Lusitania* and the bombing of Pearl Harbor.

The Machiavellian reality, then, is that elites have an interest in maintaining the popular legitimacy of the use of warfare. In the modern era, elites have utilized both official and officially sponsored propaganda in order to influence and direct public opinion about the use of war and the necessity of "defense" (but rarely "offense"). Also, in societies such as the United States with independent media organizations who produce popular entertainment and enlightenment, the effort is made to sway news organizations to report and editorialize about war as government elites would wish, and also to enlist the various entertainment industries in the project of war legitimation. If a newspaper editorial or network news anchor has the confidence of readers and viewers, a newsworthy stance that supports the use of warfare gives credence to the government's military agenda. Similarly, famed celebrities and entertaining stories that support an organized war effort are useful for the government's purposes. Over the course of the past century, American political elites in the government and military have learned how to use the organs and personalities of popular culture in order to garner popular support for the conduct of warfare. Even though warfare may be a highly rational act decided by elites in pursuit of some national interest, an emotional basis for that political act must be created through the mobilization or acquiescence of the populace in its collective attitude toward warmaking.

Government elites who seek to legitimate the use of warfare are thus in the business of attempting to influence people's ideas and images of war. This is complicated by the fact that people are interested in *war as a story*. The theme of war has always been a significant part of the world's literature, at least as far back as Homer's *Iliad* (Chandler 1969). Even though most people in any age have not had direct experience with war, it is apparently easy for them to imagine war as drama. Warfare is, after all, a significant form of conflictual endeavor, perhaps the prime example of what Walter Ong has called "adversativeness," a "relationship in which beings set against or act against one another" (Ong 1981: 15). War is perhaps the ultimate form of adversativeness, since it involves large-scale killing of those the antagonistic actors set against. The adversaries in warfare involve themselves in agonistic life-and-death struggles resulting in victories and defeats, involving heroic and cowardly acts, decisions leading to cunning maneuvers and stupid blunders, desperate combat and abject surrender, ironic outcomes and betrayed peace, new enemies and allies among old adversaries. War, therefore, has all the elements of drama, and has been a major subject of popular storytelling since Homer first told of Achilles's anger.

There are different ways to translate war into dramatic form suitable for popular storytelling. *The Iliad*, for example, is an epic, but it involves a great many of the attributes of story-telling—romance, abduction, treachery, heroic single combat, familial strife, great adventure, low comedy, Greeks bearing gifts. In modern popular literature and art, we are used to three distinctive dramatic forms. First, we are familiar with the image of war as tragedy. War can be dramatized as tragic for the individual, a unit or an army, or for a nation. Novels such as *The Red Badge of Courage* or *The Naked and the Dead* or films such as *All Quiet on the Western Front*, *Paths of Glory*, or *Platoon* come close to being tragedy, with the destruction of individual lives in meaningless combat for at best dubious reasons. Even John Huston's documentary film *San Pietro*, shot ostensibly for propaganda purposes, has a tragic tone to it, with so many young lives lost over such an insignificant place. Much of the Vietnam literature and many of the films have this tragic tone, not only in terms of what the war did to individuals but also what it did to the nation. Such treatments are not tragedy in the classical or "high" sense, but are attempts to speak to warfare as an event that has tragic consequences in the destruction of people and national rectitude and honor.

More commonly, war has been dramatized as melodrama, with a plot, perilous adventure, group camaraderie, intense struggle, starkly drawn friends and foes, heroes and villains and fools, often wartime romances as subplot, and usually leading to death for some and heroism and survival for others, including the defeat of the enemy and the emotional return home for glory, reunion, and well-deserved peace. A glance at the typical "G.I." World War II movies of the post-war period—*Battle Cry*, *Battleground*, *Sands of Iwo Jima*, *Hell Is for Heroes*, among some of the most memorable—were made with Pentagon assistance and often script approval, and remained well within the melodramatic formula. This does not mean they glorified war necessarily or were recruiting propaganda, although sometimes they did so do. War melodrama allows for a wide range of touches, some gritty and brutal, some romantic and improbable (recall all the beautiful nurses who seem to be near the battlefield, such as the group in the TV series "China Beach"). In any case, melodramatic war stories tend toward the pathetic rather than the tragic, emphasizing the trials of ordinary people caught up in war, including separation of lovers, the death or mutilation of soldiers, the agony of families back home, the male bonding of the military group, the civilians who are caught in the middle, and so on.

We are also familiar with the dramatic motif of war as comedy. Since war is serious and deadly business, this may seem a strange approach to the subject. But this kind of story tells of war as absurd, an idiotic enterprise that is in itself insane. War becomes a kind of theatre of the absurd, in which those unwitting people who are unlucky enough to be caught in it can only view it as black comedy. Perhaps the most famous such comic treatment is Joseph Heller's novel *Catch-22*. In the movies, we may include here perhaps the greatest of all war films, the Marx brothers' *Duck Soup*, satirical movies such as *Dr. Strangelove* and

M*A*S*H, and also the TV series "M*A*S*H." Comic views of war have
a serious subtext of anti-war sentiment, seeing war as something so
dumb that the only way to combat it is to show war as stupid beyond
belief. These familiar ways of telling war stories reminds us that we as
popular audiences want to see war placed in some kind of dramatic
context so we can make sense out of it. Popular depictions of warfare
are responses to that mass desire, and in recent times a canon of for-
mulaic conventions and expectations have developed about the war
genre. Since most of us only experience war second-hand through accounts of it, we are seeking vicarious experience about warfare: We want
to know something of what it is like, what it means, and what the
consequences of it are without the direct danger of being in battle and
having our lives at risk. In that sense, modern popular auditors, whether
readers, listeners, or watchers, are *voyeurs of warfare*. A voyeur of sex
gains emotional excitement and vicarious information by watching something in which he or she does not directly experience, nor may ever
have. A voyeur of war gains emotional excitement and vicarious information by watching war, in either fictional or documentary form, an
experience they only know through witnessing stories about war. For
one reason, motive, or another (some of them likely pathological), we
are *interested* in seeing war depicted, and seek and find popular formulas
that put it in narrative structures that hold our interest. As civilian
audiences, we expect war to be great drama, whether we prefer war as
tragedy, war as melodrama, or war as comedy. In fact, it may not be
great drama, as some of the work on war suggests. The great director
D. W. Griffith visited the Western Front in 1917 while shooting a pro-
Allies film, eventually titled *Hearts of the World*, for the British government. Griffith took a quick look at the muddy trenches, the decimated
front, and the shell-shocked soldiers, and concluded that in dramatic
and cinematic terms the war was a bust (Schickel 1984: 346–47).

For a very long time, the only way non-combatants could experience
war was through story-telling that was decidedly second-hand and after
the fact, often months and years later. People would listen to "war
stories" told by returning veterans or read books that gave fictional or
factual accounts of war. Such retrospective story-telling, either oral or
in print, was often much embellished. The post-war Southern version
of the Civil War and its aftermath was different from Northern or other
versions. Confederate veterans spun tales of gallant cavalier heroics and
Yankee cowardice and brutality, and indeed the myth of the noble "lost
cause" found its way in print, in such novels as Thomas Dixon's *The
Clansman* (1905), which made the war and Reconstruction into a "racial
epic." But it had many patently melodramatic motifs too—lovely young,
virginal white women threatened by rapacious ex-slaves, heart-rending
homecomings, the ride of vigilantes (the hooded Ku Klux Klan) to save

threatened womanhood and to restore Southern honor (in the guise of white supremacy). Such popular melodrama appealed to audiences in and out of the South at the turn of the century, and Dixon's novel was performed first on stage and then, most powerfully, as a movie directed by the itinerant stage actor and fledgling movie director, D. W. Griffith. The movie *Birth of a Nation* (1915) was a sensation, not only because of the salacious touch of threatened women, but also because of its star- tlingly kinetic vision of warfare, the first "moving picture" look most people had ever had of war. *Birth of a Nation* really began Hollywood's development of the war movie, a genre that continues down to the present (Carter 1983: 9–19). For all its power, however, Griffith's *Birth* was not the first movie image of an American war. Let us survey some of these developing visual images of war Americans have seen with a view to what this history tells us about the media and the Gulf War. In so doing, let us recall Griffith, who was able to imaginatively recreate a past war that had become for many a romantic conflict, translatable into melodrama, with sweeping epic context of warring armies and he- roic figures such as Lee and Grant, and thus a good story that audiences would like to see again. For Griffith the popular artist, war on film must live up to the quickly developing conventions of visual storytelling as a form of screen entertainment. Like those before him who spun oral tales about war for the benefit of the tribe or group, or those who wrote books and poems about war, Griffith sensed that a war story properly told attracted people's attention, if it could appeal both to people's vicarious curiosity about war and their dramatic expectations as to what it is like.

The motion picture gave kinetic power to our imagination of warfare as no medium, including photography such as Matthew Brady's, had ever done before. But recall also that Griffith shot *Hearts of the World* as an employee of, and with the cooperation of, the British government in the midst of a desperate war in which they needed continued American support; thus that government, and the American government that ap- proved the release of the film in the United States, had a vested political interest in what story the movie told about the war, approving the propaganda element in its depiction of the Allies and the Germans. A war film is always made in both a popular and political context, chal- lenging filmmakers to understand both popular desires to witness war and political constraints on what can be, and is expected by rulers to be, shown. In these chaotic and creative early days of the movie industry, film was becoming both part of American narrative tradition and Amer- ican political culture (Fell 1986).

As well, at this time popular film was becoming a part of people's everyday lives, as a source of both social information and diverting entertainment. In that sense, like oral and print media before it, this new form of visual culture was quickly experienced as *play*. People wanted to see movies because they were "ludenic" activity, forms of communication-pleasure pursued in the interstices of leisure in everyday life (Stephenson 1967: 45–59). Moviemakers discovered very quickly, in accord with popular narrative traditions and conventions, that this desire for movie play included fare that was horrific, frightening, sensational, and repugnant; the "taste culture" that attended the movies were not necessarily in good taste. As we shall see, this playful curiosity included a wish to see again and again *war as play*. Movie voyeurs could safely witness deadly warfare without risk but with interest at the emotional spectacle of war on the screen. We may also infer that from the very beginning of the movies people found them a source of popular learning, providing people a visually powerful medium of social information. War movies became important not only because war stories made good movies but also because that entertaining fare about war also let people learn something about it, including whether it was good or bad. In our terms, war on screen can help legitimate or delegitimate war if people are in fact learning from it. This appears to have been the case from the very beginning.

THE MOVIES GO TO WAR ON SPAIN

By the 1890s, there was already a fledgling but growing and quite opportunistic film industry, which realized that it was in the business of producing entertainment that catered to immediate interests. In 1898, when tensions increased between the United States and Spain over Cuba, the popular media (such as the Hearst papers) helped to inflame public opinion during the period of national debate. The new "flickers," appearing at carnivals, little theaters with canvas screens, and nickelodeons, were crude films that lasted only a few minutes. But the promotional gifts of filmmakers were considerable, and they were able to make films that appealed to people's immediate interest in the impending war. These earliest war films provided both information, however phony, and emotional experience for a country quickly developing a "war fever."

It seems that these enterprising filmmakers went to great lengths to find, or manufacture, film footage that catered to popular war interest. With their background in or at least familiarity with vaudeville and other forms of popular theater and promotion, they sensed that potential audiences existed who would be drawn to such an immediate, and exciting and dangerous, subject. And they were shameless in their visual recreation of the war for the benefit of those audiences. After the battleship *Maine* exploded and sank in Havana harbor, one early movie exhibitor found footage of other American battleships at sea or anchor, and simply relabeled one or another as the *Maine*. Other hustling companies, armed with their primitive but mobile equipment, quickly made it down to Cuba to photograph the sunken hulk of the *Maine*, and indeed the Edison Company got a film crew to Key West in time to film *Burial of Maine Victims*. Another shot a film called *War Correspondents*, which apparently staged real correspondents in a fake race to a cable office (presumably in Havana) to telegraph a story (presumably the sinking of the *Maine*) back to their newspapers, in perhaps our first movie glimpse of the drama of war news. The *Roosevelt Rough Riders* were filmed galloping around on horses at an army base near Tampa. Indeed, in this pre-war period, the new medium of the movies seemed to have at least the tacit cooperation of the military, since they were able to obtain or shoot footage of military events on bases. One can imagine Theodore Roosevelt being quite happy to oblige the publicity. In any case, they were able to get on bases to film moving images of the launching of the battleship *Kentucky*, army cavalry riding at Ft. Meade, and the like. During and after the short Spanish-American War, moviemakers were able to film staged battle scenes, again presumably with regular army troops, on the proving grounds of Ft. Meade, making little combat films recreating the American heroics in the war, with titles such as *Last Stand*, *In the Trenches*, and *Defense of the Flag*. In the pre-war period, images of the military or the *Maine* disaster would be complemented by patriotic pageantry such as graphics of Uncle Sam or the American flag on screen, which were lustily cheered, and juxtaposed with a picture of President McKinley, who was reluctant to go to war, which was jeered and hissed. Advertisements outside tents and nickelodeons would blare: "Peace at Any Price! Do We Want It? Read the Answer in the Wonderful Biograph." "The patriotic feelings of the audience," notes Charles Musser, "invariably got plenty of fresh and sterling material for frequent outbursts" (Musser 1990: 247). The earliest filmmakers were quite willing to exploit the aroused feelings of people in a tense political situation, and appeal to jingoistic sentiments and the marital spirit. The earliest audiences of war movies wanted blood.

When war broke out in Cuba, actual footage of the "splendid little war" was impossible. But this did not dissuade filmmakers from faking it, as with the combat films shot at Ft. Meade. Another company filmed naval battles in a tank with miniature ships. But their ads implied that what people were seeing was an actual battle, somehow shot with "telescopic lenses" that captured the naval spectacle. When the war ended with a quick American victory, film exhibitors toured with a program of sixteen to twenty short films, offering a "panorama of the whole war," with "Thrilling Animated Pictures" of the "Great Cuban War," calling these staged or animated films, variously, "wargraphs," "warscapes," and "warshow." The notion that a visual medium reporting a war could improve upon or even manufacture the vents occurred to moviemakers early on. Further, the idea that people are interested in the story and spectacle of war was also evident. By attempting a panoramic story on film or faking a naval battle *as if* what was being seen in some sense corresponded with or actually was what happened, the filmmaker appealed to a willing suspension of disbelief that combined patriotic or "war fever" emotions with a thirst for visual information about an immediate and important event outside the purview of everyday life. The desire for war as play may have been so great that people were willing to eschew incredulity in order to believe they were somehow seeing the actual war story and spectacle for themselves. The purveyors and voyeurs of war had found each other.

After surveying this enthusiastic participation by the fledgling movie industry in the Spanish-American War, Musser concludes that this early interaction between a moving image medium and war, "on an unprecedented and previously unimagined scale," did demonstrate "cinema's value as a visual newspaper and as propaganda. Moving pictures had a tangible effect on the way Americans experienced a distant war. . . . Moving pictures projected a sense of national glory and outrage." The movies had found a political role beyond "narrow amusement," since the rise of the new popular industry had "coincided with a new era of overseas expansion and military intervention. Who can say what fantasies of power audiences experienced in those darkened halls and how those emotions continued to resonate outside the theater?" (Musser 1990: 247–61).

Who, indeed? Erik Barnouw has reflected on the cultural implications of the early development of the movies. The movies developed out of magic shows, he argues, and eventually "magic turned into 'media'." With the movies, "the appetites that drew crowds to magic theatres continued to be served-by movie palaces." And in the movies, "the elements of magic are all there—the flights into the future, nightmares of the past, hopes that maintain us, fears that threaten, and all the mythologies that tell us of our heritage and destiny." Since then, he asks, does not our "magic industry—via drama, documentary, docudrama—still summon up ghosts of yesterday and use them for present purposes, whether of statecraft, religion, commerce?" (Barnouw 1981: 104–05). The magic of media, we may surmise, is the magic of theater, projecting ephemeral images and voices for interested auditors. The movies, and other mass media such as radio and television, have the potential of drawing audiences into their magical play. But further, a magic show is usually best conducted with a unitary dramatic structure, offering the audience a singular, compelling narrative voice and mesmerizing, vivid narrative imagery. If the show is organized in such a way as to communicate a singular authority whose word and imagery may be believed, whose ability to manipulate and master reality is not contradicted, and who is able to conduct the narrative in an entertaining and instructive manner, audiences are quite willing to believe in the power and efficacy of authoritative magic. As magic turned into the movie medium, the films about the Spanish-American War became not only a way of seeing but also a way of learning about the war. This may have been our first example of the movies as an "emotion medium," with our national hopes and fears, our embrace of patriotic mythology, our desire for military vengeance, the nightmare of imagined defeat and humiliation, the sorrow of death and destruction, the ecstasy of glorious and righteous victory, all projected up there on the screen for all non-combatants to see and enjoy (Snow 1983: 169–209). Americans at that time were witnessing our first magic warshow.

WORLD WAR I

By the time of the outbreak of World War I in 1914, the movie industry was already a flourishing and lucrative enterprise. Filmmakers had long since learned how to respond to audience expectations and moods and how to interpret and adjust to the reception of film genres, stars, and narratives. This was never better illustrated than in the agonizing pre-involvement debate in the United States as the European war raged on year after year. Since it was clear that audiences were interested in the war, the movie industry responded with films replicating the ground and aerial combat "over there." But if the movies are any indicator of public opinion, Americans divided very much on "hawk" and "dove" lines in the war years before 1917. Films such as *Battle Cry of Peace* (1915) and *The Nation's Peril* (1915) conjured up the specter of German espionage and invasion, with the former enjoying war department cooperation. (General Leonard Wood put 2,500 Marines at the director's disposal as extras.) On the pacifist side were such notable films as Ince's *Civilization* (1916) and Griffith's *Intolerance* (1916), with both directors believing they were making a statement consistent with Wilson's "too proud to fight" moral rectitude. The political atmosphere did change quickly, and with American entry into the war the marriage of a powerful new medium and its industry and a government at war became astonishingly cozy. For Hollywood became a major vehicle of official propaganda, giving visual credence to American entry into the war. Virtually all of the techniques and themes of film propaganda were created at this time, under the guidance of the government's Committee on Public Information. Indeed, the official sanction given the war film after American entry suggests that politicians and the military recognized the power of the movies to provide visual and verbal "information" by framing in emotional and imaginative terms the nature and conduct of the war. War movies produced by an industry–government alliance at this time are an early indication of Jacques Ellul's argument that a good deal of what we take to be straightforward information is in fact propaganda, here in the guise of entertaining fare about the war (Ellul 1973).

These World War I war films, in either melodramatic or comedic form, employed all the polarizing visual and verbal languages of propaganda. In their more lurid form, they portrayed the Germans as Prussian monsters bent on rape and pillage, executing civilians, flogging women, starving children, and burning villages. The Americans, and often Allies, are stalwartly heroic, warmed by unit camaraderie (and British nurses and French peasant girls) and urged on in battle by the atrocious behavior of their foe. The Germans had all the attributes of the perfected enemy—as godless and immoral, barbaric, destructive, undemocratic, subhuman with menacing superhuman traits, and exploitative (Keen 1985). "The Hun" was an enemy of civilization itself, and thus could be destroyed at all costs. As sponsored propaganda, the industry–government alliance gave anxious audiences a unified perspective on the war. Further, it gave audiences a recurrent recruiting call in some of the war movies, with young men devoted to their mothers finally overcoming their domestic duties to join the comradeship and derring-do of a democratized army unit. In retrospect, then, the war films of the active period of American involvement included both the propaganda of repugnance, portraying an enemy worth fighting and killing, and the propaganda of recruitment, urging young men to join their friends in the fight. Political learning from the films included not only vicarious imaginings of a nefarious and fearsome enemy, but also fantasies of group bonding and individual heroics, themes that would become staples of war propaganda down to the present (Ward 1985).

In the post-war disillusionment, the war film almost entirely disappeared. Veterans returned with the scars and stories of battle, and the promise of the peace turned out to be a dismal failure. It was not until well into another political era did retrospective on World War I begin to appear. Beginning with *The Big Parade* (1925), a cluster of films emerge that take a very different, and unofficial viewpoint: war is an existential nightmare, an utter waste of brave young men and by implication a stupid exercise in political futility. Writers such as Ernest Hemingway and Erich Remarque gave credence to the popular view that war is hell, and that American involvement was a mistake. The war films of the 1920s and 1930s—*What Price Glory?*, *Wings*, *Lilac Time*, and into the sound era with *All Quiet on the Western Front*, *Hell's Angels*, *A Farewell to Arms*, and *Duck Soup*—in one way or another took the view that the Great War had been a grave mistake, and that the sacrifices on all sides had not been worth it. True, these films continued the image of war as an arena of heroism, but included the other side as equally heroic and equally doomed to futility and death. The camaraderie of the unit is tempered by the loss of one's buddies one by one in meaningless death in combat, as in *All Quiet on the Western Front* and *The Dawn Patrol*. Attacks and trench warfare, such as the costly assault on machine gun positions in *The Big Parade*, are envisioned as horrifying and randomly deadly. The other side is accorded humanity and a common fate of death or dismemberment, symbolized by death salutes to each other, the respect accorded fellow soldiers, as in *The Grand Illusion*, and death watches with a dying enemy soldier in the trenches, as in *The Big Parade* and *All Quiet on the Western Front*. Although these films retain romantic and adventuristic elements, they now include in their retrospective on the war the grittier existential aspects of warfare. Even if they cannot be called "antiwar" films, nevertheless they do represent a harder look at war, and likely reflect something of the popular attitude about the Great War, indicating that " a considerable number of Americans retained an ambiguous relationship to the war experience" (Isenberg 1988).

The retrospective war films of this post-war period, then, offer us the first example of a sober second look at a recently past war experience. Even if they cannot be called pacifist films, nevertheless they had none of the propagandistic "recruitment" thematics of the films made during wartime at government behest. But it did take an interval, a time of reflection on what turned out to be a horrible and bitter experience, both individually and politically, for artists to begin to retell the story of the war and what it means. This is "serious play" at the movies, offering an image of warfare with the implicit message of "Never Again!" Devoid of war fever and official propaganda, the war film can reach for both artistic maturity and political skepticism in the portrayal of war.

WORLD WAR II

At this point, we can identify several popular functions the war film seems to serve. As early as the Spanish-American War, the war film, however bogus, provided people with immediate information about the war. Also, war films became a medium through which people my exercise emotions such as patriotism, desire for revenge, bloodthirstiness, and fear of alien threats, as well as regretful and bittersweet pathos about a recent war that involved personal and national suffering and that turned out ironically to not have the outcome that was the political justification for the commitment and sacrifice. In a pre-war period, war movies can become a vehicle for dramatic debate about the advisability of going to war, taking either a hawkish or dovish position. War films may serve a definite governmental propaganda function, propagating the official justification for the war, the culpability of the enemy, the motivation for joining up to fight, the fruits of certain victory, and so on. And, more basically, war films allow people to experience war vicariously, an extraordinary event of which most people have no direct experience. The war film permits you to be there, but also, as Huck Finn observed about pirate stories, without the dangerous parts.

By the late 1930s, then, the war film had developed many of the melodramatic conventions and alternatives we still associate with it. With the rise of the Nazi threat, Hollywood and the nation reluctantly began again to play with the possibility of renewed warfare in Europe. The movies entertained a variety of stories, with both texts and subtexts relating to "the gathering storm" in Europe. Newsreels showed Americans images of the European and Asian situation, and feature films cautiously began to treat again the subject of war and aggression. The war film had almost disappeared in the late 1930s, apparently because the cycle of war films we discussed above had exhausted the painful subject of the previous war. In some cases this new treatment of war was oblique, often in historical "cautionary tales" (*The Adventures of Robin Hood, The Sea Hawk, Santa Fe Trail, Gungha Din*) which included covert messages about appeasement, fanatical movements, and desires for world conquest. But most amazingly, the just discredited World War I becomes again a mythic referent justifying intervention to stop German aggression. The heroic figure of *Sergeant York* is revived in 1941 as a model of principled warmaking against the German war machine. York personally met with President Roosevelt and went on a speaking tour in support of such righteous intervention. Sergeant York (Gary Cooper) of the movie has to undergo an agonizing choice as whether to overcome his religious pacifism; he does to the extent of winning the Medal of Honor for killing 20 Germans and almost singlehandedly capturing 132 more. This attitude of grim resolve in feature films seemed to capture a growing national sense of existential resignation, that we had to reluctantly fight again, and this time we'll be so ruthless that we'll insure permanent peace. In *Casablanca*, for instance, the surrogate "grand alliance" at Rick's place are all committed save for the isolated American, who finally intervenes again against Germany on the side of European culture and democratic values. "Welcome back to the fight," Rick is told by the Czech anti-fascist, "now I know our side will win." Even though many of the war films included stereotypes of the Germans, Italians, and Japanese, it was common to portray Americans, both soldiers and civilians, as grittily committed to the fight against the Axis, in a kind of popular "unconditional surrender" stance, but without a great deal of the simple-minded innocence of the previous world war's films (Combs 1990).

It was during the active period of World War II that the documentary propaganda film began to take shape in the form with which we are familiar. In some way, the war movie from its inception at the Spanish-

American War always had a documentary "feel" about it, since it involved glimpses of warfare that were deemed somehow actual. Moviemakers used film of real war such as footage of marching armies, battles, generals in action, and the aftermath of carnage interspersed with fictional or mythological storytelling. A movie can give visual documentation to life, so a documentary about war can document an aspect of life in which there is vicarious interest. But in order to sustain audience interest, the documentary has to have narrative force, telling an entertaining story that interweaves documentation with character, plot, and sequences of events that add up. If so, such a "docudrama" can communicate the representation of a persuasive reality. Factual and fictional data can be combined in a form that eliminates any distinction between them, and allow the film's perspective to acquire visual authority as a persuasive voice. The drama of war has a documentary basis, and the documentation of war has a dramatic logic.

The war documentary was given great impetus by the aesthetic sophistication brought to it by the directors enlisted in the American war effort—John Ford, William Wyler, John Huston, and perhaps most of all, Frank Capra. Capra's *Why We Fight* series set a standard for using footage (much of it shot by the enemy!) in a coherent narrative that makes a case for fighting to defend democratic values, admiring courageous Allies such as the British and Russians, and having contempt for the ambitions, and societies, of the enemy. Other documentaries were even more remarkable in merging an important story about the war with actual combat experience. William Wyler's *Memphis Belle* and John Huston's *San Pietro* told of the air war over Europe and the foot soldier on the ground by narrating the story, respectively, of one B–17 crew and one small unit in action in Italy. However, as propaganda films these two films were too graphic for American audiences. The *Memphis Belle* (the movie) showed airplanes being shot down as well as the *Memphis Belle* with Wyler nearly lost on a mission. *The Battle of San Pietro* depicted combat so graphically that the Pentagon effectively kept it out of circulation for many years (German 1990: 237–48; Edgerton 1987: 27–41).

By the end of World War II, a great deal of documentary footage existed, as well as skill at inclusion of such film in not only the making of "factual" documentaries but also fictional features. A feature film such as *Sands of Iwo Jima* could incorporate the extensive footage of the actual battle with the familiar war story of a tough sergeant who whips a unit into shape. The existence of so much war film was not only directly useful to filmmakers as incorporable footage, but also because it gave them, and indeed all of us who had seen such film, an idea of what we should expect from war films. Not only did such films find their way into television documentaries with Cold War purposes such as "Victory at Sea" or the Pentagon's "The Big Picture," they also were made available to studios who were making retrospective war films. Since World War II had seemed such an American triumph, post-war Hollywood war films would use such footage in the narrative celebration of "the good war." Now, however, war movies had to be good, since audiences had such a fund of experience with seeing war depicted on screen that their expectations were educated, and after so much war, and war movies, perhaps a bit jaded. In any case, by now in the history of the war film we may surmise that Americans had an imagistic and narratalogical repertoire of what war is supposed to be, and look, like. As with some of the other persistent and cumulative genres Hollywood created (e.g., the Western, the swashbuckler, the "woman's picture," *film noir*), the war movie had acquired a set of generic conventions.

THE COLD WAR

During the dynamic early phase of the Cold War, those conventions were applied, however obliquely, to the contemporary anxieties of the struggle against Communism. By this time, Americans were used to interchangeable enemies, since now the Germans and Japanese had been rehabilitated through defeat, and the former heroic Allies of World War II, the Russians and Chinese, were the new embodiments of evil. The Cold War era war films, some set in World War II, a few during and after Korea, others in training camps, rarely directly confronted those enemies, but they did seem designed to allay anxieties about these new alien threats. Films such as *Battle Cry*, *Take the High Ground*, and *Battle Circus* revived the "recruitment" and training theme, producing soldiers, pilots, and so forth who were battle-worthy; James Stewart gave up being the St. Louis Cardinals's third baseman to man the aerial barricades in the *Strategic Air Command*; and war retrospective, usually on World War II, reassured us that the American military formula of democratic camaraderie, organizational talent, technological superiority, and willingness to kill insured triumph in the current struggle. This was the peacetime period of the most stable Pentagon–Hollywood cooperation, with the former being able to count on the latter to say and image the right thing on screen. There were a few notable exceptions, such as *Attack!*, *The Quiet American*, and one of the greatest of all anti-war films, Stanley Kubrick's *Paths of Glory*.

Even though genre conventions may become well established, both conventionally and politically, they are subject to changes in the movie process, who makes movies and who sees them. A mature genre such as the war movie may become highly ritualized, if there is no fresh experience of warfare to revivify the genre. If that new experience of war does not conform to past experience and dramatic expectations, however, it may renew the genre in ways that the authorities do not like. If war is thought so terrible as to be insane, or is parodied as idiotic, then it may change the genre into an anti-war or disarmament story devoid of the heroic merits the political and military authorities prefer. The comfortable relationship between Hollywood and the Pentagon came to be threatened by the wave of "anti-nuclear" war films, beginning largely with *On the Beach* (1959), and continuing through *Fail-Safe* and *Dr. Strangelove* (both 1964), all of which envisioned the nuclear standoff of the Cold War ending in disaster. The military was even deemed capable of a *coup d'état* in *Seven Days in May* (1964). If war movies were at this time beginning to express popular skepticism about the military, it makes the intervention in Vietnam all the more astonishing. Although Vietnam obviously constituted no nuclear threat, it did extend the Cold War into a conflict that seemed to confirm popular doubts about the wisdom and even sanity of those committed to the global struggle. Anti-nuclear films would be a subgenre of the war film, reappearing again and again as fears of nuclear holocaust were rekindled, as in the "evil empire" heyday of the Reagan years, with such films as *Testament* and the made-for-TV "The Day After." But Vietnam was different.

During the Korean War, Hollywood had responded to the American intervention in 1950 in a positive manner, attempting to "frame" that puzzling conflict in both conventions of the World War II combat film and the ideological rationale of the Cold War. These movies (*Retreat Hell!*, *One Minute to Zero*) were topical but undistinguished, still being made on the premise that war was interesting and that Hollywood was responsible for educating the public on the necessity of the conflict. Even though the Korean War ended in a bitter stalemate, it remained in the movies for awhile as a new setting for conventional stories of war heroics, if with a more "realistic" tinge, in, for example, *Pork Chop Hill* and *War Hunt*. But the intervention in Vietnam inspired no movies made during its initial years. The relationship between Hollywood and the Pentagon had changed, and the attitudes and expectations of moviegoers were changing too. As the Vietnam War continued on and on, there were no war films made about it, with the notable exception of John Wayne's *The Green Berets* (1968), made with full government cooperation. Although Wayne's movie did well at the box office, Hollywood, like the rest of the country, little understood the war, and likely thought that it could not be fit into the war genre. So no others were produced. *The Green Berets* itself attempted to legitimate Vietnam not only as part of the struggle against Communism but also as a continuation of the Western and war genres so richly associated with the aging Wayne, complete with mythic references to G. I. heroics and frontier conflict with the Indians. As John Hellmann has noted, the audience for Wayne's film "apparently welcomed two hours of escape into a Vietnam that resembled Wayne's earlier westerns and war films. . . . Afflicted with doubt, Americans were now regarding the American mythic landscape in terms exceedingly close to nostalgic, self-conscious fantasy" (Hellmann 1986). The fund of experience of the war movie genre did not seem sufficient or "mythically adequate" to make Vietnam into a coherent story that could be plausibly told and understood as the war was happening. Moviemakers sensed that Vietnam was a new experience that would only look ridiculous if framed in generic conventions for a new and skeptical audience, many of them young.

Another constraint on Vietnam films was the proliferation of television news. Television had begun war coverage with the Korean War, relying largely on crude maps, approved footage flown in from Japan, and verbal retelling of a grim and frustrating war story. Even though news organizations were largely uncritical of the war and sometimes enthusiastic about it, even if as confused as everyone else as to what it meant, the facts spoke for themselves: The war was rough going for the American soldiers; casualties, although not shown, mounted; and victory in the World War II sense was impossible without escalation beyond the limited war aims. It was hard to sustain public support for such a limited but vicious little war, and many either wanted to quit or, more commonly, to widen it to bomb China and use nuclear weapons. In retrospect, news, and the new TV news organizations in particular, tended to depict the Korean war as pathos, as a pathetic struggle without victory against a nefarious Asian enemy who could be killed without guilt but whose power of numbers and fantacism made him impossible to defeat in conventional terms. Although crude in presentation, Korea was the first television war.

Korea was not only news, it was also entertainment. Aside from the topical movies, it was also grist for the TV documentary mill, framed as part of the global struggle with communism. Indeed, the much-heralded documentary "Victory at Sea," ostensibly about the naval victory in World War II, had as an immediate subtext the "lesson" of halting aggressive totalitarian powers through strong defense and war if necessary. More broadly, the Cold War provided the context for counterespionage dramas such as the series "I Led Three Lives." All these television formats provided a new medium for the communication of visually powerful stories which gave imaginative legitimacy to the conduct of the Cold War, and of military interventions such as Korea and NATO (McDonald 1985; Parenti 1992).

The news coverage of Vietnam became controversial because some argued that the story that came to be told in the many years of the war was of futility and carnage. It is now well known that the networks developed the habit of "shooting bloody," telling a mournful story of small-unit actions in the field. Reporters constructed stories on the "ironic model," telling a story of military futility, death and destruction, and a sense of endlessness that conveyed a narrative conclusion of ironic resignation to a war of attrition. Although it has been argued that large events such as the Tet offensive of 1968 were misreported as more disastrous then they were, it may well have been the cumulative effect of visual narration (now in livid color, blood and all) over the years that wore down public acceptance of a war that was going nowhere and meant nothing (Turner 1985).

In any case, Vietnam seemed to many people to be the ultimate fruition of the Cold War mentality and the power of the national security state. But for those who doubted, Vietnam also seemed the ultimate strangelovian insanity, the "perfect war" conducted without moral or political restraints, but perfecting only the savagery of military power applied in a small Asian country and the self-delusionary "groupthink" that rationalized it. In any case, Vietnam represented the first time television brought war into American living rooms, at least in the sense that it enjoyed enormous media coverage, and unlike Korea, the "turnaround" of information and images of events unfolding in the war could be viewed on TV news very quickly. Even though there was military censorship and other elite and journalistic constraints, people were for the first time seeing disturbing and "unsupportive" visual narratives about a war that no one seemed able to win or stop. Vietnam was to have a devastating effect on American politics, and strain mightily the myths of American power and civilization. The fall of Saigon in 1975 was the end of a major story in American political life since 1945, and indeed in retrospect seems one of the culminating events of the Cold War, a struggle that began to collapse of its own dinosaurial weight and length on both sides of the conflict, if for no other reason that it bankrupted, both morally and financially, both the United States and the Soviet Union (Gibson 1986).

It was after the fall of Saigon that the younger artists of "political Hollywood," and the changing movie environment in which they now operated, began to deal with Vietnam. In the years after the fall of Saigon there was mature reflection on what the war meant, since now it was clear that Vietnam had been an historical watershed different from all previous war experience. These films did share with the war films of the 1920s the conviction that war was an existential nightmare, and that this war—World War I or Vietnam—was a mistake, since the war had been robbed of its meaning, if it ever had any meaning at all. But Vietnam was a lost war, and one that seemed to constitute a threat to all the political assumptions that flowed from American national mythology. Moviemakers, as well as novelists and other artists, now were free to confront the agonizing question, what kind of story was Vietnam? There was no clear answer, and there were many stories that were inspired by the Vietnam experience. The movies alone, from 1977 to 1990 or so, seriously attempted to make some sense out of what to many had seemed senseless—*The Deer Hunter*, *Go Tell the Spartans*, and *Apocalypse Now* down to *Platoon* and *Born on the Fourth of July*—comprised a cluster of films that did constitute the post-war question of meaning in a mythically shattering experience. We may recall that many of these films showed American soldiers as capable of atrocities (*Platoon*, *Casualties of War*), of the military as capable of destroying their own people (*Apocalypse Now*), of neglecting those maimed by the war (*Born on the Fourth of July*), of turning troops into war machines (*Full Metal Jacket*), and destroying convival and familial groups back home (*The Deer Hunter*, *In Country*). In terms of the politically "supportive" traditions in more conventional war films of the past, the major corpus of Vietnam films denied that there were many valorous paths of glory in war.

Many of the Vietnam war films did well at the box office, suggesting that there was widespread interest in a war that in retrospect deserved serious treatment, since its effects on the United States had been so great as to inspire the phrase "Vietnam syndrome." Concomitant with this interest is the fact that audiences were now much more willing to witness, and believe, negative depictions of the military establishment, once an entity almost beyond political reproach. One study has suggested that if one looks at the many war films made from the end of World War II to the present, the U.S. military is increasingly depicted negatively, and that officers are now depicted more negatively than before. This began to change in the mid–1960s, with the appearance of more films that were critical of the military establishment, often with a theme of anti-authoritarianism and the celebration of individuality. Indeed, the implication in many such films is that if anything gets done, it has to be done by a lone individual who defies authority (*Heartbreak Ridge*) or leads an irregular unit of misfits (*The Dirty Dozen*). The legitimate authority of the military, and by implication the civilian authorities who command, is suspect, something to be defied or circumvented. Even the most bellicose films of the Reagan era were premised on this theme, including *Rambo, First Blood Part II* and *Top Gun*. But then so were ostensibly "anti-war" films, such as *Good Morning, Vietnam* and *Platoon*, which also focused on personal growth and even redemption in spite of the insanity of war and in particular the military system. After Vietnam, war films lost the ability to portray the military hierarchy in a positive light, small-unit camaraderie and soldierly loyalty disintegrated, and patriotic motivation disappeared (Rothman, Rothman, and Powers 1990: 79–84).

Such disbelief in, or mutation of, a major popular genre that at key points in American military history was deemed useful to legitimate the conduct of war was an alarming development for those national security elites who are charged with the successful conduct of warfare and the nurturing of a climate of popular opinion to support that conduct. For the Vietnam experience brought in its aftermath such alterations in the war film as to suggest the emergence of a "counter-myth" that would undermine popular confidence in not only the ability of the American military to fight a war, but also the legitimacy of American warring at all. The "formula" for the war film no longer could be counted on to appeal to the romance of war, and the melodramatic themes that story entails—war as a righteous enterprise, a grand adventure, a place for comradeship and individual heroics, the menace of a demonic villain, the *agon* of armed struggle, the vindication of right, the rewards of glorious victory. Anti-authoritarian individualism, whether that of the Robin Williams character in *Good Morning, Vietnam* or that of Sylvester Stallone in the *Rambo* films, is antithetical to military norms of authority and discipline. Also, focus on the extent to which war becomes an existential nightmare and a setting of senseless carnage and random death that potentially undermines support, not to mention recruitment.

Yet our post-war movie contemplation, not to mention books and TV, on Vietnam did not undermine old myths of national rectitude and redemption through violence. If anything, we may speculate, the spectacular and agonizing failure of the Vietnam War made them all the more salient for segments of the populace, and also key political elites. Hellmann argues that popular war stories after Vietnam did not confine themselves to agonizing over what was lost by the war, but rather began to reformulate a new myth of heroic warfare, one that reintegrated the essence of old myths of American "innocent" warfare with new myths based in technological superiority. Such a new mythic paradigm prepares the way for a new military vision and political visionary "to restructure American history according to that pattern" (Hellmann 1986: 208). *Star Wars*, for instance, combined the fantasy of innocent Americans fighting again for a good cause in an exotic setting, succeeding not only by the usual heroic combination of luck and pluck, but also through mastery of technological power. In this way, Vietnam becomes a "passage," a learning experience, that is not to be repeated but can point to a new kind of warfare that retains mythic adequacy from the past and acquires dramatic interest and justification in the present. Such a reformulation has both dramatic and political possibilities, since potential audiences for heroic possibility, as *Star Wars* demonstrated, and political interests wishing to relegitimate warfare exist.

The much-televised Iranian hostage stalemate of 1979–80 was a catalyst for the desire for "war realities" that reacquired mythic adequacy in a dramatically satisfying setting and restricted time period. The national anger and frustration over the hostage stalemate revealed a deep desire for our traditional and supportive war mythology to prevail once again.

Vietnam had been long, mysterious, inchoate, and without a simple and desirable denouement, and hence now the stuff of mature movies, a medium suited to the scope of such a protracted and multidimensional war, and the mythic consequences of a lost war. Vietnam did not reduce well to television news, with its immediate and factoidal focus; that war was too "storied," with too many voices telling too many stories over too long a time to absorb and make sense of. As the king said to Mozart in *Amadeus*, there were too many notes. It took a decade and a half of Vietnam veterans writing books (Ron Kovic, Larry Heineman) and making movies (Oliver Stone) about it for us to begin to comprehend the many notes. But even as we attempted, the new myth, one suited more for television, was being developed.

THE GRENADA MODEL

The long national contemplation over Vietnam was accompanied by the appearance of war stories that suggested a desire to relegitimate warfare. Indeed, one of the subgenres of the Vietnam war film was the "return and revenge and rescue" movie, in which commandos would return to Vietnam in order to reconnoiter the alien terrain, strike out at those who defied and defeated us, and rescue those Americans still held there against their will as in *Missing in Action*, *Rambo*, and *Uncommon Valor*. But these were fantasy interventions, in which an elite unit or superheroic individual accomplishes what the American war machine could not do during the war. And there were other themes: the high-tech combat of *Top Gun*, intervention against Middle Eastern enemies (*Iron Eagle*), fantasies of occupation and resistance (*Red Dawn*), fears of a Sorcerer's Apprentice starting World War III (*WarGames*), and so on. But it was this commando, or *blitzkrieg*, theme that now seems most intriguing. For such an action is "minimalist," involving a story that is confined in both scope and timeframe, includes concerted and heroic military action that is quick and successful, and leads to a clear victorious denouement at minimal costs and within an understandable narrative and imaginative structure. In short, such a war story is suited to television, although its conventional roots are in the war movie.

Further, such a war story is suitable for two distinctive television genres: Breaking News, especially in the "special report" or "instant documentary" formats; and Docudrama, that bastardized formula that gives symbolic and histrionic ordering to an event or biography (e.g., the Israeli rescue raid on Entebbe, the lives of the various Kennedys, Eisenhower in love and war, the *Challenger* disaster, Jimmy Carter and the hostage crisis), often a story of recent vintage that lends itself to the blending of news and drama, fact and fiction, personal and spectacular motifs. Such a story becomes "instant history," made soon after the event with the conviction that the story was of enough popular interest, and lent itself to dramatization, to warrant retelling the story. Many such stories involve pathetic personal agony in the context of a sweeping or significant historical event. War is obviously one such historical spectacle, offering the range of melodramatic touches that make a popular story appealing (Nimmo and Combs 1990).

This new docudramatic television format has been able to include both old and new war myth. It is rooted in the conventions of the war movie, but is able to include contemporary uses for the mythic format of the war story. The oft-repeated miniseries "Ike" was able to portray the spectacle of the great struggle against the Nazis in the framework of the personal biography and wartime love story of Eisenhower; the fictional Pug Henry of "The Winds of War" moved through a variety of spectacular settings including the Russian front and Pearl Harbor, and met a breathtaking array of leaders: Hitler, Stalin, and Roosevelt. But hitherto the TV docudrama has depicted war in the past. What if one could conduct, as it were, a docudrama in the present *as it happened*? If a government or whomever had the power to conduct the narrative of a story, it might be able to go the traditional TV docudrama one better by transforming a real war story into a palatable and interesting war story on TV as the event unfolded. Given the right circumstances, and the proper controls, the government could become the belated narrator of war theater as a coherent docudrama in progress as breaking news. Such military theatrics could serve the interest of rulers by involving audiences in the conduct of war against designated enemies, in a sense legitimating warfare as something that was both necessary and entertaining. The show becomes a "designed experience" of sorts, allowing the viewer to see selected aspects of warfare as if the observer were seeing it for himself or herself without the distorting "filter" of media interpretation and skepticism. By becoming a direct voyeur of war virtually as it happens, one feels as a participant-observer witnessing a dangerous and exciting mega-event in which "our side" wins, militaristic and nationalistic values and interests are triumphant, and the story has the proper mythic outcome and cathartic effect. Even though such controlled storytelling is based in the conventions of the "positive and patriotic" war story, it involves no time lag, no negative appraisals nor agonizing interpretations after the event, no aesthetic reflection by artists who might portray the war as something other than as another glorious victory, no independent news people casting doubt or shooting bloody. Such a media event may be based in, and conjur up, images and expectations of warfare drawn from movie and docudramatic conventions, but in a sense it is a new kind of war, *war as a performance art*. It is a war in which the attention of its *auteurs* is not only the conduct of the war, but also the communication of the war. With their political and military power to command, coerce, and coopt the mass media, the national security elite can make the military event go according to script, omit bad scenes and discouraging words, and bring about a military performance that is both spectacular and satisfying. In the wake of the Vietnam debacle, the national security elite had to conceive of warfare that was conductible without undermining public support and media criticism. This could only be a war that was quick, efficient, and victorious, and revived the canons of popular warfare as it was long ago conceived by "supportive" war stories. Further, it had to appeal to a news-saturated public's habit of desiring to witness big events, be told information, however trivial, about such events, and to identify with a single narrative voice and imagery. A war that was too long or with too many notes was impossible, at least in the immediate wake of Vietnam. Indeed, a war that resembled Vietnam was impossible. The Reagan administration made noises and spent money and sent advisors to Central America, but the situation and terrain so reminded both Congressional elites and much of the public of Vietnam that a large commitment of troops fighting a protracted war was out of the question. Nuclear war, despite all the big talk about "winnable nuclear wars" and suchlike, was also constrained by public fears, fed over the years by the scary tales of nuclear war and its aftermath.

What was required, of course, was a "splendid little war." Such a war would essentially be an action that would allow for a virtuoso performance by the military in a setting in which there was little doubt about the outcome, but which demonstrated American resolve, willingness to use the military option, and dispel the "Vietnam syndrome," at least initially on a limited and quick basis. For the Reagan administration, the opportunity for such a theatrically satisfying action came with the postage-stamp island of Grenada in 1983. In the wake of another American interventionist disaster, the death of the marines in Lebanon, an uprising on this obscure Caribbean island became the pretext for American military action. Even though in retrospect the reasons for the intervention remain dubious at best, at the time it hit a responsive public chord as a decisive and victorious victory by American troops over a familiar foe (Cubans and communists), with the good guys being seen (in approved footage) doing the things American soldiers had once done well, with the proper results ("liberation" of the island, threatened American students kissing the ground when flown home, the liberators being greeted by happy natives, the Cuban prisoners sent abjectly home, and so on). Grenada was likely a preposterous military action producing no real results in terms of the array of power in the world, but it did help to relegitimate the idea of intervention as beneficial and successful, without producing a quagmire, nuclear exchange, large casualties, and financial sacrifice by the citizenry. Presidential and military action had now been re-expanded to include the possibility of committing troops to actions in which they can at least appear to be decisive, and in a large sense can be watched by the viewing public in so doing. War was now to be conducted with not only concern with military tactics, but also with how the war looked as dramatic narrative seen almost instantaneously back home. (Some of the inspiration for this may have come from the British episode in the Falkland Islands.)

The Grenada model was expanded by President Bush in the invasion of Panama in 1989. This action was taken ostensibly to oust Panamanian strongman Manuel Noriega from power, but it also served the purpose of demonstrating both Bush's willingness to take military action as a touch and decisive leader who takes no national guff from the likes of Noriega, and that the Grenada model is repeatable, eliciting public interest and support and getting the news media used to their new role as conveyor of a war story in which the president and the Pentagon control, and conduct, the narrative. Since they have defined and portrayed the situation, it is they who get to show and tell.

THE GULF WAR

It is a relatively short historical period from the fall of Saigon in 1975 to the fall of Kuwait City to American and Allied troops in 1991, but it is light years in public enthusiasm for American military commitment. The latter event occurred after a long military build-up and national debate, especially with reference to Vietnam. But in terms of both rhetoric and imagery, the presidential and Pentagon narrative that took hold was one that referred to older conventions of the war story. It was old myth, "the New World Order," in new bottles in terms of justification—appeasement against aggression, Munich and the new Hitler, and so on. Desert Shield gave us the time to re-imagine war as such, to see the G.I. faces, the melodramatic stories of separation, the anxiety of relatives, their resolve to right to need be, their apparent mastery of high-tech equipment, the resolute but comradely commander-in-chief out there in the field with his troops. In that sense, the visual and verbal imagery conjured up was that of World War II—Americans from all across this broad land brought together in an exotic and alien setting to fight for the right against a demonic and aggressive dictator who is a threat to world peace.

The Gulf War was the fulfillment of the Grenada model. It was a war narrated by the authorities, the national security elite who had successfully relegitimated warfare. Military planning now included careful attention to how the war is being imagined, and communication confined to those authoritative sources of word and image which become the news of the event. In this case, the news is propaganda, propagating the messages about the war that cohere for the narrative thrust chosen for the story. Drawing on the old myth of American military rectitude, and the new myth of technological warfare as the means, and proof, of national and military virtue and dominance, the impending and actual conflict is framed in a "strategy of persuasion" that is interwoven into the words and images selected for communicating the official, and only, story of the war (Alexander and Deutsch 1991). With the official *auteur* in command of the narration without fear of significant contradiction, with a series of profiles of highly sympathetic protagonists, with a stereotyped or shadowy protagonist menacing, and a complicit press acting merely as the messenger for the official story, then we should expect an involved and expectant audience for "The Gulf Warshow." The fund of supportive war story conventions became the mythic frame for the Gulf drama, but the story also followed the canons of romance, the romance of war: a wish-fulfillment dream of heroic actors in concert against demonic enemies, which, after numerous adventures into exotic lands and encountering strange peoples, triumphs through the agony of conflict, the pathos of death-struggle, and the exhilaration of overcoming peril and doubt, in this case "licking the Vietnam syndrome." "The perennially child-like quality of romance," wrote Northrop Frye, "is marked by its extraordinarily persistent nostalgia, its search for some kind of imaginative golden age in time or space" (Frye 1957: 186). Licking the Vietnam syndrome through the Grenada model meant the eventual recovery of a pre-Vietnam mythology that signals a new kind of warfare now repeatable whenever national security elites deem it necessary. Since it will enjoy popular support and exclude as harmful unromantic images and information that might undermine the mythic adequacy of the war story.

The political uses of such a war story will not be restricted to purely military objectives. The new mass-mediated performance art of warshow can be expanded to include the lack of political morale, serving a therapeutic function. Defense Secretary Cheney noted after the war that it was a "catharsis . . . that sort of lifted the burden that the country had borne, almost without being aware of it, since the war in Vietnam" (Cheney, 1991). The war produced a moment of national euphoria and following period of national self-congratulation, and there were even intimations that now it should not only make us willing to fight more such wars, but also enjoy a period of prosperity at home through the creation by the war of national "confidence." Since according to conventional storytelling, war is supposed to produce not only victory but also in the aftermath the fruits of victory in prosperity, the old myth was supposed to magically conjur up the nostalgic golden age produced by victory abroad, the confident and prosperous Fifties after World War II repeated now.

From the perspective of 1992, it is clear that this effect, if intended, did not happen, and the euphoria and self-congratulation have long since vanished, like Bush's approval ratings, in the lingering and deepening recession. We also now know a great deal more about the war we were not allowed to see—the soldiers killed by friendly fire, the smart bombs that turned out to be as dumb as any others, the high-tech equipment, including the Patriot missile, that didn't work as well as billed, not to mention the Iraqi soldiers buried alive by army plows, the mounting civilian casualties, the hopeless plight of the Kurds, the fact that Saddam Hussein remains firmly in power, and that because of the war, Iran now dominates the region. But therapeutic war, undertaken for purposes of political morale or re-election, is an immediately experienced event, and later on is forgotten or sublimated, since it is no longer enjoyable, involves messy facts, and is not mythically adequate. The political elite now armed with its legitimacy is now concerned with its next possible use in some other context for some future immediate purpose, both foreign and domestic.

"In the post-modern world," predicted Lewis H. Lapham, "maybe war will come to be understood as a performing art, made for television and promoted as spectacle" (Lapham 1991: 15). In some ways, post-modern warfare conducted in the official light of media spectacle will be continuous with those people watching the movies of the real, and imagined, Spanish-American War long ago. But it will be discontinuous also, since in the "wired" world of post-modernity, it may be the case that the primary function of war will be the warshow. War may continue to be directed at easy targets—Third World dictators, drug lords, revolutionary or terrorist groups—but the military purpose may be subordinated to the domestic purpose of swaying, and commanding, opinion through the use of "play-events" such as media war shows. It is obvious that such a practice has Orwellian overtones. But in a world, both at home and around the world, increasingly divided between the haves and have-nots, TV war now may well have political uses undreamed of by previous military and political elites. If bread is not in the offing, then circuses will have to do; the practice of therapeutic warfare will then be an integral part of policy carried out by an obliging military seeking new justifications for large budgets, new technologies, and recruitments. For potentially restless and bored populaces, war shows will be a welcome relief from the dreariness of the post-modern world. The military performance art of the future will be witnessed by the many who momentarily forget their plight and who is responsible for it, agreeing as they see the dazzling light show and follow the thrilling war story that what they are seeing is a splendid little war, in which for a brief euphoric time all other forms of human endeavor, including more mundane and intractable problems, shrink into insignificance.

BIBLIOGRAPHY

Alexander, Yonah, and Robert D. Deutsch. "Media and the War of Imagery."
    Chicago *Tribune*. January 19,1991, 14.
Barnouw, Erik. *The Magician and the Cinema*. New York: Oxford University Press,
    1981.
Carter, Everett. "Cultural History Written with Lightning: The Significance of
    Birth of a Nation (1915)." In *Hollywood as Historian: American Film in a
    Cultural Context*, ed. Peter C. Rollins. Lexington: the University Press of
    Kentucky, 1983.
Chandler, Alice, ed. *The Theme of War*. Dubuque, Iowa: William C. Brown, 1969.
Cheney, Dick. "War Was Good for Country in Some Ways, Cheney Says."
    Roanoke *Times and World-News*. August 2, 1991, A2.
Combs, James E. *American Political Movies*. New York: Garland, 1990.
Edgerton, Gary. "Revisiting the Recordings of Wars Past: Remembering the
    Documentary Trilogy of John Huston." *Journal of Popular Film and Television*
    15, 1 (Spring 1987): 27–41.
Ellul, Jacques. *Propaganda: The Formation of Men's Attitudes*. New York: Vintage
    Books, 1973.
Fell, John L. *Film and the Narrative Tradition*. Berkeley: University of California
    Press, 1986.
Frye, Northrop. *Anatomy of Criticism*. Princeton, N.J.: Princeton University Press,
    1957.
German, Kathleen M. "Frank Capra's *Why We Fight* Series and the American
    Audience." *Western Journal of Speech Communication* 54 (Spring 1990): 237–
    48.
Gibson, James W. *The Perfect War*. Boston: Atlantic Monthly Press, 1986.
Hellmann, John. *American Myth and the Legacy of Vietnam*. New York: Columbia
    University Press, 1986.
Isenberg, Michael T. "The Great War Viewed from the Twenties: *The Big Parade*
    (1925)." In *American History/American Film: Interpreting the Hollywood Image*,
    ed. John E. O'Connor and Martin A. Jackson. New York: Frederick Ungar
    Continuum, 1988.
Keen, Sam. *Faces of the Enemy*. New York: Harper & Row, 1985.
Lapham, Lewis H. "Trained Seals and Sitting Ducks." *Harper's Magazine* (May
    1991): 10–15.
McDonald, J. Fred. *Television and the Red Menace*. New York: Praeger, 1985.
Musser, Charles. *The Emergence of Cinema: The American Screen to 1908*. New York:
    Charles Scribner's Sons, 1990.
Nimmo, Dan, and James E. Combs. *Mediated Political Realities*, 2d ed. New York:
    Longman, 1990.
Ong, Walter J. *Fighting for Life*. Ithaca: Cornell University Press, 1981.
Parenti, Michael. *Make-Believe Media: the Politics of Entertainment*. New York: St.
    Martin's Press, 1992.
Rothman, Stanley, David J. Rothman, and Stephen P. Powers. "Hollywood
    Views the Military." *Society* 28, 1 (November/December 1990): 79–84.
Schickel, Richard. *D. W. Griffith: An American Life*. New York: Simon and Schus-
    ter, 1984.

Snow, Robert P. *Creating Media Culture*. Beverly Hills: Sage, 1983.

Stephenson, William. *The Play Theory of Mass Communication*. Chicago: University of Chicago Press, 1967.

Turner, Kathleen J. *Lyndon Johnson's Dual War: Vietnam and the Press*. Chicago: University of Chicago Press, 1985.

Ward, Larry Wayne. *The Motion Picture Goes to War: the U.S. Government Film Effort during World War I*. Ann Arbor, Mich.: U.M.I. Research Press, 1985.

Selected Bibliography

Albritton, Robert, and Jarol Manheim. "Public Relations Efforts for the Third World: Images in the News." *Journal of Communication* (Winter 1985): 43–59.

Altemeyer, B. *Right-wing Authoritarianism*. Winnipeg, Canada: University of Manitoba Press, 1981.

Altemeyer, B. *Enemies of Freedom: Understanding of Right-Wing Authoritarianism*. San Francisco: Jossey-Bass, 1988.

Altheide, David L. *Creating Reality: How TV News Distorts Events*. Beverly Hills, Calif.: Sage, 1976.

Altheide, David L., and R. P. Snow. *Media Logic*. Beverly Hills, Calif.: Sage, 1979.

Altheide, David "Iran Versus TV News: The Hostage Story Out of Context." In *Television Coverage of the Middle East*, ed. William Adams, 128–57. Norwood, N.J.: Ablex, 1981.

Altheide, David L. "The Impact of Television Formats on Social Policy." *Journal of Broadcasting and Electronic Media* (Winter 1991): 3–21.

Andreasen, Margaret. "Listener Recall for Call-in Versus Structured Interview Radio Formats." *Journal of Broadcasting and Electronic Media* (Fall 1989): 421–30.

Arkin, William, Damian Durrant, and Marianne Cherni. *On Impact: Modern Warfare and the Environment, A Case Study of the Gulf War*. Washington, D.C.: Greenpeace USA, 1991.

Arlen, Michael. *Living Room War*. New York: Viking, 1969.

Atwater, Tony. "News Formats in Network Evening News Coverage of the TWA Hijacking." *Journal of Broadcasting and Electronic Media* (Summer 1989): 293–304.

Avery, Robert, Donald Ellis, and Thomas Glover. "Patterns of Communication on Talk Radio." *Journal of Broadcasting* (Winter 1978): 5–17.

Ball-Rokeach, S. J., and M. L. DeFleur. "A Dependency Model of Mass-Media Effects." *Communication Research* 3, 1 (1976): 3–21.

Barber, James David. "Empire of the Son." *The Washington Monthly* (October 1991): 25–29.

Barnouw, Erik. *The Magician and the Cinema*. New York: Oxford University Press, 1981.

Barrett, Marvin, ed. *Broadcasting Journalism: 1979–1981*. New York: Everest House, 1982.

Barry, Brian, and Russell Hardin. *Rational Man and Irrational Society?* Beverly Hills, Calif.: Sage, 1982.

Battaglio, Steven. "Gulf Crisis Triggers Ad Assault." *Adweek*, January 21, 1991, 9.

Boot, William. "The Pool." *Columbia Journalism Review* (May/June 1991): 24–27.

Braestrup, Peter. *Battle Lines: Report of the Twentieth Century Fund Task Force on the Military and the Media*. New York: Priority Press, 1985.

Campbell, D'Ann. "Servicewomen of World War II." *Armed Forces and Society* 16, 2 (Winter 1990): 251–70.

Carragee, Kevin. "News and Ideology." *Journalism Monographs* (August 1991): 1–30.

Chandler, Alice, ed. *The Theme of War*. Dubuque, Iowa: William C. Brown, 1969.

Chen, A. C., and R. G. Chaudhary. "Asia and the Pacific." In *Global Journalism: Survey of International Communication*, ed. J. C. Merrill, 2d ed. New York: Longman, 1991.

Clausewitz, Carl Von. *On War*. Princeton, N.J.: Princeton University Press, 1976.

Cohen, A. A., H. Adoni, and C. R. Bantz. *Social Conflict and Television News*. Newbury Park, Calif.: Sage, 1990.

Colford, Steven W. "Hopping onto Parade Bandwagon." *Advertising Age*, April 22, 1991, 10.

Collins, Ronald K. "Media Images Pitch War for Profits." *Media and Values* 56 (1991): 7.

Combs, James E. *American Political Movies*. New York: Garland, 1990.

Conover, P. J. "The Influence of Group Identifications on Political Perception and Evaluation." *The Journal of Politics* 46 (1984): 760–85.

Copetas, A. Craig. "Conquering Heroines." *Mirabella* (June 1991): 26–35.

Corry, J. "TV News and the Neutrality Principle." *Commentary* 91, 5 (1991): 24–27.

Cotton, J. L., and R. A. Hieser. "Selective Exposure to Information and Cognitive Dissonance." *Journal of Research in Personality* 14 (1980): 518–27.

Cranberg, Gilbert. "A Flimsy Story and a Compliant Press." *Washington Journalism Review* (March 1990): 48–49, 52–53.

Crumley, Bruce. "Iraq as Hot Ad Market." *Advertising Age*, March 4, 1991, 48.

Dennis, Everette, David Stebenne, John Pavlik, et al. *The Media at War: The Press and the Persian Gulf Conflict*. New York: Gannett Foundation Media Center, 1991.

Denton, Jr., Robert E. "Primetime Politics: The Ethics of Teledemocracy." In *Ethical Dimensions of Political Communication*, ed. Robert E. Denton, Jr. New York: Praeger, 1991.

Dionne, E. J. "Are the Media Beating the War Drums or Just Dancing to Them?" *The Washington Post National Weekly Edition*, September 10, 1991, 23.

Dobkin, Bethami A. "Paper Tigers and Video Postcards: The Rhetorical Dimensions of Narrative Form in ABC News Coverage of Terrorism." *Western Journal of Communication* (Spring 1992): 143–60.

Dobkin, Bethami A. *Tales of Terror: Television News and the Construction of the Terrorist Threat*. New York: Praeger, 1992.

Doty, R. M., B. E. Peterson, and D. G. Winter. "Threat and Authoritarianism in the United States, 1978–1987." *Journal of Personality and Social Psychology* 61 (1991): 629–40.

Edelman, Murray. *Constructing the Political Spectacle*. Chicago: University of Chicago Press, 1988.

Edgerton, Gary. "Revisiting the Recordings of Wars Past: Remembering the Documentary Trilogy of John Huston." *Journal of Popular Film and Television* 15, 1 (1987): 27–41.

Elliott, Deni. "Family Ties: A Case Study of Coverage of Families and Friends During the Hijacking of TWA Flight 847." *Political Communication and Persuasion* (1978): 67–75.

Ellul, Jacques. *Propaganda: The Formation of Men's Attitudes*. New York: Vintage Books, 1973.

Enloe, Cynthia. *Does Khaki Become You? The Militarisation of Women's Lives*. London: Pluto Press, 1983.

Entman, R. M. "Framing U.S. Coverage of International News: Contrasts in Narratives of the KAL and Iran Air Incidents." *Journal of Communication* 41, 4 (1991): 6–27.

Fell, John. *Film and the Narrative Tradition*. Berkeley: University of California Press, 1986.

Fisher, G. *American Communication in a Global Society*, rev. ed. Norwood, N.J.: Ablex, 1987.

Fisher, Walter. "Narration as a Human Communication Paradigm: The Case of Public Moral Argument." *Communication Monographs* 51 (1984): 1–22.

Fite, D., M. Genest, and C. Wilcox. "Gender Differences in Foreign Policy Attitudes: A Longitudinal Analysis." *American Politics Quarterly* 18 (1990): 492–513.

Fitzgerald, Frances. *Fire in the Lake*. New York: Vintage, 1972.

Foltz, Kim. "Agencies and Clients Plan Strategies If War Occurs." *The New York Times*, January 16, 1991, C16.

Foltz, Kim. "Agencies Caution Clients on Using Patriotic Themes." *New York Times*, March 11, 1991, C1, 3.

Fund for Free Expression. "Freedom to Do as They're Told." *Index on Censorship* 4/5 (1991): 36–38.

Gameson, William A. "News as Framing: Comments on Graber." *American Behavioral Scientists* (November/December 1989): 157–61.

Ghareeb, Edmund. *Split Vision: The Portrayal of Arabs in the American Media*. Washington, D.C.: American-Arab Affairs Council, 1983.

Gibson, James. *The Perfect War*. Boston: Atlantic Monthly Press, 1986.

Golding, P., and P. Elliott. *Making the News*. London: Longman, 1979.

Goodman, Walter. "Arnett." *Columbia Journalism Review* May/June (1991): 29–31.

Granger, Rod. "Ads in War News Don't Upset Viewers, Study Says." *Electronic Media*, February 25, 1991, 4.

Gurevitch, M. "Comparative Research on Television News: Problems and Challenges." *American Behavioral Scientist* 33 (1989): 221–29.

Gurevitch, M., M. R. Levy, and I. Roeh. "The Global Newsroom: Convergence and Diversities in the Globalization of Television News." In *Communication and Citizenship: Journalism and the Public Sphere in the Media Age*, ed. P. Dahlgren and C. Sparks. London: Routledge, in press.

Hale, Katherine, and Michael Mansfield. "Politics: Tastes Great or Less Filling." In *Politics in Familiar Contexts*, ed. Robert Savage and Dan Nimmo, 75–95. Norwood, N.J.: Ablex, 1990.

Hallin, D. C. "Network News: We Keep America on Top of the World." In *Watching Television*, ed. Tod Gitlin, 9–41. New York: Pantheon, 1986.

Hallin, D. C. *The "Uncensored War:" The Media and Vietnam*. New York: Oxford, 1986.

Halloran, Richard. "Soldiers and Scribblers Revisited: Working with the Media." In *Newsmen and National Defense: Is Conflict Inevitable?*, ed. Lloyd Matthews. New York: Brassey's, Inc., 1991.

Hammond, William M. *The Military and the Media 1962–1968*. Washington, D.C.: Center for Military History, 1988.

Head, S. W. *World Broadcasting Systems: A Comparative Analysis*. Belmont, Calif.: Wadsworth, 1985.

Hedges, Chris. "The Unilaterals." *Columbia Journalism Review* (May/June 1991): 27–29.

Heiberg, R. E. "Public Relations as a Weapon of Modern Warfare." *Public Relations Review* 17, 2 (1991): 107–116.

Heider, Fritz. *Balance Theory*. New York: Springer-Verlag, 1988.

Hellmann, John. *American Myth and the Legacy of Vietnam*. New York: Columbia University Press, 1986.

Hertsgaard, Mark. *On Bended Knee: The Press and the Reagan Presidency*. New York: Schocken, 1989.

Hester, A. "The Collection and Flow of World News." In *Global Journalism: Survey of International Communication*, ed. J. C. Merrill, 2d ed., 29–50. New York: Longman, 1991.

Hollihan, Thomas. "Propagandizing in the interests of War: A Rhetorical Study of the Committee of Public Information." *Southern Speech Communication Journal* 49 (1984): 241–57.

Hudson, J. C., and S. Swindel. "TV News in Saudi Arabia." *Journalism Quarterly* 65 (1988): 1003–6.

International Centre on Censorship. *International Freedom and Censorship: World Report 1991*. Chicago: American Library Association, 1991.

Jarvie, Ian. *Movies as Social Criticism: Aspects of their Social Psychology*. Metuchen, N.J.: Scarecrow Press, 1978.

Jeffres, Leo W. *Mass Media Process and Effects*. Prospect Heights, Ill.: Waveland Press, 1986.

Jervis, R. *The Logic of Images in International Relations*. Princeton, N.J.: Princeton University Press, 1970.

Johnson, DeWayne B. "Vietnam: Report Card on the Press Corps at War." *Journalism Quarterly* 46 (Spring 1969): 9.

Karnow, Stanley. *Vietnam: A History*. New York: Penguin, 1984.

Katz, Jon. "The Air War at Home." *Rolling Stone*, March 7, 1991, 93–100.

Keen, Sam. *Faces of the Enemy*. New York: Harper & Row, 1985.

Kellner, Douglas. "Film, Politics, and Ideology: Reflections on Hollywood Film in the Age of Reagan." *The Velvet Light Trap* 27 (1991): 9–24.

King, J. "Visnews and UPITN: News Film Supermarkets in the Sky." In *Crisis in International News*, ed. J. Richstad and M. E. Anderson, 283–98. New York: Columbia University Press, 1981.

Knightley, Phillip. *The First Casualty*. New York: Harcourt, Brace, Jovanovich, 1975.

Komarow, Steven. "Pooling Around in Panama." *Washington Journalism Review* (March 1990): 45, 49.

Kurian, G. T., ed. *World Press Encyclopedia* (2 vols.). New York: Facts on File, 1982.

Gitlin, Todd. *The Whole World Is Watching*. Berkeley, Calif.: Free Press, 1980.

Lamb, Brian. *C-SPAN: America's Town Hall*. Washington, D.C.: Acropolis Books Ltd., 1988.

Lamb, David. "Pentagon Hardball." *Washington Journalism Review* (April 1991): 33–36.

Larson, J. F. "International Affairs Coverage on US Evening Network News." In *Television Coverage of International Affairs*, ed. William Adams, 15–41. Norwood, N.J.: Ablex, 1982.

Larson, J. F. *Television's Window on the World: International Affairs Coverage on the U.S. Networks*. Norwood, N.J.: Ablex, 1984.

Lee, M. A., and T. Devitt. "Gulf War Coverage: Censorship Begins at Home." *Newspaper Research Journal*, 12 (1991): 14–22.

Lent, J. A. "Telematics in Malaysia: Room at the Top for a Selected Few." In *Transnational Communications: Wiring the Third World*, ed. G. Sussman and J. A. Lent, 165–99. Newbury Park, Calif.: Sage, 1991.

Levin, Murray. *Talk Radio and the American Dream*. Lexington, Mass.: Lexington Books, 1987.

Levinson, Nan. "Snazzy Visual, Hard Facts, and Obscured Issues." *Index on Censorship*, 4/5 (1991): 27–29.

Lewis, Justin. *The Ideological Octopus: An Exploration of Television and its Audience*. New York: Routledge, 1991.

Lewis, Justin. "Decoding Television News." In *Television in Transition*, eds. P. Drummond and R. Patterson, 205–34. London: British Film Institute, 1985.

Lewis, Justin, S. Jhally, and M. Morgan. *The Gulf War: A Study of the Media, Public Opinion & Public Knowledge*. Amherst, Mass.: The Center for the Study of Communication Research Archives, 1991.

Lofton, John. *The Press as Guardian of the First Amendment*. Columbia, S.C.: University of South Carolina Press, 1980.

Mander, M. S. "Narrative Dimensions of the News: Omniscience, Prophecy, and Morality." *Communication* 10 (1987): 51–70.

Manheim, Jarol, and Robert Albritton. "Changing National Images: International Public Relations and Media Agenda Setting." *American Political Science Review* 78 (1984): 641–57.

Mann, Patricia S. "Representing the Viewer." *Social Text* (1990): 177–84.

"Marketers Slash Ads as War Erupts." *Advertising Age*, January 21, 1991, 1, 54.

"Marketers Welcome Home Troops." *Advertising Age*, March 11, 1991, 4, 8.

Martin, L. A., and A. G. Chaudhary. "Goals and Roles of Media Systems." In *Comparative Mass Media Systems*, ed. L. J. Martin and A. G. Chaudhary, 1–31. New York: Longman, 1983.

Marwick, A. "Print, Pictures, and Sound: The Second World War and the British Experience." *Daedalus* 111, 4 (1982): 135–55.

Massing, Michael. "Another Front." *Columbia Journalism Review* (June 1991): 23–24.

McCann, S. J. "Authoritarianism and Preference for the Presidential Candidate Perceived to Be Higher on the Power Motive." *Perceptual and Motor Skills* 70 (1990): 577–78.

McCann, S. J., and L. Stewin. "Threat, Authoritarianism, and the Power of U.S. Presidents." *The Journal of Psychology* 121 (1987): 149–57.

McDonald, J. Fred. *Television and the Red Menace*. New York: Praeger, 1985.

McGee, Michael C. "Some Issues in the Rhetorical Study of Political Communication." In *Political Communication Yearbook 1984*, eds. Keith R. Sanders, Linda L. Kaid, and Dan Nimmo 155–82. Carbondale: Southern Illinois University Press, 1985.

McLuhan, Marshall. *The Medium is the Message*. New York: Bantam Books, 1967.

McMasters, P. "The Pentagon and the Press: The War Continues." *Newspaper Research Journal* 12 (1991): 2–9.

Military Strategy: Theory and Application. Carlisle Barracks, Penn.: U.S. Army War College, 1983.

Moody, Randall J. "The Armed Forces Broadcast News System: Vietnam Version." *Journalism Quarterly* 47 (Spring 1970): 27.

Morin, Richard. "The New War Cry: Stop the Press." *Washington Post National Weekly Edition*, February 11, 1991, 38.

Morsy, Soheir. "Politicization Through the Mass Information Media: American Images of Arabs." *Journal of Popular Culture* 17, 3 (1983): 91–97.

Mott, Frank L. *American Journalism*. New York: Macmillan, 1966.

Mott, P. "New King of the Hill." *The Quill* (March 1991): 14–16.

Nasser, M. K. "New Values Versus Ideology: A Third World Perspective." In *Comparative Mass Media Systems*, ed. L. J. Martin and A. G. Chaudhary, 44–66. New York: Longman, 1983.

Negrine, R., and S. Papathanassopouolos. *The Internationalisation of Television*. London: Pinter, 1990.

Newcomb, Theodore. *Social Psychology: The Study of Human Interaction*. New York: Holt, Rinehart & Winston, 1965.

Nimmo, Dan, and James E. Combs. *Nightly Horrors: Crisis Coverage by Television Network News*. Knoxville, Tenn.: University of Tennessee, 1985.

Nimmo, Dan, and James E. Combs. *Mediated Political Realities*, 2d ed. New York: Longman, 1990.

Noelle-Neumann, Elisabeth. *Spiral of Silence*. Chicago: University of Chicago Press, 1984.

Oberdorfer, Don. *Tet!* New York: DeCapo Press, 1984.

Oberlander, Kate. "Advertisers Snap Up CNN's Pricier Ads." *Electronic Media*, February 25, 1991, 3, 37.

Ogan, C. "The Middle East and North Africa." In *Global Journalism: A Survey of*

International Communication, ed. J. C. Merrill, 2d ed., 129–53. New York: Longman, 1991.

O'Heffeman, P. "Television and Crisis: Sobering Thoughts on Sound Bites Seen 'Round the World." *Television Quarterly* 25, 1 (1990): 9–14.

O'Heffeman, P. *Mass Media and American Foreign Policy: Insider Perspectives on Global Journalism and the Foreign Policy Process*. Norwood, N.J.: Ablex, 1991.

Paraschos, M. "Europe." In *Global Journalism: Survey of International Communication*, ed. J. C. Merrill, 2d ed., 93–128. New York: Longman, 1991.

Parenti, Michael. *Make-Believe Media: The Politics of Entertainment*. New York: St. Martin's Press, 1992.

Pearson, Judy C., Lynn Turner, and William Todd-Mancillas. *Gender and Communication*. Dubuque, Iowa: William C. Brown, 1985.

Peled, T., and E. Katz. "Media Functions in Wartime: The Israeli Homefront in October, 1973." In *The Uses of Mass Communication: Current Perspectives on Gratifications Research*, ed. J. G. Blumier and E. Katz, 46–69, Beverly Hills, Calif.: Sage, 1974.

Pendakur, M. "A Political Economy of Television: State, Class, and Corporate Confluence in India." In *Transnational Communications: Wiring the Third World*, ed. G. Sussman and J. T. Lent, 234–62. Newbury Park, Calif.: Sage, 1991.

Powell, JoAnne. "At Last, A Happy Ending." *Life: In Time of War*, March 18, 1991, 38–39.

Priest, Dana. "A Woman's Place in a Time of War." *Washington Post National Weekly Edition*, March 25–31, 1991, 35.

Prince, Stephen. *Visions of Empire: Political Imagery in Contemporary Hollywood Film*. New York: Praeger, 1992.

"Public Affairs Guidance on Refueling of C–141 Aircraft in India." U.S. Department of Defense. January 31, 1991.

Pyle, Richard. *Schwarzkopf: In His Own Words*. New York: Signet Books, 1991.

Raden, D. "Authoritarianism Revisited: Evidence for an Aggression Factor." *Social Behavior and Personality* 9 (1981): 147–53.

Ray, Robert B. *A Certain Tendency of the Hollywood Cinema, 1930–1980*. Princeton, N.J.: Princeton University Press, 1985.

Richstad, J. "Transnational News Agencies: Issues and Politics." In *Crisis in International News*, ed. J. Richstad and M. E. Anderson, 242–57. New York: Columbia University Press, 1981.

Roberts, James. "The Power of Talk Radio." *The American Enterprise* (May 1991): 56–61.

Roeh, I. "Journalism as Storytelling, Coverage as Narrative." *American Behavioral Scientist* 33 (1989): 162–68.

Rosen, Phillip. *Narrative, Apparatus, Ideology*. New York: Columbia University Press, 1986.

Rosenberg, E. "TV and the Gulf War." *The Quill* (March 1991): 17–19.

Rothman, Stanley, David J. Rothman, and Stephen P. Powers. "Hollywood Views the Military." *Society* 28, 1 (1990): 79–84.

Rusciano, Frank Louis, and Roberta Fiske-Rusciano. "Towards a Notion of 'World Opinion.' " *International Journal of Public Opinion Research* 2 (1990): 305–22.

Said, Edward. *The World, the Text, and the Critic*. Cambridge, Mass.: Harvard University Press, 1983.

Salwen, M. B., B. Garrison, and R. T. Buckman. "Latin America and the Caribbean." In *Global Journalism: Survey of International Communication*, ed. J. C. Merrill, 2d ed., 267–310. New York: Longman, 1991.

Schudson, M. "The Politics of Narrative Form: The Emergence of News Conventions in Print and Television." *Daedalus* 111 (1982): 97–112.

Schwartz, Tony. *The Responsive Chord*. New York: Anchor Books, 1973.

Semetko, H. A., J. G. Blumler, M. Gurevitch, and D. H. Weaver. *The Formation of Campaign Agendas: A Comparative Analysis of Party and Media Roles in Recent American and British Elections*. Hillsdale, N.J.: Erlbaum, 1991.

Servaes, J. "European Press Coverage of the Grenada Crisis." *Journal of Communication* 41, 4 (1991): 28–41.

Shaheen, Jack. "The Arab Image in American Mass Media." *American-Arab Affairs* 2 (1982): 89–96.

Shaw, M., and R. Carr-Hill. "Mass Media and Attitudes to the Gulf War in Britain." *Electronic Journal of Communication* 2 (November 1991).

Sherif, M. *Group Conflict and Cooperation: Their Social Psychology*. London: Routledge & Kegan Paul, 1966.

Sidle, W. Testimony of Major General Winant Sidle (U.S. Army Ret.), Chairman, Joint Chiefs of Staff Investigation of U.S. News Policy During Invasion of Grenada. Hearing on *Pentagon Rules on Media Access to the Persian Gulf War*, 52–54. U.S. Congress, Senate, Committee on Governmental Affairs, 102nd Congress, 1st. Session, February 20, 1991.

Siebert, Fred. *Freedom of the Press in England 1476–1776*. Urbana, Ill.: University of Illinois Press, 1972.

Siebert, Fred, T. Peterson, and W. Schramm. *Four Theories of the Press*. Urbana: University of Illinois Press, 1956.

Sifry, Micah, and Christopher Cerf, eds. *The Gulf War Reader*. New York: Random House, 1991.

Smith, A. *The Age of Behemoths: The Globalization of Mass Media Firms*. New York: Priority Press, 1991.

Smith, Larry D. "Narrative Styles in Network Coverage of the 1984 Nominating Conventions." *Western Journal of Speech Communication* 52 (1988): 62–74.

Smith, Larry D., and Dan Nimmo. *Cordial Concurrence: Orchestrating National Party Conventions in the Telepolitical Age*. New York: Praeger, 1991.

Smith, T.W. "The Polls: Gender and Attitudes toward Violence." *Public Opinion Quarterly* 48 (1984): 384–96.

Snidal, Duncan. "Coordination Versus Prisoners' Dilemma: Implications for International Cooperation and Regimes." *American Political Science Review* 79 (1985): 923–42.

Snow, Robert. *Creating Media Culture*. Beverly Hills, Calif.: Sage, 1983.

"Special Report." *Congressional Quarterly* (January 5, 1991): 42.

Sperry, Sharon. "Television News as Narrative." In *Understanding Television*, ed. Richard P. Adler, 292–312. New York: Praeger, 1981.

Steele, Richard. "News of the 'Good War': World War II News Management." *Journalism Quarterly* (Winter 1985): 707–83.

Stephens, L. F. "The World's Media Systems: An Overview." In *Global Jour-*

nalism: Survey of International Communication, ed. J. C. Merrill, 2d ed., 51–71. New York: Longman, 1991.

Stephenson, William. *The Play Theory of Mass Communication*. Chicago: University of Chicago Press, 1967.

Stevens, John D. *Mass Media Between the Wars: Perception of Cultural Tension*. Syracuse, N.Y.: Syracuse University Press, 1984.

Straubhaar, J. D., C. Heeter, B. S. Greenerg, et al. "What Makes News: Western, Socialist, and Third World Television Newscasts Compared in Eight Countries." In *International and Intercultural Communication Annual*, vol. 16, ed. F. Korzenny and E. Schiff. Newbury Park, Calif.: Sage, in press.

Summers, Harry. *On Strategy: A Critical Analysis of the Vietnam War*. Navato, Calif.: Presidio Press, 1982.

Tannen, Deborah. *You Just Don't Understand: Women and Men in Conversation*. New York: William Morrow and Co., 1990.

Taylor, Philip. *Munitions of the Mind: War Propaganda from the Ancient World to the Nuclear Age*. Northhamptonshire, England: Patrick Stephens, 1990.

Teeter, Dwight. "King Sears, the Mob and Freedom of the Press in New York, 1765–76." *Journalism Quarterly* 41 (1964): 539–44.

"The Media: In War and Peace." *Media & Values*, 56 (Fall 1991): 1–24.

Thompson, Mark. "With the Press in the Persian Gulf." *Columbia Journalism Review* (November/December 1991): 40–45.

Tramer, Harriet, and Leo Jeffres. "Talk Radio—Forum and Companion." *Journal of Broadcasting* (Summer 1983): 297–300.

Tuchman, Gaye. *Making News*. New York: Free Press, 1978.

Tunstall, J. *The Media Are American: Anglo-American Media in the World*. London: Constable, 1977.

Turner, Kathleen J. *Lyndon Johnson's Dual War: Vietnam and the Press*. Chicago: University of Chicago Press, 1985.

Turow, Joe. "Talk Show Radio as Interpersonal Communication." *Journal of Broadcasting* (Spring 1974): 171–79.

"TV and the Gulf War." *The Quill* (March 1991): 17.

U.S. Congress. House of Representatives. Subcommittee on Telecommunications and Finance, Committee on Energy and Commerce. Hearing on *Globalization of the Media*. 101st Congress, 1st. session, November 15, 1989. Serial No. 101–98.

U.S. Congress. Senate. Committee on Governmental Affairs. Hearing on Pentagon Rules on Media Access to the Persian Gulf War. 102nd Congress, 1st. Session, February 20, 1991.

Vasquez, Juan. "Panama: Live From the Marriott!" *Washington Journalism Review* (March 1990): 44–47.

Wallis, R. and S. J. Baran. *The Known World of Broadcast News: International News and the Electronic Media*. London: Routledge, 1990.

Wallis, Victor. "Media War in the Gulf." *Lies of Our Times* (February 1991): 3.

Ward, Adrienne and Alison Fahey. "Retailers Rallying 'Round the Flag'." *Advertising Age*, February 11, 1991, 4.

Ward, Larry W. *The Motion Picture Goes to War: the U.S. Government Film Effort During World War I*. Ann Arbor, Mich.: UMI Research Press, 1985.

"War Over, the Press Looks Back." *Presstime* (April 1991): 40.

Williams, P. Testimony of Peter Williams, Assistant Secretary for Public Affairs, U.S. Department of Defense. Hearing on *Pentagon Rules on Media Access to the Persian Gulf War*, 6–11. U.S. Congress, Senate, Committee on Governmental Affairs, 102nd Congress, 1st. Session, February 20, 1991.

Wilson, Stan Le Roy. *Mass Media/Mass Culture*. New York: Random House, 1989.

Woll, Allen, and Randall Miller. *Ethnic and Racial Images in American Film and Television*. New York: Garland, 1987.

World Radio TV Handbook. 1992 Edition. London: Billboard Limited, 1992.

Wyatt, Clarence R. "At the Cannon's Mouth: The American Press and the Vietnam War." *Journalism Quarterly* 13 (1986): 104.

Zavarzadeh, Mas'ud. *Seeing Films Politically*. Albany, N.Y.: State University of New York Press, 1991.

Zelizer, Barbie. "CNN, The Gulf War, and Journalistic Practice."*Journal of Communication* (Winter 1992): 66–81.

Index

ABC News, and coverage of Gulf War, 107–21

advertising: and Persian Gulf War, 213–30; Persian Gulf War implications, 226–30; reactions to Persian Gulf War, 219–26; and referent systems, 214–16; relationship to Persian Gulf War, 216–19

Arnett, Peter, 12, 49, 56, 102

attitudes toward the Gulf War, 145–61

authoritarianism, 146–47

BBC (United Kingdom), 182–85

bloodless war, 236–38

Bush, George, xv, 1, 47, 48, 49, 50, 58, 60, 65, 98, 99, 107, 115, 116, 117, 118, 119, 123, 132, 136, 174, 181, 185, 244, 246, 279

callers, and talk radio/television, 93–105

CBS News coverage of Gulf War, 185–88

Cheney, Dick, 3, 18, 34, 49, 50, 181, 185, 201, 280

CNN, and coverage of Gulf War, 107–21

co-hosts, and talk radio/television, 95–99

C-SPAN: call-in shows of, 129–30; coverage of Persian Gulf War, 123–42; debates about the war on, 127; military briefings, 127; the network of, 124–26; as open pipeline, 128–29; primary themes, 131–33; styles of discourse on, 135–38; subordinate themes of, 134–35

diversity of perspectives on the Gulf War, 59–60

docudrama television format, 277–78

Doordarshan (India), 174–76

experts. See guest

exposure to television coverage, 147–48

film: Cold War movies, 270–76; films of Spanish-American conflict, 262–65; Gulf War movies, 279–81; ideologies of Middle East films, 239–41; images of Arabs in, 243; link between film discourse and

political discourse, 243–55; of Middle East, 239–41; World War I films, 265–67; World War II films, 267–70
forms of reporting, 4–5

globalization, 166–67, 170–91
Grenada, media coverage of, 8–9, 47
guests, and talk radio/television, 95–105

historical models of media coverage, 44–48
Hollywood, and the Persian Gulf War, 235–55
hosts, and talk radio/television, 93–105
Hussein, Saddam, 1, 22, 34, 44, 48, 60, 77, 79, 80, 81, 82, 85, 94, 98, 99, 102, 115, 123, 136, 148, 156, 180, 184, 187, 188, 189, 246, 247, 250, 281

instant history, 29

Jordan Radio and Television, 172–74

Kelly, Thomas, 63
King, Larry, 9, 100, 103, 104
Korea, media coverage of, 6–7

language and war, 135–36
legitimation of warfare, 257–81

media coverage: ABC, 107–21; balance in, 53–58; C-SPAN, 123–42; challenges of war and, 61–62; Chile, 179–81; CNN, 107–21; in Germany, 181; of Grenada, 8–9, 47; historical models of, 44–48; in India, 174–76; international environment of news, 167–70; interpretations of, 149–51; in Jordan, 172–74; key actors in, 50–51; of Korea, 6–7; in Malaysia, 176–78; narratives of, 172–88; of soldiers' children, 199–202; of women, 197–210; of Panama, 10; of

Persian Gulf War, 49–65; problems of, 18–23; seven country comparison of, 165–92; talk radio, 89–105; television, 89–105; in the United Kingdom, 182–85; in the United States, 185–88; of Vietnam, 7–8, 45–47, 56–57; and women's roles in war, 202–7; of World War II, 5–6, 44–45
media management, 62–63
media perspectives on world opinion, 71–86
military ground rules, 11–18
military news management, 4–11
military, and women, 198–99
moral components of world opinion, 78–80
Murrow, Edward R., 5, 6, 15, 18, 62

narrative, of Persian Gulf War coverage, 172–88. See also quest narrative
news: balance in, 53–58; key actors in, 50–51; quest narrative of, 115–20
news management, military history of, 4–11
news narratives, 107–21; as structural frames, 109–11
news pool system, 13–15
New York Times, perspective on Gulf War, 71–86

Panama, media coverage of, 10
Persian Gulf War: and advertising, 213–30; authoritarianism and support for, 146–62; globalization of coverage, 166–67; and Hollywood, 235–55; link between film discourse and political discourse, 243–55; media coverage of, 49–65; media ground rules, 11–18; media narratives of, 172–88; media problems of, 18–23; phases of news coverage, 58–61; as "prime-time war," xvi; rules for press, 1–26; and talk radio, 89–105;

and television, 32–34; world
  opinion on, 71–86
phase I of Gulf War coverage, 58–59
phase II of Gulf War coverage, 59–61
phase III of Gulf War coverage, 61
political information and TV news,
  30–32
politics and television, 28–32
politics of speculation, 111–15
popular entertainment, and
  legitimation of war, 257–81
Powell, Colin, 34, 47, 185, 201
pragmatic components of world
  opinion, 78–80
press, rules for, 1–26
press management, 62–63
press performance, reports on, 51–53

quest narrative, of news, 115–20

reporting, forms of, 4–5

Saddam Hussein. *See* Hussein,
  Saddam
Schwartzkopf, Norman, 18, 47, 49,
  52, 62, 185
Sidle Commission, 12, 14; rules of,
  10–11
Stone, I. F., 4, 5
styles of media discourse, 135–38
support for Gulf War, 146–62

talk radio: and Persian Gulf War, 89–
  105; egoism of, 90–92; format of
  agreement, 93–95; format of
  confrontation, 95–99; format of
  instruction, 99–105; formats of, 93
talk television: format of agreement,
  93–95; format of confrontation, 95–

99; format of instruction, 99–105;
  formats of, 93
telediplomacy, 35
television: coverage of the Persian
  Gulf War, 49–50; docudrama
  format, 277–78; egoism of, 90–92;
  and the Persian Gulf War, 32–34;
  as instant history, 29; as an
  instrument of war, 27–42
television and politics, 28–32
television news: comparison of
  coverage, 165–92; international
  environment of, 167–70; narratives
  of, 172–88; and political
  information, 30–32; viewing and
  attitudes toward war, 145–61
Times of India, perspectives on Gulf
  War, 71–86
TVN (Chile), 179–81
TV3 (Malaysia), 176–78

Vietnam: as first TV war, 27–28;
  media coverage of, 7–8, 45–47, 56–57

war: and advertising, 216–19;
  bloodless, 236–38
warfare, legitimation of, 257–81
Williams, Pete, 3, 8, 10, 12, 13, 16,
  17, 51
women: in combat, 207–9; media
  coverage of, 197–210; and the
  military, 198–99
world opinion: media perspectives
  on, 71–86; moral and pragmatic
  elements, 78–80; and threats of
  isolation, 80–83

ZDF (Germany), 181–82

About the Editor and Contributors

JOANNE CANTOR is a professor in the Department of Communication Arts and Associate Dean in the College of Letters and Sciences at the University of Wisconsin at Madison. Her research interests are in developmental studies of cognitive and emotional reactions to mass media. She has published numerous book chapters and articles in such journals as *Journal of Communication, Journal of Broadcasting and Electronic Media,* and *Communication Monographs.*

JAMES COMBS is a former professor in the Department of Political Science at Valparaiso University. He is the author or coauthor of ten books and numerous scholarly articles. His most recent books include *American Political Movies* and *The Political Pundits* (with Dan Nimmo) (Praeger, 1992).

ROBERT E. DENTON, JR. is professor and head of the Department of Communication Studies at Virginia Polytechnic Institute and State University. In addition to numerous articles, he is the author/editor of several books, including *The Primetime Presidency of Ronald Reagan, Political Communication in America,* second edition (with Gary Woodward), and *Ethical Dimensions of Political Communication* (Praeger, 1988, 1990, and 1991). Denton serves as associate editor of *Presidential Studies Quarterly* and as editor for the Praeger Series in Political Communication and Presidential Studies.

BETHAMI A. DOBKIN is coordinator of Media Studies and assistant professor in the Department of Communication Studies at the University of San Diego. She is author of *Tales of Terror: Television News and the Construction of the Terrorist Threat* (Praeger, 1992) and has published articles in communication and legal studies journals. She teaches and writes in the areas of media theory and criticism, television news, and political communication.

MARK HOVIND is a Ph.D. student in political communication in the Department of Communication at the University of Oklahoma. He has worked in journalism photography for *The Advocate* in Newark, Ohio, and as a business and pension plan consultant.

ANNE JOHNSTON is assistant professor in the Department of Radio, Television, and Motion Pictures at the University of North Carolina at Chapel Hill. She has written chapters on the use of mass communication in childhood, presidential campaigns, and on recent trends in political communication research. She has co-authored chapters on content analysis, political advertising, and political themes in music videos.

MARIE-LOUISE MARES is a doctoral candidate in the Department of Communication Arts at the University of Wisconsin at Madison. Her research interests include emotional and cognitive responses to mass media content, with particular emphasis on the responses of elderly adults. She has published in *Communication Research*.

SHANNON E. MARTIN is a Ph.D. student at the School of Journalism and Mass Communication at the University of North Carolina at Chapel Hill. She was a reporter and special writer for several newspapers and magazines, including the *Louisville Courier-Journal*, the *Indiana Times*, and the *Charlotte News and Observer*.

MATTHEW P. McALLISTER is assistant professor in the Department of Communication Studies at Virginia Polytechnic Institute and State University. He had published book chapters and articles in the *Journal of Communication* and the *Journal of Popular Culture* about popular culture and medical communication.

JANETTE KENNER MUIR is the basic course director and assistant professor in the Department of Communication at George Mason University. She has published articles in a variety of communication journals, and is currently editing a volume on the uses of C-SPAN in the communication classroom.

DAN NIMMO is professor in the Department of Communication at the University of Oklahoma. He is author or co-author of several books in political communication. Among those examining the relationship of politics and the news media are *Cordial Concurrence* (with Larry David Smith) and *The Political Pundits* (with James E. Combs) (Praeger, 1991 and 1992).

MARY BETH OLIVER is an assistant professor in the Department of Communication Studies at Virginia Polytechnic Institute and State University. Her research interests include audience enjoyment and interpretation of media content, with particular emphasis on content involving scenes of violence and/or sexuality. She has published in *Social Psychology Quarterly*.

STEPHEN PRINCE is an assistant professor in the Department of Communication Studies at Virginia Polytechnic Institute and State University. He has written articles for such publications as *Cinema Journal*, *Wide Angle*, *Journal of Film and Video*, and *Journal of Popular Culture*, and is the author of *The Warrior's Camera: The Cinema of Akira Kurosawa* and *Visions of Empire: Political Imagery in Contemporary Hollywood Film* (Praeger, 1992).

FRANK LOUIS RUSCIANO is an associate professor of political science at Rider College. He is the author of "Isolation and Paradox: Defining the Public" in *Modern Political Analysis*. His articles on world opinion, rational choice, and political methodology appear in such journals as *Western Political Quarterly*, the *International Journal of Public Opinion Research*, and *Comparative Politics*.

DONALD L. SHAW is the Kenan Professor at the School of Journalism and Mass Communication at the University of North Carolina at Chapel Hill. He is the author of numerous studies of communication history, theory, and journalism practice. He served for nearly a decade as associate editor or editor of *Journalism Quarterly*. Shaw, a retired colonel, served two short tours of duty with the Chief of Public Affairs, Department of the Army, during the period of the Persian Gulf War and was at the Pentagon during the briefing by Secretary of Defense Dick Cheney and General Colin Powell, Chairman of the Joint Chiefs of Staff, on the January evening the Allied forces counterattacked Iraq with an air war.

LARRY DAVID SMITH is assistant professor in the Department of Communication at Purdue University. His articles on presidential nominating conventions, presidential rhetoric, political and product advertising and popular culture have appeared in a variety of scholarly journals. He is co-author (with Dan Nimmo) of *Cordial Concurrence: Orchestrating National Party Conventions in the Telepolitical Age* (Praeger, 1991).

DAVID L. SWANSON is professor in the Department of Speech Communication at the University of Illinois at Urbana-Champaign. He is the author of numerous articles and book chapters on topics concerning the social and political influence of mass communication. He edited *The Uses and Gratifications Approach to Mass Communication Research* and *New Directions in Political Communication* (with Dan Nimmo). He is co-author of *The Nature of Human Communication* (with Jesse G. Delia).

GARY C. WOODWARD is professor in the Department of Speech, Communication and Theater Arts at Trenton State College in New Jersey. In addition to numerous articles in the areas of communication and rhetorical theory, he is the author of *Persuasive Encounters* (Praeger, 1990) and co-author (with Robert E. Denton, Jr.) of *Political Communication in America*, 2d ed. (Praeger, 1990) and of *Persuasion and Influence in American Life*.